RUSSIAN IDEA · JEWISH PRESENCE

RUSSIAN IDEA · JEWISH PRESENCE

Essays on Russian-Jewish Intellectual Life

BRIAN HOROWITZ

Boston 2013

Library of Congress Cataloging-in-Publication Data:
A catalog reference for this title is available from the Library of Congress.

ISBN 978-1-61811-819-6
ISBN 978-1-618110-52-7 (electronic)

Copyright © 2013 Academic Studies Press
All rights reserved

Cover design by Ivan Grave
Book design by Adell Medovoy

On the cover:
Synagogue at Preobrazhenskoe Jewish Cemetery.
Photograph by William Brumfield.

Published by Academic Studies Press in 2013
28 Montfern Avenue
Brighton, MA 02135, USA
press@academicstudiespress.com
www.academicstudiespress.com

To Benjamin, Rebecca, and Sophia, whom I love.

Contents

Introduction   13

I. Varieties of Russian-Jewish History: Liberals, Zionists, and Diaspora Nationalists   16

1. The Russian Roots of Semyon Dubnov's Life and Works   18
2. Maxim Vinaver and the First Russian State Duma   37
3. What is "Russian" in Russian Zionism?: Synthetic Zionism and the Fate of Avram Idel'son   54
4. An Innovative Agent of an Alternative Jewish Politics: The Odessa Branch of the Society for the Promotion of Enlightenment among the Jews of Russia   72
5. Politics and National Self-Projection: The Image of Jewish Masses in Russian-Jewish Historiography, 1860-1914   87
6. "Both Crisis and Continuity": A Reinterpretation of Late-Tsarist Russian Jewry   105
7. Crystallizing Memory: Russian-Jewish Intelligentsia Abroad and Forms of Self-Projection   124

II. M. O. Gershenzon and the Intellectual Life of Russia's Silver Age   139

8. M. O. Gershenzon — Metaphysical Historian of Russia's Silver Age: Part 1   141
9. M. O. Gershenzon — Metaphysical Historian of Russia's Silver Age: Part 2   171
10. "...To Break Free of Centuries-Old Complications, of the Abominable Fetters of Social and Abstract Ideas": M. O. Gershenzon's Side in the *Correspondence Across a Room*   198

11. Unity and Disunity in *Landmarks* (*Vekhi*): The Rivalry between Pyotr Struve and Mikhail Gershenzon — 213
12. M. O. Gershenzon and Georges Florovsky: Metaphysical Philosophers of Russian History — 229
13. From the Annals of the Literary Life of Russia's Silver Age: The Tempestuous Relationship of S. A. Vengerov and M. O. Gershenzon — 239
14. M. O. Gershenzon, the Intellectual Circle, and the Perception of Leader in Russia's Silver-Age Culture — 258

Bibliography — 275

Appendix A: Jewish Monuments in Russia at the Turn of the 20th Century — 288

Appendix B: Rare Photographs of Gershenzon and his Family — 294

Index — 301

List of Illustrations

1. St. Petersburg Choral Synagogue (Photograph by William Brumfield) — 18
2. The exhibit of the Society for the Promotion of Enlightenment at the 1893 Fair in Novgorod (reproduced courtesy of Michael Beizer) — 36
3. The lawyer and activist, Maxim Vinaver (reproduced courtesy of the Jewish Studies Department of the European University in St. Petersburg). — 53
4. Medal coin from the Society for the Promotion of Enlightenment (reproduced courtesy of Michael Beizer) — 71
5. Jewish Arc in front of the St. Petersburg Choral Synagogue (Photograph by William Brumfield) — 86
6. The historian and writer, Semyon Dubnov (reproduced courtesy of the Jewish Studies Department of the European University in St. Petersburg) — 104
7. The civic activist and writer, Mikhail (Menashe) Morgulis (reproduced courtesy of the Jewish Studies Department of the European University in St. Petersburg) — 123
8. Mikhail Osipovich Gershenzon (reproduced courtesy of Mikhail Chegodaev) — 140
9. Mikhail Osipovich Gershenzon and family (reproduced courtesy of Mikhail Chegodaev) — 170
10. Mikhail Osipovich Gershenzon (reproduced courtesy of Mikhail Chegodaev) — 197

Acknowledgements

I would like to thank the following individuals who gave me advice to improve the book: Shaul Stampfer, Jeffrey Veidlinger, Maxim Shrayer, Hugh McLean, Ezra Mendelsohn, Edith Frankel, Antony Polonsky, Samuel Ramer, Oleg Budnitsky, Shai Ginsburg, Vladimir Lukin, Scott Ury, Dragan Kundzic, Shulamit Magnus, Kathryn Shield, Zvi Gitelman, Deborah Dash-Moore, Marat Grinberg, Shaul Stampfer, Viktor Kel'ner, Bettina Kaibach, Urs Heftrich, Vladimir Levin, Edward Kasinec, Robert H. Davis, Taro Tsurumi, Heinz Dietrich-Loewe, Joachim von Puttkamer, Włodzimierz Borodziej, Irina Paperno. I must also mention my friend and colleague, Seth Appelbaum, who gave me much help with notes and bibliography. I also need to acknowledge my mentor, colleague, and friend, William Craft Brumfield. Needless to say, any mistakes in the book are mine alone.

I would also like to acknowledge those institutions that have given me direct aid. The Dean's Office of Liberal Arts at Tulane University, The Jean and Samuel Frankel Center for Advanced Judaic Studies at the University of Michigan, The Imre Kértesz Kolleg at the University of Jena, The Alexander Von Humboldt Foundation, Yad Hanadiv Foundation, the Posen Foundation USA.

Essay 1 appeared in Hebrew in *Zion* 3 (2012): 341–358.

Essay 2 appeared in German in *Von Duma zu Duma. Hundert Jahre Russischer Parlamentarismus*. Ed. Dittmar Dahlmann and Pascal Trees (Bonn: Bonn University Press, 2008), 115-131.

Essay 4 appeared in *Place, Identity and Urban Culture: Odessa and New Orleans, Occasional Papers of the Kennan Institute*. Ed. Blair Ruble and Samuel Ramer (Washington DC: Woodrow Wilson International Center for Scholars, 2008), 9-18.

Essay 5 appeared in *The Jews of Eastern Europe: Studies in Jewish Civilization*. Ed. L. Greenspoon, R.A. Simkins, and B. Horowitz (Omaha: Creighton University Press, 2005): 168-189.

Essay 6 appeared in Russian in *Vestnik Evreiskogo Universiteta* 11, no. 29 (2006): 89-112.

Essay 11 appeared in *Studies in East European Thought* 51, no. 1 (March 1999): 61-78.

Essay 12 appeared in *Canadian-American Slavonic Studies* 34, no. 3 (2001): 365-374.

Essay 13 appeared in *Wiener Slawistischer Almanach* 35 (1995): 77-95.

Essay 14 appeared in *Wiener Slawistischer Almanach* 29 (1992): 45-73.

Permission for the republication of articles appearing in this volume has been attained from the publishers or individuals holding copyright.

Note on transliteration:

I use the Library of Congress system in transliterating from Russian, with the exceptions of the adjectival ending "ii," for which I use "y" (so Dostoevsky, not Dostoevskii), and yo in Semyon. Also I use English standard forms of names when conventional forms exist. For Hebrew and Yiddish I observe the Library of Congress system.

INTRODUCTION

This book has two goals. One is to present the varieties of Jewish identities that were normative in tsarist times, and the other is implicitly to compare American- and Russian-Jewish consciousness. Despite the differences in the two countries and their times, Russian Jewry serves as a model in the attempt of secular Jews to integrate into the host society and still find a way to express their Jewish identity.

In some instances integration and identity were overtly political. Maxim Vinaver, among others, persuaded liberals in the Constitutional Democratic Party to give priority to Jewish rights. In another direction, Avram Idel'son, a Zionist, invented the doctrine of *Gegenwartsarbeit* (*Doigkeit*) in order to release Jewish political energies in the struggle for rights in the diaspora. Lastly, Semyon Dubnov looked to Russian culture as a source for his ideas of cultural nationalism. These various ideas were meant to promote a politics of synthesis (Jewish integration and separation simultaneously).

From another perspective, culture came to the forefront. Mikhail Gershenzon, for example, employed his "Jewish genius" in explicating Russian intellectual life of the nineteenth century. He was accused of "universalizing" and "de-nationalizing" Russian intellectuals, such as Pyotr Chaadaev and the Slavophiles. By refusing to convert, this "Jew in the Russian elite" functioned as a mirror of Russian chauvinism. In this regard he entered into polemics with Vasily Rozanov and also invited debates with Pyotr Struve, Georges Florovsky, Viacheslav Ivanov, and Nikolai Berdiaev on the meaning of Slavophilism, Russian Orthodox Christianity, and Russian power.

Historical scholarship offered an opportunity for secular Jews to "perform" Jewish identity. The study of Jewish history and the establishment of institutions for the publication of historical research supplanted more traditional, religious forms of Jewish expression. For example, the Jewish Ethnographic and Historical Society had its own journal, *Evreiskaia starina* (Jewish Antiquities). Philanthropy also played an operative role. For example, in Odessa of the 1880s and 90s, Mikhail Morgulis rebuilt the Jewish community through involvement in educational reform and direct aid to the city's poor.¹

It should already be fairly clear that the kind of Jewish identities depicted in the book depart from the familiar preconceptions of Russian Jews either as religious (orthodox or Hasidic) or anti-religious (revolutionary, socialist, or anarchist). They were neither assimilated nor traditional, they did not live in shtetls or avoid Russian culture. They were not rabbis or canters, moneylenders, industrialists, or merchants, and not musicians, artists, or writers. The Jews examined in this study lived primarily in Russia's capital cities, Moscow and St. Petersburg. Some were lawyers, others were journalists, teachers, and historians. The rise of an intellectual class reflects the maturation of Jewish society from a religious community into a multifarious, occupationally diverse and ideologically pluralistic body.²

The book also examines methodology and historiography. I employ a contemporary form of intellectual history that emphasizes the role of individual and inimitable experience in the construction of ideology. Ideas matter but they are not divorced from the context in which they originate and function. In this case, ideas such as nationalism, socialism, and liberalism operate in more than just a political context; they also play a part in other debates over economics, social change, religion, and gender. These debates in turn shaped individual discourse and identity.

Several essays deal with the approach of Jewish historians toward the topic of Jewish history in Russia. Research methods, knowledge, and identity evolved in response to, among other things, tsarist government policies. Historians from the era, such as Dubnov, had a preponderant influence on our understanding of the Jewish past. In recent years Jewish historians have liberated themselves from Dubnov's grasp.

The emphasis in these essays is on Jewish liberals who have been neglected by Jewish historians in their studies of the extreme political left or right. The liberal center has not received enough scholarly attention in part because its truncated existence following the October revolution. However, a Jewish political and ideological center has grown strong in the United States, and this Jewish center, removed by time and space from its Eastern-European origins, has much to gain from examining a

---

1   Brian Horowitz, *Jewish Philanthropy and Enlightenment in Late-Tsarist Russia* (Seattle: University of Washington, 2009).
2   Jeffrey Veidlinger, *Jewish Public Culture in the Late Russian Empire* (Bloomington: Indiana University Press, 2009).

Russian Jewry similarly engaged in the difficult synthesis of uniting the human being and Jew, citizen and Jewish interests, universalism and particularistic identities.

The collection is composed of two parts: 1) seven selected essays on Jewish history and historiography in Russia and 2) seven studies on the life and work of Mikhail Osipovich Gershenzon in the context of Russia's modernist culture. Although some of the essays have appeared elsewhere, a number were published in foreign languages (Hebrew, German, and Russian). For the majority of the essays this is the first English-language publication.

I
Varieties of Russian-Jewish History: Liberals, Zionists, and Diaspora Nationalists

1. THE RUSSIAN ROOTS OF SEMYON DUBNOV'S LIFE AND THOUGHT

Although it might seem self-evident to claim that Semyon Dubnov reflects the Russian environment from which he came, the subject of Dubnov's attitude toward Russia is not as simple or as clear as one might think. In his memoirs and other works, Dubnov emphasized European influences, chiefly the English philosopher John Stuart Mill, the German-Jewish historian Heinrich Graetz, and the French writer Ernest Renan.[3] In fact, scholars have considered the subject of Russia as part of their general studies on Dubnov, but the question of Russia's meaning in Dubnov's work has not yet been the object of a concentrated study.[4] What was the influence of Russia on Dubnov's life and work, and what was Dubnov's attitude toward Russia, the country in which he lived most of his life, and Russian, the language he preferred to all others. How does he use Russian themes in his self-presentation, when and why does he refer to Russian culture, and what do these allusions mean? In a general way, Russian influences can be divided into those that are direct and indirect. At the same time that one finds salient and easily documented parallels, one can also discover subtle and hidden borrowings in theme, structure, and language.

A re-examination of Dubnov's life and thought from the viewpoint of his borrowings from Russian sources demonstrate the degree to which Dubnov participated in and was influenced by the ideological, religious,

---

3   See S. Dubnov's memoir, *Kniga zhizni: materialy dlia istorii moego vremeni, vospominaniia i razmyshleniia* (Moscow-Jerusalem: Gesharim, 2004), 113-16, 154-56, 181-85, and elsewhere.

4   V. E. Kel'ner, *Missioner istorii: zhizn' i trudy Semena Markovicha Dubnova* (St. Petersburg: Mir, 2008); Robert Seltzer, "Coming Home: The Personal Basis of Simon Dubnow's Ideology," *Association for Jewish Studies Review* 1 (1976); also Seltzer, "Simon Dubnow: A Critical Biography of his Early Years" (PhD diss., Columbia University, 1970); Sophie Dubnov-Erlich, *The Life and Work of S. M. Dubnov, Diaspora Nationalism and Jewish History* (Bloomington: Indiana University Press, 1990); Jonathan Frankel, "S. M. Dubnow: Historian and Ideologist," in *Crisis, Revolution, and Russian Jews* (Cambridge: Cambridge University Press, 2008), 239-75; Benjamin Nathans, "Russian-Jewish Historiography," in *Historiography of Imperial Russia: The Profession and Writing of History in a Multinational State*, ed. Thomas Sanders (Armonk, NY, London: M.E Sharpe, 1999); Yahudah Rozental, "Ha-historiografiya ha-yehudit be-rusya ha-sovyetit ve Shim'on Dubnov," in *Sefer Shim'on Dubnov*, ed. Simon Rawidowicz (London: Arat Publishing Company, 1954), 201-20; Jeffrey Veidlinger, "Simon Dubnov Recontextualized: the Sociological Conception of History and the Russian Intellectual Legacy," *Simon Dubnov Institute Yearbook* 3 (2004): 411-27.

1. St. Petersburg Choral Synagogue (photograph by William Brumfield).

and artistic ferment that took place in Russia. I hope to illuminate some of the contexts in which the larger Russian-Jewish interaction took place, contexts that helped shape Dubnov's worldview.

Dubnov was hardly a passive receiver. Mixing ideas and genres to build his original ideas of diaspora nationalism, he turned for inspiration to poetry, fiction, philosophy, and historiography. Russian literature in particular contributed to the development of his intellectual potential.

In contrast to the usual dichotomies in nineteenth-century Russian intellectual history—East versus West, Slavophiles against Westernizers, the idealists of the 1840s and the radicals of the 1860s—Dubnov takes ideas and approaches from contradictory sources. Engaging with Russians and Ukrainians of his own time, he also admires the poets and writers of the past, such as Mikhail Lermontov and Ivan Turgenev, and the radical critics of the 1860s. He was aware of the renaissance of secular Jewish culture that was occurring in Russia with the rise of Yiddish as a serious literary language and the expansion of Hebrew literature (in fact he announced the arrival of this renaissance).[5] He did not appreciate the Russian avant-garde of the day (Bely, Blok, and Merezhkovsky).

In the first part of this essay, I will discuss Dubnov's formation as an intellectual and treat the way he presented himself in his memoirs. Then I will turn to an analysis of his political theories of diaspora nationalism and its relations to Russian-Jewish life. Then I will examine indirect parallels, treating Dubnov's attitude toward the title "Russian writer," and concluding with a discussion of Dubnov's professed love for the Russian language.

In his memoir, *Book of Life* (*Kniga zhizni*), Dubnov expresses awareness of the tension between his inner world and the external events that occurred during his life. He writes from exile, geographically distant from Soviet Russia and intellectually alienated from Communism. "Due to a historical cataclysm, the century's intellectual currents, that were interwoven in my life and the lives of my contemporaries, have temporarily been interrupted. And we, the last representatives of this former epoch, are obligated to produce a monument to it. I am publishing my memoirs as the 'material for a history of my life'; at the start [it is] a

---

5   See Shmuel Niger, "Simon Dubnow as Literary Critic," *YIVO Annual of Jewish Social Science* 1 (1946): 335-58.

history of an intellectual struggle and at the end, a political struggle."⁶

In this passage, written in the early 1930s while Dubnov was preparing the first volume of his memoirs for publication, one can sense the historian's emotional condition. He feels ripped from the intellectual world that gave order to his life, and feels an obligation to memorialize earlier times.⁷ There are reasons why Dubnov cherished his life in Russia. Young maskilim in the 1860s and 70s, such as Dubnov, were animated by the changes taking place there. Committed to breaking with the past, they read forbidden books, joined reading circles, and found purpose in spreading the word about the possibilities of life outside the religious community.⁸ The influence of the revolutionary movement was more important than the government, since young people emulated the behavior and discourse of the revolutionaries. The rise of a secular Jewish culture in three languages inspired many intellectuals of the time, and provided them with a sense of mission and purpose.

Russian culture played a large part in Dubnov's intellectual development. In *Book of Life* he wrote about his early teen years, "Having little work to do in school, I devoted myself again to reading books from the library of our [literary] circle. The universal melancholy of the young Lermontov was of course more to my liking than Pushkin's stylized poetry. Turgenev's romanticism captivated my imagination, and I found myself under its spell many years later. I was hopelessly in love with all those dreamy heroines of Turgenev's stories."⁹

As this passage shows, Dubnov was attracted to realist fiction and had significant limitations in his literary taste and sophistication. In his preferences he shows a strong attraction to Populist literary criticism of the 1860s.

Dubnov's interest in Russian realist literature had significant consequences for the development of his worldview since in his youth he attributed to literature a more profound purpose than mere entertain-

---

6 Dubnov, *Kniga zhizni*, 23. All translations by Brian Horowitz except where noted. For more on Dubnov's life in Western Europe, see Simon Rabinovitch, "The Dawn of a New Diaspora: Simon Dubnov's Autonomism from St. Petersburg to Berlin," *Leo Baeck Institute Year Book* 50 (2005): 267-88; Cecile Kuznits, "The Origins of Yiddish Scholarship and the YIVO Institute for Jewish Research" (PhD thesis, Stanford University, 2000), 61-111.
7 On Dubnov in European exile, see Simon Rabinovitch, "The Dawn of a New Diaspora," 267-88.
8 Two paradigmatic narratives of rebellious maskilim, who fight Orthodox Jewry can be seen in the lives of Moses Leib Lilienblum and Shimon An-sky.
9 Dubnov, *Kniga zhizni*, 63.

ment or even art. Literature, he asserted, conveyed the emotional dimension of the human spirit and stood as a bulwark against an unlimited confidence in reason. He wrote in *Book of Life* about the mid-1880s:

> In essence I attributed to poetry a religious function in the realm of the unknowable and therefore assigned it serious demands: it should be an intellectual poetry of world problems and universal melancholy. In those summer days I allowed myself a treat: I reread Turgenev's stories and Goncharov's novels that I had read in my youth without giving them proper attention. Once, having finished Turgenev's "An Unhappy Girl," I covered my head in my pillow and cried.[10] There was no one in the room, but I was ashamed of my tears that brought me down to the level of the crowd and sentimental schoolgirls. Nonetheless, there was a lesson for me: I understood that it was wrong to separate reason and emotion so sharply, that a true work of art, even one without a definite underlying idea, can serve as a source for deep thoughts just like a fine philosophical treatise.[11]

The novella relates the life of a young Jewish girl, the illegitimate issue of a Jewish woman and a French nobleman who has moved to Russia. After her mother's death, she is left in the hands of hostile caretakers who inhibit her chances for love. The story ends with the young girl's suicide and a funeral that erupts in a senseless brawl. The girl's life is shown as bereft of joy and deeply tragic.[12] What is typical of the period is the attribution to literature of functions that are outside literary significance. The critics of Dubnov's time looked to literature to provide political commentary, a guide for behavior, and philosophical import.[13]

---

10   Ivan Turgenev's story, "Neschastnaia," published in 1869, can be found in I. S. Turgenev, *Polnoe sobranie sochinenii i pisem v dvadtsati vos'mi tomakh*, 28 vols. (Moscow-Leningrad: Nauka, 1965), vol. 10, 71-160.
11   Dubnov, *Kniga zhizni*, 125.
12   The girl's Jewish background does not matter because she lives among non-Jews who are indifferent to her origins. Although it is hardly one of Turgenev's best stories, the treatment of Suzanna is at least not hostile to Jews, as is for example his infamous story, "Kike" ("Zhid") (1847).
13   Literature in nineteenth century Russia fulfilled many supra-literary functions. For a study of

An important stage in Dubnov's development was signaled by the shift from the binary opposition of universalism and national particularism, Western thought and Jewish culture, to the realization that Jewish history and culture could serve as a path to reach a higher universalism.[14] By studying Jewish history, he realized that he was better able to see the totality of world history since the Jews had existed since nearly the time of earliest documentary evidence and had lived in the largest and most important empires from ancient to modern times.

In the 1880s, Dubnov took over as *Voskhod*'s literary critic, a position that defined his intellectual path.[15] He concluded that, just as Western culture was thriving in its Jewish context, so too a study of the central issues of Western society could take place through a focus on Jewish history. He wrote in *Book of Life*:

> I felt that the fateful tortures of self-definition had come to an end, that I finally had to define my vocation, decide on one of the many plans of action that drew me in different directions. The twenty-seventh year of my life was a decisive moment for me. Until that time my ideas still dissolved in universal literary plans, although in fact I was working in Jewish literature. [...] It became clear to me that the general knowledge I had acquired and my universal strivings could give productive results when combined with the inherited treasures of Jewish knowledge and national ideals that had not yet been defined.[16]

Secular Jewish culture of the 1880s opened Dubnov's eyes to the idea that Jews could embody and contribute to the highest European ideas. Dubnov witnessed an explosion of secular Jewish creativity in such authors as Semyon Frug, Mendele Moicher Sforim, Itzak Leib Peretz, Sholem Aleichem, Lev Levanda, and Ben-Ami. In memoirs (published separately from *Book of Life*) Dubnov showed how he perceived Russian-

---

the social critics, see Victor Terras, *Belinskij and Russian Literary Criticism: The Heritage of Organic Aesthetics* (Madison: University of Wisconsin Press, 1974).
14   Sophie Dubnov-Erlich treats this development; see *The Life and Work of S. M. Dubnov*, 52-59.
15   This argument is not entirely new and was first promulgated by Shmuel Niger in his article, "Simon Dubnow as Literary Critic," 335-58.
16   Dubnov, *Kniga zhizni*, 146-47.

Jewish culture as bridging two separate worlds. Writing about the poet Frug, Dubnov remarked, "Frug wrote primarily in Russian, masterfully using the Russian poetic language, but nevertheless remained a Jewish national poet—this is his main characteristic and huge advantage. He stood on the border between two literatures—Jewish and Russian—and if he had devoted himself solely to presenting general, I mean, exclusively poetic themes, he could occupy a central place in the 'Russian Parnassus,' where many people situated him."[17] Dubnov himself had such a double vision.

In presenting his own intellectual development in *Book of Life*, Dubnov used Russian paradigms that reflected the influences that guided his behavior and thought.[18] He depicts himself as a rebellious teenager in Mstislav with an image of generational conflict. He clashed with his grandfather, a religious scholar, who brought him up in place of his father. While living in Mstislav, he refused to go to synagogue on Yom Kippur, thereby wounding his grandfather. Dubnov writes, "Our break with the old world was even sharper than what a young Russian experienced, because for us it involved the destruction of both the religious and national connection with the people..."[19]

For one familiar with *Haskalah* literature, the allusion to *The Sins of Youth* by Moshe Leib Lilienblum is obvious.[20] However, once again nineteenth-century Russian literature is also relevant. Dubnov admits to modeling his own life on Ivan Turgenev's *Fathers and Sons*, the novel that foregrounded an ideological conflict between the nobility and *raznochintsy* (men of various ranks and classes), the old generation and the new. Dubnov explains, "Russian literature was generally speaking my hobby. [...] We had a philosophy of life in the types of heroes from Turgenev's novels and those of other writers. Bazarov and Rakhmetov (heroes from Turgenev's *Fathers and Sons* and Chernyshevsky's *What Is To Be Done?*) were symbols of the 'new men,' 'nihilists,' i.e. repudiators

---

17 S. Dubnov, "Vospominaniia o S. M. Fruge," *Evreiskaia starina* 4 (1916): 448.
18 Russian literature was often read as a how-to book for life. Irina Paperno has studied the life-art issue in nineteenth-century Russian culture. See her book, *Chernyshevsky and the Age of Realism* (Stanford: Stanford University Press, 1988).
19 Dubnov, *Kniga zhizni*, 78.
20 M. L. Lilienblum, *Hat'ot neurim, o, Vidui ha-gadol shel ehad ha-sofrim ha-'ivrim* (Vienna: Buchdruckerei von Georg Brög, 1876). For a discussion of generation gaps in Hebrew literature, see Alan Mintz, *Banished from their Father's Table: Loss of Faith and Hebrew Autobiography* (Bloomington: Indiana University Press, 1989).

of the old world and creators of a new order, where the free 'critically-thinking individual' set the tone."[21]

It was typical among Russian intellectuals to emulate the lives of literary characters, as Irina Paperno has shown.[22] Similarly, as the literary critic for *Voskhod*, Dubnov mimicked radical writers. "[...] At that time [in the 1880s] I got pulled into the orbit of ideals from the Russian intelligentsia of the time whose radical wing had its origins in Belinsky up through Dobroliubov, Chernyshevsky, and Pisarev."[23] According to Jeffrey Veidlinger, Dubnov was also influenced by the sociological approach of the 1840s and 50s in his own research methodology, especially his view of the nation that he may have borrowed from the Slavophile Konstantin Aksakov.[24]

In his nearly forty years of journalism, Dubnov branded the tsarist regime as medieval, backward, repressive, and vindictive. In 1891, the government closed *Voskhod* for six months because of one of Dubnov's articles, depriving him and his colleagues of income.[25]

It is intriguing to consider the extent to which Dubnov's political and historical ideas emerged as reactions to actual events of his time.[26] For example, although he explained the meaning of assimilation in his analysis of the French Revolution, he learned about assimilation firsthand in Odessa in debates over funding for a national school in 1901-02. There Dubnov clashed with Mikhail Morgulis and other leaders of the Odessa branch of the Society for the Promotion of Enlightenment among the Jews of Russia, who adamantly upheld the principle that subsidies

---

21 Dubnov, *Kniga zhizni*, 77. The critically-thinking individual was the watchword of Petr Lavrov, the radical and leading theorist of the Socialist Revolutionaries.
22 Paperno, *Chernyshevsky and the Age of Realism*.
23 Dubnov, *Kniga zhizni*, 77.
24 Veidlinger, "Simon Dubnov Recontextualized," 422-23.
25 John Klier, "S. M. Dubnov and the Kiev Pogrom of 1881," in *A Missionary for History: Essays in Honor of Simon Dubnov*, eds. Kristi Groberg and Avraham Greenbaum (Minneapolis: University of Minnesota Press, 1998), 65-66; S. Dubnov, "Iz pisem A. E. Landau (1884-1894) s predisloviem i primechaniiami S. M. Dubnova. Materialy dlia istorii *Voskhoda* (1884-1896)," *Evreiskaia starina* I (January-March 1916): 106. Dubnov's objectionable article was published in *Nedel'naia khronika 'Voskhoda'* 13 (March 20, 1891). It is worth recognizing that today's historians reject Dubnov's claim that the government was directly responsible for pogroms. In fact, they claim, no evidence has been found that the government actually planned or carried out violence against its Jewish subjects.
26 For the classic study of Dubnov's political ideas, see Koppel S. Pinson, "Simon Dubnow: Historian and Political Philosopher," in *Nationalism and History: Essays on Old and New Judaism by Simon Dubnow* (Philadelphia: Jewish Publication Society, 1958).

should only go to schools that offered a curriculum of "universal" subjects (math, science, world history, Russian literature) and had none, or at most, only a few hours of Jewish subjects per week.[27]

In his view, such a school fostered assimilation, and during debates, Dubnov fashioned a definition of assimilation. In *Letters on Old and New Judaism* (*Pis'ma o starom i novom evreistve*) he wrote, "Assimilation is not so much a doctrine as a fact of life, unavoidable under the present circumstances against which nationalism struggles. It is the direct practical result of the rejection of the national idea. If you are not a Jewish nationalist, you inevitably will become assimilated, if not in the first, then in the second generation. And that is why we have a full moral right to call those who reject Jewry's national evolution facilitators of assimilation, whether they are conscious of it or not."[28] In this case Morgulis and the other leaders were incorrigible "assimilationists."[29] These debates also helped Dubnov formulate a theory of national education. In "Letter Nine" he expressed his ideas about the ideal Jewish school and its relationship to the national program:

> Our old school, the heder and yeshiva, educated only the Jew, but not the individual, and it educated even "the Jew" in an extremely one-dimensional way, affecting only his religious feeling and thought. The new secular school has it the other way. It completely forgets about "the Jew" and educates only "the individual," that is factually, a Russian, Pole, or German, in view of which spirit and language dominate in that particular school. This is the thesis and its antithesis. The synthesis comes out by itself: the simultaneous education of "the individual" and "the Jew." A school should prepare a youth for the struggle [to defend] his own individuality and his national individuality since in a Jew's life the struggle for the former is tightly connected with the latter. The hostile world persecutes us not only as individuals who

---

27 A study of Mikhail Morgulis can be found in my book, *Empire Jews: Jewish Nationalism and Acculturation in Nineteenth and Early Twentieth Century Russia* (Bloomington: Slavica, 2009).
28 S. Dubnov, "O rasteriavsheisia intelligentsii," *Pis'ma o starom i novom evreistve*, *Voskhod* 12 (1902): 74-75.
29 Ibid., 87.

collide with it on the basis of personal interests, but also as members of a certain nation."[30]

As this passage shows, Dubnov's approach to nationalism was founded on synthesis, a rejection of the *maskilic* division of Jew inside and individual outside, and valorization of the unity of Jew and person, universal and particular. What Dubnov would reject in the situation of French Jews was precisely their one-sidedness, their rejection of national difference in the rush to integrate into the majority.[31]

The Russian philosopher, Vladimir Solov'ev, was an important influence in helping Dubnov conceive of a nationalism characterized by tolerance. In *Book of Life* Dubnov wrote, "I modified Vladimir Solov'ev, the Christian humanist's formula—'Love all people as you would your own'—to this: respect the national individuality of every person as you would your own."[32] In his book, *The Nationality Question in Russia* (*Natsional'nyi vopros v Rossii*), Solov'ev expressed the view that the separation of morality from politics was particularly harmful because politics bereft of morality led to the domination of one group over another. Solov'ev wanted morality to guide a nation's treatment of other nations. Instead of national "egoism," Solov'ev advised powerful nations to respect others on the grounds that all peoples compose individual parts of a single whole. "Moral duty demands from a people above all that it repudiate national egoism if it has surpassed its natural borders [...]. A people must recognize itself for what it genuinely is, i.e. merely a part of the cosmic whole. It must acknowledge its solidarity with all other living parts of the whole—solidarity with the highest universal interests—and not serve its own self-interests, but others' interests in accordance with the quantity of its own national forces and national qualities."[33]

Solov'ev distinguished between "*narodnost'*" (national qualities) and "*natsional'nost'*" (nationality). *Narodnost'* refers to the nation's positive dimension, its national creativity and inspiration. Solov'ev's example

---

30 S. Dubnov, "O natsional'nom vospitanii," *Pis'ma o starom i novom evreistve*, *Voskhod* 1 (1902): 82-83.
31 S. Dubnov, *Epokha pervoi emansipatsii, 1789-1815, Noveishaia istoriia evreiskogo naroda*, vol. 1 (Jerusalem: Gesharim, 2002), 57-64 (reprint from the 1937-39 edition).
32 Dubnov, *Kniga zhizni*, 228.
33 V. Solov'ev, "Natsional'nyi vopros v Rossii," in V. S. Solov'ev, *Sobranie socheinenii v desiati tomakh*, vol. 5 (Bruxelles: Foyer Oriental Chrétien, 1966), 4.

for England includes Shakespeare, Byron, and Newton. As an example of *natsional'nost'*, he points to Warren Hastings and Lord Seymore.[34] Hastings, the first English Governor-General of India, and Edward Seymour, Home Secretary under Victoria, represented the egotistic side of nationality, the desire to "destroy and murder." True universal brotherhood, Solov'ev maintained, can only be attained through an understanding and celebration of distinctions among individuals of different nations.

In *Letters on Old and New Judaism*, Dubnov describes a vision of nationalism that alludes to Solov'ev.[35] "A Jewish nationalist says, 'As a citizen of the country, I participate in its political and civic life in accordance with the rights given to me. But as a member of the Jewish spiritual nation, beyond those rights I have my own internal national interests, and in this sphere consider myself autonomous to the degree that autonomy is permitted for political dependent nationalities in the state and in the realm of interests.'"[36] Dubnov's conception of "autonomy" bears Solov'ev's influence in that it valorizes spirituality and culture (as opposed to government), gives preference to pacifism over militarism, and upholds the equality of all the nationalities.

Following the 1905 Revolution, Dubnov tried to realize his ideas. He helped establish a new political party, the Folkspartai, to participate in the new State Duma.[37] As a small party, however, the Folkspartai needed to be part of a coalition. Therefore, Dubnov drew up a program for cooperation with the Constitutional Democratic Party in order to gain seats in the Duma, while simultaneously struggling for Jewish collective rights that would include the right to separate educational and cultural institutions, civil courts, and political institutions for administrating internal Jewish issues.[38]

His demand for collective national rights brings him closer to figures in the empire who struggled for national liberation, such as the Polish nationalist, Roman Dmowski.[39] However, Dubnov's claims for

---

34 Ibid., 13.
35 David Fishman, *The Rise of Modern Yiddish Culture* (Pittsburgh: University of Pittsburg Press, 2000), 67-68.
36 S. Dubnov, "Avtonomizm, kak osnova natsional'noi programmy," *Pis'ma o starom i novom evreistve*, *Voskhod* 12 (1901): 10.
37 Simon Rabinovitch, "Alternative to Zion: the Autonomist Movement in Late Imperial and Revolutionary Russia" (PhD diss. Brandeis University, 2007), 66.
38 S. Dubnov, *Volkspartei: Evreiskaia Narodnaia Partiia* (St. Petersburg: Ts. Kraiz, 1907), 12.
39 On Dmowski, see Krzysztof Kawalec, *Roman Dmowski: 1864-1939* (Wrocław: Zaklad Narodowy, 2002).

the rights of citizens in a democracy, his respect for the individual, and his rejection of class struggle and revolutionary excesses, link him in part to ideas that appeared in 1909 in *Landmarks*, the volume criticizing the revolutionaries and favoring individual conscience. However, it is important to note that the promotion of Great Russian nationalism by right-wing Kadets repelled Dubnov.[40]

Allusions to Russia are palpable in theoretical discussions in *Letters on Old and New Judaism*, since Dubnov selected aspects from the experience of Eastern European Jewry to present his overall vision of Jewish purpose. As one may recall, in *Letters on Old and New Judaism*, Dubnov evaluated the development of nations according to a developmental hierarchy: racially linked tribes stood on the lowest step, while territorially and politically connected groups occupied a higher stage.[41] He attributed the highest level to the spiritual nation. It is impossible not to sense that he had Eastern-European Jews in mind when he lauded a people who retained their national identity and heritage, despite the loss of territory, political independence, and a common language. He exclaims, "If, despite an external break, the people nonetheless exist and through many centuries creatively develop an organic way of life, showing a stubborn desire for further autonomous development, this people has reached the highest rung of cultural-historical individualization. Even under conditions of increased pressure on their national will, they can be considered indestructible."[42]

Although the *Letters* are supposed to describe Jewish nationalism unconnected to any particular geographical area, Dubnov seems to allude to the experience of Eastern-European Jews when he promulgates national autonomy as the optimal basis for the development of Jewish culture. He writes, "Jews consistently paid the state regular and extraordinary taxes that were hardly compatible with the poverty of civil rights that were provided them, and therefore considered themselves free [of any inner obligation]. They did not have political rights or civil equality, but they preserved one right that was more valuable than anything else—the right to their own national life derived from communal self-

---

40   See P. Struve, "Intelligentsiia i natsional'noe litso," in *Patriotica: Politika, kul'tura, religiia, sotsialism* (Moscow: Respublika, 1997), 206-8; originally published in *Slovo*, 10 March 1909.
41   S. Dubnov, *Pis'ma o starom i novom evreistve*, 2nd ed. (St. Petersburg: Obshchestvennaia pol'za, 1907), 1-2.
42   Dubnov, "Avtonomizm kak osnova natsional'noi programmy," 5.

government."⁴³

Dubnov refers to institutions that were established when the Jews of Poland had been politically autonomous. He looked to the traditional *kahal*, the institution of Jewish self-governance in Eastern Europe, as a model for modern Jewish politics on the local level and to the Council of the Four Lands in late medieval Poland as a supreme legislative body.⁴⁴ However, he was perfectly aware of the anachronism in selecting these institutions—the Council of the Four Lands had been in disuse for at least two centuries and the *kahal* system had been abrogated by czarist decree in 1844. Furthermore, he fully acknowledged the excesses of the *kahal* in earlier times, when it was used as a brazen tool of oligarchs, and had no illusions about the ambiguities of the Polish state vis-à-vis Jews in the sixteenth and seventeenth centuries.

Nevertheless, Dubnov believed the two institutions could be useful in a significantly modified form in the twentieth century. He maintained in his program for the Folkspartai (1907) that Jews should possess their own national parliament in which Jewish representatives would be elected democratically with full suffrage for the entire adult community, including women.⁴⁵ He explained that in his conception of the *kahal*, representatives would be democratically elected and therefore responsive to the electorate.⁴⁶ Furthermore, he asserted that national autonomy worked best in a constitutional state, where the individual rights of citizens were fully protected.⁴⁷

In discussions of the Jewish nation, Dubnov employed rhetoric that parallels the search for spirituality that was widespread among Silver-Age Russian intellectuals with their syncretism, eliding religious differences and mixing traditions. Already in the early 1890s, for example, Dubnov engaged in this kind of religious rhetoric, by explaining that secular Jewish history gives spiritual, even messianic, meaning. He writes in "What is Jewish History," "The purpose of Jewish survival is ultimately

---

43   Ibid., 4.
44   S. Dubnov, *Volkspartei: Evreiskaia Narodnaia Partiia* (St. Petersburg: Ts. Kraiz, 1907), 12. For more on this, see Israel Bartal, "Dubnov's Image of Medieval Autonomy," in *A Missionary for History: Essays in Honor of Simon Dubnov, Yearbook Supplement* (Minneapolis: University of Minnesota, 1998), 11-18.
45   Needless to say, women's suffrage had been restricted in elections to the tsarist Duma. Vladimir Levin, "Russian Jewry and the Duma elections, 1906-1907," *Jews and Slavs* 7 (2000): 234.
46   Dubnov, *Volkspartei*, 12.
47   Ibid., 13.

transcendence." Dubnov emphasizes the next sentence by writing it entirely in italics; "Really, *the history of the Jews is the most philosophical, ideological, and didactic part of general history*. Before you appears a picture of the continuous development of the spirit that overcomes the sufferings of the flesh."[48] Alluding to Pushkin's "Elegy" (1830) and the famous phrase, "to ruminate and suffer"—"мыслить и страдать"—to evoke the idea that suffering leads to spiritual growth, Dubnov affirms his idea that modern Jewish identity gets its meaning from a sense of shared history and not religion. Consciousness of history should give tribute to the people's suffering in the past. Dubnov argued that the German historian Heinrich Graetz also used the concept of suffering to describe a Jewry that was abused externally, but internally was productive, creative, and profoundly alive.[49] Later in his memoirs he would attribute the same paradigm to his own development. "Maybe that was how it had to be: the Jewish writer could not take advantage of the privileges of a diploma, but had to suffer together with the Jewish masses. Then from his own experience he could depict this suffering in the critic's book of 'great anger' and with the controlled pathos of the historian."[50]

Alluding here to Akim Volynsky's writings on Dostoevsky, Dubnov affirms Volynsky's idea that the great novelist experienced the depths of personal anguish and also the heights of spiritual idealism.[51] Volynsky helped Dubnov find a solution to a "human yearning for internal freedom."[52] At the same time Dubnov, formally imitating Volynsky, uses religious rhetoric and invokes Christianity to describe a path to salvation. Such ecumenical expressions were typical of the Silver Age, in which authors portrayed a thirst for spirituality as a general human attribute.[53]

---

48 S. Dubnov, *Ob izuchenii istorii russkikh evreev i uchrezhdenii Istoricheskogo obshchestva* (St. Petersburg: 1891), 8.
49 Heinrich Graetz, *Geschichte der Juden von den ältesten Zeiten bis an die Gegenwart: Aus den Quellen neubearb* (Leipzig, 1874–1902).
50 Dubnov, *Kniga zhizni*, 95.
51 Akim Volynskii, "Tsarstvo Karamazovykh," in *Dostoevskii* (St. Petersburg: Akademicheskii proekt, 2007), 264. Interestingly, Akim Volynsky and Dubnov had been friends in the early 1880s when Flekser (Volynsky's real name) was not yet a Symbolist.
52 V. Kotel'nikov, "Skvoz' kul'turu (Akim Volynsky kak ideolog i kritik)," in Akim Volynsky's *Dostoevskii*, 57; see also Elena Tolstaia's masterpiece, *Apollon v snegu: Sintezy Akima Volynskogo*, unpublished manuscript.
53 Akim Volynsky's book is *Kniga velikogo gneva: kriticheskie stat'i, zametki, polemika* (St. Petersburg: Trud, 1904).

In addition to his thoughts, it would be valuable to depict Dubnov's feelings regarding Russia. An opportunity to do this appears in his reaction to an invitation in 1913 from Semyon Vengerov, the well-known literary scholar, to contribute an autobiographical entry in the illustrious *Critical-Biographical Dictionary of Russian Writers*.[54] In two letters to Vengerov, Dubnov poured out his objections to his inclusion in the dictionary. Because of the significance of these documents (and their unfamiliarity to the public), I will quote at length. The first excerpt is from March 25, 1913 and the second, longer one from April 8, 1913.[55]

> 1. Unfortunately I cannot take the opportunity to respond to your invitation in the letter I received concerning giving biblio-biographical information about myself for your *Dictionary of Russian Writers*. Not considering myself a Russian, but a Jewish national writer—although by the force of the historical tragedy of Jewish culture I write primarily in Russian—I contend that my name should not figure in the *Dictionary of Russian Writers*.[56]
>
> 2. The expression "Russian writers" (russkie pisateli) allows for two interpretations: 1) the writers are Russian, leaders of a Russian national literature or 2) all who write in the Russian language.[57] However much the editors of the *Dictionary* may explain to the reader that they conceive of this term in the second technical meaning, the first national meaning will always become attached to the epithet "Russian" in the book's title. The term's ambiguity can give cause to think that a Jewish writer, by force of fatal circumstances and writing his scholarship in Russian, at the same time considers himself in the

---

54 Semyon Vengerov, ed., *Kritiko-biograficheskii slovar' russkikh pisatelei i uchenykh*, 2nd ed. (Petrograd, 1915).
55 Vladimir Levin alerted me to these letters; I thank him for the aid.
56 Letter from S. Dubnov to S. Vengerov, March 25, 1913, located in Semyon Vengerov's archive in the Russian National Library, St. Petersburg (377-7-1398).
57 Dubnov uses the adjective "Russian." Scholars often speak of a distinction between "russkii" and "rossiiskii," although "russkii" is used most often and "rossiiskii" was used mainly in official documents.

family of Russian writers and his work part of Russian literature. This would contradict the national-historical principle of the spiritual unity and indivisibility of world Jewry as a "nation among nations" that the *unity of a multi-lingual Jewish literature* presupposes. It would be especially wrong in similar cases to permit ambiguity on the part of the Jewish historian who, contemplating the meaning of history, has arrived at a strict national conception of Jewry and developed his conception in a series of essays.[58]

That is why, even now after your explanation, I cannot decide to supply you with the biblio-biographical information and help you include my name in the *Dictionary of Russian Writers*.[59] Of course I have no right to prevent the editors of the *Dictionary* from using information about me that is available in other sources for the sake of the completeness of the reference book. But then I ask of you that, if you do quote autobiographical excerpts in your editions, please quote the main content of this and the other letter in order to dispel the ambiguity that I mentioned.[60]

Vengerov did as Dubnov wished. He gathered enough information independently to publish an entry, and he honored the request by printing that Dubnov "considered himself a Jewish national writer."[61]

Recalling this episode, Dubnov limited his remarks to his reasons for refusing to fill out Vengerov's questionnaire. "I admit that my feelings were more persuasive than any firm conviction. My spirit was seething in anger at what was happening in Russia and I gave this feeling release

---

58 Dubnov is obviously referring to *Letters on Old and New Judaism*.
59 Presumably Dubnov's second letter is a response to a second letter from Vengerov in which the critic explains that by Russian writers he includes writers of the Russian language only and is indifferent to content.
60 S. Dubnov to S. Vengerov, April 8, 1913. Letter located in Semyon Vengerov's archive in the Russian National Library, St. Petersburg (377-7-1398).
61 An entry on Dubnov can easily be found in the reprint, *Russkaia intelligentsiia: avtobiografii i biobibliograficheskie dokumenty v sobranii S. A. Vengerova: annotirovannyi ukazatel'*, vol. 1 (St. Petersburg, 2001), 385-86. It says that, "D[ubnov] considers himself a Jewish national writer." The first edition was published in 1891.

in a small protest."⁶² One may recall that it was the time of the Mendel Beilis Trial, and the St. Petersburg censor banned one of his historical volumes.⁶³ Dubnov also felt a personal animus toward Semyon Vengerov for converting to Russian Orthodox Christianity. He wrote in his memoirs about it that, "Painful pages in the memoirs of his mother Pauline Vengerov (*Memoirs of a Grandmother*) give a clear understanding about the family tragedy caused by his conversion."⁶⁴

The two very different reactions reflect, I think, two different periods in Dubnov's life, but also two irresolvable positions that competed for dominance in his identity. The attitude of 1913 is clear: he felt anger. A Jewish nationalist, he could not consider himself a member of the Russian intelligentsia. Moreover, he was aware that his reputation might be soiled by giving the impression that he desired inclusion in Vengerov's dictionary. However, in the early 1930s, he felt differently. In emigration there was a large group of Jews who were using the Russian language. Unexpectedly, Dubnov sent Vengerov the completed questionnaire in 1919 (the postage stamp on the envelope clearly reads Petrograd, May 26, 1919).⁶⁵ One can only speculate why he did this, although it would seem a sign of reconciliation and respect.

Viewing Dubnov's reactions another way, one can conclude that the historian had two visions of his place in Russian culture. He conceived of himself as outside it, a Jewish nationalist whose allegiance extended to Jews around the world. In this case Russia was only one Diaspora home, perhaps only a temporary one. At the same time, as a Russian-language writer, he felt himself a member of a multi-national Russian-language family that consisted of writers of various nationalities whose members shared a politics of liberation for all.

Dubnov passionately loved Russia. He describes his feelings in his *Letters on Old and New Judaism*: "This natural feeling of love of fatherland is within everyone of us, regardless of whether we were happy or unhappy there.... Birth is not the only factor that binds us to a country.

---

62   Dubnov, *Kniga zhizni*, 353.
63   Ibid., 352.
64   Ibid., 106. Semyon Vengerov's conversion to Russian Orthodox Christianity is described by Shulamit Magnus in the introduction to volume 2 in *Memoirs of a Grandmother: Scenes from the Cultural History of the Jews of Russia of the Nineteenth Century* by Pauline Wengeroff, trans. and ed. Shulamit Magnus (Palo Alto: Stanford University Press, 2010-2012).
65   See the letter from S. Dubnov to S. Vengerov, May 25, 1919. Letter located in Semyon Vengerov's archive in the Russian National Library, St. Petersburg (377-7-1398).

It is also the cherished national relics, the graves of our ancestors, our sacred places, our historical monuments, the places connected with poetic folklore which so often in our youth filled us with joy or sadness—all these and many more are factors that nourish deep devotion to the fatherland."[66]

Russia's strong influence on Dubnov has support in the work of Sophia Dubnov-Erlich, Jonathan Frankel, and, more recently, Viktor Kelner, who also emphasizes the Russian environment in depicting the development of Dubnov as a historian and thinker.[67] One consequence of linking Dubnov and Russia's Silver-Age culture is that Dubnov appears more messianic and utopian than he might through a different lens. In later years he moved toward a more sociological approach that emphasized a strict rationalism. In his essay in 1910, "On the Contemporary State of Jewish Historiography," he emphatically repudiated theology and teleology, "the twin flaws," as he calls them, of nineteenth-century historiography.[68] He even acknowledged that he himself had been guilty of methodological mistakes and expressed hope that Jewish historiography would become more objective, analytic, and scientifically verifiable.[69]

However, one cannot accept Dubnov's statement that he expunged the utopian ideals of the earlier period. Even with his sociologically-based ideas of "mobile centers" Dubnov hinted that Jewish history expressed a higher, spiritual, or (one might call it) mystical purpose because the Jewish people are in his view "unique," and their fate weighted with meaning. In "The Survival of the Jewish People" (1912), he writes, "We find in the history of Israel a spiritual attracting force and a repelling force. The Jewish people goes its own unique way, attracting and repelling, beating out for itself a unique path among the routes of the nations of the world, a path that continues on from the beginning of

---

66   S. Dubnov, *Nationalism and History*, 367.
67   Kel'ner, *Missioner istorii*, 382-476. Frankel, "S. M. Dubnov," 239-75.
68   Dubnov, "O sovremennom sostoianii evreiskoi istoriografii," 151-58. Jeffrey Veidlinger has written well about this: "Simon Dubnow Recontextualized," 411-27.
69   Dubnov, "O sovremennom sostoianii evreiskoi istoriografii," 157. "I have to say that I do not believe in the very rapid success of this reform. It is very difficult. Even for those who admit the flaws of the old methods, it is difficult to reject what has become second habit to them. I have to admit that in the beginning of my scholarly activity I myself was not free of the old methods and now I would not be able to sign my name to much of what I wrote twenty years ago on the philosophy of history."

history, to go on perhaps to its end. And when we ask: 'Are the days of this people indeed like the days of the heavens above the earth?' a voice comes out from the depths of history and replies: 'They are, indeed!'"[70] Is this a metaphor? Maybe. But even if it is, Dubnov asserts that the Jews remain the chosen people whose fate is unique among all the peoples of the world. If I am right—and I think that I am—it would show that the mysticism and messianism of Russia's Silver-Age culture had a lasting influence on Dubnov's thought.

In the final analysis, Dubnov's contributions should be characterized as more than merely Jewish, Russian, or European, but reflect intersections of multiple intellectual strands from multifarious sources. Dubnov's mixture of humanism and belief in a Jewish Diaspora reflects a complex worldview, and his successes as a scholar and thinker point to the existence of a cultural climate that was rich and, despite official anti-Semitism, able to provide a suitable ground for cultural cross-fertilization. Neither West nor East, neither just Russian or Jewish, Dubnov's creations absorbed many sources and reflected something new, unique, and alive. Although I consider the Russian influence a predominant one, Dubnov's contributions embody the intersections and reworking of traditions that characterized the Jewish renaissance in Russia as a whole.

---

70   S. Dubnov, "The Survival of the Jewish People: The Secret of Survival and the Law of Survival," in *Nationalism and History*, 327. This article was originally published in *Heatid* 4 (1912).

2. The exhibit of the Society for the Promotion of Enlightenment at the 1893 Fair in Novgorod (reproduced courtesy of Michael Beizer).

2. Maxim Vinaver and the First Russian State Duma

The name, Maxim Vinaver, became associated with the First Russian State Duma. He wrote two books on the subject, *Conflicts in the First Duma* (*Konflikty v pervoi Dume*) (1907) and *The History of the Vyborg Appeal* [Memoirs] (*Istoriia vyborgskogo vozzvaniia* [*vospominaniia*]) (written in 1910 and published in 1913). This output, emerging in the years following the closure of the First Duma, memorializes the short period between spring and fall of 1906. At the same time, these two memoirs reflect the time in which they were written, and allude to new realities in Russian political life between 1906 and the First World War. They are redolent of internecine disputes within the Russian Constitutional Democratic Party (Kadet), the difficulties of organizing a unified Jewish politics, and the relentless struggle with the government.

In this essay I discuss the content of Vinaver's memoirs while trying to reconstruct the political context in which they were written. My goal is not to provide an exhaustive description of Vinaver's activities in the Duma or to provide a full description of the memoirs' content. Rather, I outline Vinaver's perception of the First Duma and illuminate the political goals contained in these two books.

Lawyer, politician, and memoirist, Maxim Vinaver was born to a middle-class Jewish family in 1862, in Warsaw. After graduating with a degree in law from the University of Warsaw, he settled in St. Petersburg, where he was active both as a trial lawyer and editor of and contributor to the most prestigious legal journals in Russia, including *Iuridicheskii vestnik* and *Vestnik prava*. Because of regulations affecting the advancement of Jewish lawyers, he was unable to rise beyond the rank of lawyer's assistant for fifteen years, until regulations were changed in 1904.[1] In St. Petersburg he was active in Jewish political circles, helping form the Defense Bureau in 1902.[2] This organization was dedicated to defending Jews by non-violent means, including civil trials and the print

---

1 S. L. Kucherov, "Evrei v russkoi advokature," *Kniga o russkom evreistve ot 1860-kh godov do revoliutsii 1917 g.* (New York: Soiuz russkikh evreev, 1960), 407.
2 B. Nathans, *Beyond the Pale: The Jewish Encounter with Late-Tsarist Russia* (Berkeley and Los Angeles: University of California Press, 2002), 329.

media. Early in 1905, Vinaver reacted quickly to lend support to the Revolution. In February 1905, he urged the Society for the Promotion of Enlightenment among the Jews of Russia to join the Union of Unions, and in March, he and the Jewish lawyer, Henrik Sliozberg, arranged an illegal meeting in Vilna "in order to set up an independent Jewish political organization."[3] At the so-called Vilna Congress, the Union for the Attainment of Full Equality for the Jewish People in Russia (*Soiuz dlia dostizheniia Polnopraviia Evreiskogo Naroda v Rossii*) was founded, and soon after, it also joined the Union of Unions. In October 1905, when the Constitutional Democratic Party was established, Vinaver became one of its leaders and was elected as a representative from St. Petersburg to the First Duma.

In order to understand Vinaver's perspective on the First Duma, one has to consider his attitude toward the Revolution of 1905, the politics of the Kadet party, and his activities within the Jewish community. Of primary importance is the fact that Vinaver viewed the Kadets as the authentic heirs of the Revolution. He believed that the work of the Kadets in establishing the Union of Unions, leading the 1905 Revolution, fighting in the First Duma, and organizing the Vyborg Appeal reflected a new stage in the heroic revolutionary tradition. The right to represent the Russian people had shifted away from the radicals to the Constitutional Democrats. Moreover, unlike radicals, the Kadets adapted to the new situation and understood that with the establishment of a Duma, the methods of struggle had changed. To wrest control of political power from the tsarist government, revolutionary violence would have to cede its place to peaceful negotiation.

One reason that Vinaver wrote memoirs about the First Duma was no doubt to express disappointment. In his memoirs Vinaver remembered not only what occurred, but also the way he felt. Comparing the first efforts to scaffolding at a large building site, Vinaver writes:

> When we carried out the work of the First Duma day after day, then it seemed to us only like the scaffold of a grandiose building, a scaffold that we would soon re-

---

[3] C. Gassenschmidt, *Jewish Liberal Politics in Tsarist Russia, 1900-1914: The Modernization of Russian Jewry* (New York: New York University Press, 1995), 21. For more on Sliozberg, see B. Horowitz, "Henrik Sliozberg: A Mirror of Petersburg Jewry in Late Tsarist Days," in *Empire Jews*, 139-52.

move, although now it has already become fossilized in memoirs as something that has receded from life's background. Is it worthwhile to print onto the memory of our descendents the outline of the scaffold, the history of the first cautious creative movements, when behind the scaffold something was hidden that would soon shine as an eternal monument to the work of the first people's democracy and, impervious to decay, would live forever?[4]

In the years following the closure of the Duma, when Vinaver's ideal of yoking revolutionary passion to parliamentary democracy grew further from attainment, he valorized the First Duma as reflecting a better time. In addition, Vinaver glorified the Duma for its role in advancing the political and social life of the country generally and for uniting the left and the center in the struggle against the government. In *Conflicts in the First Duma*, he emphasizes the Duma's significance by referring to the renunciations of its detractors.

Skeptically inclined individuals, having read the whole history of the imperceptible and controversial work to extend the life of the first Russian People's parliament and recalling that in the end the Duma did die, will turn away from our useless efforts with a disdainful smile: what good is that masterful exquisite pattern on cloth which a bayonet can rip apart with such ease? In response we quote two or three lines that belong to the leaders of the party which boycotted the Duma more vigorously than the others [Social Democrats]. "The State Duma lived only 72 days, but its role was huge in developing the struggle for freedom. The Duma pulled away the heavy curtain that hid the holy of holies of Russia's state power from the sight of the people… The Duma was a national agitator of enormous strength."[5]

---

4   M. Vinaver, *Konflikty v pervoi dume* (St. Petersburg: 1907), 6-7.
5   Ibid., 183-84.

While a reader today can understand the subjective importance of the First Duma for its participants, one hesitates to assign it major historical significance. In fact, looking back over a century later, it is easier to accept the claim that Vinaver created an idealized image that did not coincide with reality. The Kadet, Vasily Maklakov charged that, "Vinaver was not only a participant, but he preserved the ecstatic cult of the Duma. He became its singer. He illuminates with the light of dreams anything and everything connected with it."[6]

Vinaver's excitement can be excused. After all, a number of generations of patriotic Russians had been waiting impatiently for the chance to establish democratic institutions of government. The Duma provided the first experiment of a democratic legislature in modern Russian history. Here was the first chance to hold genuine elections, design legislation, and speak directly to the public through a relatively free press. This idea of "firsts" gripped Vinaver and other leaders in the First Duma. Pavel Miliukov has written, "M. M. Vinaver was not a professional politician. Not a single person who went into the fight for Russia's social and political liberation was one. The possibility itself of such a fight—in that constitutional context in which we found ourselves assigned to lead it—came into being so recently and suddenly that our generation could not rely on any previous experience. Our experience was the first one; we had to feel our military position on the run and learn from our own mistakes."[7]

Besides portraying the First Duma as part of an exercise in personal accounting, Vinaver used the memoir form to express his political ideals in the context of the struggles in the years immediately following the Duma's closing. In order to understand these contexts, we must examine Vinaver's political position after 1905.

Politically, Vinaver stood on the left flank of the Kadet party. As one may recall, the groups that coalesced to become the Constitutional Democrats included leftist-leaning liberals, members of various professional unions, including the union of railroad workers and employees of the Zemstvos. The right wing consisted mainly of business leaders, many of whom left the Kadets later to form the Union of October 17,

---

6 V. Maklakov, "1905-1906 gody," in *M. M. Vinaver i russkaia obshchestvennost' nachala XX veka* (Paris: 1937), 60. See also V. Maklakov, *Pervaia Gosudarstvennaia Duma, 27 aprelia-8 iiulia 1906 goda* (Moscow: Tsentrpoligraf, 2006).

7 P. Miliukov, "Vinaver kak politik," in *M. M. Vinaver i russkaia obshchestvennost' nachala XX veka*, 19.

known generally as the Octobrist party.[8]

Although Vinaver shared with his Kadet colleagues a respect for rule of law, he also identified with the revolutionary intelligentsia, considering its values sacred. Vinaver's sympathy for the revolutionary left was shaped by a desire for a more equitable division of resources and equal rights for all the national minorities, including Jews. In addition, he bore the tsarist bureaucracy a great deal of ill will both for personal reasons and because of its hostile treatment of Jews. In his Duma speeches, he expressed anger at the tsar's anti-terrorist campaign, the fomenting of pogroms, and the government's inability to help the peasantry with a reasonable plan for agricultural reform.[9] He was disappointed in Pyotr Stolypin, whom he accused of intentionally undermining the Duma.[10] St. Ivanovich and D. Zaslavsky, authors of a book on the Kadets and the Jews, described Vinaver's views accurately when they wrote, "The Constitutional Democratic Party broke with the political and social traditions of the heroic period of the Russian intelligentsia, but those traditions were still alive among Jewish liberals."[11] In other words, Jews still expected the Kadets to fight for liberation even after the party had set a course of compromise with the government that did not include equal rights for Jews.

One of the central ideas of *Conflicts in the First Duma* was that the Kadets offered the best political leadership in the country because they alone walked the fine line between aggression and conciliation with the government, and were therefore able to nudge the government toward greater concessions. Thus, what was needed in the First Duma, according to Vinaver, was to tame the revolution and channel its energy into productive parliamentary work. With a revealing but complicated metaphor, Vinaver ends *Conflicts in the First Duma* this way:

> Understand that these 72 days of the Duma's survival were spent largely occupied with meticulous parliamentary work. Don't reject frivolously the "fine mechanism."

---

8   L. Menashe, *Alexander Guchkov and the Origins of the Octobrist Party: The Russian Bourgeoisie in Politics, 1905* (New York: New York University Press, 1966).
9   M. Vinaver, *Rechi M. M. Vinavera (partiia narodnoi svobody)* (St. Petersburg: 1907).
10 *Konflikty*, 182-83.
11 D. Zaslavskii and St. Ivanovich, *Kadety i evrei* (Petrograd, 1916), 8–9. St. Ivanovich is a pen name for Semyon Osipovich Portugeis (1880-1944), who was a well-known Menshevik.

> Realize that when you pass from fighting with a nightstick to a Mauser rifle, then you cannot jump into a fight with a rifle as though it were a nightstick. You have to use the rifle aware of all the rules of the art. You must calculate the aim in millimeters and you cannot disdainfully dispose of the fine mechanism in the middle of the fight and coarsely and senselessly wave the gun's butt around in empty space, putting your bare chest in the sights of the enemy aiming his arrow skillfully and precisely…
>
> But all this of course only serves good cause until they take the rifle from your hands…[12]

The meaning of this extended metaphor refers to the conflict with the government; the image of the rifle is well chosen. Although the Kadets had chosen parliamentary methods, for Vinaver the opposition was still engaged in a lethal duel with the government. Thus he mixes metaphors, using revolutionary language to describe the mechanism of legislation, which he describes as "mundane parliamentary work" ("*melkotkannaia parlamentskaia rabota*"). Vinaver lauded negotiation, compromise, and tactical skill, but still he hoped to vanquish the enemy, i.e. the government. The fight continued until, as Vinaver says, your opponent "takes the rifle out of your hand,." i.e. closes the Duma. This passage sums up Vinaver's attitudes about legality, revolution, and leadership in the First Duma and the Kadet party's skills in operating their weapon.

As the largest party in the Duma, the Kadets had the main responsibility for charting strategy.[13] However, not having enough seats to govern alone, they had to form a coalition with other parties. While some Kadets preferred to join with the parties of the right, Vinaver argued that one could not join hands with those who rejected equality for Jews, repudiated women's suffrage, and accepted the government's summary executions of radicals. Vinaver played an instrumental role in leading the Kadets to form a coalition with the parties on the left, such as the Trudoviki, and so-called unaligned leftists.[14]

Vinaver was aware of the First Duma's flaws. He lamented the way

---

12 *Konflikty*, 183-4.
13 The Kadets with their 180 deputies and the Trudoviki with 84 deputies commanded a majority in the parliament of 497.
14 *Konflikty*, 170.

Trudoviki and other leftists obstructed Kadet initiatives, referring as often to the fissures in the Kadet-Trudoviki bloc as to conflicts with the government.[15] He describes how Trudoviki used dissimulation and deceit to slow down legislation on military appropriations, agricultural reform, and even the nationalities question. He was also repelled by their public-relations campaign to denounce the Kadets and obfuscate their role. Describing the so-called Throne Speech in which Nicholas II demanded that the Duma representatives acknowledge his unconditional power, Vinaver complained about the way leftists reacted to the Kadet decision to respond without fulfilling the tsar's demand.

> Our response [to the Throne Speech] served as a signal for the beginning of the attacks on our party, which continued without a break until the dissolution of the Duma and which in my opinion played a decisive role in the Duma's fate. It was only in Vyborg, at the last session of the party committees that [the attacks] were reversed with dithrymbs in praise of the party and all its Duma activities. Not only the Social Democrats and Socialist-Revolutionaries, but as we will see, all the independent leftists and especially the independent leftist press participated in these attacks at the time.[16]

According to Vinaver, while the government bore responsibility for the Duma's closing, the failure to organize effectively lay with the leftists who, unwilling to compromise, acted arrogantly and irresponsibly. Vinaver, therefore, spoke directly in his memoirs: in elections to future parliaments, voters should shun the obstructionist left and support that party which was capable of leading the country competently and effectively, i.e. the Kadets.

Vinaver believed that the Kadets were more heroic than the radicals. In *The History of the Vyborg Appeal* Vinaver emphasized that the Kadets had organized the meeting of Duma deputies in Vyborg, and formulated, then proliferated the manifesto that called for civil disobedience. Moreover, in an act of self-sacrifice, the Kadets risked their own lives in order

---

15   Ibid., 7.
16   Ibid., 47-48.

to save the Duma. "Distributing [the manifesto] for which we were tried and sat in prison hardly bothered us, as I said. We were entirely certain that it would get enormous distribution without any effort. And if we had realized that one needs to make an effort to distribute the farewell manifesto, we would still have chosen to do it. In reality, it turned out that we were not wrong."[17]

Despite the deputies' good intentions, the manifesto did not have the effect that the signatories had hoped for. When Vinaver arrived in Vyborg, the manifesto was already ready, having been written by Pavel Miliukov. Vinaver wrote:

> I found the plan weakly conceived, the manifesto should have rang out the cry of rebellion more sharply; like a bolt of lightning it should have illuminated the true meaning of what had happened before the population. There wasn't any of that elemental enraged force in it. The second part—the appeal that played such a fatal role later on—did not draw any attention. It certainly seemed, especially at the first minute, that this [manifesto] was elementally the simple and natural minimum, pathetic minimum, of action that remained in our power. And exactly because it was so small we felt a special need to use decisively and boldly what was left to us: to publish our cry of rebellion which, so it seemed, corresponded to the strength of the blow that we had taken and which would gain vast momentum in the country.[18]

It is clear that Vinaver wanted a more vibrant document that would startle the nation with its expression of anger and frustration. Disappointed that the appeal to the population not to appear for military service was ineffective since the recruitment induction was some ten months away and the call not to pay income taxes had little relevance, since most taxes were collected from retail sales and taxes unrelated to income, Vinaver predicted that their appeal to the people would fall on

---

17   M. Vinaver, *Istoriia vyborgskogo vozzvaniia (vospominaniia)* (Moscow: 1913), 75-76.
18   Ibid., 15-16.

deaf ears. In fact, the manifesto's publication did not lead to any displays of civic disobedience.

Inevitably, Vinaver's memoirs became involved in polemics over the memory of the First Duma that reflected internal debates within the Kadet party itself and issues related to the so-called "Jewish Question." In particular, after 1905, Vinaver became the object of criticism by Kadets on the right, such as Vasily Maklakov and Pyotr Struve, who disagreed with Vinaver's conception of a heroic Duma.[19]

Maklakov, for example, criticized Vinaver for refusing to recognize that the unwillingness of the leftists to cooperate with the government had caused the failure. According to Maklakov, by yielding to the demands of the leftists, Vinaver and the Kadet party had written the Duma a death sentence, unforgivably squandering a rare opportunity.

> There was a total lack of understanding of one's own and the other's strengths in the First Duma. Frivolous self-assuredness, a passion for loud phrases and gestures led to contempt for real achievements. The Duma, in the words of a poet, had an aversion to "the ant-like deeds of man" and considered itself only worthy of "heroic action." The real style of the First Duma, not Vinaver's idealized one, consisted of a tense relationship of both sides. One may pity nearsighted people who because of the Duma's flaws did not perceive its qualities and were incapable of understanding the reasons for the halo that encircles it. But admiration for it should not stop one from the sad conclusion: the Duma was not appropriate for the duty assigned to it by the people's trust. One could have expected something else and something more.[20]

---

19 See also Dittmar Dahlmann, *Die Provinz Waehlt: Russlands Konstitutionell-Demokratische Partei und die Dumawahlen, 1906-1912* (Koehn: Boehlau, 1996); Terence Emmons, *The Formation of Political Parties and the First National Elections in Russia* (Cambridge, MA: Harvard University Press, 1983); Antony Kroener, "The Debate between Miliukov and Maklakov on the Chances for Russian Liberalism," *Revolutionary Russia* 7, no. 2 (1994): 239-71.

20 Maklakov, "1905-1906 gody," 89. Although these remarks were published only in 1936, they represent views that Maklakov held at the time. Proof of this assertion can be found in the speeches that he gave and in his own memoirs about the period. See *Rechi: Sudebnye, dumskie i publichnye lektsii, 1904-1926* (Paris: 1949); and *Vlast' i obshchestvennost' na zakate staroi Rossii (vospominaniia)* (Paris: 1936).

Maklakov's disagreement with Vinaver pivoted around his interpretation of the government's intentions.[21] According to Maklakov, the government was actually trying to come to an agreement with the First Duma, but had to weigh offers of compromise against the leftists' desire to spread disorder and anarchy. One can sympathize with a government that put its responsibility for domestic order above other goals. In contrast, Vinaver did not believe that the government had acted in good faith, maintaining that there was never any intention of cooperating with the Duma. In fact, government repression had actually started before October 17, 1905. The so-called "Throne Speech" and the final dispersal of the deputies served as incontrovertible proof of this claim. Convinced of the government's permanent hostility, Vinaver maintained that only a revolutionary overthrow of power would enable the Duma to wrestle power from the uncompromising government.

In fact, the two had contradictory perspectives. Whereas this was a time of tremendous positive energy and enormous potential for Vinaver, Maklakov viewed it as doomed by decadence and immorality.[22]

> "The style of the First Duma was not a characteristic of it or in general a characteristic of that year. It was a general phenomenon. In different doses and combinations it is the style of all those colorful, overly bright, and unhealthy epochs, which one conventionally calls "renaissances," "breaks with the past," "springs" and similar laudable names. Often the best sides of a person are revealed in these times: faith, energy, and heroism. But in these times its opposite and weaknesses are also revealed: vanity, envy, malice and most importantly, an inability to be fair, i.e. that principle quality which is taught in every political contest and which for some reason is called the "Hottentot" moral. But it is exactly these negative qualities that motivate people in dark epochs."[23]

---

21 Georgii Adamovich, *Vasilii Alekseevich Maklakov, politik, iurist, chelovek* (Paris: 1959), 157-59.
22 On Maklakov's attitudes see Nikita Igorovich Dedkov, *Konservativnyi liberalism Vasiliia Maklakova*, (Moscow: Airo-XX, 2005); David Arwyn Davies, "V. A. Maklakov and the Problem of Russia's Western Modernization" (PhD diss., Ann Arbor, University Microfilms, 1968).
23 "1905-1906 gody," 89.

Although one may agree with Maklakov's negative characterization of the political left, it is interesting that the perspective of those Kadets who moved to the right did not sway Vinaver, who held fast. In *The History of the Vyborg Appeal*, which appeared in 1913, Vinaver depicted the First Duma as a beacon of the best values, the sole institution capable of uniting the left and right, characterized by heroism and self-sacrifice. "My soul shined. The fruit of suffering and painful contemplation grew ripe. The First Duma did not dissipate without a trace. Once again it became welded into a unity that will leave the people a will and testament to the struggle for rights that have been trampled."[24]

Vinaver's disagreement with the Kadets on the right intensified at this time over the calls for the dominance of Russian nationalism and skepticism about Jewish equality. It is essential to know that in the Jewish political context Vinaver found himself uncomfortably positioned between individuals who were more radical on both the left and the right. In 1905, Vinaver became a leader of the Union of Equal Rights (*Soiuz polnopraviia*) which was composed of Jewish leaders who hoped to gain equal rights as a consequence of the Revolution of 1905.[25] Soon enough, however, this coalition split into the Jewish People's Group (*Evreiskaia narodnaia gruppa*), which remained loyal to the liberal line, and the Jewish People's Party (*Evreiskaia narodnaia partiia*), which was composed of groups further to the left. In 1907, however, Vinaver's Jewish People's Group itself splintered when Zionists decided to leave to seek election to the Second Duma separately.[26]

Having failed to unite all the Jewish groups under the liberal banner, Vinaver faced a new threat from members of the Kadet party that had been perceived as friendly to Jews and was even called a "Jewish Party" by ultra-right groups.[27] In 1909, the Kadet ideologist Pyotr Struve published an article in the liberal newspaper, *Slovo* (Word) entitled "Intelligentsia and the National Face" ("Intelligentsiia i natsional'noe litso") in defense of Russian nationalism and the dominance of Russian culture, raising doubts about whether Jews could be fully integrated.[28] Struve

---

24 Vinaver, *Istoriia vyborgskogo vozzvaniia*, 58.
25 Gassenschmidt, *Jewish Liberal Politics in Tsarist Russia*, 22.
26 Ibid., 48.
27 D. C. Rawson, *Russian Rightists and the Revolution of 1905* (Cambridge: Cambridge University Press, 1995), 69.
28 P. Struve, "Intelligentsiia i natsional'noe litso," in *Patriotica: Politika, kul'tura, religiia, sotsialism* (Moscow: Respublika, 1997), 206-8.

made a distinction between individual Jews who joined Russian culture, whom he lauded, and Zionists and other Jewish nationalists, toward whom he was hostile.

Vinaver was critical of the article's timing since it was likely to add to the general anti-Jewish feeling that was intensifying in cultural circles due to the Chirikov Affair. Referring to Struve's comparison of the two artists, Isaac Levitan and Karl Briullov, Vinaver wrote,

> In your examples Briullov is beaten by the "undilutable" Jew Levitan... Incidentally, I repeat, I understand and am inclined to respect Suzdal nationalism, but therefore I have to ask: from whom are you protecting yourself? Why have you entered into battle majestically with trumpets and banners? Why do you connect your sermon precisely with us? [...] It is a sin against truth and a particularly heavy sin because your false connection of ideas will be used maliciously to harm the weakest side.[29]

While Struve had been rethinking his position on the nationalities and now stood in favor of a renewed principle of state power with preferred place for the Russian people, Vinaver remained faithful to the idea of equal rights for all nationalities in a cosmopolitan rule-of-law state.[30]

By challenging expectations for full equality, Struve indirectly prompted Vinaver to justify his commitment to the Kadet party and explain why the Kadets should be perceived as defenders of Jewish political interests. Later Vinaver wrote a book, *The Kadets and the Jewish Question* (*Ka-dety i evreiskii vopros*), published in 1912, devoted to propagandizing the virtues of the Kadet party for Jewish voters. Alluding to objections that Kadets had not fought hard enough for Jewish rights, Vinaver recalled the days of the First Duma: "[...] Did the Kadets act correctly with regards to the Jewish people, did they do for it what they were obligated to do? To this question I answer yes unconditionally. And I am sure that

---

29 M. Vinaver, "Otkrytoe pis'mo P. B. Struve," in *Po vekham: Sbornik statei ob intelligentsii i "natsional'nom litse"* (Moscow: 1909), 83-84.
30 Exactly at this time Struve was expressing ideas about the need for a great Russia. See his articles, "Velikaia Rossiia: Iz razmyshlenii o probleme russkogo mogushchestva" and "Otryvki o gosudarstve," both of which appeared in his volume, *Patriotica: Politika, kul'tura, religiiia, sotsializm* (1911).

the source of accusations now falling on the Kadets are nothing but simple ignorance of the facts."[31] Among the facts that people are unaware of, Vinaver points to a resolution passed by the pre-Duma Kadet congress in which the "principle of civil equality was raised as the foundation stone of the whole transformation of the state...."[32] The Kadet tactics on the Jewish question was to "use the ministry's legislative proposal on freedom of conscience." "This way the Constitutional-Democrats could immediately begin to resolve the Jewish question. Since the ministry's legislative proposal removed all restrictions connected with religious confession, [it was possible] to put the Jewish question on the table and remove immediately all Jewish restrictions."[33]

Although many critics accused Kadets of cowardice for attempting to attain equal rights for the Jews in a "backdoor" way, i.e. by subsuming their interests in those of the whole, Vinaver was convinced of the rightfulness of this approach. Incidentally the strategy was unsuccessful; the Kadets were unable to gain increased rights for the country's Jews. Nonetheless, Vinaver defended liberals. "But I consider the unproven and unjustified accusations against the party raised in the name of the Jewish people as not just unfair, but also politically harmful. The party has up to now fulfilled and continues to fulfill its political obligations regarding the Jewish people, if not with more, than in no manner with less consistency and energy than all the other opposition parties."[34]

Because he was convinced that by struggling on behalf of Russian democracy he was serving Jews and by working on behalf of Jewish emancipation he was serving Russians, Vinaver was offended by Struve's remarks that revealed lines of division. Maklakov wrote, "Vinaver felt both joy and bitterness when he could speak as a representative of Judaism and a deputy from Petersburg, when he could link the fate of Judaism in Russia with the victory of the rule-of-law principle that was needed not only for them, but for everyone."[35]

Incidentally, Zionists were highly critical of Vinaver, whom they accused of selling out Russia's Jews. In a number of newspaper articles,Vladimir Jabotinsky mocked Vinaver for continuing to cooper-

---

31 M. Vinaver, *Ka-dety i evreiskii vopros* (Odessa: 1912), 3.
32 Ibid., 4.
33 Ibid., 8.
34 Ibid., 9.
35 "1905-1906 gody," 63-64.

ate with the Kadets after party leaders had announced the desire to turn Russia into a nation state at the expense of the rights of its minorities. Jabotinsky wrote, "Mr. Vinaver in the same issue of *Rech'*, March 13, 1908, nonetheless also offers for the future Jewish services warmed by mutual love, 'precisely love.' By all means. The gentle calf sucks on two teats. We grant Mr. Vinaver and the other gentle people to live Mathuselah years in that curious position where they, looking into the eyes of their 'Pan,' emotionally speak out: 'Nonetheless you love us!' But Mr. Struve and Miliukov answer, 'Mm... not really.'"[36]

Probably because of accusations that Kadets were not doing enough to support the Jewish cause, during a conference of the Kadet Central Committee in January 1909 in Moscow, Vinaver demanded that the party make greater efforts to defend Jews. Arguing that the continuing indifference would lead to a loss of voters and serious damage to the party's reputation, Vinaver called for a change of tactics. According to Christoph Gassenschmidt, the "venture was met with success: the Central Committee of the Kadets nominated the Duma deputies [V. A.] Karaulov and [N. V.] Nekrasov to speak on behalf of the Jews in the name of the Kadet Duma faction."[37] Gassenschmidt continued, "How successful Vinaver's move was became evident in the fact that from early 1909 onwards Kadet leaders such as [F. I.] Rodichev and Maklakov not only defended Russian Jews against the right-wing anti-Semitic outbursts in the Duma, but also became active outside parliament by meeting Jewish community leaders for feedback and material to defend Russian Jewry appropriately."[38]

It should perhaps not come as a surprise that Vinaver introduced the Jewish question in his memoirs to underscore his conception of the unity of Russians and Jews. Heading a Duma commission to investigate the Bialystok pogrom (1905), Vinaver gave a fiery speech on June 2, 1906, in which he accused the government of instigating violence with the motivation of punishing Jews for allegedly "making the revolution." Arguing that the country had to choose between the tsarist government and the principle of rule-of-law, he pointed out that a government that wreaks violence on innocent citizens represents the antithesis of a just

---

36 V. Jabotinskii, *Fel'etony* (St. Petersburg: 1913), 66.
37 Gassenschmidt, *Jewish Liberal Politics in Tsarist Russia*, 85.
38 Ibid.

government whose function it is to protect its citizens and defend its laws.³⁹ Vinaver ended his speech by claiming that the horror of Bialistok linked Jews to the Russian people who felt similar horror about their government. "There are few of us but we have a single enormous force—the force of despair, and one ally—the entire Russian people filled with true humanity."⁴⁰

Although Zionist and Jewish nationalist leaders disagreed with his claim about the unity of the Jewish and Russian peoples, Vinaver did not cede on this point. Similarly, he did not yield to the contradictory views of Russian nationalists or, as we have seen, members of his own party. For Vinaver, the First Duma embodied the common cause that joined Russians with the members of all the national minorities, including Jews.⁴¹

In the years that followed the closing of the First Duma, Nicholas II changed the franchise laws, truncating the voting rights of workers and peasants in order to insure a conservative majority in subsequent Dumas. At the same time radical parties decided to participate in future elections, while the Octobrists formed their own party. The numbers of Kadets elected and their overall percentage in the Duma decreased. In an atmosphere of renewed competition between the left and right, Vinaver wanted to legitimate the Kadets as the party that embodied the proper combination of sympathy for radicalism tempered by pragmatic restraint. His memoirs about the First Duma provide a tribute to the Kadets for their unfailing attempts to "save the Duma," i.e. to save that Kadet-centered Duma capable of confrontation, idealism, heroism and self-sacrifice.

When the Provisional Government took power in 1917, Vinaver was tapped once again for his expertise, assigned to the commission for organizing the elections to the Constituent Assembly.⁴² After October

---

39   In his speech from June 26, 1906, Vinaver said, "Power that announces: I am powerless to suppress the Revolution,—has already condemned itself to death. But the power that announces: I am powerless to openly fight with the Revolution, and therefore I will engage in hidden moves; I will distribute secret brochures, place my true state advisors, the Rachkovskys and Lavrovs, in hidden underground places and from there I will let fly poisoned arrows onto innocent people. Such a government has not only condemned itself to death, not only acknowledged itself incapable of governing, but has criminally undermined the foundation of that power which one is obligated to support." (M. Vinaver, *Rechi M. M. Vinavera [partiia narodnoi svobody]* [St. Petersburg, 1907], 58).
40   Ibid., 69.
41   Vinaver's Jewish identity has not been the subject of study. Suffice it to say here that a great deal more can be said on this theme than has been discussed in the context of the First Duma.
42   Vinaver's activity from 1917-1918 is described in William G. Rosenberg's *Liberals in the Russian*

1917, he left Petersburg for Moscow and from there fled a Bolshevik arrest warrant. Arriving in Crimea, he joined the local anti-Bolshevik government, becoming its first Minister of Foreign Affairs. He described his Crimean experiences in *Our Government: Crimean Memoirs, 1918-1919* (*Nashe pravitel'stvo: Krymskie vospominaniia, 1918-1919*) (1928).[43]

Looking back at the First Duma from the perspective of the spring of 1917, Vinaver had regrets. Relating a conversation from the spring of 1917 with the lawyer F. F. Kokoshkin, Vinaver claimed that the failed parliament in Russia was a tragedy, but less for the individual than for the country as a whole.

> "We were born to be parliamentarians, but fate placed us in a situation when the struggle had to be waged by other means. That is how it's always been [how it was] in 1905-06, that's how it is now." [...] In these words told to me in one of our intimate conversations in the still early months of the Revolution, a deep tragedy in the life of this outstanding man was hidden. The tragedy here was not, however, in his personal experience; the harmony of his nature had inoculated him from any internal drama. The tragic aspect was Russia's fate that, possessing such a pearl at the dawn of its free parliamentary life, [Russia] could not take from it all its brilliance and in stupid madness allowed her [fate] to be crushed.[44]

That sentiment represents Vinaver's lasting view of the First Duma period. A time of amazing possibilities, the Duma changed the terrain of Russian politics, but with this change came great expectations for the attainment of participatory democracy and equality that ultimately remained unfulfilled at that time and in the intervening two decades before his death in Paris in 1926.

Revolution: The Constutional Democratic Party, 1917-1921 (Princeton: Princeton University Press, 1974).

43 A discussion of Vinaver in the Crimea can be found in Oleg Budnitskii's *Russian Jews Between the Reds and the Whites, 1917-1920*, trans. Timothy J. Portice (Philadelphia: University of Pennsylvania Press, 2012), 153-55.

44 *Nedavnee*, 135.

3. The lawyer and activist, Maxim Vinaver (reproduced courtesy of the Jewish Studies Department of the European University in St. Petersburg).

3. What Is "Russian" in Russian Zionism?
Synthetic Zionism and the Fate of Avram Idel'son

The history and character of the group of intellectuals who gathered around the Zionist journal *Rassvet* between 1905 and 1917 deserves recounting. Among them were extremely talented individuals who had a strong impact on the history of Zionism in Russia—Avram Idel'son, Daniil Pasmanik, Yuly Brutskus, and Vladimir Jabotinsky among them. But their talents as individuals were overshadowed by their feverish energy as a group: their cultivation of a Zionist press, their success in Helsingfors in articulating a new approach to Zionism, their participation in Russian politics, and their contributions to political theory.

These individuals (with the exception of Jabotinsky) are hardly remembered today. Nonetheless, there are good reasons to recover this history. The story composes a part of the history of Russian intellectual life in general and the history of the Jewish intelligentsia in particular.[1] However, when scholars approach Zionism in Russia, it is usually to deal with the earlier period, that of Hibbat Tsion with its major thinkers, Leo Pinsker and Ahad-Ha'am, or with the group associated with the Cultural Opposition since its leaders became important in later times (Hayim Weizmann, Martin Buber, Menachem Usishkin and Ben Gurion).[2] Few people have taken an interest in the *Rassvet* group of activists and writers because their story belongs as much to Russian as Jewish history, and does not fit the Zionist narrative in which the dedicated activist makes Aliyah and transforms himself from a Russian, German, or American Jew into an Israeli. Avram Idel'son in particular did not make Aliyah. However, Idel'son's story has a central role

---

1 The exceptions are Yossi Goldshtein and earlier, Itzhak Maor, who looked at Russian Zionism for its own sake. Despite their efforts, Russian Zionism is still an under-researched subject. The best book exclusively dedicated to the history of Russian Zionism is Yosef Goldshtein, *Bin tsionut medinit le-tsionut ma'asit: ha-tnuah ha-tsionit be-rusiyah be-ra'ashita* (Jerusalem: Magnes Press, 1991).

2 For example, Gideon Shimoni, *The Zionist Ideology* (Hanover: University Press of New England, 1995); Yossi Goldstein, *Usishkin: biografiyah*, vol. 1, *Ha-tekufah ha-rusit*, 1863-1919 (Jerusalem: Magnes, 1999); Jehuda Reinhartz, *Chaim Weizmann: the Making of a Statesman* (New York and London: Oxford University Press, 1993).

in Russian-Jewish and Russian-Zionist history.[3]

Idel'son came of age in the period of political upheaval and cultural renaissance known as the Silver Age, in which writers, poets, philosophers, artists, and revolutionaries were at the forefront of Russian life. This ferment strongly influenced other young Zionists, including Pinkhus Rutenberg, Leo Motzkin, and Hayim Weizmann. Politics was only one part of a larger intellectual scene in which literature, music, and art were joined to an intense social life of drinking, friendships, and conversation. An examination of private life is imperative if one hopes to understand this generation of Russian-Jewish Zionists.

Like others of his generation, Avram Idel'son was strongly rooted in Russian intellectual life. In fact, despite years of intense activity on behalf of Zionism, he remained in Russia at the same time that the Halutzim of the Second Aliyah put their ideas into practice in Palestine. Nonetheless, his life and thought typify a central group of Russian Zionists now referred to as the "Rassvet group."

Although Idel'son alone is hardly remembered now, in the introduction to a 1946 volume dedicated to him, an editorial board that included Leib Jaffe, Yuly Brutskus, and Abraham Goldshtein, wrote, "Idel'son's personality and teachings were among the reasons leading to the development of the national idea and the Zionist movement at a brilliant time for Russian Zionism. The revolution that began in Zionist thought set down roots for the movement's [later] ideology. Whether we are aware of it or not, our path moved along those that Idel'son had already blazed."[4] Vladimir Jabotinsky, his colleague and friend, praised him this way:

> I am sure that it is no exaggeration if I say that to describe Idel'son the word "talent" is inadequate—that man stood on the border of "genius." "Acid all-corroding brain"—[Oscar] Gruzenberg once said to me speaking of Idel'son, and he was right. But that was merely one facade of a multifaceted crystal. His "acidity" consumed

---

3 My study of the life and ideas within Russian political contexts has precedents. See Steven Zipperstein, *Elusive Prophet: Ahad-Ha'am and the Origins of Zionism* (Berkeley: University of California Press, 1993).

4 *Sefer Idelsohn: Divre ha`arakhah ve-zikhronot, toldot hayav u-khtetavav* (Tel Aviv: Va'ad le-hotsaat, 1946), 1.

only the shells; into the kernels he knew to inject vivifying magic fluids. The curse of his destiny, the fate of a pauper—as were most of the members of our circle—or perhaps also, and to a certain extent the self-neglect originating in that same "acidness," prevented him from explicating his ideas in the form of a definite treatise. From him I heard the wistful phrase: "Would the Lord [have it] that I be imprisoned for a couple of years, then I might perhaps be able to write my works"... But to us youngsters even without his "works" his company was like a university.[5]

This passage provides us with an evaluation. Jabotinsky expresses the view that Idel'son was the group's leader and that his ideas had an enormous influence on the younger members. He notes that Idel'son never presented his ideas in a consistent and orderly way, but rather transmitted them in conversations. Although an oral method may have been effective during Idel'son's life, now, a century later, the absence of a coherent exposition makes it hard to reconstruct his ideas.

Since my goal is to explain the social context for Idel'son's thought, I have compiled the facts of his biography.[6] In addition to his own collections of articles, *On Zionist Themes* (1914), *On Jewish Social Democracy* (1917), and *Collected Works* (1919), two volumes about him were published after his death. The first volume appeared in Russian in Berlin in 1925, and the second in Hebrew in Tel Aviv in 1946.[7]

Born in 1865 to a religious family in Vekshni, Lithuania, Idel'son grew up in Zhagory, Kovno Province, located next to Courland.[8] This northwestern region was famous for its German influence and also its openness to European cultural trends.[9] Having studied in a heder and

---

[5] Vladimir Jabotinsky, *The Story of My Life*, unpublished manuscript located in the Vladimir Jabotinsky Institute, Tel Aviv. Translation modified by Brian Horowitz.
[6] For example, there isn't even an entry in the two-volume English-language *Encyclopedia of Zionism and Israel*. One should also not confuse Avram Idel'son with his namesake, Abraham Zevi Idelsohn, the musicologist and collector of Jewish music who lived from 1882-1938.
[7] *Sbornik pamiati A. D. Idel'sona* (Berlin: 1925); *Sefer Idelsohn: Divre ha'arakhah ve-zikhronot, toldot hayav u-khtetavav*.
[8] L. Cherikover, "Avram Davidovich Idel'son," in *Sbornik pamiati A. D. Idel'sona*, 8.
[9] Several important Jewish intellectuals came from Zhagory, including "Russia's first Jewish university student," Leon Mandelshtam, his brother Benjamin, the author of *Chason Lamoed*, and the Talmudic scholar, Shneer Zaks. See L. Mandel'shtam, "Iz zapisok pervogo evreia-studenta

yeshiva, Idel'son turned his attention to secular subjects in his teens.[10] In search of higher education, Idel'son matriculated in Moscow University's law school in 1886, just before the most stringent quotas restricting Jews were imposed a year later. Well versed in German culture, he knew Russian only from books; apparently he never lost his "thick [Yiddish] accent." In Moscow he lived in the Jewish "ghetto," an area inhabited mainly by Jewish merchants, students, and artisans. However, instead of practicing law, "he lived a bohemian life surrounded by young people and friends either in the hotel, Blesk on Marosejka Street, or the famous Zakharinka with its furnished rooms occupied by young Jewish students."[11]

The 1890s were complicated for Moscow's Jews. The massive expulsion of Jews from the city in 1891 affected Idel'son deeply.[12] At the same time, he noticed that assimilation was building momentum among Jewish young people too. These two dangers—anti-Semitism and assimilation—made him conscious of his own position; no longer religious, he began to take an interest in the Hovevei Tsion (Lovers of Zion) movement. As Idel'son described it, the movement took possession of the best, most idealistic Jewish students who began to immerse themselves in traditional Jewish customs, "even attending synagogue."[13]

When Theodor Herzl came to prominence in the mid-1890s, Idel'son embraced his brand of political Zionism.[14] Nonetheless, Idel'son joined the Democratic Fraction in 1901, working with Ahad-Ha'am and Hayim Nachman Bialik as a member of Russian Zionism's Cultural Commission.[15] Idel'son was very interested in education, and in the decade

---

v Rossii," *Perezhitoe: sbornik, posviashchennyi obshchestvennoi i kul'turnoi zhizni evreev v Rossii*, 1 (1898): 3-50. *Chason Lamoed* was published in 1877. For more on Shneer (Senior) Zaks (1816-1892), see *Evreiskaia entsiklopediia: svod znanii o evreistve i ego kul-ture v proshlom i nastoiashchem*, vol. 7 (St. Petersburg: Brokgauz & Efron, 1907-1913; reprinted The Hague/Paris: Mouton, 1971), 653-54.

10 Cherikover, "Avram Davidovich Idel'son," 10. But he never experienced the irreversible break with Judaism that earlier intellectuals had since the conflict between Haskalah (Enlightenment) and religion was never as sharp in Courland as elsewhere. Moreover, by the 1880s, the conflict lacked the animosity of earlier years. Nonetheless, Avram's elder brother expressed surprise that his father and grandfather did not object to Avram's request to attend a Russian gymnasium since they had hoped that as an acknowledged "iluj" (Talmudic genius), Avram would become a rabbi.
11 Ibid., 14.
12 As a holder of a diploma from the university, Idel'son had a legal right to live in Moscow.
13 Cherikover, "Avram Davidovich Idel'son," 15.
14 See Yosef Klausner, *Opozitsyah le-Hertsl* (Jerusalem: Ha-Ahiaever, 1960).
15 Zipperstein, *Elusive Prophet*, 144-45.

before the Revolution of 1905, he helped open secular Jewish schools and so-called "improved heders."[16] He even designed a curriculum for instruction in Yiddish (which was an innovative position) as well as in Hebrew.[17] Along with Pinkhas Marek, he joined the Moscow branch of the Society for the Promotion of Enlightenment among the Jews of Russia, which had expanded a school program at this time.[18] It was the Moscow branch that published the first journal devoted to Jewish pedagogy in Russia, *Evreiskaia shkola* (*The Jewish School*, 1904-05).[19] Idel'son was also active in the movement for Jewish self-defense during the Revolution of 1905.[20]

Moving to St. Petersburg to take over the editorship of the Zionist journal, *Evreiskaia zhizn'* (later renamed *Rassvet*), Idel'son gathered under his wing a talented group of writer-activists, V. Jabotinsky, S. Gepshtein, A. Gol'dshtein, A. Zaideman, I. Naidich, A. Gurevich, and M. Soloveichik.[21] About Idel'son's importance as a journalist, Cherikover has written: "In the course of several years under his leadership, *Rassvet* reached an unimaginable number of Jewish readers, 15,000 copies, leaving the weekly *Voskhod* (*Novyi Voskhod*) far behind... [...] *Rassvet* became the central organ of the party [General Zionists], and the Petersburg group with A[vram] D[avidovich Idel'son] at its head also became the party's institutional center [...]."[22]

After 1906, Idel'son occupied positions in the national and interna-

---

16 The government placed quotas on Jewish enrollment in Russian schools in 1887. For details, see Brian Horowitz, *Jewish Philanthropy and Enlightenment in Late-Tsarist Russia* (Seattle: University of Washington Press, 2009), 85, 88, 102, 110.
17 Yiddish had long been condemned as a retrograde language that had to be jettisoned. For a discussion of modern Jewish schooling in Russia, see Brian Horowitz, *Jewish Philanthropy and Enlightenment*, 95-158.
18 Ibid., 80-83, 208-10.
19 The *Jewish School* appeared from 1904-05. Yehudah Slutzky, *Ha-itonut ha-yihudit-rusit bemeah ha-esrim (1900-1918)* (Tel Aviv: ha-Agudah le-Heker Toldot ha-Yehudim ha-Makhon le-Heker ha Tefutsot, 1978), 437-38.
20 I have not been able to find out more about Idel'son's role in the self-defense movement, although clearly the issue deserves more investigation.
21 For a discussion of the paper's role, see Slutzky, *Ha-itonut ha-yihudit-rusit bemeah ha-esrim*, 203-67. In fact, his home became a center for Zionist intellectual life. "In Petersburg his house was far from a stuffy English 'home.' Once again the bohemian character prevailed. His apartment became a real club and center for Zionists, and not only Zionists, but for the nationalist-leaning Jewish intelligentsia in general, those young people who used to live in Moscow. The personality of the host and his wife, Frieda Abramovna, the whole atmosphere of 'free intellectualizing,' attracted a large and varied group of people."
22 Cherikover, "Avram Davidovich Idel'son," 23.

tional Zionist organization. Internationally he participated in the Actions Comité from 1905 until his death in 1921; in Russia Idel'son became a member of the "Merkaz" of General Zionists. During World War I, he revived *Evreiskaia zhizn'*, which had been closed since 1907. After the February Revolution, Idel'son campaigned hard for Zionist candidates in the elections to the All-Russian Jewish Congress and in the elections to the Constituent Assembly.[23]

Under Bolshevik rule, Idel'son continued his activities. However, in February 1919, he managed to get out of Russia, traveling to Berlin and then Paris in order to participate in the Peace Conference. In 1919, he was sent to London to become the editor of *Ha-Olam*, the weekly Hebrew newspaper of the World Zionist Organization. In October 1921, his wife finally gained permission to leave Soviet Russia. In December 1921, Idel'son died in Berlin, where he is presently buried.

* * *

In the context of Zionist theory, Idel'son's most important contribution was his articulation of Synthetic Zionism and its confirmation as the movement's official policy at the Helsingfors Conference in 1906.[24] One essential dimension of Synthetic Zionism was what Russians called the program of "small deeds," which means concrete efforts to improve Jewish life in Russia through education and social activism. The other central thrust of Synthetic Zionism was the importance of the Galut as a training ground for emigration to Eretz-Israel.

The rationale for Helsingfors rested on a number of factors, above all on the changed political situation in Russia itself. Although the policy of *Gegenwartsarbeit* (Doigkeit [Yiddish])—defense of work in the diaspora in the present—had been previously articulated by Idel'son in 1903, it

---

23 *Rassvet* appeared until September 1919.
24 On the Conference, see *Katsir: kovets le-korot ha-tenu'ah ha-tsiyonit be-Rusyah* (Tel Aviv: Masadah be-shituf ha-va'ad ha-tsiburi le-toldot ha-tenu'ah ha-tsionit be-Rusyah, 1964), 66-67. It was in *Evreiskaia zhizn*'s editorial offices that Idel'son introduced his ideas. In his memoirs A. Goldshtein describes his experience hearing the proposal in 1904. "I remember that morning when Idel'son came to explain for the first time what would be called later by everyone as Synthetic Zionism. It was a short time after he had come to meet the members of *Rassvet*'s editorial board. As the head he was not supposed to lecture, but he opened with a request to express his ideas and he explained his point of view. The debate continued at the next meetings as well, and Jabotinsky was the first to agree with Idel'son's idea. After that [Shlomo] Gepshtein, [Arnold] Zeideman, Zeitlin and me" (Alexander Goldshtein, *Zichronot*, quoted in Y. Slutzky, *Ha-itonut ha-yihudit-rusit bemeah ha-esrim*, 219).

had not been implemented because the Zionist organization had been illegal.²⁵ However, a different climate existed in 1906, and legalization of political activity made all the difference.

Although the long-term goal of a Jewish home in Palestine remained unchanged, Synthetic Zionism placed emphasis on the short-term goal of strengthening Jewish national life in Galut.²⁶ The theory went that Eretz Israel had to be built up so that it could provide Jews with exclusive space for the development of their own language, economy, and culture. But who would build the Yishuv? The answer: Jews in the Galut. Paradoxically, at the same time that the diaspora offered no long-term future, it had to be developed. In his recollections about Idel'son, Vladimir Jabotinsky wrote:

> For example, our ideal consisted in preserving only what is alive in Judaism, the energy that at one time was transferred into our workshops, i.e. they shook the dust of the diaspora from their feet. That [goal] is still true. But now we bend down and pick up from the ground the clumps of this "dust" and try to analyze them. We immediately see that it is full of valuable organic ingredients that turn out to be productive when used properly. Let us analyze the ghetto. A terrible institution that has poisoned us physically and morally—but at its base is found the healthy principle of estrangement, and it is worth cultivating this principle in a different form. At the same time, take assimilation: an indisputable illness, moral gangrene—but it put into our hands the whole cultural arsenal of modernity without which we would not even be able to dream of any building. Take the Jew's cowardliness and physical passivity, his response to a pogrom, "the dark cellar." It is shameful and an invitation to other pogromists, but in certain conditions it is precisely the very best method for a weak minority's self-defense.²⁷

---

25   See A. Idel'son, *Sionism: Lektsiia pervaia (teoreticheskoe obosnovanie)* (Saratov, I. M. Rotshtein & S. I. Ginzburg, 1903).
26   Itzhak Maor, *Sionistskoe dvizhenie v Rossii*, trans. O. Mintz (Jerusalem: Biblioteka Aliyah, 1977), 243.
27   V. Jabotinsky, "U kolybeli Gel'singforskoi programmy," *Sbornik pamiati*, 90.

Zionist participation in the first State Duma in 1906 was a centerpiece of Synthetic Zionism. Although the Jewish Bund agitated against involvement, hoping thereby to harness anti-tsarist forces to continue the revolutionary struggle, Idel'son saw tactical value in joining a coalition with liberals in 1905.[28] Acknowledging that in a normal society different classes would challenge one another over economic interests, Idel'son argued that Jews of all classes had to unite to pursue the struggle for national rights.[29] They also had to seek allies among other groups; liberals offered the best chance of gaining such rights.

Synthetic Zionism emerged at a unique historical moment, when nationalism was becoming a political force in the Empire.[30] The idea that Jews could take their place at the political table was beguiling for those Jewish nationalists who also felt close to Russian culture. Expectations for increased rights for Jews were high indeed. But these expectations were not fulfilled. Although the strategy of support for the Kadet liberals had seemed realistic when thirteen Jewish representatives were elected to the First Duma, by the end of the Second Duma in 1907, the Zionist-Liberal alliance had fallen apart.[31] Zionists could no longer refrain from criticizing the compromises that liberals were making, including silence on the Jewish question, in order to pursue agreements with the center-right Octobrists.[32] After 1907, with the restrictions on suffrage, Zionists and Jews generally had a hard time getting elected. There were only two Jews elected to the Fourth Duma and little or no legislation was initiated to relieve pressure on Russia's Jews.[33]

With practical political activity shown as futile, Idel'son turned to the world of ideas and a theoretical exploration of Synthetic Zionism.[34] For example, in "Somewhat A Heresy" ("Nemnogo eresi") (1916) he writes:

---

28 The coalition did not last long and by the end of 1907 it was finished. One of the reasons certainly was the Kadet swing to the right and support for Russian nationalism, which alienated Jewish nationalists. See Christoph Gassenschmidt, *Jewish Liberal Politics in Tsarist Russia*, 64-66.

29 Idel'son, pseudonym, A. Davidson in *Evreiskoe natsional'noe sobranie* (St. Petersburg: Vostok, 1906), 7

30 Heinz Dietrich-Loewe, "Poles, Jews, and Tartars: Religion, Ethnicity and Social Structure in Tsarist Nationality Policies," *Jewish Social Studies* 6, no. 3 (2000): 52-96.

31 Vladimir Levin, "Russian Jewry and the Duma elections, 1906-1907," *Jews and Slavs* 7 (2000): 253-54.

32 Alfred Levin, *The Third Duma: Election and Profile* (Hamden, CT: Archon Books, 1973), 54.

33 Hans Rogger, *Jewish Policies and Right-Wing Politics in Imperial Russia* (Berkeley and Los Angeles: University of California Press, 1986), 224-28.

34 Hayim Greenberg mentions this paradox in his article, "Sholel ha-galut," in *Sefer Idelsohn*, 97. On Helsingfors, see also Itzak Maor, *Sionistskoe dvizhenie v Rossii*, 238-43.

> Our "social movements" have the aim of assimilating Jews into the economy, politics, and culture. And even if they do not want to, they cannot do otherwise since it is impossible to achieve an improvement in our situation in the diaspora by creating a Jewish economy, a Jewish political, independent, and autonomous organism or a living Jewish cultural union in day-to-day life, as we say. [...] The wealth of a Jewish merchant or industrialist depends on the success of the non-Jewish peasant economy and with his activity, he contributes not to Jewish society, but to the land at large, to the entire population in the same measure. Therefore, there are no possible actions, even in our imagination, that could be directed to [bringing about] a rise in the economic position of the Jewish collective, which in essence does not exist.[35]

Idel'son came to the conclusion that there could be no real Jewish collective in the diaspora because the interests of economic survival diluted feelings of Jewish cohesion and encouraged assimilation. "Reality pushes us to general schools, Russian, German, and Polish culture, and—let's be direct—to cultural assimilation. Cultural assimilation is a very significant factor in a Jew's private life and provides him with some gain. It is sad, but we cannot change this."[36] Despite the often-heard argument that progress and enlightenment provided the only chance for minority rights, Idel'son held fast to the opposite view that the modern state produced irresistible pressures on minorities to assimilate.[37]

Idel'son was convinced that Jewish nationalists tended to overstate the masses' striving for social difference. Although Ahad-Ha'am or Semyon Dubnov proclaimed that Jews had national interests, Idel'son countered that the average Jew only obeyed the laws of egoism. Jewish nationalism in Galut represented an abstraction that survived in the

---

35 A. Idel'son, "Nemnogo eresi," *Sobranie sochinenii* (Petrograd: Kadima, 1919), 146-7. An appendix to *Sbornik pamiati A. D. Idel'sona* gives the original date of publication as 1916 and the location as *Rassvet*.
36 A. Idel'son, "Golus," in *Sbornik pamiati A. D. Idel'sona* (Berlin, 1925), 232.
37 Otto Bauer, for example, argued in favor of minority rights in multi-national empires. See O. Bauer, *The Question of Nationalities and Social Democracy* (Minneapolis: University of Minnesota Press, 2000). On Idel'son and Bauer, see *Sefer Idelsohn*, 42.

realm of ideas, but was inoperative in reality.

> Any person, a Jew too, lives above all for himself, and only dreamers could imagine that a Jewish cobbler or storekeeper thinks eternally about the fate of the Jewish people and its culture, and fears that the Jewish people will sooner or later disappear. From morning to night a cobbler thinks about his workshop, a shopkeeper about his store, and when they have free time, they devote it to civic activity and not always out of purely civic inclinations. This is the law of life and if we imagine that we can squeeze from a Jew more civic energy than the English can from an Englishman, or that we will be able to convince the individual Jew to arrange his personal life according to the goals and future tasks of the Jewish people, then we expect some force that just does not exist.[38]

In the argument that egoism trumps national consciousness, one can easily recognize a polemic with Diaspora Nationalists, such as Territorialists like Israel Zangwill, or Autonomists like Dubnov. Dubnov argued that Jews could lead a national life in Diaspora and that national identity depended above all on historical consciousness independent of economic factors.[39]

Idel'son's position may seem out of joint with the times, since, at least in Tsarist Russia, anti-Semitism—pogroms, legal disabilities, and educational discrimination—seemed a greater threat than assimilation. However, he was convinced that in the long run economic development would cause national differences to diminish. He abided by a general conception of capitalism that said that the formation of nation states was carried out precisely to facilitate commerce.[40] Thus, in the *longue durée* the danger of assimilation was stronger. He believed that discrimination was aimed primarily to pressure minorities to integrate, and anti-

---

38 Idel'son, "Golus," in *Sbornik pamiati A. D. Idel'sona*, 233. An appendix to *Sbornik pamiati A. D. Idel'sona* gives the original date of publication as 1916 and the location as *Rassvet*. "Golus" was published in *Rassvet* in 1911.
39 S. Dubnov, *Pis'ma o starom i novom evreistve* (St. Petersburg: 1907).
40 A. Idel'son, *Sionism: Lektsiia pervaia (teoreticheskoe obosnovanie)*, 27.

Semitism the specific result of Jewish reluctance to assimilate.[41]

Idel'son was convinced of the reality of the nation as the operative concept in history. In particular, he analyzed the Jewish nation, concluding that because of their idiosyncratic way of life, values, and ideas, Jews cannot melt into the general population. It was the anomalous position of Jews in Europe, where, in Idel'son's words, they were actually a state within a state that had caused Zionism. Although one may recall that the concept of "a state within a state" was always used pejoratively to mean that Jews were not loyal, Idel'son maintained that the inability of Jews to assimilate had made Zionism inevitable: "If anti-Semitism is the projection of a tendency by the dominating nationality to create a nation state, then the appearance of the same tendency on the part of the oppressed people, the Jewish people, is Zionism."[42] In other words, just as other nations have a state of their own where they can fulfill their economic, social, and cultural mission, so too Jews need the same.

Idel'son conceived that education would play a central role in Synthetic Zionism. In 1904, an editorial in *Evreiskaia zhizn'* spelled out his view: "We see in a national education the cardinal point in the Zionist Program. Teachers and schools will decide the fate of the people and its future will be the task of the generation that is coming of age. To awaken among the teachers and parents the true Jewish national spirit, to inculcate in them healthy understanding of physical and ethical education, to facilitate the process by which our school will become a truly national institution—these will be our primary aims."[43] Regarding the Hebrew language, he repeated that every nation had a right to cultivate its own national language. Although it would seem paradoxical to promote Hebrew in the Galut since it was hardly an essential means of communication, Idel'son would not back down: "Society can struggle to acquire the national language in the school, the courts, and administrative institutions. It is [...] a struggle for the essential interests of life. The nation demands that it have a necessary chance for spiritual development in its own language."[44]

In contrast to others, who saw a contradiction between the long term

---

41   Ibid., 28.
42   Ibid., 29.
43   "O zadachakh 'Evreiskoi zhizni'," *Evreiskaia zhizn'* 1 (1904): 6.
44   I. Idel'son, "Nemnogo eresi," in *Sbornik pamiati*, 255.

and the short term, construction of a Jewish Yishuv in Palestine and the cultural activity in Galut, Idel'son thought it advancement on political Zionism alone because he was convinced that it was dangerous to wait for a miracle from above (a charter from the Sultan); endless waiting led to passivism.[45] Although he had rejected the Uganda proposal in 1903, Idel'son nevertheless lent his support to political Zionism, advocating activity on multiple fronts simultaneously; political and practical ideology, Hebrew study, culture, and self-defense.[46]

Like others of his generation, Idel'son was strongly influenced by the national cultural autonomy model from the Vienna School, which provided him with a model of what a nation is, and the role of culture and language in the development of national identity.[47] Clearly, Idel'son acknowledged the existence of non-territorial nations in diaspora, among them the Jews. He was clearly pessimistic about the long-term possibilities for the successful political autonomy of national minorities. He believed that "territory" would ultimately trump "personality," and nationalities without territories would come under intense pressure to assimilate.[48]

Idel'son found in Leo Pinsker's ideas similar pessimistic pronouncements that Jews are a nation that will always be persecuted as economic competitors.[49] Although one might look to Ahad-Ha'am as a teacher—who else if not Ahad-Ha'am promoted Hebrew in the Galut—in fact Idel'son was a critic. Doubting that a small avant-garde living in Palestine could have a potent role as a model for Jews around the world, Idel'son rejected the effectiveness of culture alone in the national struggle. He writes, "Various words, such as progress, civilization, culture, and so forth, are crowned with an areole so that one needs to possess a large dose of confidence to regard them critically or deny their absolute significance. [...] The word, 'culture' with the loud epithet national was always the idol of the nationalists, a severe God, implacable, demanding

---

45 Klausner, *Opozitsyah le-Hertsl*, 45.
46 On the attitude of Russian Zionists to Herzl, see Yosef Goldshtein, *Bin tsionut medinit le-tsionut ma'asit*, 186-214.
47 Ephrain Nimni, "Introduction: the National Cultural Autonomy Model Revisited," in *National Cultural Autonomy and its Contemporary Critics*, ed. E. Nimni (New York & London: Routledge, 2005), 1-14.
48 Karl Renner, "State and Nation," in *National Cultural Autonomy*, 15-46.
49 Leo Pinsker, in *The Zionist Idea: a Historical Analysis and Reader* (Philadelpia: Jewish Publication Society,1997), 178-98.

absolute submission. Whoever is able to doubt these holy dogmas of the national code is proclaimed a heretic and rebel."[50]

Among Russian Jews of the earlier generation, the one closest to him was Moshe Leib Lilienblum.[51] Idel'son admired Lilienblum's effort in turning the Haskalah from an abstract and romantic ideology without any clear focus to one obsessed with down-to-earth questions of life, economic issues, social roles, and personal happiness. However, although few attribute to Lilienblum innovations in Hebrew, Idel'son asserts that Lilienblum's major achievement was to transform the Hebrew language to make it serve the needs of real people in real living situations. "He was the first among the Jewish writers who began to 'ruin the language,' inserting Talmudic and even foreign words into it [Hebrew]. This seemingly innocent step caused a whole revolution in the worldview of the period. The emphasis that language exists exclusively to express to another person one's thoughts and not for the sake of abstract and lifeless thoughts was a break with the whole sentimental-romantic lifeless movement of Jewish thinking of the time."[52]

Besides Lilienblum, Idel'son admired Theodor Herzl and agreed with the need to put politics at the center. Herzl's ideas paralleled Idel'son's that anti-Semitism was the logical result of the striving for nation-states that left no room for Jews in Europe. Sooner or later Jews would feel enough pressure from anti-Semitism to take their destiny into their own hands and seek a political solution in the form of a national state.[53]

As a result of the government's repressive actions against Zionism in 1907, including prohibiting official participation in politics and the shekel donations, *Evreiskaia zhizn'* was closed. After that, the opportunities for Idel'son in politics were limited: he could join the illegal Socialist Jewish nationalist parties, but for adult men with families, risk of prison in Siberia was too great. Idel'son devoted himself to the only legal activity still left to him, education. He involved himself in expanding the Tarbut Zionist school network.

When *Evreiskaia zhizn'* was reopened in 1915, he got back into jour-

---

50 I. Idel'son, "Rassol (doklad 'chitannyi v Moskovskom Kruzhke, 'Kadima')," in *Sobranie sochinenii*, 24.
51 I have to thank Taro Tsurumi for this insight; personal conversation.
52 A. Idel'son, "V epokhu pereloma," *Rassvet* 6 (1910): 9.
53 Avineri, *The Making of Modern Zionism: The Intellectual Origins of the Jewish State* (New York: Basic Books, 1981), 93-94.

nalism full swing.⁵⁴ Idel'son took control of the paper, placing the editorial board in Moscow to avoid the stricter censorship in St. Petersburg. During World War I, *Evreiskaia zhizn'* was a center for the discussion of the language question generally.⁵⁵ It was also a forum for discussions about post-war politics. In 1916, he wrote: "A critical moment has arrived. The Jewish question whether we like it or not has penetrated the international realm. A large group of Jews with land and wealth is awaiting [the future]; but so too awaits an even larger movement of Jews without land, alienated and thrown out of their homes [...] And there is no doubt that in the coming European revolution, when the fates of many small and large nations will be decided, the fate of the Jewish people will be decided in the only way possible, the Herzlian way."⁵⁶ "Herzlian" here refers to the Basel Program and a Jewish homeland.

Interestingly, in 1917, only a few months before the publication of the Balfour Declaration, a new translation of the Basel Program of 1897 was published in Russian with Idel'son's introduction. Idel'son felt that the text needed reworking, because the conventional translation of the word Heimstätte, which in Russian was rendered "asylum" (ubezhishche), created a mistaken impression, implying that Palestine was merely another asylum for sad, poor, and powerless immigrants. "We got used to it and do not feel the linguistically absurd and false Russian formulation: 'Zionism aims to create a legally assured asylum' [...] 'Asylum!' The word 'Heimstätte' was translated with this humiliating term. It is not entirely translatable. In ordinary usage it signifies 'house,' 'homeland.' English Zionists followed the latter meaning of 'Heimstätte' choosing the English word 'home.' But 'Heimstätte' in political usage has the meaning accurately rendered by 'national territory.'"⁵⁷ Although the publication was issued in order to propagandize Basel as the solution to the "Jewish problem," the Balfour Declaration undermined the need for the translation, since it essentially established Basel as the policy of the British Empire, which adopted the League of Nations mandate over

---

54   For a description of *Evreiskaia zhizn'*'s various closings, see Slutzky, *Ha-itonut ha-yihudit-rusit bemeah ha-esrim*, 203n3.
55   See B. Horowitz, "Russian-Zionist Cultural Cooperation, 1916-1918: Leib Jaffe and the Russian Intelligentsia," *Jewish Social Studies* 13, no. 1 (Fall 2006): 100-09. Idel'son attacked Jewish organizations that created schools for Jewish refugees in languages other than Hebrew.
56   A. Idel'son, "Na povorote," in *Voina, evreistvo i Palestina: stat'i* (Petrograd: Vostok, 1916), 34-35.
57   A. Idel'son, "Predislovie," in *Bazel'skaia programma* (Petrograd, 1917), 3-4.

Eretz-Israel at the end of World War I.[58]

The Bolshevik Revolution drastically changed Idel'son's life. Although Zionists were the most popular among Jewish political parties, with 140,000 individuals represented at the Zionist conference in Petrograd held in May 1917, after the October revolution, Bolshevik repression was immediate.[59] By 1921, most of the senior leaders had fled the country. Idel'son was appointed by the Russian Zionist organization as a representative to the Paris Peace Conference, and in 1919, took over the editorship of *Ha-Olam*, a Hebrew newspaper that was projected to appear in London. From his perch in England's capital, he was supposed to influence public opinion worldwide.

What becomes clear is the full extent to which the Bolshevik revolution undercut Idel'son's position as a leader and spokesman. First of all, he lost his audience. *Ha-Olam*'s tiny readership cannot be compared with the influence that *Rassvet* (*Evreiskaia zhizn'*) had on the five-and-a-half-million strong Jewish population of Russia. His decisive role as a theorist of the Zionist movement also diminished. In addition, forced to leave Russia, he lost contact with his native environment and therefore could no longer respond decisively to events taking place there. Memoirists describe him in London as full of anger.[60]

In truth, multiple factors, and not only the October Revolution, made Idel'son's position obsolete. Despite his personal happiness about the announcement of the Balfour Declaration, changes in Zionism caused a need for reorientation. The announcement annulled the Helsingfors Program. If Eretz-Yisrael became a national home under a British charter, the focus of exclusive attention had to be placed on building the Yishuv.

In the first issue of *Ha-Olam*, Idel'son underscored the sense that Jews were set to embark on a new life and would now put behind them the hate, violence, and despair of the war years. "Let us say that a new age is coming to the world, new subjects and new aspirations have arisen in the present that have already overturned previous social ideas. The old world is already gone, cut off, as far as one can imagine. It is not for us to predict the future. [...] In this hour we see only chaos, a waste of

---

58   See Jonathan Schneer, *The Balfour Declaration: the Origins of the Arab-Israeli Conflict* (New York: Random House, 2010), 245.
59   Gepshtein, "Avram Idelsohn," 39.
60   Goldshtein, "Shanot-hayav ha-achronot," 57.

ideas, a mixture full of expressions and phrases that are bereft of substance. The old world stands in revolt and what is more terrible, it hides its nakedness in a rotten girdle of wisdom and morality, in high ideals and lofty aspirations."[61]

Hebrew-language papers in the Diaspora often had difficulties attracting a large readership and not surprisingly this paper closed within twenty-four months. However, the cause for the failure cannot solely be attributed to language. *Ha-Olam* was the official paper of the Histadrut (the Zionist Labor Exchange or, in other words, the Labor Zionists) and, despite Idel'son's reputation for sharp analysis, the articles were on the whole predictable and pedestrian. Moreover, Idel'son's own articles—written under the pseudonym A. Davidson—were primarily focused on present-day politics and especially the immediate situation in Palestine. Here we find none of the broad scope and sociological lens of his better works. The titles of his articles will give one an impression of his interests: "Questions of the Arabs," "San Remo and the Society of Eretz-Israel," "Demands," and "Zionism and the Work of the Yishuv." In the latter piece, Idel'son writes, "All of Jewish society is occupied with the Yishuv, with the strength of its fitness. I am pleased with its independence and drunk from its spirits. However much the Zionist party is occupied with the Yishuv, in essence it is only one group in the Yishuv and needs to work on the same basis as any other group. For it, then, practical tasks should be the foundation, such as the possibility of attaining more productive results with the means at its disposal, to improve its markets with increased quantity and quality."[62]

It is impossible not to notice a drop in quality in Idel'son's writing in *Ha-Olam*.[63] The cause was not merely Idel'son's Hebrew, which was well regarded. I attribute his diminished power to his honest attempt to serve the movement as a propagandist. But there is another problem. Without the tension of the relationship of Galut and Eretz Yisrael, his work was lifeless. It seems clear that his paradoxes were nourished exactly by the problems of Synthetic Zionism. Now, with the Balfour Declaration opening Palestine for Jewish occupancy, his muse weakened.

Idel'son's fate was not unique; there was an entire generation of indi-

---

61 "Ha-Olam," *Ha-Olam* 1, October 19 (1919): 1.
62 A. Davidson, "Ha-tsionut ve-avoda ha-yishuv," *Ha-Olam* 43 (August 13, 1920): 2.
63 My viewpoint is not shared by Alexander Goldshtein, who claimed that Idel'son was able to transmit his inimitable style in Hebrew. "Shanot-hayav ha-ahroniot," *Sefer Idelsohn*, 53.

viduals who found themselves around fifty years old at the time of the Balfour Declaration, and for whom 1917-18 represented a tragic watershed. The Bolshevik victory ended an era. To succeed in the post-war era, one either had to transform oneself entirely or leave the scene. Looking at various Russian Zionists one can observe how much the October Revolution changed their lives. Rabbi Jacob Maze died in Soviet Russia in 1924 and Yechiel Tschlenow died in London in 1918. Daniil Pasmanik, who had been one of the major theorists, became estranged from Zionism, siding in the 1920s "with the counterrevolutionary White armies of generals Denikin and Wrangel, who were responsible for anti-Jewish pogroms."[64] I would argue that Menachem Usishkin never regained a position of real power in Palestine. Jabotinsky succeeded, but he was helped by his younger age. Moreover, even he had to break out from under the official organization to become a major leader of his own Revisionist Zionist Party.

Just before his death, Idel'son moved to Berlin to begin work on a Yiddish newspaper; but he was somehow broken by the failure of *Ha-Olam*, his emigration from Russia, and his loss of status.[65] Despite his love for Palestine and years of work in the Zionist movement, Idel'son underwent ideological regression at exactly the moment of Zionism's greatest success. The reason for this may be that he was a Russian Zionist with an emphasis on the adjective "Russian." The collective joy for the British charter was accompanied by a private grief at the victory of Bolshevism and the eviction of Zionists and then Zionism from Communist Russia. His death, representative of a generation's, marked at once the beginning of a new era in which Russian Zionists—as opposed to Zionists from Russia—would play a much smaller role in the development of Eretz-Yisrael as a Jewish homeland.

---

64 J. B. Sch[echtman], "Pasmanik Daniel," in *Jewish Encyclopedia*, 13: 160-61.
65 Goldshtein wrote, "In the history of the Zionist movement Idel'son remains a teacher of the Zionists of Russia," "Shanot-hayav ha-achroniot," 62.

4. Medal coin from the Society for the Promotion of Enlightenment (reproduced courtesy of Michael Beizer).

4. An Innovative Agent of an Alternative Jewish Politics: The Odessa Branch of the Society for the Promotion of Enlightenment among the Jews of Russia[1]

In the historical literature, the Odessa branch of the Society for the Promotion of Enlightenment among the Jews of Russia became famous thanks to the struggle for Jewish nationalism on the part of Ahad-Ha'am and Semyon Dubnov.[2] Supposedly the outrage of the Zionists against the "assimilators" brought some life to a dead institution. However, nothing could be farther from the truth.

The Odessa branch of the Society for the Promotion of Enlightenment was a powerful tool for the expansion of Jewish communal and educational funding from 1867-1903. The practical achievements of the Odessa branch were based on grassroots efforts that promoted civic participation in philanthropy and educational reform that, while not uncommon in late tsarist Russia, brought effective results.[3] A study of the branch shows that by seeking gradual improvement in real lives, the branch members provided a model for Jewish philanthropists in St. Petersburg and other cities.[4] In fact, the success of the Odessa leadership was confirmed when, in the first decade of the twentieth century, the older members of the society were able to repel an attack from young Zionists. The old guard continued to win the leadership posts that showed the popularity their program based on a compromise be-

---

1 I want to thank Steven Zipperstein for his suggestions and advice and Blair Ruble and Sam Ramer for originally editing this article.
2 I. Levitats, *The Jewish Community in Russia, 1844-1917* (Jerusalem: Posner and Sons, 1981), 69; D. Vital, *The Origins of Zionism* (Oxford: Clarendon Press, 1980), 123, 125-26; A. Orbach, *New Voices of Russian Jewry: A Study of the Russian-Jewish Press of Odessa in the Era of the Great Reforms, 1860-1871* (Leiden: E. J. Brill, 1980), 99-100.
3 In his book, *The Jews of Odessa*, and in several articles, Steven Zipperstein and John Klier have studied the significance of Odessa's Jewish institutional life in its early period, during the 1860s and 70s; Steven J. Zipperstein, *Jews of Odessa: A Cultural History, 1794–1881* (Stanford: Stanford University Press, 1985); and "Transforming the Heder: Maskilic Politics in Imperial Russia," in *Jewish History: Essays in Honour of Chimen Abramsky*, ed. Ada Rapoport-Albert and Steven J. Zipperstein (London: Peter Halban, 1988), 87-110; John Klier, "The Jewish Den' and the Literary Mice, 1869-71," *Russian History* 1 (1983): 31-49 and "Krug Gintsburgov i politika shtadlanuta v imperatorskoi Rossii," *Vestnik Evreiskogo Universiteta v Moskve* 3, no.10 (1995): 38-56.
4 See my book, *Jewish Philanthropy and Enlightenment in Late-Tsarist Russia*.

tween integration and Jewish identity.

By looking at the Odessa branch, one can gain new perspectives on the centrality of Odessa as an engine of change in Jewish life from 1880s onward. The branch's activity in organizing members and resources for improving the lives of the city's Jews can be construed as an alternative politics. The branch's members did not contact the government as an intercessor (*shtadlan*), since by the 1880s that *shtadlan* was perceived as ineffectual and even collaborationist. They also did not seek separatism either in Zionism or another nationalist ideology, which was viewed as hopelessly unrealistic for a small minority in a huge Empire. Furthermore, the branch's bourgeois leaders rejected Bundist socialism and radicalism of all kinds. Instead, by fostering pragmatic action the branch was able to offer leadership that simultaneously provided a path to integration (as much as that was possible) and some of the benefits of the new nationalist political orientation, such as reliance on independent Jewish effort alone.

The Society for the Promotion of Enlightenment was established in St. Petersburg in 1863 by the country's wealthiest Jews, who devoted themselves to philanthropy, giving direct aid to individuals, especially Jewish university students.[5] Located far from the Pale of Settlement and the heart of Jewish life, the St. Petersburg grandees wanted to gain a foothold in the south. Therefore, in 1867 the leadership granted the request of a group of Odessa intellectuals to become part of the society. The St. Petersburg leaders even offered the branch one-eighth of the society's total budget for their use. Although established by members of the elite, principally Abraham Brodsky and Odessa's rabbi, Shimon Aryeh Shwabacher, the branch soon came under the control of young intellectuals, who were imbued with the spirit of the Haskalah (Jewish Enlightenment) and had more energy than the wealthy Shtadlonim (Jewish intercessors with the government) to spend on concrete civic initiatives.

Ideologically, the *Haskalah* still dominated the Jewish landscape in Russia in the 1860s, with its program for the full integration of Jews into Russian society, the dissemination of secular knowledge in modern

---

5   E. Cherikover, *Istoriia Obshchestva dlia rasprostraneniia prosveshcheniia mezhdu evreiami v Rossii* (History of the Society for the Promotion of Enlightenment among the Jews of Russia) (St. Petersburg: 1913), 41; see also my monograph, *Jewish Philanthropy and Enlightenment in Late-Tsarist Russia*.

schools, and Jewish political emancipation. Although traditional Jews viewed the *Haskalah* as dangerous to the unity of the Jewish people, the *maskilim* (advocates of the *Haskalah*) believed that only by reforming the Jewish community's structure and changing its goals could Jews improve their lot in Russia. Thus, the *maskilim* criticized the irrationality and injustice of religious authorities, but these modernizers were still proud of the achievements of the Jewish people and wanted to contribute to the health of the community in the present.[6]

In contrast to earlier maskilim, the intellectuals in control of the Society in Odessa adopted the radical position of full-scale Russification. The leaders, Lev Pinsker, Emanuel Soloveichik, I. Tarnovsky, and Reuven Kulisher, supported the publication of a Russian translation of the Hebrew Bible (the Tanach), explaining, "As long as we do not use Russian to teach our children religion, as long as Jews are forced to turn to foreign languages to study everything that concerns their religion and customs—as is the case now—the Russification of the Jews will be merely a pretty phrase without any fundamental content" (emphasis in the original).[7] The intellectuals' desire to disseminate a Russian version of the Hebrew Bible among Russia's Jews was motivated by the view that such translations had contributed to the political success of Western European Jews who were able to speak the language of the country in which they lived.

The intellectuals undoubtedly believed that the translation would promote more than Russification—perhaps also a relaxation in the practice of religious rituals, which they claimed contributed to the separation of Jews from their neighbors. In Germany, after all, linguistic assimilation had spurred religious reform and encouraged Jews to modify their own rites and even imitate some Christian practices.[8] The Odessa Jewish community had already installed a "reform" synagogue, and had hired a German-educated rabbi to lead the congregation.[9]

Arranging for the sale of an existing translation or gaining permis-

---

6   Mordechai Zalkin, *A New Dawn: The Jewish Enlightenment in the Russian Empire, Social Aspects* [Hebrew] (Jerusalem: Magnes Press, 2000).
7   Cherikover, *Istoriia Obshchestva*, 67.
8   See Michael Meyer, *Response to Modernity: A History of the Reform Movement in Judaism* (Oxford and New York: Oxford University Press, 1988). Steven Zipperstein notes that the leaders in St. Petersburg tried to discourage the Odessa group from publishing religious works in Russian translation; S. Zipperstein, "Transforming the Heder," 96.
9   Zipperstein, *Jews of Odessa*, 38.

sion for a new translation was no simple matter. Lev Mandel'shtam, the head of the imperial government's Jewish school program, had published a Russian version of the Tanach in Germany in 1862, but government religious censors had banned its importation and sale.[10] The Holy Synod argued that until an official Russian Orthodox translation appeared, it could not allow the publication of a "Jewish" translation, suspecting that the Jews might use it to convert Russians to Judaism.[11] Fear of *Judaizers*, however remote in reality, was real and alive among the state's religious authorities.[12]

Although Mandel'shtam's translation was published in Russia in 1872, the Society for the Promotion of Enlightenment could not recoup its outlay with sales.[13] This financial failure did not necessarily reflect a lack of interest in learning the Russian language, since the use of Russian among Jews was on the rise. However, it seemed to show that Russian Jews made a distinction between religious and secular texts. When the younger generation studied Russian, it apparently preferred texts devoted to economics, politics, mathematics, and natural history.

The members of the Odessa branch also desired to do something about the lack of opportunities for young people to gain a secular education. The branch's members faced a situation in which there were only two options: the traditional heder, which was unacceptable to the *maskilim*, and the secular government schools for Jews created in the early 1840s, which were unpopular and considered by some to have the goal of converting Jews to Christianity. Borrowing ideas from pro-

---

10   Leon Mandel'shtam, *Zakon ili Piatiknizhie Moiseevo. Bukval'nyi perevod L. I. Mandel'shtama, kandidata peterburgskogo universiteta. V pol'zu russkikh evreev* (Berlin: 5622 [1862 g.]). The Holy Synod viewed the Hebrew Bible as part of its patrimony. For more on this incident, see Horowitz, *Jewish Philanthropy and Enlightenment in Late-Tsarist Russia*, 41-43. For more about Lev Mandel'shtam, see S. M. Ginzburg, "Iz zapisok pervogo evreia-studenta v Rossii," *Perezhitoe: sbornik posviashchennyi obshchestvennoi i kul'turnoi istorii evreev v Rossii*, vol. 1 (St. Petersburg: 1908-1913), 1-50.
11   See I. Chastovich, *Istoriia perevoda Biblii na russkom iazyke* (St. Petersburg: 1873), 5–15. Ilya Trotskii argues that Orthodox rabbis raised a "sharp protest" against the project, "seeing in the translation of the Bible a blasphemous infringement on the holy Jewish Torah" ("Samodeiatel'nosti' i samopomoshch,'" in *Kniga o russkom evreistve ot 1860-kh godov do revoliutsii 1917 g.* [New York: Soiuz russkikh evreev, 1960], 473).
12   Iulii Gessen, *Istoriia evreiskogo naroda*, vol. 2 (Leningrad: 1925–26), 77.
13   "Protokoly OPE," May 19, 1874, list 89, Russian State Historical Archive (RGIA) St. Petersburg, 1532-1-11. The society also wanted to publish an advertisement offering a subscription to its Bible translation, but was still denied permission by a censor who considered such an advertisement "religious propaganda."

gressive Russian educators, the branch's members tried to promote an alternative, taking up vocational and literacy schools for both children and adults.¹⁴ However, because the branch's leaders could not get government permission to create permanent schools, they decided to open courses "wherever and whenever they were needed."¹⁵ In time, however, the government discovered this evasion of the law and demanded compliance; the courses were closed.¹⁶ In 1870, branch members suggested reforming heders (traditional religious schools) to make them places where students could acquire both religious and secular knowledge. Soon enough, however, the leaders discovered that the heder could not easily be transformed. Parents who sent their sons to a heder did not, in most cases, want to send them to a school. This fact contradicted one of the cardinal beliefs of the intellectuals that once parents understood what a school could offer, they would turn their backs on the heder.¹⁷

On May 27, 1871, a major pogrom took place in Odessa. Steven Zipperstein summarized the result: "Within four days, 6 people were killed and 21 wounded, and 863 houses and 552 businesses were damaged or destroyed. Not a single street or square in the Jewish neighborhoods was left untouched, according to a report in the *Jewish Chronicle*, and thousands were rendered homeless. The damages came to 1.5 million rubles, twice as much as would be caused by Odessa's 1881 pogrom."¹⁸

As a result of the pogrom, the Odessa branch decided to close. In a letter of May 7, 1872, to the St. Petersburg board, Emanuel Soloveichik asked permission to liquidate the branch and transfer the remaining funds to the local chapter of the Society for the Promotion of Crafts and Practical Knowledge in Odessa, an organization devoted to training Jews in handicrafts that was known in Russian as Trud.

Invited to St. Petersburg for an "emergency meeting," Soloveichik

---

14 Zipperstein, "Transforming the Heder," 102-3.
15 Protocol July 6, 1869: list 21, Russian State Historical Archives (RGIA) St. Petersburg, 1532-1-10. Steven Zipperstein has written very perceptively about the educational initiatives of the OPE in the 1860s and early 1870s. See "Transforming the Heder," 98-106.
16 Zipperstein shows that the government's repression of the Sunday School movement influenced its attitude toward the Society for the Promotion of Enlightenment's school reform and also frightened the notables in St. Petersburg. See "Transforming the Heder," 103.
17 In May 1870, the branch created a special committee headed by the editors of the Odessa Jewish newspaper *Den'*, Ilya Orshansky and Menashe Morgulis, to study the heder question. Orshansky and Morgulis solicited information from all the heders in the city, and the results were published in *Den'*. See issues 41–42 (1870): 664–66, 679–80.
18 Zipperstein, *Jews of Odessa*, 114.

informed the St. Petersburg board that the Odessa branch would agree to continue its work, but only on the condition that they be allowed to "strive for the improvement of elementary education received by the poor." "But for this," he argued, "[the branch] would have to be better funded and made less dependent on the fluctuations in the annual contributions [provided] by the small number of members in Odessa."[19] Since St. Petersburg was unwilling to make such a financial commitment, the Odessa branch temporarily closed.

Despite the lack of achievement, one may consider the establishment of the branch itself as its greatest success. Odessa's intelligentsia fashioned an institution meant to help the Jewish community to modernize. But this function was only of potential benefit.[20] The great hopes of transforming Jewry though education had led nowhere. Certainly it did not help that the branch had an inadequate budget (less than 1,500 rubles annually). Nonetheless, one should not view it as a marginal institution.[21] The branch enlisted the help of the Brodsky and Poliakov families, the wealthiest Jews of the city, who helped cover the chronic budget deficits. Moreover, in its ideology and activities, the branch was representative of popular attitudes. In the 1860s, Jews in the city understood the need for change, education, and even Russification, but they were guarded, unsure of the government's intentions and fearful of mass assimilation.

* * *

In 1878, Menashe Morgulis, an intellectual and civic leader, proposed reopening the branch, explaining that in Odessa one could find many poor students who needed help paying for tuition, books, clothes, and food. Describing how he had started a fund to aid these students and

---

19 Protocol 6 July 1872: list 24, Russian State Historical Archives (RGIA) St. Petersburg, 1532-1-11: "These provisions could be attained in part through the fulfillment of the third resolution of the charter of the Odessa branch, in which the society provided for the branch's use no less than one-eighth of the Society for the Promotion of Enlightenment's entire funds, reaching at present 6,000 rubles, which include the dues of the members of the Odessa branch."
20 Zipperstein, "Transforming the Heder," 103. Zipperstein notes that in their efforts to provide Jews a secular education, the Society for the Promotion of Enlightenment was stopped not only by pressures from Orthodox Jewry, but also by a suspicious government that kept a close watch for anything that "seemed vaguely contentious, let alone seditious."
21 Protocols of the Society for the Promotion of Enlightenment for 1869-1871, list 38, Russian State Historical Archives (RGIA) St. Petersburg, 1532-1-10.

had collected money from 120 individuals, Morgulis announced his intention to revitalize the branch on the basis of this core group of donors. While the St. Petersburg board agreed to renew the branch's membership in the society, it no longer felt obligated to share resources because the branch was "occupying itself with philanthropy" rather than engaging in activities that "would aid all of Russia's Jews."[22]

Morgulis had become convinced of the effectiveness of "small deeds" that improved the lives of concrete individuals. In the mid-1870s, he became the director of Trud, an organization that revitalized a defunct trade school in Odessa, where Jewish boys and girls also received instruction in general subjects.[23] Around 300 students were enrolled. It seems paradoxical that Morgulis, previously a vocal critic of philanthropy, now became its advocate, and the St. Petersburg board, previously in favor of philanthropy, now became a critic. However, in the decade since the Odessa branch had closed, many things had changed.

As a result of the "May Laws," streams of immigrants had begun to arrive from those areas where decrees had forced Jewish families out of the countryside.[24] Odessa's famed economic opportunities attracted the newcomers, who soon overwhelmed the city's ability to provide social services for them. One journalist, for example, described a situation in which the number of students who sought entrance to schools far exceeded capacity. The result was that "hundreds of children walk the streets without any possibility of becoming literate."[25]

The branch acted quickly to meet the increased need for basic services. In the early 1880s, when the St. Petersburg center fell into stagnation, the branch leaders began to facilitate elementary education and provide financial aid directly to students and their families.[26] Odessa's leaders reacted better to the situation in the 1880s than their counterparts in St. Petersburg because the pogroms of 1881–82 had a less debilitating

---

22 Protocols of the Society for the Promotion of Enlightenment, 1876–1878, list 91, Russian State Historical Archive (RGIA) St. Petersburg, 1532-1-12.
23 Menashe Morgulis, "O professional'nom obrazovanii evreev v Odesse" (On the Professional Education of Jews in Odessa), in *Sbornik v pol'zu nahal'nykh evreiskikh shkol* (St. Petersburg: 1896), 389–90.
24 The Temporary Laws of the Third of May 1882 were essentially an edict that imposed severe restrictions on the kinds of jobs Jews could hold and pursue and where they could live. These regulations were temporary, never having been deliberated by the tsar's own senate.
25 "Korrespondentsiia, Odessa," *Nedel'naia Khronika Voskhoda* 48 (1887): 1289.
26 "St. Petersburg," *Nedel'naia khronika Voskhoda* 3 (1887): 58.

psychological effect on them; they had already recovered from paralysis after 1871.

In 1884, the branch's expenditures on education more than quadrupled, to 21 percent of the budget. They grew another 10 percent in the following year before topping off at 51 percent in 1889. This permitted subsidies for five schools in 1887, and seven in 1888. Unfortunately, the budget did not completely meet the ever-expanding needs of Odessa's Jewish poor; the branch's budget for 1890 was only 10,000 rubles. Nevertheless, the shift in priorities is revealing.[27]

The members of the branch also decided to help provide vocational training for adults, thereby remedying their lack of employment skills. By 1893, Odessa's Jewish civic elite had organized four schools devoted to training craft workers of both genders and paid the salary of a seamstress who taught a class at all the schools.[28]

The branch's leaders took particular pride in the elementary school in Peresyp, the poorest section of the city. In 1889 there were 125 students attending this school, 90 percent of them enrolled free of charge. The school offered a three-year course of study, the equivalent of the two-year curriculum at a Russian gymnasium, with courses in French, German, arithmetic, and history.[29] In addition, it had a craft studio, and provided additional instruction in woodwork and agriculture. Since one of the goals was to create fluent speakers of Russian, instruction in the language included singing, which was supposed to help students perfect their pronunciation. Several hours a week were devoted to physical education, an entirely new phenomenon. The price of running the school was high, 9,974 rubles per year, but costs were offset by a generous donation from G. E. Veinshtein, a rich engineer-industrialist.[30]

Menashe Morgulis's singular role as the Odessa branch's inspiration reflected changes that had brought intellectuals to dominate institu-

---

27 D-v. (pseudonym unknown), "Iubilei 'Prosveshcheniia': O dvadtsatiletnei deiatel'nosti Odesskogo otdeleniia obshchestva rasprostraneniia prosveshcheniia mezhdu evreiami v Rossii (1867–1892)," *Voskhod* 7 (1893): 22.

28 Morgulis, "O professional'nom obrazovanii evreev v Odesse," 397-99.

29 Surprisingly, the pedagogical experts believed that knowledge of European languages would be indispensable to the future artisans and workers of Odessa. See *Spravochnaia kniga po voprosam obrazovaniia evreev: posobie dlia uchitelei i uchitel'nits evreiskhikh shkol i deiatelei po narodnomu obrazovaniiu*, (St. Petersburg: 1901), 27-46.

30 Peter Shaw, *The Odessa Jewish Community, 1855–1900: An Institutional History* (Unpublished PhD dissertation, Hebrew University, Jerusalem, 1988), 219.

tional life in the city. As a result of the abrogation of the *kahals* (community self-government) in 1844, the government had become dependent on local Jewish representatives for advice regarding the collection and distribution of taxes and the organization of communal institutions.[31] Although the government turned to the wealthy notables, their numbers were limited, and they were often too busy to serve. Therefore, the Jewish intelligentsia was enlisted. Mikhail Polishchuk describes the intelligentsia's growing political influence in the second half of the nineteenth century:

> In Odessa the *maskilim* already shared power in the communal organizations and participated in the city administration with the Russian elite. Their field of activity constantly grew: in 1860, they composed fully half of one committee that served as a mediator between the [Jewish] communal and local [Russian] administration. In 1870, B. Bertenson was elected to the position of official for Jewish affairs in the City Duma. In 1873, E. Soloveichik was elected as a member of the City Administration (*gorodskaia uprava*), where Jewish questions were addressed. In 1874, ten *maskilim*, among them seven doctors… two inspectors and a single scholar were elected to the council of representatives of the Jewish community, i.e., "the Council of One Hundred." In 1879, three *maskilim* [Jewish autodidacts] and eight members of the [Jewish] intelligentsia were invited to a meeting on the question of the so-called Jewish taxes, and served in the advisory councils of the orphanage and Talmud Torah school.[32]

Since Jewish intellectuals already had experience in running the

---

31 See Michael Stanislawski, *Tsar Nicholas I and the Jews: The Transformation of Jewish Society in Russia, 1825–1855* (Philadelphia: Jewish Publication Society, 1983), 132.

32 Mikhail Polishchuk, *Evrei Odessy i Novorossi: Sotsial'no-politicheskaia istoriia evreev Odessy i drugikh gorodov Novorossii, 1881–1904* (Jerusalem: Gesharim, 2002), 21. The Council of the Hundred was a kind of local assembly that existed in Odessa during the 1870s. The distinction between *maskilim* and members of the Russian-Jewish intelligentsia pivoted on whether an individual had an education in modern schools or had studied exclusively in Jewish traditional institutions: heders, *betei midrash*, and *yeshivot*.

city's Jewish institutions, they could effectively expand their reach in the 1880s. In contrast to the 1860s, when the *maskilim* took pains to draw the attention of the public to their activities in order to gain legitimacy as community leaders, by the end of the 1870s the intellectuals enjoyed considerable authority. In earlier times they pursued projects that appeared marginal, but now they took leadership positions and devoted themselves to building institutions quietly and effectively.

What was especially unique in Odessa was the branch's positive relationship with the city's heders. Instead of the usual antagonism, there was cooperation. When there were calls to close heders in Odessa as a health measure in the mid-1880s, the branch agreed to regulate them, thus defusing the government's concerns.[33] Furthermore, in 1886, OPE leaders approached local officials with a petition for a "softening of measures against *melameds*," the heder teachers.[34] In fact, the branch engaged two of its members to collect information about the city's 80 heders and their 3,000 students. Finally, when the government closed the heders in the early 1890s, the branch's leaders opened two schools to meet the needs of the displaced students.[35]

According to Morgulis, the branch was addressing more than just the needs of the city, but those of the whole southwestern region as well, since many of the students came from nearby areas. He maintained that these schools "serve the interests of all Russian Jewry," because educators from all across Russia came to Odessa to get acquainted with the latest methods in vocational education.[36]

The population's need for modern education continued to hold the branch's attention. In particular, vocational training was viewed as an essential service, given the socio-economic profile of the immigrants. Nonetheless, the goal was still to integrate Jews by modifying their behavior, educating them in modern schools, and inculcating a secular way of life. Despite a spate of conversions to Russian Orthodoxy during the 1880s, primarily for opportunistic reasons, little thought was given to the dangers of integration, to the idea that a weakened Jewish identity might contribute to a breakdown in the Jewish collective and ultimately lead to mass assimilation. The primary difference with the 1860s, how-

---

33   "St. Petersburg," *Voskhod* 7 (1893): 21–23.
34   Ibid., 22.
35   Ibid.
36   Morgulis, "O professional'nom obrazovanii evreev v Odesse," 400.

ever, was in the attitude toward the government. Now, in the 1890s, the branch did not expect help from that quarter, looking instead for ways to bypass the government to aid the city's, and indeed the region's, Jewish population.

The vitality of the Odessa branch can be seen in its strong activity in the late 1890s and the early years of the 20th century. In 1902, there were 1,241 paid members. The budget was 31,258 rubles, and the work was divided among five committees: the Historical-Literary Committee, the Adult Education Committee, the Committee to Help Poor Students at the University of New Russia, the Finance Committee, and the School Pedagogical Committee.[37] The branch provided subsidies to 36 different of schools and to 705 students.[38]

Although the branch was more successful in terms of schools subsidized, teachers with pedagogical training, and students served, in the late 1890s the pro-integrationist ideology came under attack by the younger generation. In 1900, trying to stave off a civil war within the branch, Morgulis and another leader, Jacob Saker, agreed to a series of meetings to air differences.[39] Although the two groups met for more than a year, by 1902 open debate was breaking out at the branch meetings over the curriculum of modern Jewish schools.[40]

Challenging the ideology of integration, the "nationalists" (as they described themselves), whose leaders included Ahad-Ha'am (Asher Ginzburg), Ben-Ami (Mordechai Rabinovich), Meir Dizengoff, Yehoshua Ravnitzky, and Semyon Dubnov, launched an attack on the branch's leadership ostensibly on account of the number of hours of Jewish and secular subjects taught in schools subsidized by the branch. The nationalists wanted a school that inspired national values, one with more hours of Hebrew and fewer of Russian; anything less would amount to yielding to assimilation. Their petition read: "It is even more unnatural to recognize a school that teaches its pupils in the spirit of another nationality. Alienated from their native group and artificially assimilated

---

[37] *Otchet o deiatel'nosti komiteta odesskogo otdeleniia Obshchestva dlia rasprastraneniia prosveshcheniia mezhdu evreiami v Rossii za 1901 g.* (Odessa: Obshchestvo dlia rasprostraneniia prosveshcheniia, 1902), 1–5.

[38] Ibid., 12.

[39] Simon Dubnov, *Kniga zhizni, materialy dlia istorii moego vremeni: vospominaniia i razmyshleniia* (Vilna, Lithuania: 1930–37; reprint in a single volume, Jerusalem and Moscow: Gesharim, 2004), 234.

[40] Ibid., 252–53.

to the foreign environment that has dominated their education, pupils of such schools suffer a moral dichotomy. Later they make up that morally undefined element in society, which everywhere turns out deracinated and unstable."[41]

According to the nationalists, the proper school should propagate a strong Jewish identity. The school must not be occupied with vocational training or instruction in Russian, but should teach courses in Hebrew, Torah, and Jewish history, since these subjects instill national feeling. In addition, the school could do this best when these subjects were presented not merely as bare facts, but integrated into life, "linking the Jewish present with its past."[42] The nationalists were adamant that at least 12 of 30 hours in the week should be devoted to Jewish subjects and that Hebrew should serve as the primary focus of the curriculum, so as to spur an interest in the "customs, way of life, and literary creativity of the Jewish people."[43]

Responding to the nationalists, the branch's leadership justified the decision to limit Jewish courses by claiming a responsibility to ensure that Jewish children could make a living in difficult times. Specifically, Morgulis explained that the Society for the Promotion of Enlightenment provided funds to three professional schools for girls, which offered two or three hours of Jewish studies, and five boys' schools with five hours of Jewish content weekly. Vocational training took up the vast majority of class time. Justifying the allocation of time, Morgulis claimed that "from a pragmatic point of view the board maintains that a Jewish elementary school must give its pupils instruments for the difficult struggle of survival, and from this viewpoint, we do not find it possible to diminish the teaching of such subjects as Russian grammar, writing, mathematics, and so on."[44]

This pro-integrationist program was meant to address the difficulties of Jewish life in post-1882 Russia. The leaders were convinced that the road to survival for the individual Jew lay in economic well-being, facilitated by a secular education and vocational skills. Prosperity, it was felt,

---

41 "O natsional'nom vospitanii (zapiska, predstavlennaia v komitet odesskogo otdeleniia Obshchestva rasprostraneniia prosveshcheniia mezhdu evreiami)," *Ezhenedel'naia khronika Voskhoda* 1 (January 6, 1902): 12.
42 Ibid., 15.
43 Ibid.
44 "Mnenie komiteta odesskogo otdeleniia Obshchestva rasprostraneniia prosveshcheniia o evreiskoi narodnoi shkole," *Ezhenedel'naia khronika Voskhoda* 16 (April 19, 1902): 6.

inoculated Jews against conversion to Christianity.⁴⁵ Weighing the risks of losing Jews to assimilation caused by a lack of knowledge about Jewish culture or losing them because of economic deprivation, the branch leaders believed that poverty was the greater danger.

The actual vote in Odessa went against the nationalists.⁴⁶ The result showed that the majority of members of the Society for the Promotion of Enlightenment in Odessa in 1902 favored integration. But the vote was not the last word. The battled raged on in the city for more than a decade.⁴⁷

It is worth drawing attention to the absence of a specific Jewish content in the kind of philanthropy that was practiced and which became vilified in Zionist historiography as "assimilationist," and its representatives as "assimilators." It is easy to see how the branch's attempts to improve people's lives paralleled activities pursued by Russian social activists of the period generally: the creation and expansion of elementary schooling, job training for adults, and the establishment of institutions to help alleviate poverty. At the same time, I maintain that this philanthropy actually provided the experience for and the ideological basis of Jewish self-administration that flowered in Odessa and was later adopted, paradoxically, by Zionists in Eretz-Israel. About Morgulis's activities in the 1880s, Eli Lederhandler has written:

> The answer Morgulis offered was not auto-emancipation in the Zionist sense of the term which [Leon] Pinsker was to use four years later. But his solution was something closely akin to auto-emancipation, which he identified as a restoration of coordinated leadership on a national level, a rebuilding of political community. Only this—not temporary local philanthropy nor even civic equality—had any hope of actually changing the circumstances of Russian-Jewish life.⁴⁸

---

45   Ibid., 5–6.
46   "Po povodu vybora v Obshchstve prosveshcheniia," *Budushchnost'* 2 (January 11, 1902): 22.
47   See Brian Horowitz, "Partial Victory from Defeat: 1905, Jewish Liberals, and the Society for the Promotion of Enlightenment among the Jews of Russia," in Ezra Mendelsohn and Stefani Hoffman, eds., *The Revolution of 1905 and Russia's Jews: A Turning Point?* (Philadelphia: University of Pennsylvania Press, 2007), 117–41.
48   Eli Lederhandler, *The Road to Modern Jewish Politics: Political Tradition and Political Reconstruction in the Jewish Community of Tsarist Russia* (New York: Oxford University Press, 1989), 153.

I agree with Lederhandler, who correctly noted that positive expectations were awakened by social activism that started in the 1860s and flourished in the 1880s. This activism verged on, but did not fully become, pressure politics. Nonetheless, it helped foster civil society, develop a new Jewish leadership, and, most of all, allow Jews to dream of controlling their own fate rather than merely responding to new crises. In this sense the Odessa branch's activity had a strong Jewish dimension, helping to energize the Jewish community and providing a plan for its social recovery.

Although leaders such as Menashe Morgulis may have been cold to political Zionism and Jewish nationalism, in their activities they concretely improved the lives of many Jews, dealing with them not merely as the underprivileged, but as Jews with specific problems attributable to their Jewish status. It is easy to see that this social activism and institution building actually paved the way for post-enlightenment Jewish politics. In its activity the branch may not fit the paradigm of Jewish Odessa, since it was neither Zionist nor "assimilationist," not purely cosmopolitan, and certainly not hostile to Jewish identity. The branch's politics of the possible through self-reliance and creative solutions was viewed as a model for an effective alternative to religious piety, political radicalism, *Shtadlanut*-style intercession, and the unrealistic promises of Jewish nationalism. For these reasons, the local branch of the Society for the Promotion of Enlightenment made Odessa a dynamic center of Jewish institutional life in the Russian Empire.[49]

---

[49] Steven Zipperstein makes this same point in his book, *Imagining Russian Jewry: Memory, History, Identity* (Seattle and Washington: University of Washington Press, 1999), 48-57.

5. Jewish Arc in front of the St. Petersburg Choral Synagogue (photograph by William Brumfield).

5. Politics and National Self-Projection: The Image of Jewish Masses in Russian-Jewish Historiography, 1860-1914

At the Russian government's Rabbinical Commission of 1861, so-called "enlightened" Jews (I. Tarnopol', L. Levanda, A. B. Gotlober) advocated prohibiting the publication of Yiddish books in Russia.[1] Although the Russian Minister of Enlightenment rejected this proposition, maintaining that such a "forced prohibition . . . would be a futile and even harmful measure," the suggestion itself deserves examination. The fact is that during the 1860s the modern Jewish intelligentsia held Yiddish in contempt. They considered the "jargon," as they called Yiddish, a distorted dialect of German and blamed it for the backwardness and isolation of the Jewish people. Nearly without exception, the vast majority of these intellectuals placed their hopes in Russian as the means for realizing the modernization and integration of the Jews. If Jews were to become fully integrated citizens of the Russian Empire, it behooved them to adopt and use the national language.

Forty-seven years later, at the Czernowitz Language Conference of 1908, the majority of participants recognized Yiddish as a national language of the Jewish people.[2] Although Czernowitz symbolizes a realignment of attitudes, official recognition was the last step in acknowledging broader changes in perspective that had formed much earlier. At Czernowitz, the Jewish intelligentsia recorded its unqualified respect for the speakers of Yiddish, the Jewish people.

What had occurred that caused the Jewish intelligentsia to change its view of the Jewish masses between those periods? Historians point to four main developments. First, the pogroms of 1881-1882 evoked widespread sympathy for the victims on the part of the Jewish intelligentsia. Secondly, the repressive May Laws of 1882, denying Jews access to Russian society, led to a push toward Jewish "self-sufficiency." Thirdly, the popularity of the Bund and Zionists starting in the 1890s

---

[1] E. Cherikover, *Istoriia Obshchestva*, 71.
[2] See *Di ershte sprach konferents: barikht, dokumenten un opklangen fun der Tshernovitser konferents, 1908* (Vilne: Der Institut, 1931).

showed that the Jewish masses could be a serious political force, and lastly, the creative awakening of Yiddish literature won over the intelligentsia's sympathies for the "language of the masses."[3]

I do not deny the importance of these factors. Each contributed to the identification of the Jewish intelligentsia with the Jewish people and to the national awakening of Russia's Jews. Nevertheless, a positive image of the people had to be developed; the intelligentsia had to be educated and encouraged to shed old axioms. At least until the late 1880s, secular Jewish intellectuals found it hard to surrender the view that the Jewish people were on a low cultural level and morally less deserving than the Russian people.[4] Although one could successfully trace the development of attitudes toward the Jewish people by examining Yiddish or Hebrew literature or by studying the process of "nationalization" in political life, in this essay I fix my attention primarily on Jewish historians and Jewish historiography.[5]

Russian-Jewish historiography was inextricably connected with the government's policies. This is true not only because the personal experiences of the individual historians became embodied in their work, but more importantly, because Jewish historians linked their historical views to political concerns.[6] In fact, historians played important roles in the struggle for Jewish emancipation. It is essential to recognize that Jewish historians in Russia had no training in the study of history: Mikhail (Menashe) Morgulis and Ilya Orshansky were lawyers, and Semyon Dubnov had no university training at all. Yuly Gessen graduated from a business school. Employed as journalists, editors, lawyers, and teachers, Russian-Jewish historians never adopted a purely objective academic approach similar to the one that is prevalent in today's American universities. Rather, the events of Jewish political life, to an acute degree, influenced the evolution of their work.

---

3   See Benjamin Harshav, *The Meaning of Yiddish* (Berkeley: University of California Press, 1990).
4   In contrast to the Russian people as victims, the Jewish masses were exploiters. Moreover, while the Russians had created their own ideal social form—the commune—the Jewish masses were crowded in towns that contributed nothing to culture.
5   My goal is not to offer an exhaustive study of every major historian, but to concentrate on those intellectuals responsible for paradigm changes.
6   Benjamin Nathans makes this point clearly: "From its inception in the era of the Great Reforms, the historiography of Jews in the Russian Empire took as its central concern the Jews' legal standing, in other words, the development of official legislation regarding the Jewish population" ("Jews, Law, and the Legal Profession in Late Imperial Russia," *Evrei v Rossii, istoriia i kul'tura* 5 [Petersburg Jewish University, 1998], 104).

The attitude of the intelligentsia toward the Jewish masses slowly improved from the 1860s until the late 1890s, when it became unambiguously positive. During the first stage in the 1860s, the intelligentsia felt close to the government and distant from its own people, while in the final stage the reverse was true. In between the two poles, however, we find various degrees of identification and repulsion.

A defining moment is 1856, not because historical writing started at that time—Shmuel Feiner has done a superb job showing us the kind of historical genres that *maskilim* cultivated earlier—but because, with the crowning of Alexander II and the implementation of his reforms, the *Haskalah* (Jewish enlightenment) entered a completely new phase.[7] The primary language of the Jewish intelligentsia switched to Russian, although books in Hebrew continued to be written. The Jewish intelligentsia became a social class with a credible size, as opposed to scattered individuals. Jewish newspapers in Russian, Hebrew, and Yiddish appeared in 1860, the Society for the Promotion of Enlightenment among the Jews of Russia was opened in 1863 in St. Petersburg, and a branch was established in Odessa in 1867. This organization, especially the Odessa branch, was devoted to disseminating secular literature in Russian and one of its central goals was to cultivate a historical literature about Jews in Russia.[8]

Historical works in the 1860s, the enlighteners hoped, would be of a higher standard than previously. In the historical writings of the earlier generation, authors did not care to ascertain whether their sources were historically truthful. Instead, they featured colorful and exotic stories. The authors chose distant subjects and themes, such as the ancient world or the heroes of the Bible.[9] With few exceptions they

---

7 See Shmuel Feiner, *Haskalah and History: the Emergence of a Modern Jewish Historical Consciousness*, trans. C. Naor and S. Silverston (Portland: Littman Library of Jewish Civilization, 2002), 163-77.

8 Leon Rosenthal, *Toledot hevrat marbei haskalah beyisr'el be'erets rusiyah*, vol. 1 (St. Petersburg: 1886-90), 23-28.

9 The first volumes of historical research by Russian Jews appeared in 1866-67 under the auspices of the Society for the Promotion of Enlightenment among the Jews of Russia: *Sbornik statei po evreiskoi istorii i literature, izdavaemyi Obshchestvom dlia rasprostraneniia prosveshcheniia mezhdu evreiami v Rossii* (St. Petersburg: 1866-7), 2 issues. Interestingly, nearly all the articles in the volume deal with either earlier periods in Jewish life, especially ancient history and Biblical philology, or with foreign Jews. Contemporary Russian Jewry does not appear to have interested these scholars. For a discussion of the earliest historical research on the Jews of Russia, see Isaiah Trunk, "Istoriki russkogo evreistva," in *Kniga o evreistve ot 1860-kh godov do revoliutsii 1917 g.: sbornik statei* (New York: Soiz russkikh evreev, 1960), 12-35; see also Feiner, *Haskalah and History*, 157-203.

avoided studying the Jews of Russia or touching upon times close to their own.[10]

But in the first issue of the first Jewish newspaper in Russia, *Rassvet*, in 1860, in an ethnographic examination entitled "A Few Words about the Jews of the Western Territories of Russia," Lev Levanda expressed the pitying attitude of the educated class toward the masses.[11] Levanda writes:

> One has to see for oneself, one has to enter a crowded, half-dilapidated hut, which always houses no less than three families, which compete among themselves for the prize of poverty. One has to see how the half-naked children of all three families crowd around the unheated oven and fight over a piece of animal skin, which each child wants to wrap around himself to warm his body, freezing from the cold. One has to be there when the father of one family arrives at the door with a loaf of bread and his children jump off the oven with shouts of joy, singing and clapping their hands together. The children of the other families, whose fathers have not brought food, turn away their eyes so as not to see their comrades' happiness, which was not to be theirs.[12]

Although Levanda's searing description of poor Jews may have been elicited by a scene the author witnessed, it also displays a conventional perception. Jewish intellectuals accepted the views of Russian government officials: the Jewish masses were poor and it was their own fault. They were religious fanatics and woefully ignorant of Western knowledge. They needed to become transformed, educated, secularized and civilized.

Such intellectuals as Levanda deemed the transformation of the Jewish masses a worthy aim, since the acquisition of civil rights hinged

---

10 Heinrich Graetz acknowledged the difficulty in finding sources for a history of Eastern-European Jewry, saying that the history of that branch of Jewry was less developed than in the West. See Samuel Kassow, "Historiography," in *YIVO Encyclopedia of Jews in Eastern Europe*, ed. Gershon Hundert (New Haven and London: Yale University Press, 2008), 723.
11 L. Levanda, "Neskol'ko slov o evreiakh zapadnogo kraia Rossii. Pis'mo v redaktsiiu (Iz goroda Igumena, Minsk[oi] guber[nii])," *Rassvet* 1 (May 27, 1860): 7-9.
12 Ibid., 8.

on this change. According to the wisdom of the time, the government supposedly was prepared to lighten Jewish liabilities if Jews would transform themselves, leave their isolation and acquire Western knowledge, including knowledge of the Russian language. Changing the masses was the Jewish intelligentsia's goal. Therefore, when the "intelligenty" did describe the Jewish people, they criticized them, revealing their flaws and pointing out the qualities Jews should strive to acquire. Sometimes, writers of *Rassvet* or *Sion* praised a Jewish institution or the longevity of the religion, but the object of appreciation was always something abstract—an institution or concept (the people's will)—and not the masses living today and their present way of life.[13] Actual Jews in Russia were in need of radical transformation.

When it became clear by the 1870s that the transformation of the Jews would not necessarily lead to an expansion of rights, Jewish historians began to examine the causes for the breakdown of the "emancipation contract."[14] Although Benjamin Nathans has argued correctly that "In their reconstruction of the Russian-Jewish past, their strategies for emancipation in the future, and their search for self-definition as Jews in post-Reform Russia, educated Jewish elites relied to a remarkable degree on juridical categories and modes of thought." Yet it is also the case that Jewish historians started to recalibrate Jewish self-consciousness and reexamine culture and internal communal life.[15]

For example, a more positive image of the Russian Jew was developed as a response to the Odessa pogroms of 1871.[16] Even worse than the physical destruction of the city was the psychological crisis that Odessa's Jewish intellectuals experienced. While one had always understood that such violence was possible in the countryside, where Jews had not modernized, they were certain it could not happen in Odessa, where Jews were the most progressive in all Russia. Their experience

---

13 No matter how critical *Rassvet* got, however, one should recall the insight of Saul Ginzburg; "The lofty ideals and principles of Judaism, everything great and noble, brought down to us from the many centuries of our historical existence and composes the true basis of our singular way of life, remained for them no less sacred than for their enemies" (S. M. Ginzburg, *Minuvshee: istoricheskie ocherki, stat'i i kharistaristiki* [Petrograd: 1923], 80).

14 In the next section I do not treat Nikolai Bershadsky, since he was ethnically and culturally Russian. I acknowledge that an examination of Bershadsky would likely elicit similar conclusions to those I make about the Jewish intellectuals, M. Morgulis and I. Orshanskii.

15 Nathans, *Beyond the Pale*, 103.

16 See I. Sosis, "Period 'obruseniia': natsional'nyi vopros v literature kontsa 60-kh i nachala 70-kh godov," *Evreiskaia starina* 1 (1915): 129-42.

forced them to reexamine the premises upon which their views were constructed.

In articles written in the 1870s (collected in the volume *Questions of Jewish Life* [*Voprosy evreiskoi zhizni*] ,1886), Mikhail Morgulis, the editor of the Odessa Russian-language Jewish newspaper *Den'*, departed from the previous idea that the Jews themselves were guilty. Focusing on education in general and the government-sponsored Jewish schools in particular, Morgulis argued that emancipation had failed not because Jews were incapable of being educated, but because the government schools did not fulfill their needs. Demonstrating the schools' coercive aspect, he complained that Jewish communities had been forced to pay, although parents tended to boycott the schools. Furthermore, while the textbooks—German translations of Jewish religious texts—never found use in the classroom, they must have been costly for the debt-ridden communities (Morgulis's estimation of 200,000 rubles spent has never been independently verified).[17]

Morgulis pointed out that, although Jewish intellectuals were deeply critical of the traditional heder, government-sponsored schools had not won the trust of the Jewish people. Instead of reiterating the viewpoint that the people kept clear of the schools because they feared their children would be pressured to convert to Christianity, Morgulis argued that the schools simply did not meet the needs of the community.[18] In particular, the heder provided cheap child-care. Children arrived at the heder early and stayed until late in the evening, thereby allowing mothers to spend days in a shop or market stall. By contrast, the schools let the pupils out in the early afternoon. Furthermore, schools were very costly, and sometimes instruction offended parents' religious principles.[19]

Instead of viewing Jews as ignorant and regressive, Morgulis held

---

17 This fact is unproved. Morgulis accuses the *maskil* L. Mandel'shtam of having garnered a high salary for his work in translating the textbooks, but Mandel'shtam's biographer, Shaul Ginzburg, argues that Mandel'shtam was not well paid at all. M. Morgulis, *Voprosy evreiskoi zhizni: sbornik statei*, 2nd ed. (St. Petersburg: Tip. A. N. Mikhailova, 1903), 167; for S. Ginzburg's view, see "Iz zapisok pervogo evreia-studenta v Rossii," in *Perezhitoe* 1 (St. Petersburg: 1908-1913), 8.
18 M. Morgulis, *Voprosy evreiskoi zhizni*, 200.
19 In his review of Morgulis' book, published in 1889, Semyon Dubnov took issue with Morgulis' idea that the heder served primarily to watch over children and for that reason enjoyed popularity. Dubnov pointed to the religious aims and traditional attitudes of the heder, explaining that parents wanted to send their children to heder even when they didn't need baby-sitting. See his review of *Voprosy evreiskoi zhizn'* by Kritikus in *Voskhod* 1 (1890): 27.

that they understood their own interests. If they refused to modernize, it was not because they were backward, but because they had more to gain by remaining unchanged. What was needed, Morgulis believed, was to tailor knowledge to real conditions in order to make it useful and beneficial.

Margulis' assertions struck a blow at the *Haskalah* (Enlightenment) ideology because, instead of seeing the people as benighted, he levied his criticisms at the government and Jewish intelligentsia, which had arrogantly supported modern schools without considering the people's needs and desires. But Morgulis was still a *maskil*. He criticized the way Jews were asked to change, but not the idea of change itself. In articles written at the same time, Morgulis called for Jews "to engage in productive work, [to have] the chance to move from those places where their hands are inactive and move to those places where there is a pressing need for them."[20] By productive work, Morgulis meant farming and crafts.

Ilya Orshansky, the other editor of *Den'* and a historian, wrote a great deal on the maltreatment of Jews in the Russian legal code and government legislation. In order to combat the overwhelmingly negative portrayal, he wrote an article that was really original for the time, "Folksongs of the Russian Jews" ("Prostonarodnye pesni russkikh evreev"), in which he lauded the people's creative talent. Orshansky recognized that "simple" Jews had their own unique culture, admittedly invisible to non-Jews: "A Christian knows [the Jew] only as the exploitative trader, the money lender, tavern keeper; is it astounding that he has a rotten view of the Jew?"[21] According to Orshansky, the songs of any people reflect their culture, way of life, and worldview, and Jews are no exception. Above all, the songs of Russia's Jews mirror their unhappy reality. Jews sing of their sadness, poverty, and misery, of the conditions particular to their society—abandoned wives left by men who have emigrated, recruitment into the tsar's army, and conflicts between rich and poor.[22]

Orshansky helped shape a positive image of the Jews by adding new categories. He sketched a human portrait that contradicted the anti-

---

20   M. Morgulis, *Vosprosy evreiskoi zhizni*, 294.
21   I. Orshansky, *Evrei v Rossii: ocherki ekonomicheskogo i obshchestvennogo byta russkikh evreev* (St. Petersburg: Tip. Sh. I. Baksta, 1877), 391-92.
22   Ibid., 400.

Semitic images often printed in the Russian press. Nevertheless, as an intellectual in tune with Russian Populism, Orshansky felt that Russian and Ukrainian peasants were closer to nature and in this sense superior. He criticized the Jews' lack of a feeling for nature, attributing this flaw to their largely urban habitat and characterized their folk culture as "subjective rather than objective," "idealistic rather than realistic."[23]

Did either Orshansky or Morgulis think of the Jews as a nation in their own right? To be sure, they believed Jewish separation was artificial, caused by the government's special laws against Jews. But it is revealing that neither Orshansky nor Morgulis valorized Yiddish. They refused to relinquish their belief that Russian language was the key to a positive future, and the sooner the people accepted it as their proper language the better. Morgulis admitted that if any language besides Russian should be used for pragmatic purposes, Yiddish at least was understood by all of Russia's Jews.[24]

Orshansky and Morgulis' ambivalence toward the Jewish masses showed that little had changed from 1860 to 1880. While defending Jews against unfair accusations, they nevertheless had the same goal as earlier *maskilim*: full integration through adoption of the language, culture, and way of life of urban Russians. Similar to the *maskilim* before them, Orshansky and Morgulis felt contradictory. They were unable to find a way to reconcile their feelings of profound pride in the Jewish heritage and undiminished demands for change.

* * *

Semyon Dubnov dominated the next generation. His work went through a number of phases: in the first period, during the 1880s, he modified aspects of the earlier approaches, emphasizing ideal concepts—reason, freedom and universalism—in the Jews' historical experience. Even in this first period Dubnov was extremely innovative because of his focus on the Jewish people as the central agent of history.

Dubnov nonetheless shared the ambivalence of his predecessors. He was still reluctant to question the earlier practice of measuring Jewish

---

23   Ibid.
24   M. Morgulis, "Natsional'nyi i prakticheskii vzgliady na znachenie drevne-evreiskogo iazyka," *Den'*, 3 (1869).

against Western culture and finding the Jews wanting.[25] In his article on Sabbatai Zvi for example, published just after the pogroms of 1882, Dubnov compared the false messiah with a contemporary, Baruch (Benedict) Spinoza, writing: "The Jewish people stood at a crossroads. The Amsterdam philosopher called them to enlightenment, showed them the glowing dawn of a new life, new civilization. The kabbalist from Smyrna tempted them toward ignorance and darkness, the thick gloom of the past . . . A Judaism reborn cursed the former and followed the latter. It was a decisive, fatal step."[26] Dubnov's desire for the Jewish people to follow Spinoza reflected his commitment to progress, freedom, and rationality, ideals he imbibed from the idols of his youth, John Stewart Mill, Hippolyte Taine and Ernest Renan.

Convinced that history should record the life of the people, Dubnov rejected writing a history of ideas—exactly what he objected to in Heinrich Graetz's work, the domination of the Jewish idea over the Jewish people.[27] Dubnov's solution was to valorize the Jewish people by discovering what he called the "universal in the particular," i.e., he portrayed the Jews' endless quest for survival as a revelation of universal virtues. By universal, Dubnov referred to the ideals of European humanism.

In his long article of 1888, "The Emergence of Chasidism" ("Vosniknovenie Khasidizma"), influenced strongly by Ernest Renan's *Life of Jesus* (1863), the people become the undisputed hero of Jewish history. Instead of debunking the myth of the Bal Shem Tov, Dubnov accepted the legends of the founder of Hasidism as indisputable historical facts.[28]

---

25 In his memoir, Dubnov offered a paradigm for understanding his own intellectual evolution. In his view he went through three phases: thesis, anti-thesis, and synthesis. His period of thesis was during the 1870s, when he rejected Jewish history and advocated radical cosmopolitanism. In the 1880s, he applied Western reason to the study of Jewish history, while in the period of synthesis, after 1890, Dubnov overcame the first two phases, analyzing Jewish history as having its own unique, exclusive course, distinct from, although in places contiguous with, European history. In this last period he created his idea of "Jewish hegemonic centers." See *Kniga zhizni, vospominaniia i razmyshleniia: materialy dlia istorii moego vremeni* 2 (Riga: 1934), 145.

26 S. Dubnov, "Sabbatai Tsevi i psevdomessianism v 17 veke," *Voskhod* 7-8, (1882): 137.

27 S. Dubnov, "Istoriograf evreistva. Geinrikh Grets, ego zhizn' i trudy" *Voskhod* 3, (March 1892): 68. For more on Heinrich Graetz, see *Encyclopedia Judaica*, vol. 7 (Jerusalem: Keter Publishing, 1972), 845-50.

28 S. Dubnov, "Vozniknovenie Khasidizma," in *Evrei v Rossiiskoi Imperii XVIII-XIX vekov: sbornik trudov evreiskikh istorikov*, ed. A. Lokshin (Moscow: Jewish University in Moscow Press, 1995), 86. Fore more on Chasidism, see *Encyclopedia Judaica*, vol. 7 (Jerusalem: Keter Publishing, 1972), 1370-1432.

Moreover, Dubnov valorized sources based on oral genres, folktales, stories, and poems, the product of the people's creative energy. About Zalman Shneerson's "Eulogy for Besht," Dubnov wrote, "The Besht biography that has come down to us is a collective work and entirely by the folk. It was not created by a single person, but compiled from a mass of oral legends disseminated among the people. In this book everything essential that the people's memory has preserved, everything that the people's imagination has created [...] finds a place."[29]

In recounting the life and teaching of Besht, Dubnov certainly wrote with great sympathy, refraining from criticizing Besht's hostility to rationality. Moreover, Dubnov sympathized with the causes that contributed to the popularity of Hasidism. As opposed to the formalism, intellectualism, and elitism of the Orthodox *mitnagdim*, who had alienated the simple people from the religious leadership, Besht promoted a Jewish faith based on feeling, mystical knowledge and joy. Dubnov wrote, "The Besht's genuine optimism, expressed in the bright, optimistic picture he painted, his views on the meaning of prayer and communication with God as the essence of faith, his consciousness of the great task of his teaching—all this was embodied in the form of a magical vision."[30]

According to Dubnov, this religious orientation brought about new ideas of equality by reducing the hold of the rabbinical hierarchy. Dubnov depicted the founder of Hasidism—usually considered the most exclusive and fanatic wing of Judaism—as the embodiment of universalism; the people created a religious figure who fulfilled their need for universal religious feeling. By positing religious feeling as the basis of Hasidism, Dubnov defended Judaism itself, which at this time was strongly condemned by theologians and historians in Europe as "rationalistic" and "formalist."[31]

Like all *maskilim*, Dubnov disdained the institution of the *tsaddikim* (the heads of Hasidic dynasties), which formed after Besht's death. He strongly disliked their materialism and manipulations. Moreover, in forcing the people to communicate with God through them, the *tsaddikim* contradicted the Besht and ruined his greatest achievement, that

---

29   Ibid., 83.
30   Ibid., 144.
31   Léon Poliakov, *History of Anti-Semitism: Suicidal Europe, 1877-1930*, trans. G.Klin (Philadelphia: University of Pennsylvania Press, 2003), 6.

of enabling all Jews to attain direct contact with God through feeling.[32]

In the 1890s, having valorized the emotional appreciation of religion, Dubnov took the next step of attributing the same functions of religion to historiography. He believed that history could bring immortality and salvation. This view can best be seen in his 1891 book, *On the Study of the History of Russia's Jews and the Establishment of a Russian-Jewish Historical Society*.[33] According to Dubnov, Russia's Jews must take the first step by collecting documents, artifacts, communal chronicles, anything that provides evidence of a Jewish past in Russia. Once that is done, the process of national resurrection may take place. Alluding to the prophet Ezekiel's gathering of the Jewish armies and the restoration of Israel, Dubnov wrote:

> Dry bones, the remains of past generations are strewn in a valley. *"Will these bones come alive?"*—the prophet asks. And suddenly the bones begin to come together, veins and flesh appear, they tighten up with skin, only there is no spirit in them.... And I began to prophesy; and suddenly spirit arrives and the bones live and stood up, an exceeding great army. And the Lord said to me: "Son of Man! These bones are the entire house of Israel."[34]

Here Dubnov interjected: "Yes, we will soon witness and even participate in the great act of resurrection."[35]

Just how this secular messianism would work is not entirely clear, but if we understand him correctly, resurrection refers to an attitude toward history. By integrating the past into the present and carrying it into the future, the Jewish people rise from the dead and make themselves immortal. Resurrection here combines material and mystical aspects: material, in that the Jewish nation really awakens to its national purpose; mystical, in that this purpose is linked somehow with a secularized form of Jewish messianism. Moreover, the Jewish historian, as the interpreter of the purpose of the Jewish people, would become

---

32 Dubnov, "Vozniknovenie Khasidizma," 137-38.
33 S. Dubnov, *Ob izuchenii istorii russkikh evreev i ob uchrezhdenii russko-evreiskogo istoricheskogo obshchestva* (St. Petersburg: 1891).
34 Ibid., 88.
35 Ibid.

their leader. Amos Funkenstein has noted in this regard, "While it is true that during the nineteenth century historiography became professionalized and, therefore, less accessible to the reading public, it is likewise true that at the same time the historian was given a special position as a high priest of culture, responsible for the legitimization of the nation-state."[36]

These ideas reflect a change of focus. Instead of seeing the Jewish people as embodying universal values, Dubnov began to view Jewish history as having its own path and meaning for Jews alone. Moreover, the immortality he had in mind is not the possession of an individual, but the collective. However, Dubnov's rationalism did not abandon him. Nowhere is God visible. Rather, by surviving in history the Jewish people attain a secular, collective immortality.

Dubnov helped invent a modern idea of the Jewish nation. However, as the founder of Diaspora Nationalism, he valorized the lack of a state since this absence made the people preeminently historical; only their historical experience and not geography keeps them together. In contrast to the enlighteners' negative attitudes, Dubnov portrayed the Jewish people wholly positively; the people have become the embodiment of such ideas as historical essence, religious meaning, and spiritual accomplishment.

In this period when Jewish nationalism came to dominate the thinking of many Jewish intellectuals, it is interesting to note Dubnov's views about Yiddish. In many places—for example, at the first meeting of the Jewish Literary Society in St. Petersburg in 1908—Dubnov spoke out in favor of "tri-lingualism," the view that Hebrew, Russian, and Yiddish should all be considered national languages of Russia's Jews.[37] Similarly in his 1909 article, "The Affirmation of the Diaspora," written in response to Ahad-Ha'am's polemical article of the same year, "Negation of the Diaspora" ("Shelilat ha-galut"), Dubnov explained that Yiddish could serve as a national language.[38] Published a year af-

---

36 Amos Funkenstein, *Perceptions of Jewish History* (Berkeley: University of California Press, 1973), 19.
37 See Dubnov's own discussion of that meeting in *Kniga zhizni*, quoted in 3rd edition (St. Petersburg: Evreiskii universitet v Moskve & Rossiiskaia natsional'naia biblioteka, 1998), 297.
38 S. Dubnov, "Utverzhdenie golosa (Po povodu 'Otritsaniia golosa' Akhad Gaama)," *Evreiskii mir* 5 (1909): 58. Dubnov wrote, "When in our literature the question of language will be posed in its entire breadth, when it will be discussed not from the viewpoint of one or another party or literary group, but from the general national viewpoint, then there will be no room among the nationalists

ter the Czernowitz Language Conference, this statement of the use of Yiddish as a tool of nationalization affirmed an earlier attitude. One may remember that as the literary critic of *Voskhod* during the 1880s, Dubnov had spearheaded positive attitudes toward Yiddish literature.[39]

* * *

By 1908, the positive attitude of the Jewish intelligentsia toward the folk was entirely unexceptional. In fact, the reappraisal of the people would turn into a cult, with all the trappings typical of romantic idealization. An example of this treatment can be found in the work of Semyon An-sky (Rappaport), the creative writer, journalist, ethnographer, and political activist. In his 1908 article, "Jewish Folk Art" ("Evreiskoe narodnoe tvorchestvo"), An-sky claimed that, as opposed to Christian nations that have their origins in paganism, "such motifs as the idealization of military strength, enthusiasm for battle, praise of the glory and the victories of knights, have been entirely foreign to Jewish national and folk poetry. Similarly foreign is any admiration of triumphant physical strength."[40] "[...] Jewish creativity is entirely imbued with the idea of monotheism, which in its foundation is hostile to any struggle, and does not permit the cult of the individual, and places spiritual perfection above material and, in particular, above physical perfection."[41]

Many Jewish writers attacked An-sky, giving as examples of Jewish militarism the depictions of Joshua and Samson in the Bible and Bar Kochba after.[42] Nevertheless, An-sky's description of the Jewish people

---

who do not negate the Diaspora for such a misunderstanding [toward Yiddish]. Inasmuch as we 'acknowledge' the Diaspora, we must also acknowledge 'the jargon,' as one of the instruments in the struggle for autonomy, equal to Hebrew and other factors of our national culture." For more on Ahad-Ha'am see S. Zipperstein, *Elusive Prophet: Ahad Ha'am and the Origins of Zionism*.

39 For a description of the evolution of Dubnov's attitude toward Yiddish, see Samuel Niger-Charney, "Simon Dubnow as a Literary Critic," in *YIVO Annual of Jewish Social Science* 1 (1946): 305-17. This article was originally published in *YIVO Bleter* 23 (1944). The paper was read at a memorial meeting for Dubnow arranged by the Yiddish Scientific Institute on October 17, 1943. See also Dubnov's own work, *Fun Zhargon tsu Yiddish* (Vilna: Kletzkin, 1929).

40 S. An-sky, "Evreiskoe narodnoe tvorchestvo," in *Evrei v Rossiiskoi Imperii XVIII-XIX vekov* (Moscow: Evreiskii universitet v Moskve, 1995), 644.

41 Ibid.

42 Among those who rejected An-sky's claims were S. Shternberg and S. Ginzburg. For more, see V. Lukin, "Ot narodnichestva k narodu (S. A. An-skii-etnograf vostochno-evreopeiskogo evreistva)," *Istoriia i kul'tura: Evrei v Rossi: Trudy po iudaike, istorii i etnografii* 3 (St. Petersburg: Peterburgskii

as exclusively characterized by spiritual aims epitomizes a fundamental change in attitude of part of the Jewish intelligentsia. From an entirely negative view in the 1860s, the image of the Jewish people was now an object of idealization.[43]

This new view of the people propelled An-sky to organize the Jewish Ethnographic Expedition in 1912. Seeking the help of an assistant, two ethnographers, a composer, a musicologist, and photographer, An-sky travelled through the Pale of Settlement with the goal of collecting the tangible evidence of the Jewish past.[44] He and his assistants visited 66 sites in Volynia and Podolia. Over a two year period, An-sky collected, 2,000 photographs, 1,800 folktales and legends, 1,500 folk songs, 500 cylinders of Jewish folk music, 1,000 songs and *niggunim* without words, countless proverbs and folk beliefs, 100 historical documents, 500 manuscripts, and 700 sacred objects.[45]

The object of the expedition was to document the soul of the Jewish shtetl. However, An-sky viewed traditional Jewish life as a graveyard and its artifacts as in need of collection and preservation. He wrote the following even before the outbreak of World War I.

> Jewish life has undergone an enormous upheaval during the last fifty to sixty years and the losses in our folk creations are among the most unfortunate victims of this change. With every old man who dies, with every fire that breaks out, with every exile we endure, we lose a piece of our past. The finest examples of our traditional lives, our customs and beliefs, are disappearing; the old poetic legends, the songs and melodies will soon be forgotten; the ancient, beautiful synagogues are falling to ruin or are laid waste by fire and there the most pre-

---

Evreiskii Universitet, 1995).

43 Gabriella Safran, *Wandering Soul: The Dybbuk's Creator, S. An-sky* (Cambridge, MA: Harvard University Press, 2010).

44 Abraham Rechtman describes the expedition, "An-sky organized an ethnographical expedition with colleagues including Joel Engel, a famous composer from Moscow; J. Kiselgaf, an expert on Jewish folk music from St. Petersburg: Shlomo Yudovin, a painter and photographer, An-sky's cousin; J. Pikangor and S. Shrier, both students from the Jewish Academy in St. Petersburg, and of course, myself." ("The Jewish Ethnographical Expedition," *Tracing An-sky, Jewish Collections from the State Ethnographical Museum in St. Petersburg* [New York: Jewish Museum, 1992], 13).

45 S. Ansky, "Ot evreiskoi etnograficheskoi ekspeditsii," *Evreiskaia zhizn'* 17 (April 30, 1917): 33-34.

cious religious ornaments are either lost or sold, often to non-Jews; the gravestones of our great and pious ancestors have sunk into the ground, their inscriptions all but rubbed out. In short, our past, sanctified by the blood and tears of so many innocent martyrs, is vanishing and will soon be forgotten.[46]

Capturing the experience of the Jewish people was not an end in itself for An-sky. Rather, folklore had a deeper meaning. Convinced that modern Jews were alienated from religion and community, An-sky believed folk culture could have the same anthropological function as the Torah had in earlier times, i.e. it could serve as the spiritual source to keep the Jewish people together, and give them a vision of the ideal that Judaism could be.[47] The *Dybbuk* provides a good example of An-sky's idea of the uses of folklore, since with its "thurgic" intention (similar to Wagnerian opera) it was meant both to entertain and revitalize Jewish national identity.[48]

One can clearly acknowledge Dubnov's influence on An-sky's view that Jewish folk stories represented the height of Jewish creativity and were sacred and capable of providing religious salvation. However, An-sky's vision is ecstatic. The Jews have theurgy, with their folktales they can channel divine force. In this sense collecting artifacts is not the same as putting them in a museum, but rather collecting forms a bridge that will help those who survive to retain contact with the original theurgic power of the Jewish people.

It seems obvious that An-sky's conceptions emerge from Russia's Silver Age.[49] He was a close friend of Fyodor Sologub and was familiar with the ideas of Russian Symbolism that attributed "God-building" powers to extraordinary men, heroes, poets, and mystical seers. What makes An-sky unique, however, is his attribution of such powers to the

---

46 S. An-sky, *The Dybbuk and Other Writings*, ed. David G. Roskies, trans. Golda Werman (New York: Schocken Books, 1992), xxiv.
47 D. Roskies "Introduction," in S. An-sky, *The Dybbuk and Other Writings*, xxiv.
48 Seth Wolitz, "Inscribing An-sky's *Dybbuk* in Russian and Jewish Letters," in *The Worlds of S. An-sky: A Russian-Jewish Intellectual and the Turn of the Century*, eds. G. Safran and S. Zipperstein, (Stanford: Stanford University Press, 2006), 167-200.
49 The Silver Age represents the period of cultural renaissance in Russia between roughly 1890-1920, and included such movements as Decadence, Symbolism, and Futurism. See "Modernism," in *The Handbook of Russian Literature*, ed. V. Terras (New Haven: Yale University Press, 1985), 284-86.

Jewish people. By making the entire people the hero, An-sky reveals his long affiliation with Russian Populism.

Although the majority of his writings were in Russian, An-sky viewed Yiddish positively. Although like Dubnov he defended the use of Hebrew, Russian and Yiddish at the first meeting of the Jewish Literary Society in 1908, An-sky apparently came to understand the exclusive value of Yiddish at key historical moments, when one needed to make particular allusion to Eastern European Jewish life.[50] Therefore, An-sky used Yiddish to write his three-volume chronicle of the destruction of the Jewish communities during World War I: *The Destruction of the Jews of Poland, Galicia and Bukovina* (*Der yidisher hurbn fun Poylen, Galitsiye un Bukovine von togbuch, 1914-1917*).[51]

* * *

The evidence of the intelligentsia's positive change in its attitude toward the folk raises some questions regarding the path of Jewish nationalism.[52] The conventional goal was a state as the embodiment of the people's will for self-determination. But in the case of all these figures, they did not want a Jewish state, but rather some form of cultural autonomy and separation accompanied by liberal ideas of citizenship in the Russian Empire. In part it was this different kind of nationalism—as opposed to Zionism—that can explain the drive for a synthesis of Russian and Jewish elements, and consequently may make clear why these intellectuals struggled for a national historiography that was also deeply derivative from and aligned with Russian ideas, Slavophilism, Populism, Positivism, and anti-Positivism.[53]

For the Jewish intelligentsia to take a positive view of the masses,

---

50   An-sky's speech was entitled, "Equality of Languages in Jewish Literature" ("Ravnopravnost' iazykov v evreiskoi literature"). For more on this, see Ilya Serman, "Spory 1908 goda o russko-evreiskoi literature i posleoktiabrskoe desiatiletie," *Cahiers du Monde Russe et Soviétique*, vol. 36, no. 2 (Avril-Juin 1985), 167-74.

51   *The Destruction of the Jews of Poland, Galicia and Bukovina* appeared in volumes 4-6 of An-sky's *Gazamlte Shriftn* (*Collected Works*) (Vilna, Warsaw, New York: 1920-1925). An abridged version in English is titled *The Enemy at His Pleasure: a Journey through the Jewish Pale of Settlement during World War I*, ed. Joachim Neugroschel (New York: Metropolitan Books, 2002).

52   The following paragraph was inspired by questions from Richard Wortman at a lecture that I gave at Columbia University on March 4, 2011.

53   See Andrzej Walicki, *A History of Russian Thought: From the Enlightenment to Marxism* (Stanford: Stanford University Press, 1979).

the intelligentsia had to be taught to see, understand and value the folk. Works of history played an essential role in that formation. Once the Jewish intelligentsia began to regard the people favorably, it was not long before it would valorize Yiddish and see in it another sign of the unique and praiseworthy quality of the Jewish people. The process of change took the whole second half of the nineteenth century and ultimately led to the symbiosis of the people and the intelligentsia that brought brilliant results in Jewish political and cultural life during and after the Revolution of 1905.

6. The historian and writer, Semyon Dubnov (reproduced courtesy of the Jewish Studies Department of the European University in St. Petersburg).

6. "Both Crisis and Continuity":
A Reinterpretation of Late-Tsarist Russian Jewry

I reexamine Russian-Jewish life of the late-tsarist period to show that two periods usually viewed as unrelated, the period of Alexander II's Great Reforms and Jewish political life after 1905, paradoxically have sharply similar elements. In addition, it is my claim that the time most unrelated to these two is not the period right after the pogroms of 1881-2, but rather the late 1870s. Using as my criterion Jewish demands for individual and collective rights, I show that Jewish leaders adamantly expressed these desires in the 1860s and again after 1905. In contrast, the 1870s were characterized by a preoccupation with an individual's acculturation into Russian society, which Jewish leaders of the time maintained would occur inevitably thanks to progress in the economy. With this paradigm, it is possible to speculate about the circularity of Jewish history in Russia in which attitudes toward the present and prognoses for the future reveal repetitive traits.

This general hypothesis is significant because it contributes to the debate over whether to view Russian-Jewish history in the late-tsarist period in terms of crisis or continuity.[1] Jewish nationalism emerged

---

1   The debate pits those who emphasize elements of continuity and those who see crisis as characterizing the development of Russian-Jewish history. The dominant view regarding Jews in post-reform tsarist Russia has it that the pogroms of 1881-82 divided two historical epochs. From 1856 to 1881, Russian-Jewish politics conformed to the "liberal" model in which Jews expected to acquire equal rights as citizens and hoped to integrate in Russian society. After 1882, Jews entered a post-liberal period in which political parties formed, many of which clamored not only for personal civic and political rights, but for collective rights. Here integration became deemphasized and national goals, such as cultural autonomy, became essential demands. Semyon Dubnov is best known for this view. In his *Modern History of the Jewish People from the French Revolution to Our Time*, 3 vols. (1914), Dubnov ended one book and began another in 1881. He entitled the second part, "The Epoch of the Second Reaction: The Anti-Semitic Movement and the Great Emigration (1881-1900)." Another perspective has it that the pogroms of 1881-82 set off an inexorable movement of political self-consciousness and spurred migration to new worlds leading ultimately to the creation of a Jewish state in Palestine. Jonathan Frankel has been seen as the primary exponent of this view. In both cases, albeit for different reasons, the pogroms were seen as the central event in Russian-Jewish history of the tsarist period. See J. Frankel, "The Crisis of 1881-82 as a Turning Point in Modern Jewish History," in *The Legacy of Jewish Migration: 1881 and its Impact*, ed. D. Berger (New York: Columbia University Press, 1983), 9-22; *Prophecy and Politics: Socialism, Nationalism, and the Russian Jews, 1862-1917* (Cambridge: Cambridge University

from elements that were anchored in Russian-Jewish life and yet became radically modified after 1882. While proposals for individual and collective rights in 1905 parallel requests in the 1860s, admittedly the context was drastically different. After 1905, Jews created political parties and coalitions, and individuals representing Jewish interests participated in a State Duma, albeit at decreasing rates after the First Duma.[2] These facts allude to new conceptions of what Jewish politics was and how it should be conducted. Still, the traits that were the same in the 1860s and first decade of the 1900s are striking, and motivate one to inquire whether Jewish life in modern times is characterized by shifts between acculturation and its rejection.[3]

It is conventionally accepted that secular Jewish leaders in Russia during the 1860s desired Western-style emancipation.[4] Some individuals had attained full rights by exploiting the privileges that the government of Alexander II made available to a small number of Jews, including the right to reside in Russia's capital cities, and exemptions from the liabilities besetting the vast majority. The richest Jews took upon themselves the role of *Shtadlan* and were ever mindful of their brethren, hopeful that privileges could be expanded and codified as rights for all "citizens

---

Press, 1981). Incidentally, Professor Frankel did note that existing trends were concentrated and exaggerated as a result of the pogrom crisis, and he also mentioned the disagreements of such eminent historians as Y. Leshchinsky and E. Cherikover, who had argued that the pogroms of 1881-82 did not have the effect on average people that scholars imagined, noting that emigration from the country had begun before the pogroms, in the 1870s (J. Frankel, *Prophesy and Politics: Socialism, Nationalism and the Russian Jews, 1862-1917*, [Cambridge and New York: Cambridge University Press, 1981], 50).

Recently other historians have emphasized elements of continuity. In his book Erich Haberer argued that 1881-2 did not have a strong impact on Jews in the revolutionary movement. See E. Haberer, *Jews and Revolution in Nineteenth Century Russia* (New York: Cambridge University Press, 1995), 228-29. In addition, Benjamin Nathans heatedly attacked Frankel and the "school of crisis," underscoring the longevity of a "liberal tradition" in Russian-Jewish intellectual thought and arguing for the primacy of the Petersburg intelligentsia as a source for a vision of Russian Jewry that imparted the goals of Western-style emancipation, including individual civic rights and political democracy across the 1881 divide. (*Beyond the Pale*, 8-14).

2   See C. Gassenschmidt, *Jewish Liberal Politics in Tsarist Russia, 1900-1914*, 45-70.
3   Israel Bartal has taken a mixed approach in his new book. He writes, "[...] I concur with some of these reservations about the view that the events of 1881 caused a revolutionary leap from a premodern phase in the history of Eastern European Jewry to a totally new phase. [...] Nevertheless, the 1881 pogroms can be viewed as a significant milestone in the history of Eastern European Jewry" (*The Jews of Eastern Europe, 1771-1881* [Philadelphia: University of Pennsylvania Press, 2005], 4-5).
4   My understanding of emancipation is that it means the acquisition of the full rights of citizenry. See J. Klier, "The Concept of 'Jewish Emancipation' in a Russian Context," in *Civil Rights in Imperial Russia*, ed. O. Chrisp and L. Edmondson (Oxford: Clarendon Press, 1989), 121-44.

of the Mosaic persuasion."[5] Such rights would include freedom to reside throughout Russia, buy and sell land, live in the countryside, conduct business without restrictions, and pay taxes commensurate with their "estate" (*soslovie*) rather than as Jews. These rights approximated those enjoyed by Jews in Western Europe during this period.

While one conceives of the *Shtadlonim* as encouraging Jewish integration, Russia's Jewish leaders were also eager to secure collective rights. Baron Ezekiel Gintsburg, one of Russia's wealthiest Jews, established a Jewish community (*evreiskaia obshchina*) in 1867 in St. Petersburg, which was authorized to deal with such collective tasks as the upkeep of synagogues, collecting money to pay for the community's welfare, organizing a burial society, and funding the local Jewish school (known as Berman's school).[6]

The group that is most often associated with the promotion of integration and russification, the Odessa Jewish intellectuals, was actually unwilling to part with the idea of the Jewish community as having legally defined rights and responsibilities. Certainly Jews throughout the country resented the government's meat and candle tax, the so-called *korobka*, because, intended to pay for services for Jews, it was often diverted for other uses, and because in practice it affected the poorest members of the community.[7] Despite their call for *Haskalah*—modernization, secularization, education and integration—the progressive Jewish intelligentsia of the 1860s was not in favor of the dissolution of the Jewish community. In fact, they wanted to modernize community institutions by placing these institutions under their own control.

A good source for a study of attitudes among Jewish intellectuals is *Rassvet*, the first Jewish newspaper written in Russian.[8] Although

---

5 Sh. Tsitron, *Shtadlanim: interesante yidishe tipn fun noyentn ever* (Warsaw: 1926), 334-76.

6 Jacob Berman's school, open since 1865, had been successful in teaching over 2300 children (1200 boys and 1170 girls) in the thirty years of its existence. It was apparently well liked by high officials in St. Petersburg, who approved of the school's emphasis on teaching Russian.

7 Iu. Gessen, "Korobochnyi sbor," in *Evreiskaia entsiklopediia: svod znanii o evreistve* (St. Petersburg: 1907-1913), 9: 759-67.

8 John Klier has written about *Rassvet* that "Despite its abbreviated existence, *Rassvet* was a significant voice for Jews—or more specifically, for the Russian Jewish intelligentsia—before the Russian public." Klier, *Imperial Russia's Jewish Question*, 65-68. My analysis is based also on research by S. Gintsburg, *Minuvshee: istoricheskie ocherki stat'i i kharakteristiki* (Petrograd: Izdanie avtora, 1923), 1-50. In addition, I rely on I. Sosis, "Natsional'nyi vopros v literature 60-kh godov," *Evreiskaia Starina* 1 (1913): 38-47; Eli Lederhandler, *The Road to Modern Jewish Politics*; and Alexander Orbach, *New Voices of Russian Jewry: A Study of the Russian-Jewish Press of Odessa in the Era of the Great Reforms 1860-1871* (Leiden: E. J. Brill, 1980).

it only lasted a year (1860-61), it led a battle against Jewish isolation, Hasidism, traditional rabbis, and Yiddish. Its writers called for the abandonment of the shtetl, the study of mathematics and foreign languages, especially Russian, and the acquisition of practical skills. Even though these imperatives would seem to facilitate the alienation of Jews from the community, the writers of *Rassvet* did not want the destruction of the Jewish collective.

In fact, the writers held fully assimilated Jews in contempt. In an editorial from June 17, 1860, the editor, Osip Rabinovich, described his apprehensions about the young generation. He lamented that after seven years in a Russian gymnasium, four or five years in a Russian university without any contact with other Jews, it is understandable that "all the rituals which are linked to religion have escaped from his memory, the prayers that he babbled in childhood in Hebrew, a language he doesn't know, have passed into oblivion. All the interests of Judaism have become foreign to him and after having returned following years of absence to a group of his co-religionists, he sees himself as entirely foreign. Their rituals seem strange to him, because he doesn't understand their meaning. This is how the final alienation of an educated Jew from his fellow tribesmen occurs."[9] Although it seems premature to worry about the ultimate assimilation of the Jewish university elite—after all, in 1860 there were little more than 200 Jewish students in Russian universities—Rabinovich could predict the outcome from looking at the example of Western Europe.[10]

Rabinovich's apprehensions did not emerge from a fear of integration. In fact, a strong Jewish identity was supposed to go hand in hand with patriotism for Russia. Rabinovich exclaimed that "not only us, but thousands of our co-religionists know that loving Russia and speaking Russian, one can remain loyal to the God of Jacob and be a true Jew, in the sense that our teaching obligates, but not in the sense which some people understand it as a result of unfortunate circumstances."[11]

While he criticized Orthodox Jewish leaders, Rabinovich still conceived of the Jewish community in terms that would satisfy any future Jewish nationalist. Rabinovich expected the community to receive

---

9   O. Rabinovich, "Odessa," *Rassvet* 5 (June 17, 1860): 51-52.
10 I understand assimilation to signify the unification of a Jew with the majority to the degree that his/her identity as a Jew is dissolved completely.
11 O. Rabinovich, "Odessa," *Rassvet* 13 (August 19, 1860): 201.

money from the *korobka* (kosher meat and candle taxes) to provide philanthropic services. Even in a big city like Odessa, *Rassvet*'s place of publication, Rabinovich believed that the Jewish community had responsibility to tend to the sick and poor, bury the dead, educate the young, and elect the state rabbi. With regard to relations with the government, Rabinovich wanted more effective participation by the Jewish intelligentsia in the administration of Jewish life. Complaining about the *shtadlonim* and rabbis, Rabinovich wrote, "Individuals without an understanding and without talent get involved in communal affairs. We cannot get any improvement since there isn't anyone who can lead. Let's say that a question comes up about organizing a philanthropic institution. Who should take the initiative?"[12] Rabinovich wanted the intelligentsia to take charge of Jewish institutions, such as school boards, philanthropic committees, and government committees entrusted with the distribution of Jewish taxes. According to Mikhail Polishchuk, intellectuals in Odessa of the 1860s began to dominate such committees.[13]

Certainly John Klier is right in claiming that Rabinovich and his colleagues understood their goals in terms of *Haskalah* ideology, rather than in the framework of Jewish emancipation typical of Western Europe. Jewish intellectuals in Russia strove to achieve reproachment and merging (*sblizhenie* and *sliianie*) with the Russian population, which they considered the first step toward the equality of Jews with the other "citizens" of Russia. While at this time the concept of citizen was only theoretical, Rabinovich was convinced that once Jews transformed themselves and became worthy, full rights would be bestowed. While Rabinovich's desire for individual rights and collective rights has to be seen in the context of Alexander II's Great Reforms, nonetheless he and other members of the intelligentsia raised demands for participatory democracy and collective self-rule.[14] They were apparently convinced that their struggle to "improve" the Jews paralleled the tsar's own de-

---

12 O. Rabinovich, "Odessa," *Rassvet* 15 (December 2, 1860): 237.
13 M. Polishchuk, *Evrei Odessy i Novorossii: sotsial'no-politicheskaia istoriia evreev Odessy i drugikh gorodov Novorossii, 1881-1904* (Jerusalem: Gesharim, 2002), 102.
14 As part of the urban estate (*meshchane*), Jews were supposed to vote for representatives to town councils. However, Jewish participation was curtailed through special legislation, giving Jewish men at least by 1890 the right to only 25% of the seats and a prohibition on occupying the chairman's position. See his introduction in Ia. I. Gimpel'son, *Zakony o evreiakh, sistematicheskii obzor deistvuiushchikh zakonopolozhenii o evreiakh s raz"iasneniiami pravitel'stvennykh ustanovlenii* (Petersburg: Iurisprudentsiia, 1914).

sires and would therefore receive government support.

The reasons why the secular Jewish leadership supported collective goals had to do with conditions in Tsarist Russia. Despite the fact that the government created categories for defining individuals into classes or estates (*sosloviia*) and assigned burdens and privileges accordingly, Jews were still liable for collective taxes.[15] The kosher meat and Sabbath candle tax serve as obvious examples. Furthermore, special laws restricting Jewish habitation in the countryside and the prohibitions on certain professions (selling alcohol) marked the Jews as distinct. Such laws compelled even secular Jews to retain their connection with the Jewish collective. Religious difference was the primary basis for the government's discrimination, but other factors contributed to Jewish separation, such as language difference (Yiddish), ethnicity, and education. The government's discrimination reinforced a way of life that kept Jews separate, united, and committed to the health of communal institutions.

At the same time, Jewish intellectuals were strongly influenced by the habits of Jewish life, especially the importance of the former *kahal*—the institution of Jewish self-governance, formally abolished by Nicholas I in 1844. Like others, Rabinovich wanted the intelligentsia to lead the community to positive transformation. Rabinovich in particular understood that the struggle of his group for national leadership would have to be waged through various means, including the press, and participation in local and national governmental and non-governmental institutions, such as schools and philanthropic organizations, including the Society for the Promotion of Enlightenment among the Jews of Russia.[16]

In the late 1870s, this commitment to acculturation began to totter. The yearning for integration blinded the Jewish intelligentsia to the fact that the government had no intention of awarding equal rights. Partially, it was self-serving logic that convinced Jews that the confirmation of rights was imminent, partially they were swayed by the realization that it made no practical sense for the government to restrain Jews by denying them full rights since emancipation would turn them

---

15 See G. Freeze, "The Soslovie (Estate) Paradigm and Russian Social History," *American Historical Review* 91, no. 1 (1986): 11-36; also Klier, *Imperial Russia's Jewish Question*, 74 and elsewhere.
16 Lederhendler, *The Road to Modern Jewish Politics*, 115-20.

into useful members of Russian society. Echoing the times, Menashe Morgulis explained that the Jewish question could vanish if one could only articulate it properly. "The anchor for the resolution of the Jewish question lies in the way you formulate it. If you formulate it on the correct basis, which is how broad-minded individuals have done, it is resolved together with the universal questions that affect not only Jews. But if you formulate it on national-religious grounds, singling the Jews out from the other groups as a separate and condemned estate, there is no doubt that it will be as eternal as discrimination itself. The first path is the path of truth, while the second is the path of hypocrisy and lies."[17]

Lev Levanda in particular noticed that Jews played important roles as technical engineers and other specialists in the new industrial economy. It seemed logical that rights would have to be extended to facilitate economic growth. Furthermore, Jews were ardent patriots, calling themselves "true sons of Russia," as opposed to stepsons (*pasynki*), which is how they perceived themselves.[18] It was at this time that the term "Russian Jew" gained traction, especially in the cities. Perhaps more prescriptive than a mirror of reality, the term was supposed to indicate acceptance in the Russian state.[19] Inherent in this dual identity was the belief that Russia was on the path to becoming a modern industrial country in which all members (citizens) of the empire would receive equal rights. To prepare themselves, growing numbers of Jews attended Russian educational institutions, and Jews were proud to serve in the military and even become officers as a result of the universal conscription law of 1874.[20] That law in particular gave rise to increased expectations for equal rights, as Jews grasped the notion widespread in Europe that the privileges of citizenship should be extended to those who fulfill military service.[21]

A path to acculturation was also possible through involvement in the

---

17 M. Morgulis, "Evreiskii vopros v ego osnovaniiakh i chastnostiakh," *Voskhod* 1, (1881): 29.
18 L. Levanda's novel, *Goriachee vremia* (1872), reflects this patriotism.
19 Benjamin Nathans first made the argument that "Russian Jew" was a proscriptive identity (*Beyond the Pale*, 334-39).
20 Yohanan Petrovsky-Shtern, *Jews in the Russian Army, 1827-1914* (Cambridge: Cambridge University Press, 2009), 129-66.
21 The involvement of Baron Horace Gintsburg in the genesis of the conscription degree of 1874, and his hopes for Jewish integration as a result can be viewed in B. Horowitz, *Jewish Philanthropy and Enlightenment in Late-Tsarist Russia*, 61-62.

revolutionary movement.²² Revolutionaries offered a rare place where social, ethnic and even gender distinctions played a minimal role, and individuals tried to realize ideas of brotherhood in their own lives. But Jewish difference was not condoned; Judaism was sacrificed on the altar of universal justice for all peoples.²³ In the 1870s and 80s, the rate of conversions to Christianity also grew.²⁴ In Ilya Orshansky's view, capitalism would inevitably lead Russian Jews to assimilate and dissolve into the Russian mass.²⁵

The heightened expectations for equal rights were shattered by pogroms. This subject is too complicated to be treated fully here, but in terms of integration, the pogroms of 1881 and 1882 supposedly discredited that goal, because the violence symbolized a definite and irrepressible Russian animus toward Jews.²⁶ The government's reaction was to reduce the limited rights it had extended in the 1860s. The so-called May Laws, instituted in 1882 by the government and on the books until 1917, sharply limited Jewish economic activity in various ways and reduced further the right of Jews to live outside the urban areas of the Pale.²⁷ These laws (in fact they were regulations, never having been approved by the State Senate) were justified as punishment for "Jewish exploitation" of the peasants. Jewish leaders, however, understood them differently. Semyon Dubnov declared them "legalized pogroms,"

---

22   By acculturation I understand the idea that Jews integrated but retained a Jewish identity and were recognized as Jewish. I rely on Ezra Mendelsohn's book, *Modern Jewish Politics*, for my understanding of terms such as "integration," "acculturation," and "assimilation" ([New York: Oxford University Press, 1993], 1-11).
23   Ch. Zhitlowski, *Zichronos fun meyn lebn* (New York: Dr. Zhitlowski Jubilee Committee, 1935), 13-16.
24   M. Stanislawski, "Jewish Apostasy in Russia: A Tentative Typology," in *Jewish Apostasy in the Modern World*, ed. T. Endelman (New York: Holmes & Meier, 1987), 200; also I Cherikover, "Obrashchenie v khristianstvo," in *Evreiskaia entsiklopediia*, 11: 884-95.
25   I. Orshanskii, "Sushchestvuet li evreiskii vopros," *Rassvet* 2 (1879): 56-57.
26   Michael Aronson, *Troubled Waters: The Origins of the 1881 Anti-Jewish Pogroms in Russia* (Pittsburgh: University of Pittsburgh Press, 1990); Hans Rogger, "Government, Jews, Peasants and Land in Post-Emancipation Russia," *Cahiers du Monde Russe et Soviétique* 17, nos. 1-3 (1976): 5-21, 171-211; Rogger, "The Jewish Policy of Late Tsarism: A Reappraisal," *Weidner Library Bulletin* 25, nos. 1-2, (1971): 42-51; John Klier, "The Russian Press and the Anti-Jewish Pogroms of 1881-82," *Canadian-American Slavic Studies* 17, no. 1 (Spring 1983): 199-221; Shlomo Lambroza, "Plehve, Kishinev and the Jewish Question: A Reappraisal," *Nationalities Papers* 12, no. 1 (1984): 117-27; Lambroza, "Jewish Responses to Pogroms in Late Imperial Russia," in *Living with Antisemitism: Modern Jewish Responses*, ed. Jehuda Reinharz (Hanover: Brandeis University Press, 1987), 253-274.
27   John Klier gives a summary of the content of the May Laws in "The Concept of 'Jewish Emancipation' in a Russian Context," 138-39.

because they enshrined "in law the violence that the ruffians had perpetrated on the streets."[28] The unanimous view held that these regulations reflected "medieval prejudices" and served as the leading salvo in the Alexander III's repressive battle against his Jewish population.

Under Alexander III, the government's intensely anti-Jewish policy differed from that of other tsars because previous attempts, however contradictory and cruel, had the intention of integrating the "useful" Jews, i.e., those who were educated, rich, or willing to serve the country as soldiers or artisans.[29] Now, however, even "useful" Jews were objects of repression. Hostile decrees included such extreme measures as quotas on the number of Jews permitted to attend Russian schools, the eviction of the majority of Jews from Moscow in 1891, and a trumped-up trial against Mendel Beilis for the murder of a Christian for ritual purposes (1911-13). Although other minorities in the Empire also faced discriminatory laws, the Jews were treated worse, had a larger number of restrictions placed upon them, and were regarded by the government with intense suspicion.[30]

The devastating repression of Jews had the expected result of strengthening collective Jewish institutions. Since the government treated the Jews as a collective, the response was to act as one. Jews could no longer rely on the government to protect their interests and therefore had to forge a policy of "self-help." Concretely, Jewish activists with community support created schools, hospitals, welfare societies, and credit unions, which were independent both from religious authorities and from the state. Ironically, many of these organizations resembled the institutions of the traditional Jewish community. The example of the modern heder in the South serves well to show how an institution reflected continuity punctuated by change.[31]

Developing separate institutions that met collective needs, secular Jews inevitably borrowed from models in traditional Jewish society. The best example of this is the curriculum of talmud Torah schools fostered

---

28 S. Dubnov, *Evrei v Rossii i zapadnoi Evrope v epokhu antisemitskoi reaktsii* (Moscow and Petersburg: L. D. Frenkel', 1923), 52-53.
29 Heinz-Dietrich Loewe makes this point in his book, *The Tsars and the Jews: Reform, Reaction and Anti-Semitism in Imperial Russia, 1772-1917* (Chur, Switzerland: Harwood Academic Publishers, 1993), 127. Under Nicholas I, for example, the idea of integration included religious conversion.
30 Han Rogger, *Russia in the Age of Modernization and Revolution, 1881-1917* (London and New York: Longman, 1983), 202-3.
31 Shaul Stampfer, *ha-Yeshivah ha-Lita, it be-hithavutah* (Jerusalem: Zalmon Shazar Center), 1995.

by the Society for the Promotion of Enlightenment, in which students studied the Bible, Hebrew grammar, Russian, and secular subjects. The curriculum was intentionally designed to resemble the traditional heder, and thus to attract, or at least not repel, conservative parents.[32]

The period between 1897 and 1917, that historians identify with the struggle of Jews to attain national rights, is also marked by evidence of a strong desire for individual rights and integration. After the Revolution of 1905, all the Jewish political parties, even the Zionists, showed commitment to both the well-being of collective Jewish life in Russia and facilitation of individual integration.

Certainly different political parties supported ideas of integration for different reasons, but all groups justified integration by noting that Jews living in Russia were dependent on the non-Jewish sectors of the Russian economy to survive. For Territorialists and Zionists, integration was a necessary evil, a fact of diaspora life. For Bundists and liberals associated with the Constitutional Democratic Party (Kadets), integration had positive features. Unifying with Russian opposition parties provided the political, social, and economic context in which autonomous Jewish institutions could prosper in security.

How integrationist were Jewish nationalists? To answer this question, I would like to turn to the writings of Avram Idel'son, the Zionist theorist, and to the political program of the Folkspartai, written by Semyon Dubnov.

Starting out as a young member of Hovevei Tsion in Moscow in the 1890s, Idel'son became the architect of Russian Zionism's *Gegenwartsprogram*, according to Pyotr Marek. That program, accepted at the so-called Third Congress of Russian Zionists in 1906 in Helsingfors, announced a new strategy at odds with former rejection of Diaspora. The program outlined initiatives for the expansion of participation in state-wide Jewish political institutions and in education and culture. Among other things, delegates in Helsingfors demanded the democratization of the Russian state, full equality for the Jewish population, the right

---

32 Steven Zipperstein has written about a variant of these schools, the ideal or modernized heder which was traditionally run by local community leaders or enlightened melamdim. See *Imagining Russian Jewry: Memory, History, Identity*, 39-44. The Society for the Promotion of Enlightenment also controlled a few talmud Torah schools. See my article, "The Society for the Promotion of Enlightenment among the Jews of Russia, and the Evolution of the St. Petersburg Russian-Jewish Intelligentsia, 1893-1905," in *Jews and the State: Dangerous Alliances and the Perils of Privilege, Studies in Contemporary Jewry* 19, ed. Ezra Mendelsohn, (2004): 207-10.

to use Hebrew and Yiddish in schools, and the acknowledgement of the Jewish people in Russia as a legal entity with rights to self-rule in Jewish national affairs.[33] As a sign of his increased influence as a thinker and leader, in 1904 Idel'son was offered the editorship of *Evreiskaia Zhizn'*, the Zionist monthly in Russian.

In various articles he explained his view that Zionism could only be realized territorially, in a space where Jews were a majority and Jewish politics, economics, and culture could dominate. The goals of Zionism could not be realized in Diaspora. There, whether one liked it or not, Russian Jews needed to acculturate. In fact, their survival depended on it. In his article "The Galut," Idel'son wrote, "The condition of a Jewish merchant or factory owner depends on the success of the non-Jewish peasant economy, and he brings a profit with his business not to Jewish society, but to the given region, its entire population in equal measure. Therefore, there aren't any activities, even imaginary ones that are aimed toward the improvement of the economic situation of the Jewish collective, which really doesn't exist."[34] Like many other Zionists, Idel'son argued that the goal of Jewish politics in Diaspora inevitably fosters assimilation. The absence of Jewish parties in Germany, France, and England, where capitalism was more developed, demonstrated for Idel'son the natural process of political life in diaspora.

Although one conclusion led to a repudiation of Jewish life in the *Galut*, another spoke in favor of accepting and even cultivating diaspora. Idel'son argued that integration could have positive consequences. For example, when Jews moved to Palestine, they moved as healthy, strong, determined individuals who had successfully competed in difficult economic conditions.

Paradoxically, the nationalist Folkspartai supported the idea of integration. In a political declaration written in 1906, the historian Semyon Dubnov, the party's theorist, explained that he accepted the political program of the Constitutional Democrats, but added several emendations regarding the rights of Jews. Dubnov justified his support for Russian liberals by asserting that the party needed to participate in coalition politics unable to win power on its own. Explaining that Jews had

---

33 Yitzhak Maor, *Sionistskoe dvizhenie v Rossii*, trans. O. Mints (Jerusalem: Biblioteka Alia, 1977), 240-41.
34 A. Idel'son, "Galut," in *Sbornik pamiati A. D. Idel'sona* (Berlin: 1925), 247.

always found compensation for the lack of territory in the community's well-developed internal life, Dubnov pointed out that traditionally the Jewish community was isolated from the political institutions of the majority. This isolation inevitably reflected Jews' subordinate status. In modern times, he claimed, Jews could no longer accept this status.

Therefore, to defend their rights, they had to fight alongside liberal parties. "The new system of [Jewish] self-rule rejects all these principles. It rejects the first, [isolation], on the basis of the demand for full integration of the Jews in the civil and political life of the country, without which equal rights are senseless. It rejects religious authority on the basis of the secularization of the national idea that predominates in contemporary Judaism, i.e., purifying [the national idea] from the religious idea. Democratic principles should defend us from an oligarchic regime. These principles are formed on the basis of communal authority."[35] By adopting the Kadet program, Dubnov accepted the view that Jews were entitled full rights as citizens, including the right to vote for a parliament and protection by law regardless of race, religion, or nationality.[36] In this case, Jews in Russia would be emancipated as individuals, like Jews in Western Europe.

At the same time, Dubnov wanted the recognition of collective rights. In his view, every Jew was automatically a member of the Jewish community and even non-Jews could petition for membership. The community would have power over internal Jewish issues and would be provided with money from the general budget, calculated proportionally, for their use.[37] Among national rights, Dubnov demanded the right for Jews to rest on Saturday instead of Sunday, recognition of the rights of students in Russian schools to observe Shabbat and Jewish rituals. He demanded new policies regarding Jewish marriages, taking control over this institution from the traditional rabbinate.[38] Dubnov also expected government funding from general taxes to pay for Jewish collective institutions. The final decision of what rights would be awarded Jews should be left to the Jewish National Constitutional Assembly, the

---

35 *Volkspartei, Evreiskaia narodnaia partiia* (St. Petersburg: Ts. Kraiz, 1907), 27.
36 A description of the Kadet position on the Jewish problem can be found in Eliyahu Feldman, *Yehudi Rusyah bi-yeme ha-mahpekhah ha-rishonah veha-pogromim* (Jerusalem: Magnes Press, 1999), 13-38.
37 *Volkspartei*, 10.
38 Ibid., 13.

democratically elected legislature of the Jewish community. The entire community, including women, would have the right to vote.[39]

The order of importance in the program gives primacy to the political rights of the individual citizen. The right to control government policy through the ballot box and protection under the law provide the basis for collective rights, which are established on voluntary grounds. Jews can decide to reject affiliation with the Jewish community, but they cannot reject citizenship in the Russian state.[40]

In 1905, Jewish members of the Kadet party, Maxim Vinaver, I. V. Gessen, and Henrik Sliozberg, shared a similar approach with the Jewish national parties, since, while interested in securing collective rights for Jews, they were adamant that first of all Jews needed political rights and legal protections regardless of race, religion, or nationality.[41] This position emerged from their realization that Jews were entirely dependent on the successful acquisition of political rights by all the citizens of Russia. Once the principle was accepted that rights were inalienable to all, it would be impossible to deny them to Jews. Sliozberg describes the Jews' point of view with the help of a simile: "[...] Speaking about our national self-consciousness, I would like to compare the relation of Jews to Russia with the relation of a ship's passenger who has his own cabin to the entire ship. This passenger takes pains so that his cabin will stay in good condition, but he also understands that the fate of his cabin depends on the fate of the whole ship."[42]

It goes without saying that nineteen hundred and five was a unique time in Russian-Jewish politics. But one of its particular aspects was that dreams and hopes long kept under wraps could come into the open. It is therefore extremely significant that both the Zionists and members of the Folkspartai, i.e., Jewish parties on the political right, were in favor of various degrees of integration. The political left, the Bundists, viewed integration even more favorably.[43]

I am not arguing that the official Zionist organization embraced the

---

39 Ibid., 14.
40 As is well known, Dubnov was inspired by the ideas of Austrian thinkers like Otto Bauer and Karl Renner regarding the rights of national minorities to political autonomy.
41 Feldman, *Yehudi Rusyah bi-yeme ha-mahpekhah ha-rishonah veha-pogromim*, 56. See also *Nakanune probuzhdeniia* (St.Petersburg: 1907).
42 G. Sliozberg, *Dela minuvshikh dnei: zapiski russkogo evreia* (Paris: 1933), 1: 3.
43 Ezra Mendelsohn, *Class Struggle in the Pale: the Formative Years of the Jewish Workers' Movement in Tsarist Russia* (Cambridge: Cambridge University Press, 1970), 110-12.

Gegenwartsprogram for the same reasons that Dubnov advanced an alliance with liberal parties. Idel'son's ideas were compelling especially as a way out of a crisis that came to its culmination after Herzl's death. The goal of the immediate creation of a state as a result of high-profile diplomacy had to be replaced with a long-term strategy that took into consideration such realities as the permanent presence of the Jewish masses in the Pale of Settlement. The *Gegenwartsprogram* also answered the needs for a compromise between political and cultural Zionists, since it offered something to both. Finally, political change brought by the Revolution also made it possible to participate in elections for a State Duma, despite the tragedies of October 1905, or perhaps as a way to prevent more pogroms. Dubnov in fact had long considered the *Galut* a suitable environment for Jewish spiritual accomplishment. His idea of Jewish centers, taken from his historical writings, paralleled this positive view.[44] Jewish cultural hegemony had passed from center to center, from Babylon to medieval Spain, to Poland, and now to Russia. The modern period was only different because the struggle to acquire equal rights demanded participation in general political institutions. Incidentally, the Bund, perhaps the group most inclined toward acculturation, boycotted elections to the first Duma. However, their motives were purely tactical; they saw the Duma as a ruse by the state to defuse revolutionary action and therefore did not cooperate in the hope of continuing the Revolution and overthrowing the tsar. They joined the campaign for elections to the second Duma.

The period from 1905 to the end of tsarist rule in February 1917 was not marked by great changes in the political struggle for Jewish rights. As Jews became more and more disenfranchised in successive Dumas, they turned away from politics and found solace in cultural, philanthropic, and educational voluntary associations.[45] Even membership in the Bund decreased.[46] The reasons are obvious. After peaking during the revolutionary year of 1905, support dissipated because just like liberals,

---

44   S. Dubnov, "O sovremennom sostoianii evreiskoi istoriografii," *Evreiskaia starina* 1 (1910): 151-58.

45   See Heinz-Dietrich Loewe, "From Charity to Social Policy: The Emergence of Jewish 'Self-Help' Organizations in Imperial Russia, 1800-1914," *East European Jewish Affairs* 27, no. 2 (1997): 53-75; see also Christoph Gassenschmidt, *Jewish Liberal Politics in Tsarist Russsia, 1900-14*, 72-109. Also Jeffrey Veidlinger, *Jewish Public Culture in the Late-Tsarist Empire* (Bloomington and Indianapolis: Indiana University Press, 2009).

46   Joshua Zimmerman, *Poles, Jews, and the Politics of Nationality: the Bund and the Polish Socialist Party in Late Tsarist Russia, 1892-1914* (Madison: University of Wisconsin Press, 2004), 227.

radicals were unable to bring about changes that would give Jews either increased individual or collective rights.

The opportune moment for political change did not arise until 1917. Jews finally won equal rights when the Provisional Government abolished all limitations on the rights of minorities in the Russian Empire. In a word, the Jews received Western-style liberation—they became citizens. Significantly, they did not receive collective rights at this time, since a decision was made not to single Jews out, but to invoke civil rights as a principle applying to all individuals in the Empire. Jews received long-awaited collective rights under the Soviets, but these rights turned out to be a deception. Some collective "rights" were implemented for a while, like freedom to publish in Yiddish, the establishment of a state-supported Yiddish theater, and a Jewish autonomous republic in Birobidzhan, but these ultimately were not made with much consideration for the interests of the Jews themselves.[47]

I have tried to show that, despite many changes in Jewish life and state policies, the 1860s and the post-1905 period were characterized by attempts to acquire individual political rights and collective rights simultaneously. This assertion has consequences for our conventional understanding of a universal definition of emancipation, underscoring differences in the self-consciousness of Jews in Eastern and Western Europe. Furthermore, these findings upset conventional labels of the *shtadlonim* as integrationists or the Odessa group as russifiers, and open for question whether Zionists and Folkists (Diaspora nationalists) should be defined as liberal or nationalist. The intellectual programs of these groups had complicated courses of development that defy simple categorization.

Nevertheless, it is striking that during the early years of Alexander II's reign, Jewish intellectuals articulated a Russian-Jewish identity that had enormous staying power. The desire for integration as individuals and simultaneous membership in a Jewish collective kept its power for nationalists because it satisfied real needs. It offered modernization and acculturation, ensuring the retention of a strong Jewish identity, while preserving some of the communality of Jewish life. It also gave a model

---

[47] The list of studies is quite long, but perhaps the best work still on Jews in the early Soviet period is Zvi Gitelman, *Jewish Nationality and Soviet Politics: Jewish Sections of the C. P. S. U., 1917-1930* (Princeton: Princeton University Press, 1973).

for the intelligentsia's domination of the administration of internal Jewish life. These were all productive features that obviously meshed well with realities in late-tsarist Russian-Jewish life.

I cannot claim that circumstances in 1860 and 1905 were entirely similar. I understand that the words integration, the Jewish community, and even the leadership role of the intelligentsia came to mean different things in 1905 than they had in 1860. Clearly, the attitudes of Jews toward the state were opposite. No Jew worthy of the name could possibly look to the government of Nicholas II as at an agent of positive change. Maxim Vinaver noted that his generation departed from the past because its members demanded rights, basing their demands on threats of retaliation, as opposed to merely making requests that depended on the good will of the government.[48] Similarly, the political model after 1905 consisted of genuine democratic institutions with real elections, albeit marred by varying levels of disenfranchisement.[49] Jews did not receive rights because, in the end, Nicholas II refused to share power with representatives from the national minorities.[50]

Another important difference was that the goal of attaining collective national rights was no longer to aid the government to modernize Jews, but to provide a place for the cultivation of Jewish consciousness for its own sake. According to Dubnov, assimilation was a natural process. The only way to stop it was to pursue a national agenda.[51] This situation was entirely switched around in the 1860s, when Rabinovich had to try to convince the "stubborn" Jewish masses to accept moderate amounts of integration, such as learning Russian and acquiring secular knowledge in order to adapt to the modern world.

Since the truth is that pre- and post-1881 had elements of liberalism and post-liberalism in them, Jews wanted both integration and collective rights, we may ask why the two periods were seen as entirely distinct? Certainly, the pogroms starting in 1881 make a clean break for the periodization of Russian-Jewish history. After all, that was a momentous year for Russia as a whole. Alexander II was murdered that year

---

48 S. B. Pozner, "Bor'ba za ravnopravie," in *M. M. Vinaver i russkaia obshchestvennost' nachala XX veka* (Paris: 1937), 172.
49 C. Gassenschmidt, *Jewish Liberal Politics*, xvi-xvii.
50 G. Hosking, *The Russian Constitutional Experiment: Government and Duma, 1907-1914* (Cambridge:Cambridge University Press, 1973), 12-13.
51 S. Dubnov, "O rasteriavsheisia intelligentsii," *Voskhod* 12 (1902): 74.

and his son, Alexander III, led the country in a spirit of uncompromising conservatism. But there are other reasons why 1881 has taken on a special meaning. Dubnov's quasi-Hegelian tripartite model of thesis, antithesis and synthesis or traditionalism, assimilation, and nationalism carries some blame.

While this paradigm of development gave an accurate picture of Dubnov's own personal evolution, it inaccurately described tendencies in Jewish society as a whole. Certainly in the period of Alexander II there were Jewish assimilators, but they were much fewer than one would think. The vast majority of Jewish intellectuals, such as Lev Levanda, Judah Leib Gordon, Moses Lilienblum, Menashe Morgulis, and Alfred Landau, shunned full assimilation. It makes sense that many of these individuals became involved to a greater or lesser extent in proto-national Jewish politics in the years after 1881. It also makes sense that when the chance for civic rights seemed on the horizon in 1905, Jewish political leaders lunged at them. With equal rights as citizens, Jews would have gained security and support upon which to base their future prosperity and happiness. On these rights they could also base collective rights in order to create positive modern institutions to further Jewish national goals.

Viewed from the teleological perspective of 1948 and the creation of modern Israel, 1881-82 has huge symbolic meaning. But looking at the same date from the perspective of Jewish life in tsarist Russia, the pogroms of 1881-82 have only relative importance. Jews continued to live as before. The May Laws only made lives that were already hard even harder. Five million Jews remained in Russia, continuing to survive by overcoming the oppressive liabilities set by the state. From the point of view of Jewish politics in Russia itself, 1881-82 could not have the significance attributed to it, since the primary deciding factor, the status of Jews vis-à-vis the state, had not changed. Until that relationship changed, Jews either had to flee or wait. Significantly, the majority decided to wait, although two million did leave Russia to find refuge in other lands.[52]

I have tried to show that any attempt to regard Russian-Jewish history in the late tsarist period as either characterized exclusively by crisis

---

52 See Jacob Lestschinsky, "Jewish Migrations, 1840-1946," in *The Jews*, ed. L. Finkelstein, in 4 vols., 4 (Philadelphia: Jewish Publication Society, 1949): 198-200.

or continuity will not stand. Depending on the angle the historian takes, one may adopt one or the other approach for a time, but never exclusively and never for long. This study of individual and collective rights demonstrates the need to use a combined approach, one that permits the historian to notice the continuity between past epochs and yet accurately to isolate changes that have occurred in any single period. It makes sense not to employ a bipolar approach, but rather one based on multiplicity, something akin to that suggested by Jonathan Frankel in *Assimilation and Community*:

> The historical process is thus perceived in terms not of bipolarity but of multiplicity. Instead of the one basic conflict between centrifugality and centripetality, now a great variety of autonomous processes, independent variables, are traced as they interact in constantly new permutations. . . . Or, in other words, the focus had shifted from the extremes, from the dichotomous archetypes, to that middle ground where it is no easy task to distinguish the exceptions from the rules.[53]

---

53   "Assimilation and the Jews in Nineteenth-Century Europe," in *Assimilation and Community: The Jews in Nineteenth-Century Europe*, ed. J. Frankel and S. Zipperstein (Cambridge: Cambridge University Press, 1992), 16.

7. The civic activist and writer, Mikhail (Menashe) Morgulis (reproduced courtesy of the Jewish Studies Department of the European University in St. Petersburg).

7. Crystallizing Memory: Russian-Jewish Intelligentsia Abroad and Forms of Self-Projection

By 1921, most of the Jewish elite from Moscow and St. Petersburg had moved to new homes abroad, in Berlin, Warsaw, Paris, London, and New York. They had recently witnessed the worst genocide in Jewish history, the pogroms in the Ukraine and Belorussia by both the Reds and the Whites.[1] In emigration they took stock of their new lives, but also evaluated their former dreams and political failures. Many of them turned to writing memoirs about earlier days in Russia. Among the most famous of these texts are Maxim Vinaver's *Nedavnee* (Not Long Ago), Henrik Sliozberg's *Dela minuvshikh dnei* (Acts of Past Days), Semyon Dubnov's *Kniga zhizni* (Book of Life), and Shaul Ginzburg's *Amolike Peterburg* (Petersburg in the Past).[2] Surprisingly, in their memoirs their thoughts often turned to love for their former homeland rather than condemnation. Why this is the case and what they hoped to accomplished are questions I will address in this essay.

The individuals about whom I speak—all of them liberals—have been lionized in a number of scholarly studies, but much of their work in the emigration still needs elucidation.[3] Among them were well-known lawyers, journalists, writers, historians, and civic activists. Oscar Gruzenberg, Maxim Vinaver, Abraham Passover, and Henry Sliozberg played important roles in the defense of Jewish rights abroad.[4] V. I. Gessen, Jacob Teitel', and Mikhail Sheftel' were active as community organizers.[5]

---

1   See Oleg Budnitskii's *Russian Jews Between the Reds and the Whites, 1917-1920*, trans. Timothy J. Portice (Philadelphia: University of Pennsylvania Press, 2012).
2   M. Vinaver, *Nedavnee (vospominaniia i kharistaristiki)*, 3rd ed. (Paris: d'Art Voltaire, 1926); H. Sliozberg, *Dela minuvshikh dnei* (Paris: 1933); See S. Dubnov, *Kniga zhizni: materially dlia istorii moego vremeni, vospominaniia i razmyshleniia* (Vilna: 1932-36 vols.1-2; vol. 3, New York, 1967); *Amolike Peterburg: Forshungn un zikhroynes vegn yidishn lebn in... tsarishn rusland* (New York: 1944).
3   William Rosenberg, *The Liberals in the Russian Revolution* (Princeton: Princeton University Press, 1974); Marc Raeff, *Russia Abroad: A Cultural History of the Russian Emigration, 1919-1939* (Oxford: Oxford University Press, 1990); *The Russian-Jewish Diaspora and European Culture, 1917-1937*, eds. J. Schulte, O. Tabachnikova, and P. Wagstaff (Leiden: Brill, 2012); *Diaspora, Memory, and Identity: A Search for Home*, ed. Vijay Agnew (Toronto: University of Toronto Press, 2005).
4   See my book, *Empire Jews*, especially 139-52 and 181-94.
5   See Teitel's memoir in German, *Aus meiner Lebensarbeit: Erinnungen eines Judischen Richters im alten Russland* (Frankfurt: Kaufmann, 1929).

Writers and historians such as Sholem Asch, Semyon Dubnov, and Shaul Ginzburg, among others, believed justifiably that they were writing for a Russian, as well as a Jewish, audience. Russian-Jewish journalism was alive in Russian, Yiddish, and Hebrew, and Jewish philosophers, Lev Shestov and Aron Steinberg, continued their work in Europe.

Although liberal in orientation, the memoirists were ideologically diverse in their attitude to Jewish identity. Among them were individuals such as Vinaver, Sliozberg, Lev Katsenel'son, and Jacob Teitel', who sought full identification with the Russian elite, although without any tint of assimilation. At the other pole were intellectuals, such as Dubnov or Shaul Ginzburg, who fostered ideas of Jewish nationalism in the diaspora.[6] Among this group even Zionists could be counted; many were entirely acculturated (Vladimir Jabotinsky or Viktor Tchelnov are examples). Although most of the writers here wrote exclusively in Russian, some also wrote in Yiddish and Hebrew. However, using a Jewish language did not necessarily signify the absence of acculturation in Russian culture.[7]

Memoirs by Jewish liberals reflect a variety of aims. In this case we need to consider not only what they remembered, but how.[8] Some of what these intellectuals wrote emerged from an idealization of a world that seemed in retrospect more beautiful than it actually was.[9] For example, they were mostly silent on the violence against Jews from the Civil-War period. In fact, almost all the writers dismissed the idea that Russians were inherently anti-Semitic or that Russian culture had an

---

6 For example Dubnov acknowledged that his program for the Folkpartey was based on the Kadet program. See S. Dubnov, *Volkspartei: Evreiskaia Narodnaia Partiia* (St. Petersburg: Ts. Kraiz, 1907).

7 Because their political vision strayed from liberalism, I have excluded Bundists, Socialists, and other radicals. Although liberals oftentimes sympathized with radicals—even forming a coalition in 1905 and in the spring of 1917, they were principally opposed to radicalism because of its emphasis on class conflict and the idea that revolution would lead to a completely new society that would solve the problems of ethnic and religious difference. In contrast, Jewish liberals argued for a class-blind Jewish politics and condemned assimilation either through religious conversion or rejection of Jewish identity.

8 Some good examples of the treatment of memory include Marianne Hirsch and Leo Spitzer, *Ghosts of Home: The Afterlife of Czernowitz in Jewish Memory* (Berkeley and Los Angeles: University of California Press, 2010); James Young, *The Texture of Memory: Holocaust Memorials and Meaning* (New Haven: Yale University Press, 1994); Svetlana Boym, *The Future of Nostalgia* (New York: Basic Books, 2002).

9 This point is made by Albert I. Baumgarten in his article "Russian-Jewish Ideas in German Dress: Elias Bickerman on the Hellenizing Reformers of Jewish Antiquity," in *The Russian Jewish Diaspora and European Culture*, 101

anti-Semitic character. Instead, these writers viewed anti-Semitism as an instrument that the government used for political purposes. In this way the authors of these memoirs appear to exonerate Russians (and other nationalities). They exaggerated the extent of a Jewish-Russian cultural synthesis and maintained that their claims were subjective impressions colored by wishful thinking.

The unifying element of this disparate group was an assertion: "we are members of the Russian intelligentsia."[10] This claim hinged on the idea that the intelligentsia was not based on ethnic or religious difference, but on universal ideas such as universal justice and the betterment of humanity.[11] Regarding Jewish rights, they were quick to point out that Jews had lived for centuries in Russia and had contributed to its culture, economy, and social diversity. In fact, they stood by the principle that all the members of the national minorities should be represented in the Russian intelligentsia because Russia was principally a multi-national state, and its intelligentsia was engaged in a non-denominational, non-ethnically specific project to bring the universal values of democracy and human rights to the country.

The memoirs and other texts examined here share common features.[12] Front and center was the commitment to a liberal politics, i.e. individual rights for all citizens, including the establishment of democratic institutions protected by law, and introduction of elementary freedoms, such as protection of religious difference, freedom from political persecution, and ethnic discrimination. The vision was of a rule-of-law state, in which the monarchy, even if it were preserved, would have no real political power. Many of these intellectuals promoted national rights for the ethnic and religious minorities, insisting as well that the Jewish people should have collective rights, such as the right to separate schools and cultural institutions, as well as a Jewish parliament for deciding internal matters. These institutions, they argued,

---

10 The literature on the origins and development of the Russian intelligentsia is large. To mention an important but single example, Alan P. Pollard, "The Russian Intelligentsia: the Mind of Russia," *California Slavic Studies* 3 (1964): 1-19.
11 Benjamin Nathans, "Conflict, Community and the Jews of Nineteenth-Century St. Petersburg," *Jahrbuch für Geschichte Osteuropas* 44 (1996): 178-80.
12 It might be noted that not all the works by this group were memoirs, among them were also novels and historical studies, and not all were written after the Bolshevik Revolution. Some texts appeared already in tsarist times.

should be financed at least in part by the government.[13]

The individuals examined here portray the attainment of a dual Russian-Jewish identity as their greatest achievement. In a volume devoted to Leon Bramson, the lawyer and civic leader, Gregory Aronson offers this explanation of Bramson's talent: "Leon Bramson's spiritual development was formed under the sign of two principles—Jewish and Russian. As a result of the interaction and interpenetration of these two principles, an original human alloy was created that entered into history as the Russian-Jewish intelligentsia."[14]

Henrik Sliozberg, the St. Petersburg lawyer, gave this description of Alexander Braudo, head of the Russian department of the Petersburg Public Library and formerly a member of various Jewish organizations in the capital:

> To a superficial observer it could seem that Braudo was a divided man, a Jew and Russian citizen. But in Braudo's personality there was no division. Affiliation with Judaism and identification with Jewish suffering united with ardent love for Russia, hate of violence and legal arbitrariness, and deep sympathy for all persecuted peoples. He espied in the absence of Jewish rights an evil that poisoned not only Jewish lives, but destroyed the moral basis of society and the state as a whole. Braudo embodied a type of person motivated by ideas foretold thousands of years ago by Jewish prophets who discovered the humanity of man in man.[15]

Sliozberg's description of Braudo could serve as the "Ur-text" of the ideal intellectual, since it possesses the essential qualities valorized by the group. Braudo loved Russia and hated its government, he embodied universal values, and felt sympathy for Jews as well as other oppressed peoples. It is emblematic that Braudo, a Jew, headed the Russian section

---

13 Although the Constitutional Democratic party shared some of these positions, not all the intellectuals featured here were Kadets.
14 G. A., "Zhizn' i deiatel'nost' Leontiia Moiseevicha Bramsona," in *Evreiskii mir: sbornik 1944 goda* (New York: 1944; republished, Jerusalem: Gesharim, 2001), 13-14.
15 G. Sliozberg, "Lichnost'" A. I. Braudo," in *Aleksandr Isaevich Braudo: ocherki i vospominaniia* (Paris: Kruzhok russko-evreiskoi intelligentsii v Parizhe, 1936), 28.

of the Imperial Public Library at a time of intense anti-Semitism. But it is also strange that a Jew rose so high in official circles. The position at the library gave Braudo connections among the elite and in diverse sections of Russian society. For example, thanks to his relationships with Russian masons, he was able to unmask the revolutionary Yevno Azef as a tsarist spy.[16]

Maxim Vinaver claimed that a person from any ethnic group could be a member of the Russian intelligentsia because membership was not based on blood or social status, but only on ideas. In particular, Vinaver did not intentionally draw attention to his Jewish identity, but preferred to be perceived as a leader of all the people. Vinaver believed in the unity of interests between Jews and Russians, and was convinced that by struggling on behalf of Russian democracy he was serving Jews, and by working on behalf of Jewish emancipation he was serving Russians.

The best example of this unity may be seen in Vinaver's memoirs, *Nedavnee*, published in 1917, in which he describes his contemporaries, men who transformed the field of law in Russia. Depicting Ukrainians, Poles, Jews, and Russians, he offers an alternative vision in which multi-culturalism dominates and the personality of the creative individual, rather than group identity, receives the author's acclaim. Vinaver focuses on the gentile lawyers V. D. Spasovich, C. A. Muromtsev, V. L. Isachenko, F. F. Kokoshkin, and A. I. Shingaryov. He also describes Jews, including A. Ia. Passover, A. S. Gol'denveizer, G. F. Blumenfel'd, M. I. Kulisher, and S. A. An-sky. Vinaver's treatment of Jews reflects the same value system that he uses to describe the others. For example, when he praises a Jewish individual, Vinaver dismisses distinctions of race and religion, claiming that his hero deserves universal acclaim. Describing the Jewish lawyer from Kiev, A. S. Gol'denveizer, Vinaver writes:

> To say that he was respected and valued as an excellent lawyer and jurist is to utter a banality. The attitude of those around him can be transmitted by a single word: adoration. In this region, saturated with nationalist miasmas, Russians, Jews and Poles were drawn to him

---

16 S. Posner, "Rol' A. I. Braudo v dele razoblacheniia Azefa," in *Aleksandr Isaevich Braudo, 1864-1924, ocherki i vospominaniia*, ed. L. Bramson (Paris: Izdanie Kruzhka russko-evreiskoi intelligentsii v Parizhe, 1937), 93-102.

equally, drawn to him for advice, knowledge, or a judgment untarnished by the need for flattery. This was how things were established long ago and it was entirely natural; no one asked how and why it came to be this way. Aleksandr Solomonovich was a person beyond competition, above time and space, above race and class.[17]

The description of his mentor, Abraham Passover, is characterized more by the absence of any Jewish characteristics than a discussion of them. The only single mention of his Jewish background is connected with the reason why he became a lawyer. Vinaver presents one of Passover's witticisms: "Passover prepared for a scholarly career, but as a Jew, he had to give up the thought and become a lawyer. He would say, 'By not converting to Russian Orthodox Christianity, I converted to the Bar Association.'"[18]

One could argue, as Zaslavsky and Ivanovich do, that Jewish Kadets subdued their Jewish identity for pragmatic reasons.[19] After all, Vinaver understood the risks of being perceived as a Jewish tool. However, I do not think that this explanation is entirely accurate. In 1909, Vinaver broke party discipline and attacked his fellow Kadet, Pyotr Struve, because of the latter's glorification of Great-Russian nationalism.[20]

The importance of Russian populism as a model for the worldview of this group can be seen in their desire to help the Jewish masses, who were in the intellectuals' imagination equivalent to the Russian *muzhik*. We find this attitude among Jewish Socialist Revolutionaries such as Semyon An-sky and Lev Shternberg. For example, Vinaver has written, "An-sky's entire life was the best illustration. The same passion, the same ceaseless energy that he showed in his work on behalf of the Russian people was apparent in his attitude toward the Jewish people. Here was the same faith in the people as a kind of embodiment of absolute truth, goodness and beauty, the exact same love for the supra-rational entity."[21]

---

17 M. Vinaver, *Nedavnee*, 215.
18 Ibid., 95.
19 D. Zaslavskii and St. Ivanovich, *Kadety i evrei* (Petrograd: 1916), 9.
20 M. Vinaver, "Otkrytoe pis'mo P. B. Struve," *Po vekham; Sbornik statei ob intelligentsii i 'natsional'nom litse'* (Moscow: 1909), 83-84. See also Chapter 2 in this volume.
21 *Nedavnee*, 288.

Influenced by populism, the St. Petersburg Jews felt responsibility for their co-religionists. In some cases this meant providing direct handouts, but mainly these individuals wanted to establish schools, designing curricula, and promote changes in the legal code. They emphasized community service. Their self-consciousness was also shaped by a consideration of history. They saw themselves as continuing the work of the Russian-language exponents of the *Haskalah*, the authors of the journal *Rassvet* (1860-61), *Zion* and *Russkii evrei* (1879-83). Shaul Ginzburg exclaims, "An intelligentsia that gave its people a pleiad of such activists as, for example, I. G. Orshansky, M. I. Kulisher, M. G. Morgulis, L. I. Katsenel'son, Ia. M. Halperin, N. I. Bakst, G. B. Sliozberg, and A. I. Braudo, does not have to feel ashamed of the road that it traveled. The future historian of Russian Jewry, if only he is not blinded by party loyalty or chauvinism, will give proper respect to their work and service."[22]

Intellectuals' love for Russia can be explained in part by the central role Russian culture played in their lives. Among Jewish intellectuals, Russian literature and not the Tanakh or Talmud was often mentioned as having the greatest influence on their intellectual development. Moreover, although it might be pleasing to recount how Jews of the second half of the nineteenth century loved Pushkin, Lermontov, Turgenev, and Tolstoy, in fact many expressed higher appreciation for the "Critical Realists," Chernyshevsky, Pisarev, and Pisemsky.[23] In his novel, *Pioneers*, Semyon An-sky describes how a group of young Jews in a small city in Belorus in the 1870s use *pilpul* (Jewish methods of elucidating Talmud) to parse the critical realists.

> "Wait!" Uler went on triumphantly. "Soon I'll know Pisarev not only by heart, but also 'by finger.'"
> "What do you mean 'by finger'?"
> "You don't know what that means?" Uler asked in surprise. "You're completely ignorant! Who doesn't know what that means? Everyone knows. Probably even

---

22   Sh. Ginsburg, "O russko–everiskoi intelligentsii," *Evreiskii mir* (Paris) 1 (1939): 40.
23   A greater interest in Pushkin among Jewish writers began in the 1890s, when translations in Hebrew and Yiddish began to appear. A later generation of Jews, those in the Soviet Union, would become fanatics of Pushkin and the Pushkin legacy. See Yury Slezkine, *The Jewish Century* (Princeton: Princeton University Press, 2004), 134-36.

he knows what it is." He pointed to Eizerman who was standing there all the while, fascinated, regarding Uler with reverence and rapture.

"Of course, I know!" Eizerman blurted out. "To know 'by finger'—here's what it means. You place a closed book on the table, open it, point your finger to any place and ask: 'On such-and-such a page on the first or second side, I'm pointing with my finger—what word is it?' And you have to name that word." "That's all there is to it!"

"Exactly," confirmed Uler. "'By finger,' that's how I know six tracts of the Talmud."[24]

This fictional passage is interesting because An-sky portrays how young Jews used skills and habits learned in the Beit Midrash—such as knowing a text "by finger"—to study Russian literature. These young men represent the enormous wave of acculturated Jews that transformed Jewish life in Russia and expanded the Jewish presence in the Russian intelligentsia.

Whether it was playing "by finger," or just having these books around, Russian literature was part of the air these people breathed.[25] In her memoirs, *Bread and Matzah*, Sophia Dubnov-Erlich describes the way her father, Semyon Dubnov, the historian and theorist of Jewish nationalism, lived in the world of Nikolai Nekrasov's poetry.

> The program of our readings changed often. Papa loved civic poetry no less than lyric poetry: Nekrasov's poems about the heroism of the Decembrist wives and ardent appeals to leave "for the camp of those who would die for the great act of love" found a passionate response in him. One of our favorites was the tragic "Dostoevsky-like" poem, "Driving by Night on a Dark Street," [...] Papa did

---

24 S. An-sky, *Pioneers: A Novel*, trans. Michael Katz (Bloomington: Indiana University Press, 2013).
25 According to his biographer, Joseph B. Shechtman, Jabotinsky was an avid player of the Russian-poetry game. See *Fighter and Prophet, the Vladimir Jabotinsky Story, The Last Years* (New York & London: Thomas Yoseloff, 1961), 2: 163. One might think about the passage in Osip Mandelshtam's *Shum vremeni* (Noise of Time), when he describes his father's bookshelf. What is interesting is not just the hierarchy of the library's shelves, but the presence of German and Russian classics. These books were an essential part of the education of upwardly-mobile Jews in Russia of the second half of the nineteenth century.

not neglect Nekrasov even during work hours: walking back and forth in his room mulling over his next article, he would sing with feeling: "...That pain we call a song" or "... The harvesting was going in full force." In these poems he admired not only the idea, but also miraculous music. [...] Living in an atmosphere of "sweet sounds and prayers," I myself began to write poetry early.²⁶

Dubnov was not alone. A number of important Jewish national writers, Yehuda Leib Gordon, Moshe Leib Lilienblum, Semyon Frug, and Leib Jaffe were strongly influenced by Russian literature.²⁷

It is interesting to note that educated Jews were especially interested in Jewish writers in the Russian language; many individuals followed the careers of Lev Levanda, Osip Rabinovich, and Grigorii Bogrov in the 1870s, and Rakhel Khin, Ben-Ami, and An-sky in the 1890s. In particular, many Jews of St. Petersburg idolized Semyon Frug because he was the first openly Jewish author to achieve recognition among the Russian elite.²⁸ Thus, he was lionized as the "Jewish Pushkin" or "Jewish Nekrasov," a poet who had made it in "their world."²⁹

In the context of Russian-Jewish cultural synthesis, assimilation has a different meaning. Although individuals were acculturated, they were by no means fully assimilated.³⁰ Shaul Ginzburg explains: "One should not mix up assimilation as a fact of daily life with assimilation as a definite ideology. [...] Assimilation for us was a quotidian fact, but assimilation as a slogan, a literary-social tendency—that did not exist as it did in other countries of Europe. One could find 'Germans of the Mosaic Persuasion' or 'Frenchmen of the Mosaic Persuasion,' but there

---

26 Sophia Dubnov-Erlich, *Khleb i matsa: vospominaniia, stikhi raznykh let* (St. Petersburg: Maksima, 1994), 39.
27 Rina Lapidus, *Between Snow and Desert Heat: Russian Influence on Hebrew Literature, 1870-1970* (Cincinnati: Hebrew Union College, 2003); Hamutal Bar Yosef, "Vliianie russkoi literatury na stanovlenie i razvitie novoi literatury na ivrite," *Vestnik evreiskogo universiteta v Moskve* 2, no. 15 (1997): 114-36. The Russian influence on Jewish self-conceptions of Judaism seems a topic that has not yet been properly investigated. See my article, "Poet and Nation: Fame and Amnesia in Semyon Frug's Literary Representation," in *Empire Jews*, 51-64.
28 Horowitz, "Poet and Nation," 51-64.
29 Vasilii L'vovich Rogachevskii, *A History of Russian Jewish Literature*, ed. Alfred Levin (Ann Arbor: Ardis, 1979), 135.
30 The difference, explains Ezra Mendelsohn in his book, *On Modern Jewish Politics*, is that assimilation is defined as disappearing into the non-Jewish population completely. E. Mendelsohn, *On Modern Jewish Politics*, 16.

weren't any 'Russians of the Mosaic Persuasion.'"[31]

A characteristic of this group is the idealization of Russian life and culture. Sliozberg maintained that Russians were completely tolerant. "In Russia's political life we, Jews by nationality, did not make up a foreign element since many nationalities lived together united in Russian statehood without any attempt by the dominating nationality to swallow the others."[32] Not only did Sliozberg view Russians as partners in a common struggle for a rule-of-law state, he also claimed that Jews were instrumental in fostering a commitment to liberalism, democracy, and justice because their political struggle awakened everyone to the lack of general rights.

On the subject of anti-Semitism, it is intriguing that many Jews, shielding the Russian people, blamed anti-Semitism on the government and the conservative Russian intelligentsia exclusively. For example, in his magisterial *History of the Jewish People in Russia*, Yuly Gessen argued that, as opposed to Catholic Europe, where the priesthood incited hate for political ends, in Russia there was no religious anti-Semitism.[33] The only "real" source of anti-Jewish feeling was economic rivalry on the part of local merchants who resented economic competition. Gessen claims that the Russian peasantry actually valued Jews since the latter supplied consumer goods at cheaper prices than local merchants.[34]

Sliozberg in particular exonerated the peasantry from anti-Semitism: "All anti-Semitism is concentrated in a small group of half-intellectuals, petty clerks in the post, tax, and other bureaus, among some officers in the local garrison who with one voice expressed their indignation not over Jewish exploitation, but their political ambition."[35] Sliozberg tried to minimize anti-Semitism and portray it as grumblings of a small number of individuals. Others, for example, Oscar Gruzenberg, the leading Jewish lawyer in the Beilis trial, agreed that anti-Semitism was motivated exclusively by politics.

---

31 Ginsburg, "O russko-evreiskoi intelligentsii," 38.
32 H. Sliozberg, *Dela minuvshikh dnei*, vol. 2 (Paris: 1933), 302.
33 Iu. Gessen, *Istoriia evreiskogo naroda v Rossii*, eds. V. Kel'ner and V. Gessen (Moscow and Jerusalem: Evreiskii Universitet v Moskve, 1993 [reprint]; originally published Leningrad: 1923).
34 Gessen, *Istoriia evreiskogo naroda*, vol. 2, 37-49.
35 H. Sliozberg, *Pravovoe i ekonomicheskoe polozhenie evreev v Rossii* (St. Petersburg: 1907), xxvi.

This trial buried the childish hopes of those innocents who looked for a peaceful solution to the historical conflict between the conscience of a nation and the unscrupulous tsarist autocracy. The bearer of supreme power, who had relinquished the entire state apparatus to the gangs of the Union of the Russian People and the Union of the Archangel Michael for the sake of preserving his despotic prerogatives, did not stop even when the interests of justice were at stake. There was not a single person in those circles closest to the monarch who was not convinced of Beilis' innocence. Nevertheless, even the ancient Russian principle, "Do not use the court for vengeance or favors," was sacrificed. There was nowhere to go, for the failure to dispense justice always leads to an abyss. One can say without exaggeration that in the Beilis case the monarchy committed moral suicide. The nation saw that it had been striped to its last thread and that it must either perish or do away with this power, so ruinous to the destiny of the country.[36]

Gruzenberg, however, retained an idealized attitude toward the Russian people. "Having grown up in a Russian environment and traveled widely in Russia as a defense lawyer, I had not the slightest doubt about the outcome of the trial. I believed, indeed I knew that the conscience of a Russian would never condone the destruction of an innocent person, that it would not relinquish the task of administering justice to gangs having imperial sanction that was accustomed to working with burglar's tools and knives."[37]

Denying that the Russian people were guilty of anti-Semitism was useful for those who valorized for Jewish-Russian collaboration since such arguments preserved the legitimacy of Jewish integration and linked the struggle of Jews for their rights with the general struggle to overthrow tsarism. Moreover, by viewing the Russian peasant as essentially free from hate, Jews could retain their attachment to Russian

---

36   O. O. Gruzenberg, *Yesterday: Memoirs of a Russian-Jewish Lawyer*, trans. D.C. Rawson and T. Tipton, (Berkeley and Los Angeles: University of California Press, 1981), 104.
37   Ibid., 105.

populism, which for many was a source of tender feelings. Perhaps these views were delusionary, but such delusions composed the foundation stone of the Russian-Jewish intelligentsia's psychology.[38]

The silence in the memoirs on Jewish suffering during the Civil-War period can be explained by the following considerations. As a group they may have felt guilt for having supported the Whites (many in fact did) and thus bore some responsibility for the violence.[39] Another possibility is that having struggled against the Bolsheviks in the first years after 1917, it was now time to put this negative energy behind them; enough time had passed so that a more idealized experience remained. In any case it appears that most of the writers felt that it was time to stress the positive contributions of Russia's Jews, their activity as willful agents and not as helpless victims.

As a sign of their loyalty to Russia, many of these individuals rejected emigration and left only when absolutely forced. To them emigration was a deep injustice against their rights; they felt that they had full legitimacy to live in Russia and by no means could be considered "foreigners." "Whatever adversities Jews had to endure on their long and far-from-rosy historical path, it never came to mind voluntarily to leave that country in which the ashes of their fathers were buried and their own cradles were fashioned, despite the oppressive measures that limited their lives, the persecution they were subject to, and the burdensome financial payments that were demanded of them."[40]

Since (in their view at least) Jewish intellectuals cooperated with Russians as equals and could reach the heights of the cultural elite, it follows that the death of tsarist Russian culture was interpreted as a tragic misfortune. Shaul Ginzburg writes: "[The Jews] shared the fate of the Russian intelligentsia. The catastrophe that overtook Russia by the power-grabbing Bolsheviks destroyed the Russian-Jewish intelligentsia in part by physically eliminating it and in part by ejecting it from the motherland. Among the last Mohicans, a few will die in Russia, while the others will spend their lives abroad, ripped from their native land."[41] Memoir writers described the disappearance of the rich cultural envi-

---

38   See also H. Sliozberg, *Evrei v dorevoliutsionnoi Rossii* (St. Petersburg: 1907); on the writings of S. An-sky, see *The World of S. An-sky: A Russian-Jewish Intellectual at the Turn of the Century*.
39   Budnitskii, *Russian Jews Between the Reds and the Whites*, 275-95.
40   L. Landau, "Iz Petersburga," *Voskhod* 11 (March 12, 1882): 556.
41   Ginsburg, "O russko-evreiskoi intelligentsii," 33.

ronment as the greatest loss for them personally. Although torn from Russia physically, Jewish émigrés kept their Russian-Jewish identity alive as long as they possibly could. When their physical disintegration became inevitable, they wrote memoirs to preserve the memory of their culture forever.

However, one cannot help noticing a discrepancy between the reality of late-tsarist Russia and the picture drawn in the memoirs. Anti-Semitism is first and foremost a hard knot; why were most of these writers so sure that anti-Semitism was not deep-seated among the population as a whole? Why did they idealize the possibilities of Jewish integration? Were they victims of a collective blindness, did a positivist ideology blind them to reality? In addition, why did so many of the men not see or pretended not to see the weakness of their position as liberals, Jews, and members of the so-called free professions? None of these groups singularly and certainly together had much power or security in late-tsarist times.

However, can "faulty memory," the idea that distortion inevitably accompanies retrospection, answer all these questions? Perhaps we should also look elsewhere for answers. Although we might not be able to understand every motive, we can gain some insight by using a cultural-structural approach in which all human activity is said to have purposeful meaning as part of social codes of behavior.[42] Looked at from this perspective, the idealization of Russian-Jewish life in late-tsarist times reflects certain conditions and psychological situations as well as means of cultural performance. Without going too deeply into theories of performance, one can easily see that a central part of the liberal conception involved positivistic thinking, the idea that the liberal ideal will ultimately triumph. In this kind of thinking, those aspects of today's reality that conform to the future ideal are emphasized, while those that diverge are excised. Thus, these intellectuals offered a better reality than actually was in order to help fashion and even speed up the better future.

* * *

---

42 See Alexander and Alice Stone Nakhimovsky, eds., *The Semiotics of Russian Cultural History: Essays by Iurii M. Lotman, Lidia Ia. Ginsburg, Boris A. Uspensky* (Ithaca: Cornell University Press, 1985).

A certain revisionism is now gaining hold among historians of Russian Jewry especially in the United States, where one hears echoes of the sentiments of the first Jewish émigrés from post-Bolshevik Russia.[43] With the realization that knowledge about the *shtetl* reflects more invention than reality, scholars have begun to reconsider the myths of Russian Jewry; what functions they fulfilled and why myths resist debunking.[44]

More and more often we find scholarship that portrays Russian-Jewish culture as a golden age and the Russian-Jewish synthesis as a brilliant epoch in Jewish history.[45] Until recently, Jewish historians based arguments about Russian Jewry's greatness on its capacity for martyrdom.[46] Eastern Europe's Jews suffered in 1648, later under Tsar Nicholas I, and especially under Alexander III and Nicholas II (recall the pogroms and violence of 1881-82, 1903, 1905, 1914-17), then the Civil War 1918-21, and finally under the Bolsheviks. In this context the survival of the community was seen as a distinct achievement.[47] In addition, American Jews lauded the community's religious endurance.[48] Even secular movements were praised for their struggles; for example, the Soviet Jews of Conscience (refuseniks) in the 1960s and 70s.[49]

However, the recent reexamination of Russian Jewry comes from a realization that nineteenth- and early twentieth-century Russia was a world culture. Its brilliance in literature, music, and art spilled over into Jewish creativity as well. The names of such writers as Isaac Babel, Osip Mandelshtam, and Vasily Grossman, among others, reflected literary achievements by Jews in the Russian language.[50] Recently Maxim

---

43 See B. Nathans, *Beyond the Pale*; J. Veidlinger, *Jewish Public Culture in the Late Russian Empire*; Y. Slezkine, *The Jewish Century* (Princeton & Oxford: Princeton University Press, 2004); See also my book, *Empire Jews: Jewish Nationalism and Acculturation in Nineteenth and Early Twentieth Century Russia*.
44 S. Zipperstein, *Imagining Russian Jewry: Memory, History, Identity*.
45 A good deal of John Klier's work was dedicated to debunking the anti-Russian myths of Russian Jewry. See *Imperial Russia's Jewish Question*.
46 See Louis Greenberg, *The Jews in Russia: the Struggle for Emancipation* (New York: Schocken Books, 1976).
47 David Roskies, *Against the Apocalypse: the Responses to Catastrophe in Modern Jewish Culture* (Syracuse: Syracuse University Press, 1999), 57-66.
48 See the work of scholars such as Moshe Rosman, Gershon Bacon, and Immanuel Etkes.
49 Most of the literature about Soviet Jewish resistance is didactic, and even an objective study such as Gal Beckerman's *When They Come for Us We'll be Gone: The Epic Struggle to Save Soviet Jewry* (New York and Boston: Houghton Mifflin Harcourt, 2010), reflects "heroic" aspects.
50 See Harriet Murav, *Music from a Speeding Train: Jewish Literature in Post-Revolution Russia*

Shrayer has portrayed the group's literary creativity in a seven-hundred-page literary anthology by Jewish authors in the Russian language.[51]

The reevaluation of Russian Jewry is certainly related to the opening of the archives, but also to new questions that scholars have posed following the fall of the Soviet Union. According to Jeffrey Veidlinger, Jewish tourism to Eastern Europe dispelled some of the myths of the *shtetl*.[52] Seeing that cities like Minsk or Vitebsk were not quaint homey places, but urban centers characterized by late-Soviet architecture, made American Jews (at least potentially) realize that their preconceptions had been naïve. Research into genealogy has shown that not everything was gloom and doom. Instead of myths, those in search for true facts about Eastern European Jewish life can now find some satisfaction.

Finally, who should care about this history? I still have doubts even now that Jews in America, Israel, and Europe are prepared to acknowledge tsarist Russia as a fertile soil for Jewish creativity. There is too much baggage; conventional ideas of how badly Jews fared in Russia interfere with the account of its brilliant culture. The story of a pre-revolutionary renaissance among the elite should appeal to Jews still in Russia.[53] If historians search for examples of successful integration in Eastern Europe, part of the job of memorializing a humanistic and culturally exuberant Russian-Jewish culture will have already completed in the years before World War II. Jewish writers, historians, and intellectuals in the First Emigration tried to canonize the urban, politically liberal, secular, Russian-language Jewish culture of late-tsarist times.

(Stanford: Stanford University Press, 2011).

51 *An Anthology of Russian-Jewish Literature: Two Centuries of Dual Identity in Prose and Poetry*, ed. M. Shrayer (Armonk, NY: M. E. Sharpe, 2007).

52 Jeffrey Veidlinger, "From Shtetl to Soviety: Jews in Nineteenth Century Russia," *Kritika: Explorations in Russian and Eurasian History* 2, no. 4 (2001): 823-34.

53 Much of the scholarly work in the journal, *Zhurnal Evreiskogo Universiteta v Moskve*, over the last ten years has celebrated precisely the period from 1890-1920. See especially the fine work of Viktor Kel'ner.

II
M. O. Gershenzon and the Intellectual Life of Russia's Silver Age

10. Mikhail Osipovich Gershenzon (reproduced courtesy of Mikhail Chegodaev).

8. M. O. Gershenzon — Metaphysical Historian of Russia's Silver Age: Part 1

It is intriguing to consider Mikhail Gershenzon's historical writings in the light of Russia's Silver-Age cultural system.[1] Certainly the poetry of the time was intimately connected with the spirit of the age, but historiography? Was it also influenced by formal experimentation, an interest in religion, and a concern with psychology and the life of the individual rather than issues of politics and legal rights?[2] Above all, M. O. Gershenzon would make a perfect test case, since among historians he was perhaps the most in tune with his time; he befriended symbolist poets, studied religion, and took a deep interest in spiritual problems.

Gershenzon should be viewed as a representative of what Marc Raeff called "the Slavophile historiographical tradition," because he tried to reveal to his readers the internal, spiritual life of his heroes.[3] As opposed to the "Westernizer" tradition represented in Gershenzon's day by Ivanov-Razumnik, Semyon Vengerov or Pavel Miliukov, who saw the evolution of Russian history as revealing an on-going struggle for social progress, the "Slavophile" historians focused their attention on the "accomplishments of the spirit." Not social justice, but evidence of religious inspiration excited their interest. Of course some of the differences in historiographical approaches derived from the subjects being studied, but the choices of what to study and how to present material also characterize each group. Gershenzon was among the most prominent figures in the group, which included historians and writers as Vladimir Ern, Georgy Fedotov, Vasily Rozanov, Konstantin Mochul'sky, Lev Karsavin, Nikolai Berdiaev, and Georges Florovsky.

Gershenzon's claim to originality is primarily based on his new, sensitive depiction of spiritual portraits. Attempting to project the

---

1   There are many sources for a semiotic system, but perhaps the most appropriate in this context is Yury Lotman's *The Semiotics of Russian Cultural History*, ed. Alexander D. Nakhimovsky and Alice Stone Nakhimovsky (Ithaca: Cornell University Press, 1985).
2   For a general description of Russia's Silver-Age culture, see Victor Erlich, *Modernism and Revolution: Russian Literature in Transition* (Cambridge: Harvard University Press, 1994), 14-31.
3   M. Raeff, "Russian Intellectual History and its Historiography," *Forschungen zur Osteuropäischen Geschichte* 25 (1978): 279.

literary, social, aesthetic, and moral norms of the past in order to show historical figures from within their own value system, in this biographical genre Gershenzon featured his literary craft, historical subtlety and intellectual depth. Mikhail Tsiavlovsky described it this way: "The genre of Gershenzon's work, a genre in which he achieved a high mastery consists of the historical portraits of the leaders in literature and culture, the creation of 'Images of the Past' [Obrazy proshlogo] on the basis of archival materials published for the first time with a philosophical-artistic interpretation."[4]

The genre itself was part biography, part historical interpretation and part literary essay. It was not, however, a catch-all form, but crafted to embody Gershenzon's aim of describing the psychological condition of an individual as a mirror of the motivations of an entire epoch. Gershenzon's approach had many of the features of biography, but biography was not its main aim. He focused his attention on an individual, describing his idiosyncrasies and evolution, but the goal was always to capture the character of the epoch as a whole, its emotional and intellectual premises—in other words, the essential ideas and emotions that lie at the base of the self. Therefore, the historian is not interested in everyone, but exclusively in individuals who act as "carriers of ideals," who reflect the inner life of the entire age. Consequently, Gershenzon made a firm distinction between "history" and "biography," considering himself a historian. In his essay on Nikolai Stankevich, he writes, "Stankevich interests us not in his uniqueness, but historically. Our goal is to depict his spiritual development in so far as it appears as a full and pure reflection of the intellectual movement of the 1830s."[5] From 1900-1925, Gershenzon created finely drawn portraits of the most important thinkers of Russia's nineteenth century: Ivan Kireevsky, Alexander Herzen, Vladimir Pecherin, Nikolai Stankevich, Ivan Turgenev, Yury Samarin, and Nikolai Gogol'.

In a sense, Gershenzon produces at least three different kinds of textual modes, i.e. kinds of narratives within texts.[6] The first kind is

---

4   M. Tsiavlovskii, preface to M. Gershenzon, *Pis'ma k bratu* (Moscow, 1927), v. "Obrazy proshlogo" refers to the title of one of Gershenzon's collections of articles published in 1912.

5   M. Gershenzon, "N.V. Stankevich (1813-1840)," *Novyi put'* 11 (1904): 52. I borrow this argument from James Scanlan, introduction to *A History of Young Russia*, by M. Gershenzon (Irvine: Charles Schlacks Jr., 1986), xx-xxi. Scanlan writes, "Not individuals but types: thus Gershenzon viewed his own studies, and he wished them to be judged by the canons of history, not biography" (xxi).

6   On modes, see Alistair Fowler, *Kinds of Literature: an Introduction to the Theory of Genres and Modes*

straightforward narrative history: Gershenzon tells the reader who Kireevsky or Samarin was, and proceeds to record something about their childhood, family, career path, and so on. The second type of text flows from the very nature of his subject, which is the intellectual history of a number of complex writers, most particularly the Slavophies and their kin. The ideas that the Slavophiles professed were rarely cut and dried, and resist easy and obvious summary. They literally demand that the historian present some explication of their meaning. Here Gershenzon steps in with gusto and offers his own interpretation not simply of what those ideas were, but how they originated in the thinker's life. He doesn't make this up out of whole cloth, of course, but in making these Slavophile texts comprehensible to his readers, he's forced to rely upon his own philosophical background and his intuitive insights. Finally, the third mode consists of those times when he injects his own philosophical beliefs into the very structure of his argument. However, he tends to do this in his historical works in an almost imperceptible way. One minute you're discussing Kireevsky's life; then Gershenzon begins to present you with an explanation of the relationship between life and ideas, and, almost without missing a beat, he may begin to insert ideas or value statements that are more the expressions of Gershenzon the philosopher and participant in *Landmarks* (*Vekhi*) than of the gifted intellectual historian.

Gershenzon's method led immediately to objectivity/subjectivity questions. For example, his view that the human spirit is more complex than any logical form raised doubt about whether he could claim any objective knowledge at all (either the individual is comprehensible or he/she isn't) and whether he could know supra-individual phenomena as a result of the study of an individual (such as society, social movements, and intellectual milieu). To resolve these dilemmas, Gershenzon makes a distinction between an individual as a "type" and an individual as "typical." No one individual can be a "type, " but people can serve as typical representatives of their age. In *The Decembrist Krivtsov and his Brothers*, Gershenzon explains, "Krivtsov is not a 'type.' Actually no individual can be a type. But he has a characteristic personality that is immensely valuable for the historian. It is not easy through individual

---

(Cambridge, MA: Harvard University Press, 1982). I acknowledge the help here from my colleague at Tulane, Samuel Ramer (email from December 18, 2012).

expression to perceive the traits of an epoch, and still more difficult in an analysis of ephemeral feelings and thought to open the far horizons of history, but if it is possible at all, the task is worth the effort."[7]

Gershenzon thought that he had resolved the intractable problem of historical knowledge—how the historian can know the past—by separating knowledge into two categories, interior and exterior. Although an individual's soul can never be fully known, his external behavior and writing can inform us about the nature of his internal condition.[8] In *The History of Young Russia* he writes, "The [book] does not consist of a series of portraits, but rather an entire picture of the epoch marked by the successive change of personal experiences. That is why I call it a history."[9]

Metaphysical principles guide Gershenzon's interpretation of history and are based on his "cosmic philosophy."[10] The principal idea is that each individual has a single spiritual source and is originally spiritually complete (*tsel'nyi*). The object of the historian is to discover the spiritual completeness lying beneath the seeming divisiveness of the exterior facts of a person's life. Gershenzon sought out individuals who "unconsciously desire harmony with the universe" or its corollary, the rejection of "logical reason." In addition, his heroes try to attain that particular state of the soul when there is unity between the way one thinks and lives. Ideally there should be no cleft between reason and will, thinking and being, conceptual and instinctual life; the way one thinks should not conflict with the elemental or natural feeling that innately inheres in the individual.[11] Gershenzon thought he had found a foundation for his own ideas in Slavophilism generally and in particular in the work of Ivan Kireevsky. In his essay on Kireevsky (1910), Gershenzon writes, ". . . The highest ideal to strive for is spiritual fullness. The sacred thing that I feel in my soul cannot be just a part of

---

7   M. Gershenzon, *Dekabrist Krivtsov i ego brat'ia* (Moscow: 1914), 11.
8   M. Gershenzon, *Istoriia molodoi Rossii*, 3rd ed. (Moscow: 1928), 2. The first edition was published in 1914.
9   Ibid., 4.
10 The best source on this is Brian Horowitz, "M. O. Gershenzon and Intellectual Life of Russia's Silver Age" (PhD diss., UC Berkeley, 1993).
11 For a more detailed discussion of Gershenzon's philosophical thinking, see chapter one, "M. O. Gershenzon—Philosopher of the Cosmos," of Brian Horowitz, "M. O. Gershenzon and Intellectual Life of Russia's Silver Age."

it; it has to take over my entire being, it alone must govern my will."[12] According to Gershenzon, the "sacred object" is the knowledge that one's being has achieved the optimal psychological condition in which the hero feels at one with the universe.

An example of the perfect type of thinking in Gershenzon's understanding can be found in his study of the consciousness of the young Nikolai (Ivan) Turgenev. In his essay, "N. I. Turgenev in his Youth" ("N. I. Turgenev v molodosti") (1912), Gershenzon declares, "If Turgenev were to be asked now what would he like to become, he would answer without hestitation: a spontaneous man, undivided, with a single center of spiritual life. He had two: one was legitimate—natural reason, the will of God in man, the other was illegitimate—logic."[13] In Gershenzon's interpretation Turgenev reveals a desire to live organically and naturally with his environment. The way to achieve this optimal psychological condition is to reduce logical thinking, so that consciousness coheres with natural will. Gershenzon's heroes, we shall see, are depicted as endeavoring to acquire unity with the world and attain a quality of consciousness in which reason is subordinated to feeling.

In order to achieve the tasks he set himself as a historian, Gershenzon maintained that the historian should not focus on society or even its ideas, but rather should pay attention to emotions and feeling. Feeling, he wrote, can open a window onto the intellectual and emotional premises of a past epoch. He writes in *The History of Young Russia*:

> The key to the history of ideas always lies in the history of feeling. Just as the changes of the land in the winter are only the consequence of processes occurring in the bowels of the earth, so, generally speaking, every intellectual movement has as its source the dark and complex imperceptible sphere of the human spirit. In every epoch each civic group possesses its own special psychic orientation; [. . .] In every such group typical feelings and inclinations develop, there occur half-instinctual ways of reacting to various sides of life. However great

---

12   The original article was republished in 1923. Quoted in M. O. Gershenzon, *Istoricheskie zapiski*, 2nd ed. (Berlin: Gelikon, 1923), 26.
13   M. Gershenzon, *Obrazy proshlogo* (Moscow: 1912), 290.

the influence of ideas is on the psyche, in general one must admit that the conscious worldview of a given group is conditioned above all by an emotional experience (of course we leave out the initial influence of economic, social, and other external conditions).[14]

To understand Gershenzon, one must grasp what he means by feeling. He was adamant that emotions are connected with processes that precede thinking. Moreover, he maintained that, as the inner core of a person's true self, feeling exemplifies a person's actual psychological orientation, his/her metaphysical foundation. It is for this reason that Gershenzon was preoccupied with states that preceded conscious thought—intuition, feeling, instinct. In his 1914 monograph, *Griboedov's Moscow*, he wrote:

> We immodestly read letters from people who have died long ago, and now we enter into someone else's family, get to know their affairs and characters. What about it? Truly, there is nothing wrong in knowing and loving. And we find them [the Korsakovs] in days of mourning; a mother tortured by worries that extinguish her blossoming life, the whole family in exile: a heart-felt sympathy for these people is born right away. And with them we come upon the wide arena of history; personal sympathy for them makes us as if contemporaries of these historical events, since the family misfortunes in which we find them are connected directly with the history of the epoch....[15]

Clearly this is a strange way to read history. It is highly unusual for the historian to express his sympathy so explicitly, or exhort the reader to subscribe to his personal identification. Ordinarily, the historian tries to retain a certain distance from his subject, if only to preserve the author's objectivity, and consequently his authority. In contrast, Gershenzon strives to enter into the personal lives of his heroes, em-

---

14 Gershenzon, *Istoriia molodoi Rossii*, 249-50.
15 Gershenzon, *Griboedovskaia Moskva*, 37.

bracing the expression of his own personal sympathy as part of his historical method.

One way to penetrate inner life in the past is through personal documents. For example, letters transmit emotions of the past. In fact, Gershenzon went further, claiming that personal documents, such as letters, diaries and personal notations, are "organisms" full of the threads of actual life, which do not lose their "potency" over time. Gershenzon hears in them the live voices of the past. He comments about Varvara Aleksandrovna Korsakova, whose letter he published in *Griboedov's Moscow*:

> And that is everything that has remained from her earthly being, only this one leaf of paper! But in it she is alive even now, in it the living warmth of her feeling has not grown cold. Is this not a miracle? Every perception of a person and every idea in its essence is like an amazing organism, and that organism is immortal. Time can break only its material form, but is powerless to erase or make non-existent the inimitable set of feelings and ideas that for an instant, once and always, arose in a person's soul.[16]

According to Gershenzon, letters retain the actual emotional and intellectual core of a person, they way they lived. Feelings are immortal, their external form, the particular event that inspired them, suffers dissolution, but the inner spiritual content remains contemporary and alive. In this way, letters hold the secret to historical knowledge, allowing the reader to know the past and become "like a contemporary." Since Gershenzon insisted that it was possible to have direct access to the emotional world of his heroes, he was especially sensitive to the value of archival material, and he acquired and published a great deal—six volumes alone in his *Russian Prophilea*.[17]

In his work as a biographer and chronicler of Russian culture, Gershenzon gladly accepted several constraints. The first constraint was to focus on the individual because, in his view, only the individual

---

16 Ibid., 28.
17 M. O. Gershenzon, *Russkie propilei* (Moscow: 1918-1924).

creates history. ". . . Society does not seek, does not think or suffer, only individual people suffer and think."[18] Perhaps for this reason, Gershenzon cared little for political history, international statecraft, or economics. His other constraint was that of scope. He fixed his sights on the history of Russian culture from 1810-1850, and rarely wandered from its borders. In a 1926 article, Georges Florovsky posits the reasons for Gershenzon's limited vision: "He had a penetrating and imaginative sense of the past, but—it may have been for this very reason—he had no need to widen his historical horizon. His advance was not in space, but in depth, and his aim was not to embrace as much as he could, but to exhaust all the contents of an individual case, to uncover its typical skeleton, to get at its psychological kernel, to separate the 'essential' from externals."[19]

Interestingly, Gershenzon held that objective knowledge refers solely to bare facts or raw material, not history. It is only the subjectivity of the historian that creates history, since the historian interprets and gives meaning to facts. In a 1908 review of the lectures of Vasily Kliuchevsky, Gershenzon promotes subjectivity. "What then is science if not the interpretation of phenomena, a philosophical hypothesis about them? The simple presentation of facts is not science, but merely knowledge, the material from which science is made. And therefore knowledge is objective and dead, but science cannot and should not be objective: it is subjective as is everything living, as any individual mind."[20] Gershenzon's dichotomy of objectivity and subjectivity was a clear sign of his rejection of positivism and reproach of the leading historians of his day, Vasily Kliuchevsky, Aleksandr Pypin, and Dmitry Ovsianiko-Kulikovsky.[21]

Another reason why Gershenzon promoted a subjective method is because he believed that the study of history should satisfy the historian's own spiritual needs. Pavel Sakulin and others noticed Gershenzon's attempt to solder his personal and professional life. "The history of the intelligentsia in Gershenzon's rendering was not an objective-academic

---

18 Gershenzon, *Istoriia molodoi Rossii*, 2.
19 G. Florovsky, "Michael Gerschensohn, " *Slavonic Review* 14, 4 (1926): 319.
20 M. Gershenzon, review of *Kurs russkoi istorii*, by V. Kliuchevsky, *Vestnik Evropy* 4 (1908): 801.
21 Despite this critique, one can only imagine the extent to which Gershenzon and his generation were indebted to their teachers if only because the elders had professionalized historical study, demarcated boundaries of what is history, and introduced new sources and methodologies of dealing with these sources.

job. After all he took it up for the sake of his own 'spiritual task.'"[22]

Gershenzon's conception of Russian history involved the view that Russian consciousness experienced a break in the 1840s. Up until that time, spiritual integrity or wholeness had been taken for granted, passed down naturally from generation to generation. In the 1840s, however, the situation changed. For the first time, the individual was free to decide his own spiritual fate; each person now had responsibility for choosing his own purpose. This caused a tragic division in Russian consciousness.

> In the stormy intellectual movement of this epoch, it seems to me, for the first time the basic questions of personal and societal idealism were posed consciously and with a full feeling of responsibility in Russia. Of course earlier, among the masses frozen in the patriarchal worldview, there were people with an anxious conscience, a roving mind, but they were exceptions. Now the patriarchal worldview in principle was bankrupt for everyone, so that not a single person with the pretension of belonging to the educated classes could reject the obligation of analyzing his own life and society from the perspective of truth. It was a true revolution. And now searching for the new, rational and unshakable principles that should lie at the base of a person's conscious self-definition, the leaders of the movement needed to put before themselves with open eyes the most essential eternal questions of life and consciousness—God, the aim of history, purpose of man, etc....[23]

The spiritual breakup that occurred, divorcing the patriarchal past from the modern era, led to two distinct and contrary worldviews—Slavophilism and Westernism--"corresponding to the eternal dualism of the human spirit." One regards the individual from the religious point of view, as part of the unity of the universe, the other considers man

---

22 P. Sakulin, "Apologiia dukha, " Unpublished Essay, Sakulin's papers in TsGALI, Moscow (444-1-14).
23 M. Gershenzon, "Otvet P. B. Struve, " *Russkaia mysl'* 2 (1910): 176.

a separate "arbitrary" being in the world" and a social atom. What this means is that individuals living in the first decades of the nineteenth century satisfied Gershenzon's criterion of an ideal individual because they supposedly lived in perfect unity with their environment, at a time when there was no break between the way one lived and thought.

However, by making a sharp distinction between a pure consciousness up until 1840, and then a fragmented one afterward, Gershenzon designates himself as "romantic." He sees in Russia's past a perfect age in which people lived in innocent oneness with the universe and a "fallen" age in which individuals struggle with intellectual freedom and existential choice. Not surprisingly, Gershenzon's conception clashes with just about every other theory of Russian culture, be it Slavophile, Westernizer, Old-Believer, Populist, Liberal or Marxist. Nonetheless, this conception allowed Gershenzon to define his period of study (1800-1840) as a watershed of the modern age. It also allowed him to diagnose the disease ailing his own culture (fragmented individuality), and thus to offer the necessary cure (holistic thinking).

Given that he employed a highly subjective method and at times inserted his own philosophical position into his subjects' mouths, the question for Gershenzon's reader is whether Gershenzon was a competent historian who at times slid into didacticism, or whether he used his historical essays as a platform from which to argue his own philosophical views. If his historical inquiry is truly governed by an ambitious philosophical vision that allows him to write just about anything he wants, then we have a genuine problem in our evaluation of him as a historian. Perhaps it makes sense that before rushing to answer, we would examine further which of the two options best categorizes Gershenzon and his work.

***

Gershenzon's evolution from his origins to famous historian was not simple. Born in a middle-class Jewish family in Kishinev (present day Moldova) in the Pale of Settlement, far from Russia's urban centers, the young Gershenzon was restless. He long hoped to escape Kishinev and looked to enlightenment and Western culture as his ticket. In fact he was right to see a way out through education, since, at least until 1887, the state made Russian schools available to Jews, other minorities, and the Russian lower classes, offering graduates a path to upward mobility. However, after 1887, policy changed radically and the government placed quotas on Jewish enrollment in Russian schools (and also cut down the numbers from the lower orders). As a result of the changes, the dream of a young Jew of reaching Moscow or St. Petersburg to join the ranks of the Russian intelligentsia was stymied. Even a gold medal from high school did not guarantee enrollment in a Russian university, and Gershenzon only had a silver medal.

As a young man Mikhail Osipovich developed a boundless adoration for the heroes of Russian culture, even collecting miniature portraits that he hung in his room. In a letter to his brother, Avram, he describes the number of portraits he had collected, "And if one were to hang them along the walls, as Vasily Shchepkin does, then one would discover a genuine pantheon of Russian literature and, speaking solemnly, the room would be transformed into a temple."[24] Gershenzon was not joking. Time and again he mentioned his outright worship of the literary and cultural figures of Russia's past. To get a sense of his reverence, one may recall Vladislav Khodasevich's observation that, "Toward those whom he studied he [Gershenzon] had a special relation. It was strange and absorbing to listen to his stories about Ogarev, Pecherin, Herzen. It seemed he was speaking about his personal friends. He 'felt' the dead as if alive."[25]

Unable to matriculate in a Russian university, he went to Berlin to study at a technical institute—a common solution to the quotas for Jews at Russian universities. In Berlin Gershenzon availed himself of this European city in every way except going to classes. He attended the theater and visited the lectures of Heinrich Treitschke and Theodor Mommsen. After two years, he returned home against his parents' will, deciding that his vocation was in the humanities. Having little chance to be accepted in Moscow University because of his origins, Gershenzon applied merely for the right to audit classes. Unexpectedly, a "miracle" occurred, and he was enrolled as a full-time student.[26] It appears that Gershenzon was the only Jew courageous enough to seek entrance to the Philological-Historical department that year. Jews avoided the lib-

---

24 M. O. Gershenzon, *Pis'ma k bratu* (Moscow: 1927), 122.
25 V. Khodasevich, *Nekropol'* (Paris: YMCA, 1976), 155-56; originally published in 1939.
26 Ibid.

eral arts since a career as a professor or bureaucrat required conversion to Russian Orthodoxy.

At Moscow University, Gershenzon's focus was ancient Greece. Studying with Vladimir Ger'e (1837-1919), who introduced Gershenzon to social and cultural history, and Pavel Vinogradov (1854-1925), who taught the evolution of ideas, Gershenzon developed skills in investigation and interpretation that he put to use in two monographs on ancient Greek history: "Aristotle's *Athenian Constitution* and Plutarch's *Lives*" (1893) and "Aristotle and Ephorus" (1985); the first study won him a gold medal.

Like so many historians of the nineteenth century, Gershenzon found inspiration in the romantic historian Thomas Carlyle. One can easily see in Carlyle elements that impressed Gershenzon: the enthusiastic praise of the gifted person, the absolute belief in the moral superiority of genius, and the historian's sympathy with his protagonists. Gershenzon especially admired heroes who seemed able, as he expressed it, to "resolve spiritual problems."

In one of his numerous emotional "crises" as a young man, Gershenzon realized that "holism" (a healthy spiritual self) comes from the ability of a person to make phenomena originating in the domain of the unconscious understandable to the conscious mind. The most important matters in life, he claimed, are oftentimes hidden from consciousness and therefore so much of one's spiritual life is wasted. However, if one could learn to employ spiritual energy, one could become a great hero. The consequences of Gershenzon's views are obvious: every individual is capable of becoming a spiritual hero. In a letter to his brother from March 20, 1892, he wrote:

> My profound conviction consists of the view that a person must work out his own completely defined, strong worldview, otherwise he is not worthy of the name human being. I believe that when I have worked out my worldview, I will be capable of convincingly and passionately expressing my own judgment about each of life's phenomena and of deciding every question of the mind.... And if this will be the case, then I will be a writer in the best meaning of the word (entirely independent of how small or large my talent is); a holistic

person if he writes will be an honest writer. One has to work out his own strong worldview and then apply it with inexorable logic to the resolution of the questions of life and the mind, not stopping before anything: a person with a strong worldview is an invincible force, stronger than steel and granite. He cannot vacillate, become depressed or lose his spirit: he cannot be unhappy.[27]

The conviction that with a strong worldview Gershenzon will be able to apply his mind to the resolution of all the questions of life demonstrates his enormous confidence in "philosophy." Philosophy (a strong worldview) has the power to make him an "honest writer, " an "unconquerable force" and "holistic" man. Such an individual can become "stronger than steel and granite." The individual with a strong worldview can give answers to the questions of the meaning of life and insure happiness for himself. Consequently, the spiritually superior individual, not the actor on the world stage, became the object of Gershenzon's work.

After finishing his degree, he was invited by Pavel Vinogradov to continue studies that would lead to a doctoral degree, and likely a position on the faculty. The one caveat was conversion to Christianity. Although he understood the honor was being offered, Gershenzon refused. Vinogradov, a liberal, understood and then proposed something unexpected: Gershenzon would continue his studies privately, and Vinogradov would help him find translation and editing work. To his credit, Vinogradov, with the help of Nikolai Speransky, even arranged for Gershenzon to receive a stipend privately sponsored by the Sabashnikov brothers, owners of the well-known publishing house.[28] These were difficult years for Gershenzon because he had taken financial responsibility for his younger brother, Avram, who attended a university in Odessa.[29] However, a number of the translating jobs that Gershenzon did exclusively for money brought him recognition in

---

27 M. O. Gershenzon to A. Gershenzon, 20 March, 1892. M. Gershenzon Papers in the Manuscript Division of the Russian National Library (746-17-30).
28 See M. Gershenzon to A. Gershenzon, 31 October 1898 (746-18-22).
29 Avram ultimately became a well-known pediatrician in Odessa.

intellectual circles.[30]

By 1900, however, it became clear that whatever plan Vinogradov had in mind would not come to pass—Gershenzon would not be able to join the faculty.[31] In fact, Vinogradov would soon leave for Oxford.[32] Gershenzon faced a financial and academic crisis: who needed an independent scholar of ancient Greek? However, another "miracle" occurred. Hired to edit the first full edition of Nikolai Ogarev's poems, Gershenzon visited the Ogarev estate in Saransk, and there he met N. A. Ogareva-Tuchkova, the daughter of the Decembrist A. A. Tuchkov, Ogarev's second wife and Herzen's civil-law wife. She gave him permission to take a chest of letters—the correspondence of the men of the forties, N. Granovskii, A. Herzen, N. Ogarev, P. Chaadaev, and N. Nekrasov. Gershenzon describes his ecstasy to his brother.

> All the letters approximately from the end of the 1840s through 1865 are here. My examination, of course, was very superficial, otherwise I would have had to stay here around two weeks; but I took the most important ones. And now I am riding home, freezing in a terrible way; but an obsessive thought was stuck in my head: will she give them to me or not? ... She [Tuchkova-Ogareva] agreed. So I got 15-20 pounds of letters, the most important ones. ...I tied the letters in the same case that Satina had given me and promising to return, I left in the dark of night with the heavy pack and my soul overflowing.[33]

The intrinsic interest of these letters for Gershenzon was such that he shifted his studies from ancient Greek to modern Russian history, something that in retrospect seems almost inevitable. At least as a Russian intellectual historian there was a chance that he could scratch out a living, however precarious, writing popular and scholarly articles, while continuing to publish book reviews and translations. Indeed,

---

30 See Brian Horowitz, "M. O. Gershenzon and Intellectual Life of Russia's Silver Age," 498-99.
31 Presumably Vinogradov thought that during the time of Gershenzon's preparation for a faculty position the laws regarding Jews might have been reversed.
32 Vinogradov received his professorship at Oxford in 1903.
33 M. Gershenzon, *Pis'ma k bratu*, 134. Nataliia Nikolaevna Satina (1850-?) was the daughter of N. M. and E. A. Satin.

the results of his expedition quickly began to appear. His first serious articles on Russian culture were published in thick journals, such as *Vestnik Evropy* and *Byloe*.[34] At this time his focus was the Westernizers. Within a decade he would publish four important volumes: *The History of Young Russia* (1908), *P. Ia. Chaadaev: Life and Thought* (1908), *V. S. Pecherin* (1908) and *Images From the Past* (1912).

In treating the Decembrists, Gershenzon introduced his own conception: the Decembrists, he claimed, were "external" personalities by nature, as opposed to the next generation that was "internal." "The Decembrist type is above all a type of person internally complete with a clear, holistic and well defined psychological frame of mind, a person who internally does not need anything and therefore is entirely turned to the outside."[35] According to Gershenzon, these individuals were complete internally (spiritually). Their inattention to the spirit supposedly caused them to idealize politics and therefore led them to incite the uprising. In Gershenzon's interpretation of the Decembrist Mikhail Orlov, for example, Orlov endlessly meditated on heroism and patriotism. "His soul yearned for action, not for slow work for the general good, but precisely 'a stormy life for the motherland.'"[36]

Since Gershenzon argued that all thought comes from "lived experience," he claimed that the Decembrist mentality ("slavish patriotism") should be attributed to their gentry childhood and not to the influence of Western ideas, which these soldiers brought back with them following the War of 1812.[37] Emphasizing the importance of the Decembrist's personal life, Gershenzon perceives about Mikhail Orlov that, "We are missing one and perhaps the most important link in the chain. We can never correctly understand the Decembrist movement until we explain for ourselves the intimate history of their childhood and education."[38] According to Gershenzon, gentry estate life inculcated these individuals with the belief that the government was the sole organ of social progress and thus any change in Russia had to come from the top. Therefore,

---

34 "A.A. Tuchkov i ego dnevnik 1818 goda" [1900]; "Iz perepiski Chaadaeva 1845 g." [1900]; "Russkie pisateli v ikh perepiske: Gertsen i Ogarev" [1902]).
35 Gershenzon, *Istoriia molodoi Rossii*, 5.
36 Ibid., 24.
37 This is the conventional view. See Marc Raeff, *Understanding Imperial Russia: State and Society in the Old Regime* (New York: Columbia University Press, 1984), 99.
38 M. Gershenzon, "Sem'ia dekabristov," *Byloe* 10 (1906): 289. This article became the first chapter of *Istoriia molodoi Rossii*.

the Decembrists' developed a psychological self-identification with the government, respecting its power and responsibility.

This identification with power supposedly explains why the Decembrists were so quick to cooperate with the government when they were arrested. "In general their behavior at the inquests was also conditioned by these psychological facts. They were deeply affected by the idea that the subject of their struggles was identical with the government's own interest; they identified themselves psychologically with this power and, one can say without exaggeration that they related to it [the government] with the feelings of a loyal son."[39] For this reason, "The Decembrist confession was merely the continuation of their affair."[40]

In his article, "The Decembrist in Daily Life," Yury Lotman acknowledges Gershenzon's insightful explanation, but elects to disagree, emphasizing different social, historical and personal factors that played important roles in the Decembrist confessions.[41] In contrast to Gershenzon's interpretation (identification with government power) to explain why most of the Decembrists confessed and denounced their comrades, Lotman claims that aristocratic family ties had fundamental importance for the Decembrists' identity. When arrested and questioned, the Decembrists could not see in their political opponents a faceless repressive force, but rather encountered well-known friends and acquaintances, who belonged to the same social circles as they did. This intimate connection with the enemy gave the Decembrists no room for dissembling, lying, or evasion. Lotman explained that the Decembrist "could feel contempt for their senile obtuseness, their careerism, and their servility. But he could not see them as 'tyrants' and despots fit for the denunciations of a Tacitus. It was impossible to speak with them in the language of political pathos, a fact that disoriented the prisoners."[42]

As did Lotman, I too would have to note that it seems difficult to agree with Gershenzon that the Decembrist was an absolutely "exter-

---

39   Gershenzon, *Obrazy proshlogo*, 299.
40   Ibid.
41   Iurii Lotman, "The Decembrist in Daily Life," *The Semiotics of Russian Cultural History*, ed. Alexander D. Nakhimovsky and Alice Stone Nakhimovsky (Ithaca: Cornell University Press, 1985), 95-149.
42   Lotman, "The Decembrist in Daily Life," 143.

nal" type of person, as opposed to the "internal" types of the 1830s. In fact, one might point to the Decembrist G. G. Baten'kov, about whom Gershenzon himself wrote, "His isolation and distance from life was, I repeat, undoubtedly voluntary. He did not write even once to his closest friends, the Elagins, and he saw confirmation of his idea that God wanted him to break the tie with his former life in the fact that they did not search for him 'despite the absence of obstacles.' Baten'kov belongs to the number of those rare people to whom are given the ability to feel within themselves with tremendous force and to contemplate the elemental movements of their spirit."[43] Such is the externally oriented character of at least one Decembrist.

In his studies of the men of the 1830-40s, Gershenzon moved gradually toward spiritual concerns that would become his forté. In studies of N. Stankevich, N. Granovskii, I. Galakhov and N. Ogarev, Gershenzon revealed his ambivalence toward the Westernizers' reliance on "intellect." Although ultimately portraying them as disharmonious individuals because of the cleft between intellect and will, he also notes and lauds their spiritual searches. Such a perspective can be seen in his portrait of Nikolai Stankevich. "Religious feeling lived undeniably in Stankevich's soul. His correspondence does not give us material to define the distinctive traits of his faith, but its essence comes through with full clarity: it was an optimistic religion, bright and joyous. At its foundation lay an innate feeling of the harmony of life."[44]

Nonetheless, Gershenzon asserts that rationalism interfered with the idealist's ability to realize his philosophy in the world because it inhibited him from feeling and gaining love—a critically important concept: "All of his shrewd thrift was nothing other than a means to mask his personal cowardice; clearly love attracted him only in the abstract, real passion frightened him more than anything."[45] Despite his faults, Gershenzon applauds Stankevich for his struggle to answer the moral and religious questions of his age. "But Stankevich was precisely a model of his time: none of his contemporaries experienced the process with the same unconditional holism in such a pure form. His short conscious life was indivisibly dedicated to a solution in thought and

---

43 M. Gershenzon, *Russkie propileii: materially po istorii russkoi mysli i literatury* (Moscow, 1915-1919), 2: 23.
44 Gershenzon, *Istoriia molodoi Rossii*, 189.
45 Ibid., 186.

life of the personal moral-philosophical problem and no other question distracted his attention from this aim for even a single minute."[46]

Gershenzon's personal quest and interest in religious idealism is equally apparent in his study of Alexander Herzen. Gershenzon loved Herzen and spent a great deal of time studying his life and work. At one time, in 1907, he contemplated writing a monograph on Herzen, but the manuscript division of the Rumiantsev Museum would not provide him with sufficient new material for his book. In the end he dropped the idea, writing a shorter work instead.

Depicting an image of Alexander Herzen that conformed to Gershenzon's growing religious interests, he focused on Herzen's commitment to communal life as a form of religious faith and diminished his commitment to Westernization and especially his admiration for Peter the Great. For Gershenzon Herzen was a religious Populist, as improbable as it sounds, an ideological friend of the Slavophiles.[47] About Herzen's belief in the Russian people Gershenzon writes:

> Is this faith justified? Herzen thinks it is. He sees the promise of the great future of the Russian people in the commune. He gives a detailed sketch of the commune's structure, underlining the elements of Socialism in it and comes to the conclusion that the half-primitive way of life in Russia more closely corresponds to the ideal cherished in Europe than the cultural life of the Roman-Germanic world. All his efforts are focused on what for the West was merely a hope—the reality of our first steps on the world stage. Oppressed by the absolutism of imperial power, nonetheless we were heading toward Socialism just like the followers of Thor and Wotan, the

---

46   Ibid., 206. See also Edward J. Brown, *Stankevich and his Moscow Circle, 1830-1840* (Stanford: Stanford University Press, 1966).
47   It is Gershenzon's view that Herzen was spiritually akin to the Slavophiles. He was certainly personally close to the Slavophiles, and came from the same social circles as they did. They also shared an interest in the commune, although for different reasons. But he was hardly an ideological friend. In fact the relationship was far more complicated. According to A. Walicki, "... Herzen might be called a natural link between the Slavophiles and Westernizers of the 1840s and the Populists of the 1860s and '70s" (*The Slavophile Controversy: History of A Conservative Utopia in Nineteenth-Century Russian Thought* [South Bend, IN: University of Notre Dame Press, 1989], 580); also August von Haxthausen, *Studies on the Interior of Russia*, trans. S. Frederick Starr and Eleanore L. M. Schmidt (Chicago: Chicago University Press, 1972), especially Starr's introduction.

ancient German peoples, came toward Christianity.[48]

This view of Russia's natural spiritual superiority clashed with Herzen's admiration for Peter-the-Great. Since Gershenzon could not fully discount Herzen's respect for Peter's attempt to relieve Russia's backwardness by importing its technical advances from the West, the historian tried to undermine Peter's image as Russia's modernizer.

> Pyotr made a grave mistake: he did not understand that those elements of European civilization that incited his amazement were not only not conditioned by the political forms then existing in Europe, but, on the contrary, stood in direct opposition to those forms and that the latter were condemned to death; they awaited their own Peter the Great—the French Revolution—to disappear. Blinded by the West, Peter set about copying it; hating everything in old Russia, he considered as good everything that he imitated in Europe, the good and bad. The largest part of the foreign forms brought by him to Russia was completely alien to the spirit of the Russian people. He wanted to break, to dissipate the general stagnation and apathy that he saw around himself, and, deciding to enliven the blood flowing in Russia's veins, he took for this purpose old degenerate blood, and thereby injected Europe's infirmity into our young organism. [49]

Using the metaphor of a blood transfusion, Gershenzon implies that Herzen's confidence in the Russian people was positive, but his idealization of the West was harmful. In this way, Gershenzon distorts Herzen's humanistic liberalism and association with Western Socialism, attributing to him a greater love for Russia's primitive customs. Gradually, Gershenzon molds Herzen into a kind of Slavic patriot. Partially this is possible because he concentrated on a short period in Herzen's life, when the latter propagandized his ideas of Russian Socialism to

---

48   Gershenzon, *Obrazy proshlogo*, 216.
49   Ibid., 216.

a Western audience and partially Herzen's ideas had some affinity to populism and thus indirectly to Slavophilism.[50]

Overall Gershenzon admires at least one aspect of the Westernizer worldview: they refused to forsake or dilute their ideals. An indefatigable critic of his own culture, Gershenzon praises the idealists as socially harmonious individuals who were united by birth, class, and aristocratic pride. In fact, Gershenzon frankly confessed to a certain longing for the world of the Decembrists and Idealists. In an essay of 1907 entitled, "Letter to My Brother" ("Pis'ma k bratu"), he writes, "How I envied the people of the 1820s and 30s. I looked with an unquenchable thirst at the paintings that depicted their comfortable and peaceful life! Reading their memoirs, their books, I lived their life in a way, and really, I don't know; doesn't the magical charm of Pushkin comes from this life as an eternal living echo of that lost paradise!"[51]

Although nearly all historians of the period, including Pavel Miliukov, Isaiah Berlin, and Martin Malia idealize the generation of the 1840s, the American John Randolph takes a different stand.[52] Randolph writes:

> I myself tend to understand Russia's Idealists neither as exemplary men nor as myths but rather as myth makers. I believe that the romance of Russian Idealism was a charismatic tradition built in the 1830s, by an ambitious group of young men in and around Moscow University who sought to translate the central ambitions of post-Kantian thought—self-knowledge, autonomy, and progressive agency in society—into compelling Russian terms. Their explicit goal in doing so was to play a modern and inspirational role in Russia's intellectual development through the mastery of what they believed to be the most modern current of

---

50 Martin Malia describes the affinities between Herzen's idea of socialism and Slavophilism in *Alexander Herzen and the Birth of Russian Socialism*, 3rd ed. (New York: Grosset & Dunlap, 1971), 278-312.
51 M. Gershenzon, "Pis'ma k bratu, " *Russkaia mysl'* 2 (1907): 88.
52 Pavel Miliukov, *Iz istorii russkoi intelligentsii: sbornik statei* (St. Petersburg: 1902), 73-75; Isaiah Berlin, "The Remarkable Decade, " *Russian Thinkers*, ed. Henry Hardy and Aileen Kelly (London: Penguin, 1994), 114-209; Martin Malia, *Alexander Herzen and the Birth of Russian Socialism* (New York: Grosset & Dunlap, 1965).

European social thought. In this sense, their common reputation in Russian history as the "best" (or at least the most illustrative) "people of their time" is a form of historical distinction they actively sought. [53]

The level of conscious image-making that Randolph describes contradicts Gershenzon's view that the Idealists and Decembrists sought above all authenticity and a unity of thought and action.

Although Randolph offers a compelling reading especially by using Lotman's approach of behavioral structuralism, it is hard not to ignore the reductionism. Any philosophical movement anywhere could be attacked on similar grounds that ideas serve merely as springboards for power, fame, or fortune. At the same time, by acknowledging the Idealists' attempt to ground their behavior in philosophy, Randolph actually inches closer to Gershenzon and his focus on the realization of ideas in daily life.

One can perceive Gershenzon's valorization of spiritual values in his biography of Pyotr Chaadaev, where he depicts the philosopher as naturally embodying religious idealism, i.e. he displays a search for organic unity in the world.[54] Gershenzon perceives Chaadaev's struggle for spiritual perfection on two levels, in his life and his thinking, both of which are shown as integrated. They are two parts of a single whole, representing the integral unity of Chaadaev's persona. Gershenzon argues that Chaadaev's true contribution to Russian culture does not lie in any single aspect of his life and work, but in his "whole metaphysical teaching."

In *P. Ia. Chaadaev*, Gershenzon offers a spiritual biography. Just as in a conventional biography, in this work Gershenzon traces the philosopher's life, his physical and intellectual evolution: childhood, youth, maturity, and decline. The main contrast, however, is that Gershenzon analyzes each of these periods in terms of the spiritual world of the hero, and not as a reflection of social, political, and economic circumstances. Thus, the hero's spiritual transformation forms the central event of the story, and the other features receive their significance

---

53 John Randolph, *The House in the Garden: the Bakunin Family and the Romance of Russian Idealism* (Ithaca, NY: Cornell University Press, 2007), 14.
54 M. Gershenzon, *P. Ya. Chaadaev: Life and Thought (P. Ia. Chaadaev: zhizn' i myshlenie)* (Moscow, 1908).

in their relation to this critical theme. For this reason the events in Chaadaev's life—his youth in the country, his retirement from the army, his travels to Europe, his seclusion, and finally, his cosmopolitan active social life—have significance as parts of a single spiritual path.

To illustrate, let us look at the reasons Gershenzon gives for Chaadaev's mysterious retirement from the army after meeting Alexander I at Troppau, which occurred before the philosopher's putative religious transformation. Although most critics are "baffled" by Chaadaev's resignation from the army, some historians attribute Chaadaev's retirement from the army to a psychological cause: having informed the tsar about a revolt in the first battalion of the Life Guards of the Semenovsky regiment, Chaadaev found the tsar unresponsive on the question of political reform and decided he could no longer honestly serve him. In this version, Chaadaev's pride played an important role because his self-regard led him to take offense.[55]

Gershenzon offers a different hypothesis: "It is very possible that Chaadaev's retirement was not connected at all with his trip to Troppau. In any case the idea of retiring ripened a long time before this event."[56] At the end of his life, when Chaadaev began again to pay social visits and spend his evenings at the English Club following ten years of painful solitude, Gershenzon interprets the philosopher's socializing as evidence of his religious conversion. "Chaadaev, without a doubt, hid the pain of his failed life, that 'funny' life, as he sometimes declared not long before his death. But it is impossible to doubt that at times the providential purpose of his existence seemed clear to him and at that time the strange work made sense. He discussed and debated—can one call it work? But it is curious that his contemporaries speaking about his loquacious foolishness, without realizing it, characterized it as work and even as a vocation."[57]

By giving a religious interpretation to Chaadaev's life, Gershenzon

---

55   Richard Pipes is among those who find Chaadaev's resignation a mystery. See his *Russian Conservatism and its Critics: A Study in Political Culture* (New Haven: Yale University Press, 2005), 104. Yury Lotman offers another interpretation of the resignation, arguing that Chaadaev was acting out in his life the role of the Marquis of Posa from Friedrich Schiller's "Don Carlos," offering the tsar his friendship and impartial advice. Lotman writes, "...Chaadaev's story illustrates how the behavior of a man close to the Decembrists could be an encoded text with a literary plot as its code" (*The Semiotics of Russian Cultural History*, 119).
56   M. Gershenzon, *P. Ia. Chaadaev: zhizn' i myshlenie* (St. Petersburg: 1908), 20.
57   Ibid., 182.

presented a new image of the philosopher. Formerly the unanimous view was that Chaadaev was solidly in the liberal camp, a "Westernizer." In fact, he had become the "property of a legend," as Gershenzon puts it. Had he not, so said the legend, been a friend of the Decembrists, the writer of the "Philosophical Letters" that criticized Russia of Nikolai-The-First? Had he not been persecuted by the government and branded as insane? The legend originates with Alexander Herzen, who wrote about Chaadaev's "First Philosophical Letter" that it was "like a shot fired in a silent night." According to Gershenzon, the intelligentsia paradoxically lauded Chaadaev exactly for the things that the actual man deplored. "He decisively condemned everything that our leading intellectuals valued most of all—the exclusive positivist direction and revolutionary politics. He was counted in the synod of Russian liberalism among the glorified leaders of our liberation movement."[58]

Gershenzon's aim was to "reestablish Chaadaev's true image." "His biography is full of mistakes, lacunae, and fantasies."[59] Who then is the real Chaadaev? For Gershenzon, Chaadaev was a "social mystic" influenced by the ideas of French restoration conservatives, such as de Bonald and de Maistre. Gershenzon attributes Chaadaev's idea that Russia lacked a history (in the sense that Europe had experienced certain epochs which had left Russia untouched) exactly to his radical Christian mysticism. In Gershenzon's view, Chaadaev's theory is that history evolves according to a providential plan, and thus the individual and the state must dedicate themselves solely to serving God. Political activities and social improvement are meaningless until one understands that they are part of God's overall design.

At this point Gershenzon applied his own concepts of religion. Humanity, he maintained, must become aware of the providential force

---

58 Gershenzon, *P. Ia. Chaadaev*, 3. The efforts of scholars before Gershenzon to interpret Chaadaev as a political "reactionary" should be noted. In the English translation of Chaadaev's *Philosophical Letters* Raymond T. McNally and Richard Tempest categorize the secondary literature about Chaadaev, writing, "The opposite 'legend' of Chaadaev as a reactionary was fostered by Alexander N. Pypin, who wrote: 'In a word, alongside the contemporary movements of European thought, Chaadaev's theory appears close to the Catholic doctrine, which was more a reactionary than a progressive one" (*Kharakteristiki literaturnykh mnenii ot dvadtsatykh do piatidesiatykh godov*, 4th ed. [St. Petersburg: 1909], 189). Pavel Miliukov supported this thesis by tracing the influence of the ultramontanist de Maistre and especially de Bonald in Chaadaev's work, *Glavnye techeniia russkoi istoricheskoi mysli*, 3rd ed. (St. Petersburg: 1913), 323-42. R. McNally and R. Tempest, *Philosophical Works of Peter Chaadaev*, Sovietica 56 (Boston: Kluwer Academic Publishers, 1991), 260.

59 Gershenzon, *P. Ia. Chaadaev*, 4.

and submit to this greater will, thus surrendering to the will of God. In this way, each individual is both a social being—his/her personal destiny is subordinated to the destiny of mankind—and an individual, i.e., he/she must recognize God directly, personally. Gershenzon labeled this doctrine Chaadaev's "social mysticism." "But the duty of every person is to strive to become an active tool of Providence. History better than anything else helps us attain this goal. The unity of humanity and the unity of the process of completion in history must enter into a person not as an abstract idea, but as a guiding feeling, so that he constantly feels that he is not alone, but a part of a great moral whole, so that he is forced to act always in accordance with the development of the whole. In the elimination of the individual's self and its replacement with an entirely impersonal social-historical being, we find man's purpose on the earth."[60]

Of course this is an odd and idiosyncratic way to write history. But looking at the way Gershenzon originally conceived of his biography and the sources he used, we can see how he arrived at this unexpected portrait of Chaadaev. When Gershenzon began his search for materials in 1905, he was advised by Semyon Vengerov to contact the historian Mikhail Lemke, who had discovered letters in the archives of the Third Department. Explaining to Lemke that his goal was different from an ordinary biography, Gershenzon claimed that he wanted to "present a psychological investigation of Chaadaev's ideas."[61] Believing that he had discovered a secret diary, Gershenzon mistakably attributed to Chaadaev the *Memoir zur Geistkunde* (1824-25) that turned out to belong to D. A. Obleukhov.[62] This diary, written under the influence of the ideas of Jung-Stilling and Restoration Catholicism, embodies the perspective of a Christian mystic.[63]

Gershenzon's religious perspective apparently led him into errors of

---

60 Ibid., 81.
61 M. Gershenzon to M. Lemke, 19 March 1905, M. Lemke Papers in the Russian National Library, St. Petersburg (661-310-9).
62 See D. Shakhovskoi, "Iakushkin i Chaadaev," in *Dekabristy i ikh vremia*, vol. 2 (Moscow: 1932). Incidentally, James Scanlan is perhaps too generous when he writes about Gershenzon, "At bottom it is Gershenzon's perspective that is being challenged, not his handling of the perspective he adopts—which is to say, it is the philosophical principles governing his historical outlook that are being criticized, not his performance as a historian" (Introduction, *A History of Young Russia*, xxiii). Actually, Gershenzon made numerous factual mistakes in his work on Chaadaev.
63 For V. Praskurina's position on the mistake, see M. O. Gershenzon, *Griboedovskaia Moskva*, ed. V. Proskurina (Moscow: 1989), 372.

interpretation.⁶⁴ Besides claiming that there were two or more sets of philosophical letters, grouped according to subject, Gershenzon speculated about the content of other "lost" philosophical letters, claiming that they concerned the question of the "freedom of the church and the dogma of 'filioque.'" Once Dmitry Shakhovskoi found the final five letters and arranged the proper order of all eight letters, it turned out that these letters did not concern man's relations to God, but rather the question of serfdom and the proper political organization of the state.⁶⁵

Shakhovskoi's publication of the second letter especially supported his view that Chaadaev was a politically committed thinker who was deeply concerned with the politics of his own day.⁶⁶ "It was not the influence of Jung-Stilling that played the decisive role in Chaadaev's intellectual evolution, but the political crisis of the first half of the 1820s: the victory of reaction in the West, the path of the liberation movement in Russia that culminated in the uprising of December 14ᵗʰ. All these events with extreme sharpness brought before Chaadaev problems of the philosophy of history, forcing him to meditate intensely on the principles that form the historical process."⁶⁷

Although numerous scholars of the day, including Semyon Vengerov, V. O. Syroechkovsky, and N. O. Lerner, criticized Gershenzon's image of Chaadaev, the book won the Akhmatov prize for the best monograph in the field of history.⁶⁸ In the volume announcing the winners, N. A.

---

64 D. Shakhovskoi, "Neizdannye 'filosoficheskie pis'ma,'" in P. Ia. Chaadaev, *Filosoficheskie pis'ma*, *Literaturnoe nasledstvo*, 22-24 (Moscow: 1935), 8. According to Dmitry Shakhovskoi, the use of Obleukhov's diary was only one of several problems. Other misidentifications include Gershenzon's publication in the appendix of what he thought was Chaadaev's fourth philosophical letter, which turned out merely to be an article, "On Architecture" ("O zodchestve"). In addition, Gershenzon incorrectly numbered two of Chaadaev's *Philosophical Letters*. The letter Gershenzon refers to as the third letter is actually the seventh, and Gershenzon's "second" letter turns out to be the sixth. In addition, Gershenzon thought Chaadaev's "Fragments" ("Otryvki") were bits and pieces of undiscovered philosophical letters. According to Shakhovskoi, however, the "Fragments" were not a part of the cycle of philosophical letters, but comprised their own genre.

65 Shakhovskoi published all the letters in *Literaturnoe nasledstvo* 22-24 (Moscow: 1935). The complete set of letters along with *Apologiia sumasshedshego* have been published in the original French in Raymond T. McNally, "Chaadev's Philosophical Letters Written to a Lady," *Forschungen zur osteuropäischen Geschichte* 11 (1966): 24-129.

66 Shakhovskoi, "Neizdannye 'Filosoficheskie pis'ma.'"

67 Ibid., 2.

68 For a description of the Akhmatov prize I offer this passage from Arthur Levin's dissertation. "The M. N. Akhmatov prizes were officially announced at a public meeting of the Imperial Academy of Sciences, on Dec. 29, 1909. Awards were given annually 'for original works in all branches

Kotliaevsky lauded Gershenzon's book: "This is a psychological study, a history of a writer's soul written, however, not in defense of his [the historian's] own worldview, as critics and historians of literature often do these days, but the reconstruction of a historical persona with the careful preservation of historical perspective."[69]

Although Gershenzon remained silent with regard to his critics, in a private letter to the Pushkinist N. O. Lerner (1908) he reacted to the accusation that he distorted Chaadaev's image.

> Regarding Chaadaev here is what I would say: 1.it is impossible to criticize Chaadaev's metaphysical historiosophic views. The word "criticism" is generally inapplicable. One can only juxtapose to any metaphysics a different one, but everything is hopelessly subjective. 2.My metaphysical views differ greatly from Chaadaev's, but I did not want to present myself in the book, I wanted to present only Chaadaev. Let everyone take from his views what is needed for his soul. If I want to, I can speak of myself separately. One can criticize a rationalistic historical conception—Taine, Miliukov, Marx, but not Augustine, not Chaadaev.[70]

Gershenzon's monograph on V. S. Pecherin (1910) belongs to the same genre as P. Ia. Chaadaev, a spiritual biography. Pecherin, an idealist who became a Jesuit, left Russia and entered the Catholic Redemptist Order in Clapham, near London. Later he left the order, moving to Dublin, where he lived for twenty three years as a chaplain until his death in 1885. Gershenzon defends his choice of hero, justifying him as someone who lived through a great deal and experienced life deeply.

---

of learning and belles-lettres written by Russian subjects in the Russian language...' by each of the three branches of the Academy (Physics-Mathematics; Russian Language and Literature; and History-Philology). Each branch made four awards, one for 1000 rubles and three for 500 rubles each. 1909 was the first year of competition for the Akhmatov prizes... Sbornik otchetov o premiiakh i nagradakh, prisuzhdaemykh Imperatorskoi Akademiei Nauk, IV [SPb, 1912], 122, 145" ("The Life and Work of Mikhail Osipovich Gershenzon (1869-1925): A Study in the History of the Russian Silver Age" [PhD diss., University of California, Berkeley, 1968], 151).

69 N.A. Kotliarevskii, review of *P. Ia. Chaadaev* by M. Gershenzon, *Sbornik otchetov i nagradakh imperatorskoi akademii nauk: IV otchety za 1909 god* (St. Petersburg: 1912), 369.

70 M. Gershenzon to N. Lerner (1908), Nikolai Lerner Papers in TsGALI (Central State Archive of Literature and Art), Moscow, (300-1-119).

"Glory crowns those who achieve a great deal, created or destroyed a kingdom, built or at least burned a wonderful temple. But there is another kind of greatness that is no less worthy of glory, when a person, although he did not do anything, nonetheless lived deeply and fully. Vladimir Sergeevich Pecherin was one of these rare people."[71]

In contrast to Chaadaev, whom Gershenzon portrays in an intellectual vacuum, he shows Pecherin as part of a distinct generation. Providing a psychological explanation for Pecherin's actions by reconstructing the typical mentality of a Russian student of the time, Gershenzon emphasizes that the details of Pecherin's early life—his study of the classics, his participation in the philosophical group, "Holy Friday" (Sviataia piatnitsa), his travels to Europe, his flight from Russia, and his entrance in the Jesuit order—are natural for a young man steeped in the German idealism that penetrated Russia at the time. "The generation that was born around 1810, i.e. Pecherin's contemporaries, are a spectacle of stormy exaltation that we do not see either in the preceding or following generations. On the basis of this exaltation there was formed an immature ideal of the individual of the 1830s. It was a higher dream of the unbreakable connection between man and the cosmos, about beauty that fills the cosmos, the divine dignity of the individual, the duty to preserve in oneself God's essence in a pure form and promote its presence in all humanity."[72]

Gershenzon blames the mentality engendered by German Idealism for "confusing" Pecherin: "It is not surprising that Pecherin became intoxicated literally. We, people of the twentieth century, cannot imagine the feelings that the youth of the 1830s felt crossing the threshold of Berlin University, feelings of a desperate thirst for a philosophical synthesis that might offer an understanding of life, and feelings of an unshakable faith that a synthesis *could* be found and had *already in fact* been found. One only had to come to the source and drink it up."[73] (italics by Gershenzon) Later, when Pecherin realized the falsity of German Idealism, its inability to satisfy his spiritual needs, he turned to the Jesuits.

While admiring Pecherin for his religious conversion, Gershenzon

---

71 M. Gershenzon, *Zhizn' V. S. Pecherina*, (Moscow: 1910), 1.
72 Ibid., 11.
73 Ibid., 45.

criticizes his hero for his subsequent loss of faith. In the end he admires Pecherin's search, while both reproaching and acclaiming his hero. His ambivalence can be sensed in this culminating passage: "Pecherin, taking leave of life, remained the same as he was then: the Roman toga preserved his utopian idealism of the 1830s. He covered himself in Catholicism and became whole but like a fossil. In this was his unhappiness and also his beauty because humanity does not know anything more beautiful than the dream to which he was loyal."[74]

As James Scanlan noticed, Gershenzon's interpretation of Pecherin's "reaction against Catholicism—a rejection of papal authority and the Roman hierarchy—presumably in the name of a simpler, purer form of Christian faith" was apparently based on an error.[75] Once the full text of Pecherin's memoirs had been published (Gershenzon prepared the text and it was published with a foreword by Lev Kamenev) in 1932, one sees that Pecherin's rejection was "not simply of Catholicism, but of Christianity and even religion in general. The Pecherin of the memoirs savagely denounces virtually every aspect of his own religious past."[76]

Although some might speculate about Gershenzon's own attraction to Catholicism in light of these two books—Chaadaev and Pecherin—the assertion would be mistaken. Gershenzon was interested in these men as seekers of a more authentic spirituality and less as spokesmen for institutional religion. In this sense one might note a similarity with Lev Tolstoy. A personal, non-institutional spirituality, and not the collective rituals, caught Gershenzon's imagination.

In his review of *The Life of V. S. Pecherin*, the Marxist Georgy Plekhanov acknowledged the need to criticize the book lest one be seduced by its fine literary style and enthusiastic presentation. Plekhanov found fault in Gershenzon's ideology and method, especially his sympathy for irrationality and mysticism. This method, he maintained, was incapable

---

74   Ibid., 184.
75   Scanlan, "Introduction, " xix. This paragraph is based on Professor Scanlan's research.
76   Ibid. It is difficult to say why Gershenzon did not notice Pecherin's changed attitude, but as Scanlan says, "... failure to discern the secular core of Pecherin's mature outlook damages Gershenzon's implicit philosophical thesis in the book ..." (Ibid., xx). See V. S. Pecherin, *Zamogil'nye zapiski*, Kalinin: Kooperativnoe izdatel'stvo "Mir, " 1932; see also Natalia Pervukhina-Kamyshnikova, introduction to Vladimir Pecherin, *The First Russian Political Émigré, Notes from Beyond the Grave, Or Apologia Pro Vita Mea* (Dublin: University College Dublin Press, 2008), ix-xx; and Nataliia Pervukhina-Kamyshnikova, *V. S. Pecherin: emigrant na vse vremena* (Moscow: Iazyki slavianskoi kul'tury, 2006).

of correctly interpreting history. For example, Plekhanov was horrified to see that Chaadaev was conflated with Tolstoy and that, instead of the father of the radicals, Chaadaev had become "the progenitor of our Populists and subjectivism."[77] Plekhanov claimed that Gershenzon was fulfilling an important political function: he served as the ideologist of the ruling bourgeois class. "…It's known that in even the least civilized country the ruling class must have its ideologists. The group of writers to which Mikhail Gershenzon belongs understands this well and with feverish haste is preparing for the role of the ideologist of the Russian bourgeoisie."[78]

---

[77] G. Plekhanov, review of P. Ia. Chaadaev in *Ot oborony k napradeniiu* (Moscow: 1910), 648, 652.

[78] G. Plekhanov, review of *Istoricheskie zapiski, Sovremennyi mir* 4 (1910): 140. Arthur Levin disagreed, writing, "Plekhanov erroneously concluded, however, that in rejecting the Slavophile's political conservatism Gershenzon was acting as a spokesman for the bourgeoisie presently aspiring to expand their political rights. Gershenzon's attack on the philosophical bases of Russian socialism might have pleased the bourgeoisie, but he certainly was not its agent" ("The Life and Work of Mikhail Osipovich Gershenzon, " 183).

9. Mikhail Osipovich Gershenzon and family (reproduced courtesy of Mikhail Chegodaev).

9. M. O. Gershenzon — Metaphysical Historian of Russia's Silver Age: Part 2

After having finished his works on the history of Russian Self-Conscious, Gershenzon took up the Slavophiles. His monograph, *Historical Sketches* (*Istoricheskie zapiski*) (1910), was originally made up of the portraits of three Russian thinkers, Ivan Kireevsky, Yury Samarin and Nikolai Gogol', and contained an appended essay about the contemporary Russian intelligentsia, which was for the most part a rehashing of his article from *Landmarks*, "Creative Self-Consciousness" (1909).[1] That *Historical Sketches* and *Landmarks* came out at about the same time is no coincidence. Gershenzon's own ideas were strongly influenced by Slavophile thought (at least as he conceived of it).

Presenting the portraits of the three individual thinkers as a single doctrine, in the table of contents Gershenzon called his chapter on Ivan Kireevsky "a teaching about the individual" (*Uchenie o lichnosti*), on Samarin, "a teaching about the nature of consciousness" (*Uchenie o prirode soznaniia*), and Gogol', "a teaching about life's task" (*Uchenie o zhiznennom dele*). The aim was to show the unity of Slavophile thought in three different contexts.[2]

Gershenzon's conception of Slavophilism was extremely abstract and, honestly, alien to the conventional interpretation.[3] For this reason he was strongly criticized by contemporaries and later historians, as we shall see. As a preview, I might say here that his idea was closer to

---

1 "Tvorcheskoe samosoznanie."
2 In the second edition of *Istoricheskie zapiski* from 1923, Gershenzon included his essay on Pyotr Kireevsky and removed his didactic essay about the Russian intelligentsia of his own time.
3 The best study of Slavophilism that I know is Andrzej Walicki, *The Slavophile Controversy*; see also E. A. Dudzinskaia, *Slavianofily v poreformennoi Rossii* (Moscow: Rossiiskaia Akademiia Nauk, Institut Rossiiskoi Istorii, 1994); August von Haxthausen, *Studies on the Interior of Russia*, ed. S. Frederick Starr, trans. Eleanore L. M. Schmidt (Chicago: University of Chicago Press, 1972); Sergey Horuji, "Slavophiles, Westernizers, and the Birth of Russian Philosophical Humanism," in *A History of Russian Philosophy*, eds. Hamburg and Poole (Cambridge: Cambridge University Press, 2012), 27-51; Iu. Iankovskii, *Patriarkhal'no-dvorianskaia utopiia: stranitsa russkoi obshchestvenno-literaturnoi mysli 1840-1850 godov* (Moscow: Khudozhestvennaia literatura, 1981); Leonard Schapiro, *Rationalism and Nationalism in Russian Nineteenth-Century Political Thought* (New Haven: Yale University Press, 1967).

William James, or what might be called religious psychology, than to the Russian movement. In particular, Gershenzon neglected the relationship of these ideas with the Russian historical context that gave them life, and in particular minimized the similarities of Slavophilism to German Romanticism and especially to Russian Orthodox Church doctrine. Instead of an analysis of Nicholas I's Russia, he concentrates on the universal and, as I mentioned, psychological dimension of these ideas.

For a summary of Gershenzon's positive and negative qualities, one can turn to Abbot Gleason, who writes:

> Gershenzon tended to interpret "wholeness" in such a way as to minimize the theological, even the religious element, while continuing to insist, curiously enough, that Kireevsky was a "mystic." He ended his essay by relating Kireevsky's ideas about the structure of the soul rather vaguely to later psychological studies of the unconscious. He was nevertheless right to minimize the importance of the "national" aspect of Kireevsky's analysis and to stress the importance of "feeling" in Kireevsky's intellectual formation, the pietistic milieu in which he grew up, the significance of his remarkably close family relations. It is clear that Kireevsky's idea of "wholeness" is related to the intimacy of the world of his family and childhood and a nostalgia for it. One should not, however, lose sight of the fact that the "religiosity" of Kireevsky's last years was far from a mere extension of the "world of feeling" that Gershenzon writes about, a slide from romantic sentimentalism into Christianity. Gershenzon neglects the dour, grim side of Kireevsky, his feelings of duty, failure, and general insufficiency, which accompanied the most specifically "religious" period of his life.[4]

Gershenzon's interpretation can be paraphrased this way: a person's

---

4   Abbot Gleason, *European and Muscovite: Ivan Kireevsky and the Origins of Slavophilism* (Cambridge, MA: Harvard University Press, 1972), 284.

ideas come out of the individual's "emotional-volitional core" and not primarily from external or intellectual sources. With this assumption come two other ideas: the first is that a person is born spiritually complete (*tsel'nyi*), and the second, connected with the first, is that the intellectual life of a person emerges from actual experience in a "creative" interaction with life itself. Since a person is spiritually complete, one's ideas are always an expression and definition of an entire being. "Every moral idea is inseparable from the individual personality that gives it birth, and may be studied only in the course of its living life."[5] In this context "living life" (*zhivoe bytie*) has significance; it is a term from Russian Symbolism that is connected with living life as a creative act (*zhiznetvorchestvo*).[6] In Gershenzon's conception the Slavophiles creatively transformed life by living in unity with thought.

In his study of Ivan Kireevsky, which became his classic statement on Slavophilism, Gershenzon presented his own perspective about the centrality of will and experience over abstract ideas. According to Gershenzon, critics have misunderstood Ivan Kireevsky and his teaching. His real contribution to world culture is not his historical theories of Russia or evaluation of the Russian Orthodox Church. In fact these aspects are his errors! Rather, his achievement is his realization of a cosmic religion, that "in a person there is something compact, ancient, foundational—precisely his moral personality, i.e. the definite structure of his feelings, passions, and inclinations. The entire person is defined by it and whatever does not have a foothold in feeling is a lie for that person. A person attains higher things only in harmony with his feeling and consciousness."[7]

According to Gershenzon, Kireevsky made a distinction between spiritual thinking and logical-abstract thinking. Logical thinking does not produce any real insight, but is merely the connection of the exterior, formal attributes of things. Spiritual thinking, however, occurs when one grasps the essence of things. When one does this, a person lives according to feeling, lives in harmony with the universe, since the internal essence conforms with the basic, real nature of the universe.

---

5   Gershenzon, *Istoricheskie zapiski*, 14.
6   See Irina Paperno, "On Meaning of Art: Symbolist Theories," in *Creating Life: The Aesthetic Utopia of Russian Modernism*, ed. I. Paperno and J. Grossman (Stanford: Stanford University Press, 1994), 13-23.
7   Gershenzon, *Istoricheskie zapiski*, 19.

Thus, Gershenzon can say about Kireevsky's thought, "He teaches people according to the proper nature of things."[8]

In contrast to the philosopher who borrowed from German Romanticism and the religious pilgrim who visited Optina Pustyn', Gershenzon portrayed Kireevsky as a mystic who has insight into the construction of the universe. In particular, Kireevsky's dreams interest the historian because dreaming reveals one's internal, spiritual "I" animated by the cosmic will inhering in all things. Through his internal life a person becomes linked with the will of the universe. In dreams God "speaks to us through the internal 'I,' which is more absolutely holistic than the conscious 'I.'"[9] Gershenzon continues, "Thus dreams are a kind of window through which we can glimpse the activity of secret powers in our soul, and perhaps even more. In these minutes when all the other spiritual abilities are paralyzed and the internal 'I' lives freely and undisturbed, we hear not only the voices in it, but among them God's words."[10]

Gershenzon admits that many might find it strange that Christ and Christianity are absent from Kireevsky's teaching, but, he writes, "[...] They do not have an obligatory place in his chain of thought."[11] In fact, connecting the idea of spiritual holism to any particular religious doctrine is a "mistake." In addition, Kireevsky's supposed preference for the Russian people is also a flaw that his interpreters have produced. According to Gershenzon, when Kireevsky mentions the people (*narod*), he does not mean "*narodnost'*" or a preference for any particular folk, but merely the folk principle (*narodnoe nachalo*)—the view that the folk has created spiritual life. In this way Kireevsky merely articulated his ideas for the educated classes, while the people already knew them.

It seems clear that Gershenzon wanted to denationalize and universalize Kireevsky's thought. The following passage epitomizes his goal.

> Whoever follows the development of contemporary philosophy in the West knows that in the last two decades a great intellectual movement has been underway that takes as its subject the exclusive emotional-volitional personality in a person, that has the aim of explaining

---

8   Ibid., 30.
9   Ibid., 24.
10 Ibid.
11 Ibid., 34.

man's nature by freeing it [the personality] and assigning to it alone, as befits it, the task of conscious living creativity that had been usurped by the abstract mind. Maeterlinck and Nietzsche are unequal in strength, but similarly "recognized" leaders of the movement. The former tirelessly listens and teaches us to listen to the powerful voice of our emotional "I, " its incessant echo of the holistic unity of life; the latter teaches us to unite this emotional-volitional personality within ourselves and make it as powerful as possible. Together two hundred thinkers and poets are engrossed with the same exact striving and in the final analysis they all teach as did Kireevsky fifty years ago: to perceive and live spiritually holistically.[12]

Gershenzon believes that Kireevsky's ideas are the same ones expressed by Maeterlinck and Nietzsche; he also compares the Slavophile to the little known American psychologist Frederic W. H. Meyers as two thinkers who reveal the physiological foundations of religious faith.[13] According to Gershenzon, Kireevsky and Meyers argue that there is a physical or material explanation for man's metaphysical nature which can be proved by psychology. The fact that a person can recognize God, that he/she has a spiritual capacity or nature, these were supposedly Kireevsky's central insights.

The flaws in Gershenzon's treatment are not difficult to locate, he distorts the importance of nationalism, Russian Orthodoxy, and the Russian nation in Slavophilic thought. In fact, the Orthodox Church was a great inspiration to Kireevsky and his visits to Optina Pustyn' were legendary, as was his work with Father Makary Optinsky on the medieval Church fathers.

Nicholas Riasanovsky took Gershenzon to the mat over his one-sided interpretation:

Gershenzon admitted that Kireevsky had left only brief

---

12 Ibid., 41-42.
13 Federic Meyers has been forgotten now, but he was a clinical psychiatrist and author of a two-volume work, *Human Personality and its Survival of Bodily Death* (New York: 1903).

remarks, hints, and allusions concerning the psychological truths which he had discovered. The system, as reconstructed by Gershenzon, was more logical, clear and comprehensive than the original, and also markedly more scientific. For instance, Gershenzon paid particular attention to the fact that Kireevsky had regarded dreams as a revelation of the basic personality of man, as distinct from the mere conscious side of it, but he did not take sufficient notice of Kireevsky's view of dreams as prophetic warnings of the future, as messages from the outside. It is not at all clear what Gershenzon meant by modern psychology, of which Ivan Kireevsky was the alleged forerunner, and his mention of such thinkers as Nietzsche, Maeterlinck and William James confuses rather than clarifies the issue. The analysis also suffered from the fact that Kireevsky was studied apart from Western romanticism: using Gershenzon's approach, there is no reason why such romanticists as Baader and Novalis, and perhaps romanticism in general, should not also qualify as forerunners of modern psychology. Finally, it may be noted that Ivan Kireevsky himself would never have agreed with Gershenzon's interpretation of his doctrine: he had been convinced that his view of man formed the very essence of Orthodoxy, whereas Gershenzon claimed that there was no connection between the two.[14]

Scholars have raised other problems with Gershenzon's interpretation of the Slavophiles. For example, several critics disagreed with Gershenzon's claim that Kireevsky's ideas are dervied from experience. Peter K. Christoff writes, "It is of no small importance that Kireevsky's philosophical education began with a study of German thought. He never let it out of sight, and in a certain sense, one might say that his career ended on a German note. In the last few pages that he wrote, at the end of his posthumously published essay on philosophy, he again

---

14 Nicholas Riasanovsky, *Russia and the West in the Teaching of the Slavophiles* (Cambridge, MA: Harvard University Press, 1952), 209-10.

refers to Hegel and particularly to Schelling."[15] In his book, *Schelling's Influence in Russian Literature in the 20s and 30s of the Nineteenth Century*, Vsevolod Setschkareff writes (1939), "It is questionable whether Kireevsky would have had a religious transformation if Schelling had not given him the model, and I believe that Schelling's influence should not be underestimated."[16]

Georges Florovsky completely vilifies Gershenzon's view that Slavophilism was an articulation of natural or folk feeling: "One can find least of all in Slavophilism a spontaneous or organic reflection of 'folk' instinct (as Gershenzon in particular did) ..."[17] For Florovsky, Slavophilism is philosophical thought in a religious context. He writes in his *Paths of Russian Theology (Puti russkogo bogosloviia)* (1937): "[...] In Slavophilism the voice precisely of the 'intelligentsia' was heard and not at all the voice of the 'folk'; it was the voice of a new cultural class that had passed through the trial and seduction of 'Europeanism.' Slavophilism is an act of reflection, not an exposure of the primitive ... Slavophilism was and strove to become a religious philosphy of culture. And it can only be explained in the context of the cultural philosophical problems of the time ..."[18]

In his essay on Yury Samarin, Gershenzon argues that Samarin's logic reinforces Slavophilism, giving it a firm epistemology similar to indisputable scientific truth. Sarmarin's task is to prove that, "... The religious nature of thought and knowledge is an indisputable fact that does not permit exceptions, like the law of gravity or the theorem that the length of the sides of a triangle is equal to two right angles."[19] His other task is to show that only through religion could morality have any meaning. "If immutable principles do not exist, then one should adapt to the circumstances and not conceive of any guiding moral principles, swim with the flow, not burdening oneself with any useless struggle that leads nowhere."[20] It follows therefore that one must believe in God, since without belief there are no objective moral norms, every-

---

15   Peter K. Christoff, *An Introduction to Nineteenth Century Russian Slavophilism: I. V. Kireevsky* (Paris: Mouton, 1972), 182.
16   W. Setschkareff, *Schellings Einfluß in der russischen literatur der 20er und 30er Jahre des XIX Jahrhunderts* (Leipzig: 1939), 63.
17   G. Florovsky, *Puti russkogo bogosloviia*, 3rd ed. (Paris: YMCA, 1988), 253.
18   Ibid.
19   Gershenzon, *Istoricheskie zapiski*, 124.
20   Ibid., 104.

thing is just circumstance and expedience. In that case, how can there be morality?

Samarin says that morality begins as something objective and universal and becomes subjective and personal in its execution. According to Gershenzon, it follows that there is a religious "organ" in the person that permits universal morality to become personal. "One asks, how does a general law, a rule pass into subjective obligation? For this one needs an understanding of the moral law to the extent that it can be grasped by a single consciousness, and also the ability and capacity given to personal will to carry it out. This means that each subject stands before the face of God and not before an impersonal law because he [God] alone has more than just legislative power, but also the creative strength to rule both each person and his environment. It follows that one stands on a religious foundation."[21] According to Gershenzon, Samarin proves that humanity's proclivity for morality demonstrates that all people without exception are religious. "Here is the law that Samarin discovered, *contradictio in adjecto*: an unreligious consciousness could [potentially] exist, therefore [in reality] there are no people without faith and cannot be any."[22]

In expounding Samarin's philosophy, Gershenzon evinces clear sympathy for his subject. Often it appears as if in his description of Samarin's thinking Gershenzon were resolving the same questions that he posed to himself. For example, we find Gershenzon's idea of God's will as a substance within us and from which we cannot escape; the idea that natural religious feeling guides our every movement and thought and that it is useless to deny religion just because it is perceived subjectively. Religion is therefore a psychological fact, a kind of knowledge attained from an undeniable feeling known to everyone who has experienced it. Thus, a non-material essence directs a person's life. "And so one cannot attribute to matter the role of an exclusive bridge between the soul and the absolute principle. On the contrary, one should acknowledge that the soul directly consorts with the general source of psychological and physical life, i.e. with God."[23]

Although one can hear echoes of William James and his *Varieties of*

---

21   Ibid., 146.
22   Ibid., 140.
23   Ibid., 128.

Religious Experience, I have to note that Gershenzon neglects to deal with Samarin's very significant political activity: his work on the official committee supervising the liberation of the serfs and his letter to the tsar concerning the unlimited power of the German Barons in the Baltic region. According to B. E. Nol'de, Samarin's biographer, the Slavophile is actually most important as a political activist, a polemicist, and only secondarily as a religious philosopher. In addition, his primary influence was Khomiakov, not Kireevsky as Gershenzon maintained.[24]

While the essay on Ivan Kireevsky was dedicated to the idea of the individual and the one on Samarin deals with the epistemological underpinnings of Slavophilism, Gershenzon's essay on Nikolai Gogol' entitled, "The Study of Life's Mission" ("Uchenie o zhiznennom dele"), takes up the subject of politics. Gershenzon's aim was modest, however: to correct the mistaken evaluation of Gogol's *Selected Passages from a Correspondence with Friends*. Overturning the view of Gogol' as a reactionary conservative who cooperated with the tsarist government—a view propagated by Vissarion Belinsky in his famous "Letter to Gogol'" ("*Pis'mo k Gogoliu*")—Gershenzon proposes a radically new interpretation: Gogol' was neither a "friend of the tsar" nor a "political reactionary." Instead, he actually agreed with Belinsky in the view that society needed changing; his polemic was not over ends, but means: "Thanks to the efforts of our journalist historians, a distorted conception of the *Correspondence with Friends* has rooted itself in society and even in Russia where social thought has been almost entirely deformed for the benefit of a political tendency, the fate of this book is unprecedented. One has only to read it oneself with some attention and the fog of legend dissipates without a trace."[25]

In contrast to Belinsky, Gogol' felt that change had to be exacted first and foremost in the soul of each individual. "[...] The single real force of motion in history is the soul of the individual person: society's whole

---

24 Nol'de describes Samarin's career: "Precisely 'in his soul' Samarin was not prepared for the role to be a true continuator of Khomiakov. He was too logical to become a creator of great independent religious conceptions, and it is by no coincidence that, despite everything, life shaped him to be a political fighter and political thinker. There wasn't enough air for him in Russian politics in the last years of his life, but he wasn't made into a new man because of this. His religious views were strong and sturdy, his religious philosophy was not poor, but the strength of his views was a reflex of his strong will and their wealth-a reflex of Khomiakov's huge talent" (*Iury Samarin i ego vremia*, 2nd ed. [Paris: YMCA, 1978], 219).

25 Gershenzon, *Istoricheskie zapiski*, 118.

life in its turn influencing powerfully the individual mind is defined by the spiritual level on which the individual members stand. It follows that all the efforts that are aimed at the perfection of life should be directed at healing individual souls."[26] Each individual should dedicate his soul to the kingdom in heaven. If every individual becomes occupied with the perfection of his own spirit, if every individual lives as a true Christian, then society will raise its moral level and organically become morally perfect. Social discontentment between individuals and classes will be resolved automatically. "Do not be embarrassed about the events that occur around you. Let each pursue his tasks, praying in quiet. Society will improve when each private person takes up his own problems and lives as a Christian, serving God with those tools with which he has been given and tries to have a good influence on the small circle of people around him. Everything then will come into order, the right relations between people will be established naturally, the rightful limits to everything will become defined. Humanity will move forward."[27]

There can be no doubt that Gershenzon sympathized with this image of Gogol', since his own recommendations to the Russian intelligentsia in *Landmarks* mirror those he paraphrased in his essay on *Selected Passages from a Correspondence with Friends*. In particular, Gogol's argument that only the individual is the force of history and that each member of society must perfect his own soul before society can improve, anticipates Gershenzon's "Creative Self-Consciousness."[28] Gershenzon, however, thought Gogol' too extreme in his dogmatic reliance on the human spirit and in his unquestioning trust in the reigning forms of social life. "He [Gogol'] fell into the same extreme position as Belinsky, but it was the entirely opposite position. He juxtaposed the false idea about the saving power of social forms with the no-less false idea (in its exclusivity) of the saving power of individual morality."[29] Nonetheless, Gershenzon located in *Selected Passages* an eternal truth,

---

26 Ibid., 137.
27 Ibid., 154.
28 For example, in "Creative Self-Consciousness" Gershenzon wrote, "The crisis of the intelligentsia is only beginning. Before it starts I can say that it will not be a crisis of the collective spirit, but a crisis of individual consciousness, not society as a entire front will turn in the other direction as has happened in our past, but the individual will begin to define the direction of society." Gershenzon, "Tvorcheskoe samosoznanie," 92.
29 Gershenzon, *Istoricheskie zapiski*, 155.

forever-active and forever-valid. Gershenzon comments, "With this observation (about the individual) he expressed a great and simple truth irrevocable for all time."[30]

In Gershenzon's mind the world of the Slavophiles was inherently superior to his own. The inhabitants of that world were spiritually healthy from birth, organically united with all being. The Slavophiles naturally experienced an equilibrium between thinking and living, they did not suffer from self-consciousness. In contrast, Gershenzon found his own generation spiritually fragmented. Attributing the differences between the two epochs to the experience of childhood, Gershenzon claims his generation has difficulties understanding Slavophilism.

> It is hard for us today to understand Slavophilism because we grew up entirely differently—catastrophically. Not a single one of us developed with any consistency: no one emerged naturally from the culture of our parents' home, instead we made a dizzy-making jump out of it or made many little jumps. Coming into our adult lives, we usually did not have anything permanent, exchanging everything along the way—tastes, the need for an idea. Rare among us is the person who stays in the same place where he spent his childhood and almost no one remains in the same social circle to which his parents belonged. Such innovation comes at a high price. Like plants that have been replanted, and perhaps more than once, in new soil, we give off pale light and weak fruit and some die, having sacrificed our health and the life force in these changes![31]

Undoubtedly the fragmented modern individual that Gershenzon describes is himself. He left home in Kishinev to study and live in Moscow, he rejected the Judaism of his parents for a personal religion of the cosmos, and he changed social classes, rising to become a member of the non-aristocratic urban intelligentsia.

According to Gershenzon, the Slavophile nest created spiritually

---

30 Ibid.
31 Ibid., 45.

complete persons without any effort. The vigor and creativity of their thought reflected their background. Family was the major factor in their lives, responsible for their achievements and attitudes toward the world. "In any case the difference between us and those people is obvious. In the biography of a contemporary leader often nothing is said about his family. The biography of a Slavophile must begin with the character of the home from which he emerged."[32]

Gershenzon's overall interpretation of the Slavophiles came under intense criticism. In particular, Nikolai Berdiaev, the religious philosopher and Gershenzon's close friend, objected to his attempt to universalize Slavophilism. "One can purify Slavophilism from the foul idealization of the backward forms of life, from attributing an absolute meaning to a fleeting form of political institution, but it is impossible to purify Slavophilism from the universal truth of Christianity."[33] Moreover, the concentration on Kireevsky, Samarin, and Gogol', intentionally excluding Aleksei Khomiakov (Gershenzon believed him merely an imitator of Kireevsky), angered Berdiaev, who considered Khomiakov the central figure of the Slavophile group. Evaluating Gershenzon's faults in his 1912 monograph on Khomiakov, Berdiaev writes, "Khomiakov was above all an Orthodox theologian, a Christian thinker, a knight of the Orthodox Church. Gershenzon clearly does not like him and ignores him to the same degree that he loves Kireevsky to a passion. Such a relationship to Khomiakov prevents Gershenzon from evaluating Slavophilism as a whole, destroys historical perspective."[34] It important to recall that Gershenzon also ignored other Slavophiles, such as Konstantin and Ivan Aksakov.

The theological significance of Slavophilism as an exclusive feature of Russian religious life was Berdiaev's special subject of interest. Therefore, he objected heatedly to Gershenzon's universal perspective. "Slavophilism brought to conscious ideological expression the eternal truth of Eastern Orthodox Christianity and the historical character of the Russian land, joining them together organically. The Russian land was for the Slavophiles above all the carrier of Christian truth and the Christian truth was in Orthodox Christianity. Slavophilism signifies

---

32 Ibid.
33 N. Berdiaev, review of *Istoricheskie zapiski* by M. Gershenzon, *Moskovskii ezhenedel'nik* 9 (1910): 46-47.
34 N. Berdiaev, *Aleksei Stepanovich Khomiakov* (Moscow: 1912), 23.

the appearance of Orthodox Christianity as a special type of culture, as a special religious experience different from Western Catholicism and therefore creating a different life."[35]

Pyotr Struve, the political liberal and economist, also attacked Gershenzon for what he considered his misguided interpretation. He contended that the author had lost all historical perspective and projected onto the past his own contemporary idea of a cosmic religion. "If the Slavophiles considered the Russian people righteous and a carrier of Russian Orthodoxy, and Tolstoy sees in it a carrier of godliness and social justice, then Gershenzon interprets it [the people] as a carrier of cosmic feeling. This characteristic is the most general, the most abstract, least vivacious, and darkest of all the qualities of the folk-idolizers."[36] Various other critics also shared Struve's view that Gershenzon was using Slavophilism to disguise his own philosophy.[37]

Gershenzon replied to Struve, but his statements only seemed to dig him deeper into a hole. He explained that he believed Slavophile ideas could be used to solve the spiritual problems of contemporary Russian society. "Now we need a sermon—a sermon of personal self-definition. Until people acknowledge that impersonal moral ideas and the mechanical perception of knowledge are dead and ruined and that creative force is present only in ideas that are born in the depths of the personal spirit and only in knowledge that is digested organically like food, life will not come closer to truth and there will be no freedom, no happiness, no beauty. This is my strongest conviction and my book talks about this."[38] Gershenzon's acknowledgment that he used Slavophilism to further the political ideas of his own day shows that Struve's criticisms were not without foundation. Gershenzon, however, stubbornly refused to agree that he had used the study of history for political aims. In a letter of February 4, 1910 to his brother, he expressed his irritation: "... The February issue of *Russian Thought* came out, there is my reply to Struve. He answers me right there; it's all a big misunderstanding. It is a lesson for me—do not start a polemic. And my book still hasn't come out ..."[39]

---

35   Ibid., 9.
36   P. Struve, review of *Istoricheskie zapiski* by M. Gershenzon, *Russkaia mysl'* 2 (1910): 190.
37   See. B. I. Syromianikov, *Utro Rossii* (1909): 7; I. Ignatov, rev. of *Istoricheskie zapiski*, *Russkie vedomosti* 57 (1910): 2.
38   Gershenzon, "Otvet P. B. Struve," *Russkaia mysl'* 2 (1910): 179.
39   M. O. Gershenzon to A. Gershenzon, 4 Feb. 1910 (746-17-16).

Georges Florovsky emerged as perhaps the most cogent critic of Gershenzon's historical method. In 1926, in emigration in Europe, Florovsky formulated a principled objection to basing a history of ideas on human feeling. He writes about Gershenzon that, "History in his hands becomes a conflict between unchangeable mental types. All its wealth of content becomes obscured. But as psychology is only able to give the general background, it begins to appear to Gerschensohn [sic] that all the details that stand out against the background are something irrelevant, something that is illegitimately added to it. He does not see that not only do they grow into the background, but become part of it, create, and modify it."[40] Isolating his heroes from the conditions that created them, Gershenzon dangerously reduces people to expressions of feelings. Florovsky continues, "By, so to speak, abstracting his heroes from the concrete problems that tormented them, Gerschensohn [Florovsky's spelling] has robbed them of their personality. The vivid psychological silhouettes of the men of 'Young Russia' drawn by Gerschensohn do not form themselves into a living historical picture of the period."[41]

Florovsky claimed that Gershenzon resolved the duality of the individual and society by surrendering to an anti-historical method in which the historian seeks in individual experience not the individual, but eternal psychic life energy. Thus, in his study of history the individual loses his unique face, while psychological experience as a principle is raised as the ultimate value. Florovsky writes:

> Whenever he has the opportunity, Gerschensohn is almost pedantic in insisting that "life" is wider and deeper than all logical or metaphysical formulas and definitions, that "the key to the history of ideas is always in the history of sentiment, and every intellectual movement has its source in the obscure and complex emotional sphere of the human mind." In his search after this emotional and volitional bedrock of all philosophy, Gerschensohn did not succeed in keeping within the bounds of the partial truth that was open to him. His imaginative

---

40   Florovsky, "Michael Gerschensohn," 319.
41   Ibid., 325.

psychologism allowed him to feel the vital and actual meaning of intellectual movements. But it also induced him to regard ideas as mere safety-valves, or brakes on psychic energy. Under the influence of Bergson and of William James, Gerschensohn willingly succumbed to this temptation and goes to the bitter end in reducing history to psychology.[42]

What Florovsky means is that Gershenzon analyzed psychological experience outside of historical context. By fixating on one aspect of life (religious experience), Gershenzon disturbs the value of his work as history (i.e., the study of particular events enclosed in a particular time within a particular value system). What is left, then, are isolated experiences which are penetratingly described, but which could have occurred yesterday or a hundred years ago. Florovsky exaggerates to some degree, but it is true that Gershenzon's approach does envision a different idea of historical time. James Scanlan noted this aspect, but nonetheless defends Gershenzon in the introduction to his English translation of *History of Young Russia* (1986):

> Florovsky's charge is masterfully executed, and as with the other charges there is a sense in which it strikes home. But there is also a sense in which neither Florovsky nor the other critics of Gershenzon-the-historian do full justice to his work. Thus it is true, for example, that Gershenzon believes in the repetition of *some* of the same problems in different ages; but he does not simply deny "the reality of historical change": *Young Russia* is constructed to tell the story of a novel development in Russian history, and it tells that story with intimate attention to its unique, unrepeatable features as well as to features it may share with other times and places. What Gershenzon *does* do is interpret the reality of historical change differently from his critics.[43]

---

42 Ibid., 319.
43 Scanlan, "Introduction," xxii-xxiii.

According to Scanlan, change is connected with a culture's mentality; at specific times several ideas dominate an intellectual landscape and these ideas change with every epoch. One might compare this interpretation of evolution and society with, let's say, Mikhail Bakhtin's idea of "Chronotope, " or Wilhelm Dilthey's writings on *Geistesgeschichte*.[44] If I were asked to choose, I would side with Scanlan and say that Gershenzon concentrates on describing the dominant ideas and attitudes of society, and that these attitudes and ideas are subject to change and evolution. It seems to me unfairly reductive to claim that he merely depicts unchanging feelings.

***

Since Gershenzon claimed that an understanding of society was predicated on a history of feeling (feeling being the motivating force for thinking), it was inevitable that he would become interested in daily life, families, and domesticity, because he believed that feeling was generated there. This interest led him to investigate two family "nests, " resulting in two "fictional-like" studies of Russian life: *The Decembrist Krivtsov and his Brothers* (*Dekabrist Krivtsov i ego brat'ia*) (1914) and *Griboedov's Moscow* (*Griboevodskaia Moskva*) (1914).

In *The Decembrist Krivtsov and his Brothers*, Gershenzon's aim was to reconstruct the mentality of a generation. In a letter to Evgeny Liatsky of May 10, 1912, Gershenzon explains:

> A few years ago the private archive of the three brothers Krivtsov came into my possession: Nikolai, Pushkin's friend, Sergei-the-Decembrist, and Pavel, Gogol''s friend from Rome; mostly a collection of letters, diaries, and the like. On the basis of these papers I thought to recapture the life and psychology of a single cultural nest of Russian society between 1812 and 1840 through these three vivid representatives, their friends and relatives. On the basis of these papers and other documents that

---

44 Mikhail Bakhtin, *The Dialogic Imagination*, ed. Michael Holquist, trans. Caryl Emerson and Michael Holquist (Austin: U. of Texas Press, 1981); Wilhelm Dilthey, *Pattern and Meaning in History: Thoughts on History and Society* (New York: Harper, 1962).

I researched in state archives, I wrote a kind of family chronicle of the Krivtsov brothers, trying to unite strict accuracy with artistry in the portraits of my heroes and the depiction of life. I set down a concrete narrative about the life and fate of these people and from them the typical character traits of the epoch could be grasped without my intrusion.[45]

It is perhaps not by chance that Gershenzon calls his work a "family chronicle," since he had trouble deciding on a title for the work, hesitating between "a Chronicle of the Nobility" (*Dvorianskaia khronika*) and "Decembrist Krivtsov." The idea of a family chronicle links the work to Konstantin Aksakov's novel-memoirs, *Family Chronicles* (*Semeinaia khronika*), since both works trace the development of a gentry family from a sympathetic "insider's" perspective. In both works, the authors consider the gentry nest the embodiment of higher values and creative source of Russian cultural life.

The purpose of *Decembrist Krivtsov* was to paint portraits of the three Krivtsov brothers in order to reconstruct the epoch's "movement of social-psychological forces" and trace in bold outline the "break in Russian consciousness." In the introduction he wrote, "Such is the intention of this book—to investigate deeply one point of the past in order to [reach] the basic flows of history, to recount the fates of one family so that through them the movement of social-psychological forces could become visible. I chose for this depiction one episode from the history and circle of people at the time when the essential break in the history of Russian society took place; and I find the episode extremely typical."[46]

It is impossible not to object to the claim that he reconstructs the consciousness of an entire epoch. That is an overstatement. What he does, however, is investigate the lives of a family from the point of view of their attitudes toward career, education, romance, family, power, and money, with the aim of characterizing the consciousness of one part of the Russian aristocracy from 1812-1840. It is important to remember that the brothers represent only one class of Russian society of the

---

45 Gershenzon to E. Liatsky, 10 May 1912 (163-2-144).
46 Gershenzon, *Dekabrist Krivtsov*, 1.

time: the middle-tier Petersburg aristocracy that had opportunities for advancement but whose future was not fully secure.

Gershenzon's idea of a break in consciousness guides his interpretation. He examines the cleft between their deeds and ideas; each hero suffers a dualism of mind and feeling. Gershenzon writes about the eldest, Nikolai: "There is even no need to look ahead: within the limits of the diary, the duality of his thinking and nature could not appear more vividly."[47] However, it is hard to construe what Gershenzon means by a duality of thinking, as the brothers' desires are quite mundane. Nikolai, the celebrated officer of 1815, would like only to secure a governmental post. The second brother, Sergei, wants to do something useful for society, although he does not know exactly what, and Pavel, the youngest, would like to live in luxury, left alone from the problems of others. In their deeds Gershenzon records their laziness, weak morality, cruelty, and selfishness. About Nikolai Krivtsov, Gershenzon exclaims, "Under the well-groomed flower was the Russian soil, and in part we already saw it and will see more of it: such great egoism and arrogance that demanded inborn rights, the heavy, forceful and sharp behavior with elements of arbitrary willfulness (*samodur*) and outbursts of wild fury."[48] Nikolai, we find out, was forcibly retired from his position because he gave a vicious beating to a postmaster. His arbitrary use of power was certainly abusive, and it is therefore both puzzling and surprising that Gershenzon should so zealously defend him as an "unconscious contributor to culture":

> Ideas and convictions adopted by him in the West were immediately thrown overboard, but Western teachings developed and enriched his naturally broad mind, gave him a wide and enlightened mindset. They [Western teachings] permanently cultivated an intellectual interest and the tastes of a cultured person so that for the rest of his life he was not indifferent to books, ideas, and art, and would never profane the Russian nobility, its past and disorganized way of life. This was perhaps his best contribution to Russian life. Culture buried

---

47   Ibid., 42.
48   Ibid., 57-58.

within him, so it seemed, an inborn time for evening walks because he so clearly felt his personal "I" [at that time of the day]. This is a very important quality that he shared with all educated people of his generation: he loved to live within himself and felt himself internally rich.[49]

Gershenzon's idea of a psychological break in the generation of the 1840s permits him to perceive a metaphysical principle where other historians might only see crude egoism, careerism, or self-indulgence. Gershenzon's adoring attitude toward his characters, his emotional sympathy is not justified by the content and, to an extent, clashes with it. There is a distinct ideological dissonance between Gershenzon's loving relationship to this epoch and the character of the epoch itself. Of course he can present his heroes as having dual personalities, possessing positive and negative dimensions, but it makes no sense to idealize them. It is exactly Gershenzon's exaggerated admiration that casts doubt on the value of the book as history. Moreover, the work utilizes certain narrative devices germane to novels: depiction of internal states of mind, authorial digression, and the identification of the author with his heroes.[50]

Griboedov's Moscow belongs to the same genre as *Decembrist Krivtsov*—a novelistic-historical investigation—and shares the same aim of capturing the psychology of a family during the first quarter of the nineteenth century. In fact, A. Turkova considered *Griboedov's Moscow* a "first-rate" historical novel. "Truly after *War and Peace* not a single belletrist has given us such pleasure with a loving description of the beginning of the 19th century in which there is so much beauty and movement, mystical searching and political action."[51] In Gershen-

---

49 Ibid., 58.
50 A. Kizevetter discusses the question of form, writing, "At first glance it can seem that the author simply recounts documents of a family chronicle, admittedly thanks to his outstanding literary talent the report rises up to a full artistic painting and one reads with vivid interest as though reading a masterfully written novel. But as one reads it is impossible not to notice that in the form of a colorful story about life there enters a psychological and historical analysis of social types corresponding to the time, which gives shades of meaning to the reigning qualities of society's cultural development. Thus, a scientific study goes hand-in-hand with an artistic stylization" (review of *Dekabrist Krivtsov* by M. Gershenzon, *Russkie vedomosti* 76 [April 2, 1914]: 6).
51 A. Tyrkova, rev. of *Griboedovskaia Moskva* by M. Gershenzon, *Russkaia mysl'* 5 (1914): 167.

zon's own mind, *Griboedov's Moscow* was a study of the culture in which Griboedov lived. "The book offered here is an experiment in illustrating historically 'Woe from Wit' ('*Gore ot uma*') an attempt to present in the clearest way possible that corner of authentic reality that Griboedov, transforming creatively, depicted in his amazing comedy."[52]

Here Gershenzon self-consciously compared his historical method to that of a novelist. "He [the historian] does not make things up, he only tells: from his heroes' diaries and correspondence he carefully creates paintings of their moods in the course of the real events of their life. Excerps from their letters fulfill in his narrative the same goal that a conversation does in a novel: [they] lead the reader directly into the feelings of real people, give the reader the possibility to hear their voice and the manner of speech."[53] In fact, Gershenzon maintains that the historian has an advantage over the novelist because he has the actual letters, the writings of his heroes; there is none of the artificiality of fiction. "And one has to say: an excerpt from an old letter can be so psychologically sharp and so full of the spirit of the time that a conversation between invented people in the best historical novel cannot compare. What is particularly valuable here is the actual reality of feelings and speech."[54]

Gershenzon agrees with Lev Tolstoy, who argues in *War and Peace* that history is made up of the conglomeration of all the individual experiences occurring at any given moment. Thus, the agent of history is not the single "great" man, but all the little men and women, each deciding for himself; each individual will is as significant as any other. Gershenzon even goes further, arguing that each individual event is composed not only of the wills of all the individuals participating in it, but also the individual experiences of friends and family, including all the other incidents associated with the event, such as events in the history of each person. There is apparently no limit to the number of incidents that make up an event. "An 'event,' as Tolstoy showed in *War and Peace* dissintegrates into millions of individual episodes, breaks in the fates of many individual people, countless family upheavals, and so on; in each of these episodes is reflected the 'event' for the person able to see it."[55]

---

52   Gershenzon, *Griboedovskaia Moskva*, 3.
53   Ibid., 39.
54   Ibid.
55   Ibid., 38.

As far as plot goes, *Griboedov's Moscow* traces the evolution of one family, the Rimsky-Korsakovs, from the early years of the nineteenth century through the 1840s. Once again, Gershenzon perceives a single family as a microcosm of the entire epoch. Therefore all of Gershenzon's descriptions have a representative function; the idiosyncrasies of each individual are intended to represent a quality of Moscow's aristocracy. "Mar'ia Ivanovna's home in 1816-1823 was in all respects a typical home of Griboedov's Moscow. It was precisely in these years (1818-1823) in that circle and in the family of the Rimsky-Korsakovs that Griboedov observed Moscow society. In those years 'Woe from Wit' was created."[56]

The central figure is Mariia Ivanovna Rimaskaia-Korsakova, the devoted mother who worries anxiously about her children. She is flanked by her son, Grigory, who cares little about promotions, giving most of his thought to his personal comfort and pleasure, and her daughters, who think only about making a "brilliant" marriage. The book is certainly entertaining thanks to Gershenzon's depiction of the Epicureanism of the aristocracy. Take for example the Rabelaisian description of the quantities of food that these people consumed. "It was a time when people rarely got sick, thought little, but enjoyed themselves a great deal without care, when the size of an appetite was defined by the humorous proverb that a goose is a stupid bird—too little for two but shameful for one—when luncheons began at 3 pm, balls between 9 and 10, and only 'lions' ('l'vy') came at 11."[57]

As paradoxical at it might seem, Gershenzon attributes to these superficial people spiritual holism. Somehow in their unconscious existence the historian detects a veritable ideal. Despite the appearance of frivolity and amorality, they have an inimitable charm because they lived in Russia before the breakup of holistic consciousness; they felt at home with themselves and their epoch; their values were stable, known and considered immutable. Questions, doubts, meditation on the purpose of existence did not come into play. His own age was tragically marred by reflection and futile rationalism. Gershenzon compares his own epoch to *Griboedov's Moscow*.

---

56   Ibid., 80.
57   Ibid., 12.

Do not throw stones at Mar'ia Ivanovna. Was she guilty because she did not know? I strongly fear that a historian in a future generation will condemn us in the same way that we condemn Mar'ia Ivanovna, because after all our lives also contain too little creative work and in turn must seem unavoidably empty and superficial from the viewpoint of higher consciousness. I do not want to say that our age is as equally bad as that one: no, it is immeasurably better, closer to truth, weightier; but the same poison runs in our blood and the poison can be felt in us, just as in those people with their emptiness and frivolity. Only then it found other forms—balls and picnics, the whole pretentious juvenile debauchery of their life—while with us it is the nasty complexity and fruitless subtlety of feelings and ideas.[58]

In these two books Gershenzon focused on family. Perhaps his focus can be explained not only by his view that history is born in the emotional core of individuals, but also in his observation that "internal life" reflects history more genuinely than external events. If by internal life Gershenzon means private life, one must acknowledge that his heroes are shown as embedded or swaddled in the family, circles of friends, and larger circles of society.[59] However, their contact with the outside world was kept to a minimum.

To be sure, Gershenzon's idealization of the Russian aristocratic "nest" was a literary construct that served several functions. First, it provided a sociological justification for his claim that his heroes were spiritually holistic, since they came from the supposedly holistic world of the Russian gentry. Moreover, this idealization also had a psychological function for Gershenzon. He seems to have felt that his own life was fragmented and he envied the holism that he discovered in his heroes and which he attributed to their childhood. This explains why he saw an incomparable beauty in the aristocracy. It is nonetheless strange that Gershenzon celebrates the view that the aristocracy is the

---

58 Ibid., 173.
59 M. Shaginian has interesting views of Gershenzon's idea of family. See M. Shaginian, review of *Obrazy proshlogo* by M. Gershenzon, *Priazovskii krai* 56 (Feb. 20, 1912): 3.

only class capable of embodying and preserving Russia's intellectual and moral values since he was not an aristocrat, but also because the economic development in nineteenth century Russia was engineered by *raznochintsy* (men of various classes).

Gershenzon's positive attitude toward family and parenthood attracted the attention of Vasily Rozanov, who wrote a laudatory article about Gershenzon's historical writings.[60] Rozanov considered Gershenzon the "best" historian of the Russian past because he created an ideal image, one which "is worthy of ancient Greece with its propilea and its parthenon." He wrote, "Beyond any doubt, beyond any comparison, he is first today in the numerous swarm of those who explain and retell the former fates of our artistic, poetic and intellectual life."[61]

Although the two men became friends, their relationship soured because of a difference of opinion about Jews and the Jewish problem in Russia.[62] Despite admiring Gershenzon, Rozanov was sharply critical of him and even mocked him by comparing him to the Jewish painter, Isaac Levitan. The problem with Gershenzon and Levitan, Rozanov claimed, was that both modeled their wondrous artifacts on dead, "stylized" images and not living subjects. Their source is not life with its blemishes and fullness, but an unreal perfect image. "This is a masterful 'stylization' of a Russian landscape and also the history of Russian literature, and still deeper and more basic—a stylization of a Russian man, Russian writer, Russian historian of literature, Russian painter. The mastering is reflected in that everything is accurate and true, but also somewhat dead, not lively. There is no will, scream, despair, and joy; it's not clear from where the 'Russian saints' came because the 'Russian sinner' is hidden and in actuality has not even come to mind."[63]

Although Rozanov does not mention it outright, the hint was clear enough: Gershenzon and Levitan created stylizations and not authen-

---

60 V. Rozanov, "Levitan i Gershenzon." *Russkii bibliofil* (1916): 78-81. Rozanov also wrote a review of Gershenzon's edition of Ivan Kireevsky's *Polnoe sobranie sochinenii*, ed. M. Gersehnzon: "I. V. Kireevsky i Gertsen, " *Novoe vremia* 12544 (Feb. 12, 1912). There is a relatively large literature on Rozanov, but one article in particular is devoted to the study of Rozanov and the Jews. Brian Horowitz, "Jewish Stereotyping: Vasily Rozanov and Jewish Menace, " *Shofar* 16, no. 1 (Fall 1997): 85-100.
61 Rozanov, "Levitan i Gershenzon, " 78.
62 See Vera Proskurina, *Techenie Gol'strema: Mikhail Gershenzon, ego zhizn' i mif* (St. Petersburg: Aleteiia, 1998), 162-229.
63 Ibid., 80.

tic paintings because they were not Orthodox Christians, but Jews. Truly Russian phenomena, saints and sinners, were beyond their understanding. Acknowledging that Gershenzon was a master, Rozanov felt horror from the fact that "Jews were overtaking Russians even in the study of Russian history."[64]

In a private letter Rozanov exposed himself: "I always trusted your love for Russians, but 'the insuppressible Semitic' influence (in literature), 'the grafting-innoculation' in the Russian soul of 'shaggy' Semitism disturbed me."[65] In truth, the motivation for Rozanov's strange attitude toward Gershenzon is his fear that Russians will die out as a race, while Jews will survive.[66] For Rozanov, such a scenario is a personal "apocalypse, " and its explosive fears interfered with his evaluation of Gershenzon. Rozanov juxtaposed the Jews as people with worldly "craftiness" and a success-driven spirit with the otherworldly idealism of the Russian soul.

Incidentally in a commentary to Rozanov's article, A. Filosofov objected to Rozanov's comparison of Gershenzon and Levitan, calling it "bad taste" (1916). "To say that Gershenzon, just like Levitan, loves everything 'ordinary' and does not touch the 'rapids' of Russian literature is the same as 'not cutting the pages' of Gershenzon's many books. Otherwise, how do you call Herzen, Ogarev, Chaadaev, Pecherin—'ordinary life, ' 'Levitan's landscape'?"[67]

Between 1915 and 1925 Gershenzon published five volumes of his *Russian Propylaea* (*Russkie propilei*). The purpose of the volumes, as the subtitle—"Materials on the history of Russian thought and literature"—explains, was to make public important documents about Russian culture.[68] These works would not be of great importance for us beyond their self-evident role as useful volumes of original materials, had Gershenzon not caused controversy even in this endeavor. As an editor

---

64 Vasily Rozanov, *Angel Iegovy u evreev (istoki Izrailia)* (St. Petersburg: 1914), 11.
65 "Perepiska V. V. Rozanova i M. O. Gershenzona, " *Novyi mir* 3 (1992): 229.
66 Ibid., 234.
67 A. Filosofov, "Mimokhodom, " *Rech'* 50 (Feb. 20, 1916): 3.
68 Although volume one and two are filled with various materials, volume three is dedicated to the unpublished or hard-to-find works of Ivan Turgenev, volume four is a publication of Nikolai Ogarev's archive, and volume six is devoted to Pushkin's lyceum poetry and to A. N. Skriabin's philosophical works. Volume five never appeared. In addition, one volume of *Novye Propilei* appeared (1923) and following Gershenzon's death the personal archive of N. A. and N. P. Ogarev, prepared by Gershenzon, was published (1930).

of Pushkin's early poetry, for instance, Gershenzon attracted criticism by breaking a conventional rule of editing: the last version published by an author in his lifetime is the canonical version. In contrast, Gershenzon chose to publish the poet's early scribbles as legitimate variations of his poetry, despite the fact that the author had either rewritten or published the works in a revised form during his own lifetime. According to M. L. Gofman, this principle was wrong and could lead to a faulty precedent. "... As if the canon of Pushkin's lyceum poetry should be the 'very first version,' or as he calls it, 'the earliest layer of his lyceum creativity,' even without the many corrections that he entered in these works after he wrote them."[69] Gershenzon's historical principle that unconscious feeling is superior to conscious creation likely lay behind his preference for first drafts to those modified by the author.

In addition, Gershenzon was criticized for his publications of Ivan Kireevsky's thought (1912) and A. I. Ertel's letters (1909). Critics faulted Gershenzon with a subjective approach in both editions, complaining that Gershenzon "left out" important documents. Criticizing Gershenzon's edition of Kireevsky's collected works, Pavel Sakulin wrote: "But unfortunately in our view the respected editor showed too much subjectivity in the conception of his rights. From Kireevsky's letters that were already earlier in print, he said in his preface that some of them were not significant and so were left out. Such a declaration completely amazes us. Just considering *a priori*, we strongly doubt that the rights of an editor of a complete collection could extend so far."[70]

Gershenzon's historical method was in many ways a practical application of his ideas in the realm of philosophy. It is possible to say that he developed an eclectic "novelistic" genre in Russian letters that fulfilled his own metaphysical, historical, and literary needs. At once it allowed him to tailor a literary form to highlight his talents: his psychological penetration and lively writing style. It also permitted him to examine the past with an eye toward discovering holistic individuals and epochs. Despite the amazing changes that occurred in the first quarter of the twentieth century, especially political changes, Gershen-

---

69 M. Gofman, *Pervaia glava nauki o Pushkine*, 2nd ed. (St. Petersburg: 1922), 145.

70 P. Sakulin, review of *Polnoe sobranie sochinenii Ivana Kireevskogo*, ed. M. O. Gershenzon, *Russkie vedomosti* 12 (Jan. 16, 1911): 5. One can hear a similar complaint from V. Kranikhfel'd regarding Ertel's letters. See V. L. Kranikhfel'd, review of *Pis'ma A. I. Ertelia*, ed. M. Gershenzon, *Sovremennyi mir* 8 (1909): 156.

zon's historical approach remained immutable from his early university studies through his final works. He was faithful to his original insight that history consists of the internal experience of the individual. Developing a method that was remarkably idiosyncratic, he judged positively those who satisfied his values of psychological holism and condemned those who did not.

However, one must acknowledge that Gershenzon subjected himself to the same questions about the purpose of life, as those he posed his heroes. Thus, his own life as a Russian intellectual was deeply connected with his studies. In an unpublished essay Pavel Sakulin writes, "In one meeting of the Scientific Scholarly Institute M. O. [Gershenzon] stubbornly posed a question to the young scholars: why were they occupied with study? He waited for them to connect their work with the general question about the meaning of life. [...] To all of his historical heroes M. O. Gershenzon asked the question: why do you live, what are your higher ideals? With this question he approached the Decembrist movement, the idealists of the 1830s and 40s, the Slavophiles and Socialists."[71] The readers of his texts were apparently supposed to ask the same of themselves, and they would be able to answer correctly if they had properly understood the lessons inherent in Gershenzon's texts, lessons that he had acquired from his own studies of the Russian intelligentsia.

---

71 Sakulin, "Edinaia dusha."

10. Mikhail Osipovich Gershenzon (reproduced courtesy of Mikhail Chegodaev).

10. "...To Break Free of Centuries-Old Complications, of the Abominable Fetters of Social and Abstract Ideas": M. O. Gershenzon's Side in the *Correspondence Across a Room*

The *Correspondence Across a Room* (*Perepiska iz dvukh uglov*; 1921), the classic work of early twentieth-century Russian thought written by Viacheslav Ivanov and Mikhail Gershenzon, has been viewed most often from the perspective of Viacheslav Ivanov's career and development.[1] Although the great poet Ivanov was the more influential of the two, nonetheless, in the *Correspondence* Gershenzon is brilliant in his own right. Moreover, Gershenzon's side reflects his attitudes toward the Bolshevik Revolution, and serves as a source for understanding his intellectual path from 1914 until his death in 1925. At the same time, Gershenzon's ideas can be viewed as a contribution to the evolution of Russian philosophy.

In the years before World War I, Mikhail Gershenzon had worked hard to fashion a reputation as one of the leading intellectuals in Russia. He became widely recognized for editing *Landmarks* (*Vekhi*; 1909), the volume of essays about the ideological errors of the revolutionary intelligentsia. His major monographs, such as *P. Ia. Chaadaev: Life and Thought* (*P. Ia Chaadaev: zhizn' i myshlenie*) (1908), *The History of Young Russia* (*Istoriia molodoi Rossii*) (1909), *The Life of V. S. Pecherin* (*Zhizn' V. S. Pecherina*) (1910), and *Griboedov's Moscow* (*Griboedovskaia Moskva*; 1912), were very well respected, and his many articles on Pushkin and other poets brought him wide-spread acclaim.

The *Correspondence From Two Corners* came at a pivotal time in Gershenzon's evolution. During the war, he had decided to turn his mind primarily to philosophy and metaphysics. By philosophy I mean something like free speculation on epistemological questions. In the same year that the *Correspondence* was published, Gershenzon also wrote *The Key to*

---

[1] Examples of studies of the *Correspondence* that focus on Ivanov's contribution include Robert Lewis Jackson, "Ivanov's Humanism: A Correspondence From Two Corners," in *Viacheslav Ivanov: Poet, Critic, Philosopher*, ed. Robert Louis Jackson and Lowry Nelson Jr. (New Haven: Yale Center for International and Area Studies, 1986), 346-57, and Robert Bird's study of the history of the *Perepiska iz dvukh uglov* (Moscow: Vodolei, 2006), 90-166.

Faith (*Kliuch very*; 1921), a study of the ancient Jews and their relationship with God. A year later, *Gulfstream* (*Gul'fstrem*; 1922), a study of Alexander Pushkin in the context of ancient philosophy, appeared. These works came on the heals of his 1918 book, *The Triple Image of Perfection* (*Troistvennyi obraz sovershenstva*), and a series of metaphysical writings that in have been collected in a single volume, entitled *Palmyra*.²

In order to understand Gershenzon's side in the *Correspondence* one has to unpack a number of complex and intertwined contexts. In contrast to the book's many interpreters, I maintain that Gershenzon's side in the *Correspondence* acquires its primary meaning in the context of Gershenzon's own development rather than in its interaction with Viacheslav Ivanov.³ There is corroboration for this view among readers at the time the volume appeared. For example, Boris Shletser, a leading critic, noticed the absence of a true dialogue. "Really the actual goal of this polemic both for V. Ivanov and Gershenzon was not to change the mind of the other, but to put oneself through a strict trial, to examine oneself, clarify one's feelings and thoughts, discover their final and to the utmost, special form, explain reality and, if one needed, then to justify it or to save oneself from it and hide."⁴

Lev Shestov claimed that the book's mock-epistolary form was uncongenial because it forced Gershenzon to respond to Ivanov rather than articulate his own philosophy.⁵ Shestov perceives as the function of the *Correspondence* the chance for Gershenzon to present his ideas. "Nonetheless the dozen letters by M. O. in this little book give us immeasurably a lot: the letters teach us how to read *The Key to Faith* and *Gulfstream*. They can teach us to read other books that also treat first and last things."⁶ Gershenzon himself expressed a similar viewpoint, maintaining in a letter to Shestov from June 26, 1922, that the "*Correspondence* was inextricably connected with *The Triple Image of Perfection*."⁷

---

2   M. Gershenzon, *Pal'myra*, ed. V. Proskurina (Tenafly, NJ: Hermitage, 1997).
3   The scholar Olga Deschartes shares the point of view that the *Correspondence* is integrally connected to Gershenzon's philosophical writings at the time. For more on her views, see her introduction to V. Ivanov and M. Gershenzon, *Correspondance d'un coin à l'autre* (Lausanne: L'Age d'Home, 1979), 35.
4   B. Shletser, review of *Perepiska iz dvukh uglov*, *Sovremennye zapiski* 11 (1922): 196.
5   L. Shestov, "O vechnoi knige: pamiati M. O. Gershenzona, " *Sovremennye zapiski* 24 (1925): 237-45.
6   Ibid., 14.
7   Letter of Gershenzon to Shestov, 26 June 1922, "Pis'ma k L'vu Shestovu M. O. Gershenzona, " ed. V. Alloy, *Minuvshee* 6 (1988): 262-63.

After the *Correspondence* appeared, Gershenzon was unhappy with the result. In a letter to Lev Shestov from June 6, 1922, he writes, "Regarding the *Correspondence*, you observed subtlety and correctly. V. I.'s tone defined my own and that is why the book irritates me: ... He started the correspondence and began to coerce me to write answers to him. I didn't like it because there is something theatrical in it and I was very weak ... I did not have any desire to write."[8]

Gershenzon's main ideas in the *Correspondence* pivot around the post-World-War-I situation: having seen the values of his time drive humanity to war and mass murder, Gershenzon wondered about humanity's future. It was impossible to retain innocence about the mortal dangers that Western societies presented to humanity. Using himself as an object of analysis, Gershenzon concluded that life lacked authenticity. Maintaining that the values of cultural, technological, and intellectual achievement inhibited a true direct experience of reality, he confessed:

> Perhaps because I was weary of a burden become too heavy for me, perhaps because something of my original mind strove through the clutter there of knowledge and habit—whatever the cause, a simple, unmistakable feeling has arisen and established itself inside me, as emphatic as the feeling of hunger or pain. I am not passing judgment on culture. I am merely attesting to the fact that I feel suffocated by it. As did Rousseau, I dream of a state of bliss—no worldly cares, a complete freedom of spirit, a paradise. I know too much, and what I know weighs upon me. This is not knowledge acquired by me through personal experience; its origin is general and foreign, it is knowledge inherited from forefathers and ancestors. [...] Precisely because it is general, impersonally demonstrated, it is indisputable, and its indisputability freezes my soul. Proven facts by the million, so many unbreakable threads, imprison me in their net. They are impersonal facts, immutable, inescapable—horrible.[9]

---

8   Ibid. According to Vera Proskurina, it is significant that Ivanov edited Gershenzon's side with the goal of advancing his own perspective. V. Proskurina, *Techenie Gol'strema*, 248.

9   V. I. Ivanov and M. O. Gershenzon, *Correspondence Across a Room*, trans. Lisa Sergio (Marlboro, Vermont: Marlboro Press, 1984), 10-11.

10. M. O. Gershenzon's Side in the Correspondence Across a Room

Gershenzon's point is this: the West's cultural legacy, spanning hundreds (if not a millennium) of years, interferes with his ability to look out upon life as something new, original, and unique. Instead of interacting with things directly, a wall of prefabricated images, ideas, and reactions has arisen. Feeling that his idea would best be conveyed with a metaphor, he compares authentic experience to cold water from a mountain source, and culture to the tasteless liquid from the kitchen tap that is mixed with chemicals and sent through a myriad of pipes and ducts.[10] Culture sucks the essence out of life, giving the individual values that he himself did not create, but come ready-made for everyone without distinction. If somehow he could remove all that he had acquired through hard work, Gershenzon exclaims that he would be happy to jump into the river Lethe and forget everything.[11]

Nonetheless, he has an alternative in mind. "Yet I know of and consider possible another upsurge of creativity and another culture that will be able to forego transforming every last cognition into dogma, every blessing into a desiccated mummy, every value into a fetish."[12] His ideal is to turn to direct experience, inimitable, unique, and authentic. "I would give all the thoughts and the knowledge I have culled from books, as well as everything I have built on top of them, for the sheer joy of achieving spontaneously, through my own experience, just one piece of simple knowledge, fresh as a summer morning."[13]

Gershenzon esteems those values that the individual discovers himself, produces himself at the moment of creation. In a central passage he emphasizes the right kind of perception:

> Everyone knew that Napoleon was not born an emperor. Any ordinary woman in the crowd watching him ride by during some great parade might have said to herself: "Now he is the Emperor who almost lost his personal name: he is the ruler of whole nations. But when he was in his swaddling clothes he was nothing to the world, only his mother's child." And I, standing before a famous picture in a museum, think the same thing: the artist

---

10 Ibid., 53-54.
11 Ibid., 11.
12 Ibid., 14.
13 Ibid., 13-14.

painted it for himself, in the creative act it was inseparable from him—he was in the picture and the picture in him. Yet now the picture has been exalted into an objective value recognized universally.[14]

According to Gershenzon, the mother who sees in the emperor not the image that everyone sees, but her son, embodies the idea of authenticity. Similarly, he claims that Rafael's paintings were alive once, when Raphael painted them. The same is true for Goethe, Shakespeare, and Pushkin—their creations cannot be separated from their creators; their essence was alive only once, during their creation. The finished product—the painting, symphony or novel—is a kind of phantom; it has the appearance of spiritual richness, but is an empty vessel. The only way to bring about authenticity is through a fundamental transformation, a revolution of consciousness.

> The poor heart which gave vent to the prayer loves it still, as a mother loves her child within the tyrant he has become, but she weeps as she obeys his impersonal will. At last there comes a time when love overcomes submissiveness: the mother brings the tyrant down in order to retrieve her son. So it was that Luther with his ardent heart brought down the cult, the theology, the Church of the Pope, with the aim of liberating simple faith, personal faith from a strait-jacketing system. The French Revolution made away with the mystique of the throne and instituted a more direct relationship between the people and authority. Another rebellion is now shaking the earth: the truth of labor and of individual possession is struggling to break free of centuries-old complications, of the abominable fetters of social and abstract ideas.[15]

Gershenzon believed that a social revolution was necessary and that it would have the result of returning humanity to a better place. In his reading of history, revolutions had liberated humanity, improving a

---

14   Ibid., 32.
15   Ibid., 36.

world characterized by falseness and play-acting.

By refusing to accept Christian humanism, Gershenzon angered Ivanov.[16] The latter accused Gershenzon of indifference to logic, rebuking him for employing culture in order to destroy it. Other critics noted the contradiction that it was precisely one of Russia's best-educated and urbane individuals who relentlessly battered culture.[17] In a private letter from June 7, 1915, the philosopher Nikolai Berdiaev, who was a close friend of Gershenzon's, spelled out the contradiction: "Often it seems to me that you are saying: 'All these ideas are only silly games and fantasies—creativity, literature, philosophy, invention and revelation, and so on and so on, they are all a superstructure set on top of life. The essential life is found in elementary feelings, work, bread, in simple things.' And you wage war with your own complexity, aestheticism, literary proclivities, your love for talking about ideas. It pains me that you are almost ashamed that you are a writer and therefore so occupied with literature."[18]

Gershenzon was conscious of this paradox.[19] In fact, he confessed in *The Correspondence* to feeling an ambivalence. "I live a strangely double life. From childhood I have been in contact with European culture, I have bathed in its spirit; not only have I become thoroughly familiar with it, but there is much in it that I love. I love what I think of as its cleanliness and comfort; I love science, the arts, poetry, Pushkin; I feel at home in the cultural family, I love talking about cultural matters with my friends, with all and sundry, the themes we discuss and the methods of developing them interest me genuinely."[20]

Gershenzon's philosophy had two distinct dimensions. While rejecting ratiocination, abstractions, and art, he also envisioned a harmonious holistic way of thinking. The best expression of his thought can be found in *The Triple Image of Perfection* (1918) in which Gershenzon focuses on

---

16 In letter twelve, Gershenzon writes, "You are angry and that is a bad sign. Irritated by my obtuseness, you are now classifying me among the 'self-simplifiers' who have 'forgotten their kin, ' you even label me a member of the 'intelligentsia' (while you, O shrewd friend of mine, reserve a flattering title for yourself: son of the Russian land! And disciple of Saïs to boot!). But what irritates you most is my obstinately maintained *sic volo*—and refusal to argue" (Ibid., 63).
17 See in particular Renato Poggioli, "A Correspondence from Opposite Corners, " in *A Book of Essays about Some Russians Writers and Their View of the Self*, (Cambridge, MA: Harvard University Press, 1957), 208-28.
18 Berdiaev to Gershenzon, 7 June 1915 (736-28-31).
19 *Correspondence*, 48.
20 Ibid., 65.

two kinds of thinking. The negative way is how mankind conceptualizes now. Take for example the treatment of nature. A tree only has value by being cut up into boards and nailed into the form of a desk. The exploitation of nature, he argues, serves as the reflection of how people relate to one another. His solution is to reject exploitation by having each individual realize his own image of perfection (*obraz sovershenstva*). The image of perfection has three components: the perfect vision of oneself, the perfect vision of the world, and the perfect vision of one's place in the world. The image of perfection can be realized through love, in which one's soul becomes full. In this case man returns to his primitive state when he originally perceived the world as an organic whole, and thus he achieves spiritual completion. "He who loves, in him the image of perfection is excited to action: either he realizes himself through his beloved or at least reinforces himself actively by protecting his beloved; he who loves learns through the confirmation of the beloved to know the image of perfection in himself."[21]

By love, Gershenzon means spiritual love and not erotic love, love in which the person perceives the other as a complete individual and an end in himself and not as a means towards an end. This "holistic" perception heals man of the wounds in his spirit caused by his former way of thinking. Thus, through the perception of the other as a subject, you yourself become whole as well. "Love is the polar opposite of culture because love means precisely to perceive the other in a holistic way. The image of the beloved that is imprinted in you is the image of your living unity, it belongs to you, only you. Confirming it, you confirm the holistic originality of your own individual personality."[22]

In *The Triple Image of Perfection*, Gershenzon believed that he had discovered a new mentality founded on holistic perception and directed by an unchanging ideal. The triple image of perfection was intended to play the role of a spiritual compass leading man to a new epistemology that would heal his soul. The problem with humanity—and the cause of war for that matter—is that people think abstractly, analytically, impersonally, without feeling. Mankind needs to return to a time in history when each individual knew the holism of life, when a type of epistemology reigned in which individuals did not divide things into parts, but used

---

21   Gershenzon, *Troistvennyi obraz sovershenstva*, 28.
22   Ibid., 75.

10. M. O. Gershenzon's Side in the Correspondence Across a Room

intuition, rather than analytical reason, to understand themselves and the world.

The Bolshevik revolution is a central theme in the *Correspondence From Two Corners*. Whereas Ivanov virulently opposed the October putsch, Gershenzon initially embraced the Bolshevik revolution, marching as a supporter with the crowds on Moscow's streets.[23] In June 1920, Gershenzon meditated on its meaning of violence. In *The Correspondence* he cautiously left open the possibility that the proletariat would take up the goal of spiritual achievement and lead humanity onto a new and better path.[24] He wrote:

> What we see is the proletariat taking this hoard of values out of the hands of the few and into its own. At the same time we have no idea what the proletariat sees in them or has in mind to do with them. In them might it not see only an instrument of its timeless oppression, something it has no wish to own but needs to remove from the hands of its former masters? Or would it be that under the impact of public education the proletariat has come to place some store by culture and supposes its values worth having? Who can tell? Once the proletariat has got hold of these treasures, it may well realize that they are nothing more than chains and rubbish, and, disappointed and angry, toss them out and set to work creating different values of its own. Still another possibility is that it will lift these cultural values onto its own shoulders and carry them forward, assuming the burden of the cultural heritage in good faith. But if the old values continue in currency among the proletariat, the proletariat will infuse a new spirit into them and before long their molecular structure will have changed to the point where they are unrecognizable.[25]

Needless to say, Gershenzon's conception hardly resembled the

---

23   N. M. Gershenzon-Chegodaeva, *Pervye shagi zhiznennogo puti (vospominaniia docheri Mikhaila Gershenzona)* (Moscow: Zakharov, 2000), 72.
24   The parallel with Alexander Blok's position is obvious.
25   *Correspondence*, 54-55.

Bolshevik one. He did not approve of Lenin's suppression of political opponents, the imposition of martial law, or expropriation of private property. At the same time, Gershenzon sympathized with Bolshevism because it alone, it seemed to him, offered a radically different future. Viewing the Bolsheviks as a kind of modern Don Quixote, Gershenzon expressed his preference for a failed attempt at true change than any half-hearted or unfulfilled promise.[26]

Gershenzon's position in 1917 and later in the *Correspondence From Two Corners* was shocking to his friends. In contrast to nearly everyone in his community—Berdiaev, Belyi, Shestov, Remizov, and Khodasevich—Gershenzon alone had confidence in the Bolsheviks. In fact, he was regarded as a traitor, although by 1922, he seemed to have few illusions. He describes his position in a letter to Shestov:

> For your ears and only yours I repeat what I wrote you: "I have the same relations toward Soviet power that I had earlier regarding the tsarist [government], i.e. none at all; I have gone to Kamenev and Lunacharsky to help others, just as you would do, like Berdiaev and others have done, and I didn't try to get something for myself or use the occasion; nothing aloud, i.e. I have not expressed my approval or condemnation publicly, I have lived entirely in isolation. As a result, in Moscow [Mikhail] Pokrovsky treats me as a member of the White Guard and [Vladimir] Friche said to me, 'You are the enemy.' In Paris [Mark] Vishniak knows that I have defended censorship and he believes that. Let people judge me by my writings and my life and not by the gossip about it."[27]

---

[26] In a letter from 1917, Gershenzon expresses the reasons why he supported Bolshevism. "(Kadet liberalism) causes greater hostility in me than even Bolshevism because the Bolsheviks are ardent and often deeply honest, but the Kadets are cold, formal, calculating. Bolshevism is generally speaking a wonderful thing (I mean the extremism in our revolution, its utopian thrust). It is clear to me that the revolution will fail, but I am no less certain that our descendants will say that the reasons the Russian revolution did not succeed or hardly succeeded was the most beautiful aspect of it, in the same way that Don Quixote was insane and without doubt was the best man in Spain. I prefer such a failure because of utopianism, which will leave seeds of great promise to a Kadet success, which Miliukov wants and will probably attain." M. Gershenzon to I. V. Zhilkin, 1 August 1917, Zhilkin Papers in TsGALI (200-1-18).

[27] M. Gershenzon to L. Shestov, 13 Jan. 1923, "Pis'ma k L'vu Shestovu," 277.

The Jewish theme creeps into the *Correspondence from Two Corners* in various ways. However, Gershenzon's autobiographical statement about feeling a foreigner in Russia draws particular attention. In letter twelve, his last, Gershenzon writes: "I live like a foreigner adapted to a country that is not his own, liked by the natives and liking them in return, concerned for their welfare and exerting myself willingly on its behalf, suffering when they suffer, rejoicing when they rejoice. But I know that I am a foreigner, and in secret I miss the fields of my homeland, its different seasons, the different odor of its flowers in the springtime and the different speech of the women there. Where is my homeland? I shall never lay eyes upon it, I shall die in a foreign place. And how passionately I long for it sometimes!"[28]

Although it would be convenient to see in his yearnings the hopes of a Jew for a homeland, he was not a Zionist, although he seems to have befriended some individual Zionists.[29] Such sympathies are demonstrated by his participation in a number of Zionist publications during World War I.[30] For example, he participated in a volume entitled, *In the Light of War* (*Pri svete voiny*; 1916), a special issue of *Evreiskaia zhizn'* (1916) devoted to the twenty-fifth anniversary of Hayim Nachman Bialik's literary career, and he wrote the introduction to the *Jewish Anthology: A Collection of Young Jewish Poetry* (*Evreiskaia antologiia: sbornik molodoi evreiskoi poezii*; 1916)—all three works were subsidized by Zionist supporters.[31] Although Gershenzon expressed a positive attitude toward Zionism in these works, he changed his viewpoint one hundred and eighty degrees, publishing *The Fates of the Jewish People* (*Sud'by evreiskogo naroda*) in 1922, in which he criticized Zionism as one form of a general evil—nationalism.[32]

In truth it would surprise no one if Gershenzon did support Zionism; many individuals supported the cause who had no interest in moving to Palestine. After all, Gershenzon was angry about the way Jews were treated in Russia and felt an emotional closeness to Jews who had suf-

---

28 *Correspondence*, 66.
29 For a study of Gershenzon's attitude toward Jewish culture, see Brian Horowitz, "Mikhail Gershenzon: A Jew in the Russian Elite, " in *Empire Jews*, 214-28.
30 See Brian Horowitz, "Russian-Zionist Cultural Cooperation, 1916-18: Leib Jaffe and the Russian Intelligentsia, " in *Empire Jews*, 65-86.
31 M. Gershenzon, "Predislovie, " in *Evreiskaia antologiia: sbornik molodoi evreiskoi poezii* (Moscow: Safrut, 1918), 1-8.
32 M. Gershenzon, *Sud'by evreiskogo naroda* (Moscow, 1922).

fered from tsarist oppression. In his youth he had wanted to become a professor and was offered the opportunity on one condition, conversion to Christianity. In addition, for several years he was unable to marry because his future wife, Mariia Borisovna née Gol'denveizer, was a member of the Russian-Orthodox Church. They lived together unmarried until 1905, when she converted to Protestantism and they married.[33] Finally, Gershenzon had never forgiven the tsarist government for the need to bribe officials in order to receive a visit from his mother. However, these bouts with injustice did not promote a love for Zionism or radical socialism. While he never converted, he did not value Judaism or join with the Jewish people.

During World War I, the same state of mind that animated *The Triple Image of Perfection* also inspired his essays on Judaism. In an article entitled "A People Tried by Fire" ("Narod ispytuemyi ognem") Gershenzon expressed a belief in Jewish messianism.[34] In a display of national feeling Gershenzon wrote an entire book about the ancient Jews, *Key To Faith* (*Kliuch very*). Although it is a complicated work, the main thrust is that by resisting God's will, the ancient Jews led themselves to destruction. Although critical in his approach, Gershenzon showed his respect by considering the ancient Jews the first carriers of "cosmic consciousness," an ideal kind of holistic cognition.

Although he used an unfamiliar vocabulary in discussing metaphysical questions, on practical Jewish issues he was decidedly simpler, expressing his support for integration. In his letters and in the way he lived, one can perceive his approval of assimilation. Writing to Vasily Rozanov, the Russian author who was a friend for a time and a known anti-Semite, Gershenzon explained his perspective on the role of Jews in Russian culture.

---

33   See A. B. Gol'denveizer, "Vospominaniia," located in the Gol'denveizer Museum in Moscow or in Brian Horowitz, "M. O. Gershenzon and Intellectual Life of Russia's Silver Age," 469.
34   "Will a new myth be born in the country of exile at that hour when our oppression will finally become unendurable? There is harmony in the latest sorrow and inconsolable weeping is always sonorous; at the base of pain is a sharp life force. The first time since Yehudah Halevi, the soul of the Jewish people has already sang forth in Bialik an otherworldly song, an angelic-earthy song! Does it not presage the Jewish people's resurrection? Or is it true that only the land of Palestine can give birth to a new Jewish world? I do not know, but I strongly believe that the nation is alive in its lethargic sleep and at the assigned moment it will awaken." M. Gershenzon, "Narod, ispytuemyi ognem," *Evreiskaia nedelia* 1 (January 3, 1916): 28.

I do not hide from myself that my Jewish spirit through my writings brings a foreign element into Russian consciousness: I am clearly conscious of it; it cannot be otherwise. But I think that the life of any great and strong people, such as the Russian people, works itself so deeply, distinctively and irrevocably that not only the economic or literary influence of Jews, the force of Germans and other things, but even historical events—1612, 1812, 1905 (excluding however the greatest events, such as ancient conquests)—are incapable of moving it from its fatal path by an inch. This is like a smelting oven: whatever you throw into it, either burns and thus increases the smelting, or else improves the quality of the metal. Such is the participation of Jews and everything like it generally—insignificant in quantity comparatively with the people's life. A foreign admixture can become dangerous for the people only if it oppresses it quantitatively, as occurred in the conquest of England by the Normans; but this already is one of those great historical events in which there is the hand of God!

[...] I think further that each effort of the spirit brings profit to the people no matter what the content or form—pious or heretical, patriotic or not—if it is genuinely spiritual. Therefore any honest writings in Russian by a Jew, a Latvian, or a Georgian, benefits the Russian people. Moreover, I believe such a foreign admixture precisely "improves the quality of the metal, " because a Jew or Georgian perceives the world in his own way—the Jewish or Latvian way—turning things to society from such a side, from which society is not used to seeing them. That is why, identifying myself as a Jew, I still allow myself to write in Russian about Russian things. This is conscious, that is, in this way I intellectually, forwards and backwards, justify my work.[35]

---

35 M. Gershenzon to V. Rozanov 18 January 1912, "Perepiska V. V. Rozanova i M. O. Gershenzona, " ed. V. Praskura, *Novyi mir* 3 (1991): 228.

The key to understanding this passage is not only that Russians will absorb the Jewish element and become stronger, but also that an exorable process takes place that no individual can stop or manipulate. Believing in a kind of universal fatalism (cosmic force), Gershenzon was indifferent to ordinary distinctions between peoples and nations. At the same time referring to the "hand of God" and that the "admixture makes the race stronger, " Gershenzon reposted Richard Wagner's famous libel, and Rozanov himself, that Jews were dangerous to native cultures. The natural outcome of his worldview was cosmopolitanism, and Gershenzon was committed to the ideal of a merging of cultures and peoples.

Despite the desire of at least one scholar to draw a line between the Jewish tradition and Gershenzon's philosophical ideas, is difficult for me to see a Jewish source.[36] His rejection of culture, his penchant for neo-primitivism, and his antagonism for ratiocination have little in common with the Jewish tradition. Although he was by no means a self-hating Jew, he did not practice the religion. Moreover, few if any of his multiple allusions in the *Correspondence From Two Corners* refer to the Jewish tradition. Zionism and Jewish culture occupied a large space in his post-war work, but the role was primarily functional: he used them to engage ideas that were closer to his own thinking.

Gershenzon's side in the *Correspondence* is complicated not only because the dialogue form inhibited a direct expression of his thoughts, but also because his ideas themselves were difficult, strange, and unconventional. In addition, the way he expressed them in allegory and through historical examples did not always bring greater clarity. Moreover, many of Gershenzon's other philosophical texts have either never been published or have only appeared in the last decade.[37]

The few scholars who have treated Gershenzon's philosophical writings have been surprised by the absence of an acknowledgement of Lev Tolstoy's influence.[38] In fact, many of the ideas that Gershenzon asserts as his own echo Tolstoy; in particular, the idea of culture as a screen separating the individual from what is true and important. Although

---

36 In a conference devoted to Jewish literature in Russia in May, 2009, at Hebrew University, Leonid Katsis attempted to show Jewish sources for Gershenzon's philosophical views.
37 See V. Proskurina, *Techenie Gol'strema*, 238-83. Scholars may want to consult with M. O. Gershenzon's archive (746) in the Manuscript Division of the Russian National Library in Moscow.
38 N. P. Poltoratzky, "Lev Tolstoy and *Vekhi*, " *Slavonic and East European Review* 42, 99 (1964): 332-52.

Nietzsche was mentioned in the *Correspondence*, Gershenzon denied being his follower. However, Georges Florovsky has criticized Gershenzon for an indifference to religion and religious feeling, seeing in Gershenzon's complaints about culture something closer to a pagan expression of disappointment.[39] Vera Proskurina, a Gershenzon specialist, maintains that he was a modern "gnostic" with a dual worldview comprised of a belief in this and another more perfect world.[40]

I maintain that Gershenzon's idea of a "cosmic" spirituality governs his thought and that his ideas share a few common elements with Slavophilism.[41] In Gershenzon's philosophy, the cosmic force that seeks the unity of all has the paradoxical effect of promoting individuality. Much like the Slavophile concept of *Sobornost'*, "cosmic unity" demands the subordination of the individual and at the same time finds any kind of coercion unacceptable. Such concepts unite the principles of collective holism and individual liberty. For Gershenzon the search for spiritual holism has primary significance, and consequently, each individual should be occupied with removing all impediments to its achievement. Culture is just one impediment, although a powerful one, that must be overcome and transformed.

My criticism of Gershenzon's philosophical views focuses on his naiveté. There is so much left out of Gershenzon's philosophical position that it seems impossible to perceive any practical program. What is the role of society, social institutions, economics, or politics in connection with the cosmic force? Although he might reply that he disdains hierarchies because they interfere with the individual's immediate perception of reality, nonetheless it is not clear what would happen to society if everyone followed his advice. Furthermore, how would tolerance function? Presumably not everyone would want to subordinate his individual will to the group's needs. What would the group do about these misfits? Gershenzon does not deal with these questions and therefore we do not have answers. However, the absence of discussion regarding the consequences of a revolution in perception is likely to worry a questioning critic.

Having been diagnosed with tuberculosis, in 1922, Gershenzon de-

---

39   G. Florovskii, review of *Perepiska iz dvukh uglov*, *Russkaia mysl'* 4 (1922): 138-39.
40   V. Proskurina, introduction to M. Gershenzon, *Pal'myra*, 3-4.
41   Horowitz, "M. O. Gershenzon and Intellectual Life of Russia's Silver Age," 206-30.

cided to take his family to Germany for treatment and there make a final decision whether to return to Soviet Russia or remain in emigration. He had endured severe deprivation during the civil-war years in Moscow, including hunger, cold, and poverty. Although some of the intimate details may never be available, according to his daughter, Nataliia Gershenzon-Chegodaeva, Gershenzon took the advice of his children and decided to return to Russia.[42] He felt that he had an obligation to contribute to shaping Russia's future, at the same time doubting that he could offer much in emigration.[43] It is also significant that at the same time that Viacheslav Ivanov had to leave Russia as a *persona non grata*, Gershenzon's ideas were not hostile to the Soviet state. He was permitted to return in 1923 and moreover, given a position in GAKhN, the Academy of Arts. He died of heart failure two years later at the age of 56.

Gershenzon's side in the *Correspondence* is not unique in Russian cultural history. It echoes a group of texts by authors who bemoan their own position in the elite and articulate a preference for *tabula rasa* or return to nature. In the nineteenth century, one can point to a number of such texts, including Tolstoy's religious writings, Alexander Herzen's *My Past and Thoughts* (*Byloe i dumy*), Vasily Rozanov's *Fallen Leaves* (*Opavshie list'ia*), and Alexander Blok's "The People and Revolution" ("Narod i revolutsiia"). Gershenzon's side in the *Correspondence*, therefore, cleaves to one of the central sentiments of the Russian intelligentsia—a struggle against reigning social norms, a romanticization of ignorance—(e.g. idealization of the Russian peasant)—and a striving for a collective solution (couched in Gershenzon's text as coinciding with the individual's interests). In this sense Gershenzon's side links him to the larger context of Russian philosophy and helps one understand his ideas and intellectual evolution as a specifically Russian event.

---

42 Gershenzon-Chegodaeva, *Pervye shagi zhiznennogo puti*, 185.
43 Ibid., 228-29.

11. Unity and Disunity in *Landmarks* (*Vekhi*): The Rivalry between Pyotr Struve and Mikhail Gershenzon

Since the fall of Communism, the primary texts of nineteenth- and twentieth-century Russian intellectual history have come under intense reinterpretation.[1] Perhaps the most vivid example of renewed interest is *Landmarks* (1909), which had been republished nearly ten times since the fall of Communism.[2] In many ways, the volume's staying power is understandable. A collection of essays criticizing the revolutionary intelligentsia by seven non-Marxist thinkers, Nikolai Berdiaev, Sergei Bulgakov, Mikhail Gershenzon, Bogdan Kistiakovsky, Pyotr Struve, Semyon Frank and Aleksandr Izgoev, *Landmarks* is an ideal anti-Communist guidebook. Intentionally provocative, the authors came together to repudiate the philosophical premises of revolution. Lenin condemned it, the writers were personae non grata in Soviet Russia, and the volume was taken off library shelves and banished to those special holding rooms for dangerous books. In the West it was a favorite text of conservative anti-Soviet pundits. In today's post-Soviet Russia, *Landmarks* is still alive, since, in pursuing primarily negative criticism, the authors left a positive message relatively unstated and thus created an opportunity for contemporary readers to fill in their own positive program.

Looking at the historiography of *Landmarks,* one notes permanent

---

[1] In recent decades the volume has run the intellectual gamut, having been enlisted in defence of Russia democrats, anti-democrats, political conservatives, religious moderates, and Russian Orthodox revivalists. See Modest Kolerov, "Samoanaliz intelligentsii kak politicheskaia filosofiia: nasledstvo i naslednki 'Vekh,'" *Novyi mir* 8 (1994): 160-71. See also Vera Proskurina, *Techenie Gol'strema*, 107-61; Gary Hamburg and Randall Poole, *History of Russian Philosophy 1830-1930: Faith, Reason, and the Defense of Human Dignity* (Cambridge: Cambridge University Press, 2010), 258-52.

[2] *Landmarks* was published in monthly installments in the journal *Literaturnoe obozrenie*, put out as a single volume by the publishing house, Novosti, in 1990, and printed as an anthology with *Iz glubiny* (*Out of the Depths*) from Pravda in 1991. *Landmarks* has also been published in an English translation: *Vekhi — Landmarks: a Collection of Articles about the Russian Intelligentsia*, trans. and ed. Marshall S. Shatz and Judith E. Zimmerman, foreword by Marc Raeff (Armonk: New York: Sharpe, 1994). The introduction to this volume is particularly useful and is strongly recommended.

controversy. The majority of its readers have given it a negative evaluation. In 1909, with the exception of a few outspoken clerics and political centrists, [3] the volume was universally condemned as politically "reactionary," while later, "objective" scholars expressed the unanimous view that *Landmarks* was flawed. The best expression of the view of western scholarship can be found in Richard Pipes' 1980 book, *Struve: Liberal on the Right, 1905-1994*. Professor Pipes writes: "And yet, judged on its literary merits, *Vekhi* is not a good book, and in parts it is a very bad one. Due to the fact that the contributors made no effort to communicate with one another once they had agreed on the book's theme, and that the editor apparently exercised little if any authority, the volume is loosely structured. Its subject matter—the intelligentsia—is nowhere defined."[4]

Professor Pipes' viewpoint, that the book is "loosely structured," that the authors did not consult, and that, in the end, it can be judged a "bad book" contrasts with *Landmarks*' importance at the time it appeared and vitality up to this day as an extraordinarily influential text of Russian intellectual history. To what sources might we attribute the volume's indisputable, but unexpected power? This essay is an attempt to answer this question by looking at the origins of the volume and its cultural context. Especially pertinent in this regard will be an investigation of the personal and intellectual rivalry of Pyotr Struve and Mikhail Gershenzon, since these two individuals together organized the volume and represent the widest intellectual antipathy among the contributors.

---

[3] Archbishop Antonii wrote a positive review, "Otkrytoe pis'mo avtoram sbornika 'Vekhi,'" which was published in *Slovo*, 10 May (1909), and the well-known liberal professor of history A. Kizevetter reacted positively to the volume in "O sbornike 'Vekhi,'" *Russkaia mysl'* 5 (1909). For a thorough examination of the reactions to *Landmarks*, see Gisela Oberlander, "Die Vechi-Diskussion (1909-1912)" (PhD diss., University of Köln, 1965).

[4] Richard Pipes, *Struve: Liberal on the Right, 1905-1944* (Cambridge: Harvard University Press, 1980), 110. Other negative critiques of the structure of *Landmarks* can be found in the work of Jeffrey Brooks who has written, "The authors held seemingly contradictory views about what the intelligentsia was, but in its very vagueness the book presented a compelling image of the intelligent as an archetypical social deviant warped by an unnatural preoccupation with the ills of society" (Jeffrey Brooks, "Vekhi and the Vekhi Dispute," *Soviet Survey* 19 [1973]: 21). Andrzej Walicki in his *Legal Philosophies of Russian Liberalism* explains Kistiakosky's disagreement: "How could Kistiakovsky agree [with Gershenzon's introduction]? He [Kistiakovsky] was a thinker who stressed the importance of 'objective law,' of the 'external forms of community'; he was a theorist of the role-of-law state, namely a supporter of a definite 'principle of political order.' Consequently, his agreement with Gershenzon could only be partial" (374-75).

An examination of its origins is crucial for understanding the volume's composition. According to reliable testimonies, *Landmarks* was Gershenzon's idea, and he gave it form in conversations with Struve.[5] Gershenzon took upon himself the job of editor, and he wrote the introduction. According to several sources, especially Aleksandr Izgoev, once Struve got involved, he took control of the endeavor.[6] This, of course, cannot be totally true, since Gershenzon was the official editor, and the contributors sent their essays to him. But there are convincing grounds for partially accepting this claim. We see the struggle for control over *Landmarks* early, in the way the contributors were chosen.

Thanks to letters from Gershenzon's personal archive in the Russian National Library in Moscow, we now have a pretty clear understanding of how the writers were enlisted.[7] In personal conversations with Semyon Frank, Gershenzon had suggested the participation of Ivanov-Razumnik, Leonid Evgen'evich Gabrilovich, a philosopher and mathematician, Bodgan Kistiakovsky, and Sergei Bulgakov.[8] Accepting Kistiakovsky and Bulgakov, Semyon Frank rejected Ivanov-Razumnik and Gabrilovich, suggesting instead Yuly Aikhenval'd or Arkady Gornfel'd, either of whom could write on the topic of "The Intelligentsia and Aesthetics."[9] Struve invited Aleksandr Izgoev, while Bulgakov tried to enlist Nikolai Lossky, who refused the invitation.[10] Although Aikhenval'd and Gornfel'd's candidacies fizzled out, the fact that Frank and Struve rejected Gershenzon's candidates was significant. By the time of the volume's inception, Frank along with Struve were trying to gather together a cluster of like-minded contributors and move *Landmarks* away from Gershenzon's conception of giving ideological rivals, such as the populist Ivanov-Razumnik, a chance to participate.

The evidence that Struve and Frank were striving for intellectual unity has support in Frank's letters to Gershenzon. In a letter of Octo-

---

5   M. Kolerov, "Arkhivnaia istoriia sbornika 'Vekhi,'" in *Landmarks* (Moscow: Pravda, 1991), 12.
6   A. Izgoev, "O vinovnykh, " *Rossiia* (Paris) 31 (1928): 15; Kolerov, "Arkhivnaia istoriia sbornika 'Vekhi,'" 12.
7   See V. Proskurina and V. Alloy, "K istorii sozdaniia 'Vekh,'" *Minuvshee* 11 (1992): 249-92.
8   Leonid Evgen'evich Gabrilovich (pseud. Galich, 1878-1953), was a physicist and provat-docent at Petersburg University. He was also a writer for the journal *Voprosy filosofii i psikhologii*. Ivanov-Razumnik (real name Razumnik Vasil'evich Ivanov; 1878-1946), critic and literary historian associated with Russian Symbolism.
9   See Frank's letter to Gershenzon, 19 October 1908, *Minuvshee* 11 (1992): 232-53; Kolerov in *Landmarks*, 501.
10 Kolerov in *Landmarks*, 502-3.

ber 19, 1908, Frank describes his hopes for ideological unity, wishing for that reason to remove Ivanov-Razumnik.

> I would imagine that there will be a common introduction for all the contributors, in which the idea of the collection would be expressed, and it would be made clear that, in criticizing the intelligentsia, we are appealing to its moral and spiritual strengths and believe in the possibility of its rebirth. This would be honest and entirely sufficient. In any case it is impossible to entrust an introductory article of this kind to Ivanov-Razumnik, whose participation I consider undesirable—he himself is too much of a "contemporary intelligent," with all the defects of that type [of person].[11]

From the viewpoint of unity, Frank had a valid point. By "contemporary intelligent" Frank meant that Ivanov-Razumnik agreed with the revolutionary intelligentsia and would be antithetical to the viewpoints in *Landmarks*. Indeed, a 1907 article in *Kriticheskoe obozrenie*, the monthly literary journal in which Bogdan Kistiakovsky and Gershenzon were editors and Semyon Frank a contributor, Ivanov-Razumnik declared his appreciation of the 1905 revolution for expanding the breadth of revolutionary activity from politics to the social realm. Ivanov-Razumnik wrote: "…Our revolution is not a narrow class revolution: the peasants, proletariat and intelligentsia must consider it a 'moving force'; the struggle for democracy in the broad sense defines the character of the Russian revolution: this is a people's democratic revolution. The old formula of the People's Will Party appears as the banner of the contemporary revolutionary movement: a democratic revolution arriving at the social through the political."[12]

With such a pro-revolutionary message—praise for the People's Will Party and enthusiasm for the expansion of the revolution—clearly Ivanov-Razumnik was unsuitable for participation in a volume of which the aim was to criticize the revolutionary intelligentsia.

Why then did Gershenzon nominate him? Since Gershenzon was fa-

---

11   S. Frank to M. Gershenzon, 19 October 1908, *Minuvshee* 11 (1992): 252. A more extensive group of Semyon Frank's letters to Gershenzon have been published by M. Kolerov in *de Visu*. 3/4 (1994): 23-33.
12   Ivanov-Razumnik, "Kharakter russkoi revoliutsii," *Kriticheskoe obozrenie* 2 (1907): 16.

miliar with Ivanov-Razumnik's book, *History of Russian Social Thought (Istoriia russkoi obshchestvennoi mysli)* (1907), and had invited him to contribute to *Kriticheskoe obozrenie*'s literary section, ignorance of Ivanov-Razumnik's politics is out of the question.[13] Rather, the creation of a volume with a diversity of opinions was Gershenzon's actual intention. According to the scholar Modest Kolerov, before deciding upon the creation of a separate volume, Gershenzon had hoped to realize the project of criticizing the intelligentsia on the pages of *Kriticheskoe obozrenie*.[14] This being the case, by closely examining *Kriticheskoe obozrenie*, we can begin to understand how Gershenzon conceived of *Landmarks* and why he could nominate a political populist as Ivanov-Razumnik.

Kriticheskoe obozrenie, which ran from 1907 to 1909, was in reality Gershenzon's brainchild, and he managed to sell his idea to his close friend Elizaveta Orlova, who provided funding.[15] Associated officially with the "Commission for the Organization of Home Reading, " *Kriticheskoe obozrenie* had a different aim from that of the traditional thick journal, because it was not governed either by a single ideological viewpoint or by any political party. Instead, it was supposed to be above politics and ideology, offering its readers a wide variety of differing, even contrary viewpoints. The diversity of subjects can be perceived by the list of editors: N. Vinogradov (Philosophy), B. Kistiakovsky (Law), M. Gershenzon (Literature), N. Kol'tsov (Natural Sciences), I. Gold'shtein (Economics) and D. Petrushevsky (History). About the way the journal

---

13   In addition, a personal friendship had arisen between Gershenzon and Ivanov-Razumnik during 1908; see *Minuvshee*, 11, 283, cf. 3.
14   M. Kolerov, "Arkhivnaia istoriia sbornika 'Vekhi, '" *Vestnik Moskovskogo Universiteta* 4, History Series 8 (1991): 11. Professor Kolerov writes, "However the conception of a volume, devoted to an analysis of the ideas and way of life of the Russian intelligentsia did not immediately come to Gershenzon. Before the idea of a separate book was formed, Gershenzon thought to realize the project within the realm of those possibilities which presented themselves—the journal, *Critical Review*..."
15   Elizaveta Orlova, the granddaughter of the Decembrist Mikhail Orlov, was the official editor of *Kritcheskoe obozrenie*. About her relationship with Gershenzon, Alexander Gol'denveizer, Gershenzon's brother-in-law, writes in his unpublished memoirs, "M. O. Gershenzon was very close to Elizaveta Nikolaevna Orlova. Orlova, who was already at that time not a young woman [1901], came from an interesting family. At that time her mother was alive, she lived to be 90 and some years old. Her father was the son of the famous Decembrist Mikhail Orlov, married to Ekaterina Raevskaia, one of the three Raevsky sisters. In Elizaveta Nikolaevna Orlova, the granddaughter of Mikhail Orlov's hands were the extremely valuable archival materials about the Orlov, Raevsky families, the Decembrist Kritsov, etc. ... Thanks to his closeness with Orlova, Mikhail Osipovich used these materials widely in his works" (A. Gol'denveizer, "Unpublished Memoirs, " in the Museum of Aleksandr Gol'denveizer, Moscow).

was viewed by contributors we have the testimony of Nikolai Berdiaev, who wrote in a private letter to Gershenzon from 1908, "... I suppose that the journal in principle stands on the basis of tolerance and allows the expression of various opinions, among those my own."[16]

Although the names of Vinogradov, Kistiakovsky, Petrushevsky and Gold'shtein, all employed in universities, show the academic bent of the journal, the contributors included major writers, poets, historians, philosophers, and scientists, such as A. Bely, V. Briusov, G. Shpet, A. Veselovsky, V. Ivanov, M. Lemke, S. Frank, and A. Speransky. Taken as a whole, the journal points to the enormous diversity in Russian intellectual life at the time, reflecting the growing maturity of a part of Russia's readership. To a certain degree, it also shows a measure of intellectual tolerance among writers, since contributors found themselves appearing on the same page with ideological rivals. Had *Kriticheskoe obozrenie* been the vehicle for the criticism of the revolutionary intelligentsia, one would probably have found far more diverse opinions and greater tolerance among the authors, who would not have expected ideological unanimity from the very start.

That, however, did not come to pass. Instead *Landmarks*, probably under Struve's increased direction, became transformed into a narrower project, that of disparaging the revolutionary intelligentsia from a far more consistent philosophical perspective. Except for Gershenzon, all the writers shared a similar intellectual evolution and, relatively speaking, a unified political viewpoint. They had all been Marxists who had abandoned Social Democracy in favor of Constitutional Democracy. And except for the younger Izgoev, they had all contributed to *Problems of Idealism* (*Problemy idealizma*, 1903), and had all participated in Struve's other major publications: *Polar Star, Freedom and Culture,* and *Russian Thought*.[17] Struve's biographer, Richard Pipes, affirms that "they constituted something akin to a party of 'Struvists.'"[18]

The polemics between Struve and Gershenzon which exploded following the volume's appearance deserve full examination, since they offer an inimitable source for understanding both writers' intentions in creating *Landmarks*. Struve's intention that the volume present

---

16 N. Berdiaev to M. Gershenzon from 1908 (no exact date listed), Gershenzon letters located in the Russian National Library, Moscow, Russia (746-26-8).
17 Pipes, *Struve: Liberal on the Right*, 107.
18 Ibid., 108.

a unified message can be seen in his published responses to external criticism.[19] For example, in response to Dmitry Merezhkovsky's public talk in St. Petersburg, [20] Struve voiced his differences with Gershenzon. In the April 25, 1909 issue of the newspaper *Slovo*, Struve showed little tolerance for Gershenzon, characterizing the latter's ideas as "empty intellectualizing" and "historically invalid."[21] Comparing Gershenzon's "Creative-Self-Knowledge" with the other essays, Struve claimed that, while sharing a common orientation with Bulgakov's article, it was alien to the other five.[22] Although he continued to defend the volume's "single unity" (edinstvo), Struve rebutted Gershenzon's view of a "mystical role for the peasantry." Moreover, linking Gershenzon with intellectual rivals, Alexander Blok, Merezhkovsky, and Dmitry Filosofov, Struve blamed Gershenzon's attitudes on literary fashion and a lack of direct knowledge about the Russian folk. "The trace of something lifeless, far-fetched weighs upon [Alexander] Blok and Gershenzon's 'Slavofilism.' It is fiction. In general, in its content Slavophilism has become to a great degree exactly fiction."[23]

In "Creative Self-Consciousness, " we recall, Gershenzon had claimed that the Russian "intelligent" had become a psychological cripple as a result of a split between consciousness and will. The intellectual's neglect of his will, i.e. his emotional self, and his enslavement to logical reason had made him weak individually and ineffective in his work with others—i.e. in making the 1905 revolution. Moreover, the intelligentsia's atheistic attitudes alienated the folk and even caused the

---

19 Years later in 1956, Semyon Frank, mimicking Struve's criticisms, blamed Gershenzon for the volume's internal weakness. In *P. B. Struve: biografiia*, Frank claims that "... the possibility that the basic core of the participants of *Landmarks* cooperated with their initiator Gershenzon was conditioned by the fact that Gershenzon—in general a bizarre and capricious person—decided not to acquaint any of us with the articles of the other contributors before publication in the interests of independence concerning the separate contributor's judgments, so that each of us became acquainted with the content of *Landmarks* only after its publication; there was no prior editorial agreement or exchange of ideas" ([New York: Chekhov, 1956], 82). Frank's testimony is seriously undermined by recent evidence that at least the Petersburg participants were familiar with all the essays before publication. See Kolerov, "Arkhivnaia istoriia sbornika 'Vekhi, '" 14.
20 Merezhkovsky's lecture was published in *Rech'*, April 26, 1909, with the title, "Sem' smirennykh." In that article Merezhkovsky accused the authors of embodying several of the qualities of the intelligentsia that they rebuked; for example, the inclination toward messianism.
21 P. Struve, "Razmyshlenie, " *Slovo* April 15 (1909): 5; the article was republished in *Patriotica* (St. Petersburg, 1911), 228-32.
22 Ibid.
23 Ibid.

paradoxical situation in which the intelligentsia was fighting against the government in the name of the peasants, but actually needed the government's protection from the peasants' wrath.[24]

Against those ideas Struve shook his fist, passionately arguing that the most notable feature of the period from 1904-1909 was the closing of the abyss separating the intelligentsia from the folk and the attainment of their solidarity. Using as his proof the revolutionaries' success in mobilizing the growing proletariat and peasants for political action, Struve claimed that the government was protecting only itself and the proprietied classes. The people and the revolutionaries had formed a strong bond.

Struve's disagreement with Gershenzon was more substantive, however, than just political commentary; it touched upon both their overall conceptions of the "intelligentsia," a word overused and underdefined in *Landmarks*. While Struve meant the revolutionary elite that had its origins in the 1840s, Gershenzon had in mind every thinking person or Kopfarbeiter.[25] According to Struve's definition, the peasants were in collusion with the revolutionaries, while Gershenzon's intelligentsia, finding its origins in the reforms of Peter the Great, was historically severed from the people.

With these different definitions of the intelligentsia, a direct conflict arose over the diagnosis of intelligentsia's ills and means for its reconstruction. For example, although both Gershenzon and Struve use the terms "personal growth" and "creativity," they meant different

---

24   Gershenzon's original formulation ran as follows, "Whatever we are, it is not only impossible to think of merging with the folk, [but] we should fear it worse than all the executions of the authorities and bless those authorities who alone with their bayonets and prisons still protect us from the people's wrath." "Tvorcheskoe samosoznanie," 90, translation by Alfred Levin, quoted in A. Levin, "The Life and Work of Mikhail Osipovich Gershenzon (1869-1925): A Study in the History of the Russian Silver Age" (PhD diss. University of California, Berkeley, 1968), 156. This remark caused an outcry in the leftist press and in the second edition Gershenzon thought it better to place an explanatory footnote as to its meaning. He added the following: "The sentence was joyfully seized upon by newspaper critics as a public confession of love for bayonets and prisons. I do not love bayonets and I will never summon anyone to bless them; on the contrary, I see the Nemesis in them. The meaning of my sentence is that by [virtue of] its entire past the intelligentsia is [now] placed in an unprecedented, terrible situation: the folk, for whom it has struggled, despises it, and the authorities, against whom it has struggled, are turning out to be its defender, whether it likes it or not. 'Should' in my sentence means 'is fated': we, with our own hands, without realizing it ourselves, have woven this tie between ourselves and the authorities—here is the horror, and to it I am alluding" (*Vekhi*, 90, trans. by A. Levin, 168).
25   This paragraph is based on research by A. Levin in "The Life and Work of Mikhail Osipovich Gershenzon," 18.

things by them. For Gershenzon, the intelligent's main problem was his reliance on rational intellect. The solution for the intelligentsia in Gershenzon's view was to base consciousness upon will, subduing rational intellect in favor of religious feeling.[26] In contrast, Struve did not repudiate intellect. On the contrary, he considered rational intellect a guiding force for the individual, part of a group of elements, including ethical conscience and religious feeling, which must be actively cultivated, modified, and improved.

For Struve, the main problem of the intelligentsia was its uncompromising revolutionary ethos, which placed the goal of the revolution above all other goods. Characterized by "disassociation from society" and "hostility to the state," the intelligentsia had shown itself useless in building positive institutions or educating the people. Far from reality, the intelligentsia preferred merely to "tack its short, bookish slogans" onto the people's inchoate rumblings and, therefore, the revolution of 1905 was bound to fail, since, "when the hum subsided, the slogans were left hanging in midair."[27] The solution to the intelligentsia's ills, according to Struve, lay in education and cultural development. For this to occur, however, the intelligentsia had to change its political attitude and embrace other goals besides revolution. "On the one hand, politics will cease to be an isolated sphere, independent of all other aspects of spiritual life, as it has been hitherto. For it too will be based on the idea of a person's inner improvement rather than the external arrangement of society. And, on the other hand, the domination of politics over all the non-political aspects of spiritual life must come to an end."[28]

It is understandable why Gershenzon's article had angered Struve. Beyond differences over conceptions of the intelligentsia, Gershenzon had rejected the Westernizers' premise that consciousness or reason should direct will, that intellect must dominate feeling. For Struve this was unacceptable. He could not tolerate an attack on the neo-Kantian epistemology that served as the basis of Russian liberalism and philo-

---

26   In "Creative Self-Consciousness," Gershenzon writes, "When consciousness is turned inward, when it works upon the individual, here it, in constant contact with the irrational elements of the spirit, ceaselessly circulates with the world's essence, since through all the individual wills circulates the single cosmic will; and therefore it is necessarily mystical, i.e., religious, and now erudition will convince consciousness of the opposite: it knows infinity through spontaneous knowledge and this knowledge becomes its second nature, the unchanging method of all activity ..." (Vekhi, 82).
27   P. Struve, "Intelligent i revoliutsiia," in Vekhi (Moscow, 1991), 160.
28   Ibid., 163-164.

sophical idealism, nor would he accept Gershenzon's implicit populism which located moral superiority in the unassuming and unspoiled Russian peasant.[29]

To appreciate Struve's disagreements with Gershenzon at this time, we turn to his review of *Historical Sketches* (1910), Gershenzon's monograph on the Slavophiles.[30] By viewing this polemic—Gershenzon's response and Struve's answer were published together—we can fully realize the intellectual antagonisms lodged just under the surface of *Landmarks*. Struve was up front about his critical emphasis: "... The main interest of *Historical Sketches* is not in its historical content." The book is flawed, he wrote, since "the author wants to be more than a historiographer, he wants to be the philosopher-judge of our intellectual past and present. In concert with this [desire], he offers his own philosophy, artfully weaving it into the historical character of the spiritual development of Russia's educated class. But he does not simply present the teachers of Slavophilism, but expounds their ideas, as dear and cherished ideas for himself, which he shares with his entire being."[31]

To disclose the philosophical fallacies of Gershenzon's worldview, Struve focused on the epistemological premises of Gershenzon's cosmic religion. As Gershenzon explained in *Historical Sketches*, religious experience had its source in "cosmic feeling, " the perception by the individual of his unity with the whole of the universe.[32] Instead of basing his observation on experience, however, Gershenzon posited a "scientific law, " on which "all great world religions are based; it is contained fully in the New Testament Bible."[33] This law, he claimed, had three axioms. The first stated that in each person there is a "core of sensation and will—the essence of individuality and the vehicle of his holism, which powerfully directs his entire psychic life, including his personal consciousness."[34] Unconscious will, present in all of us, is part and parcel of the single, universal will, so that "through all the indi-

---

29 R. Pipes describes how Struve's conception of Western culture conforms with Immanuel Kant's. See *Struve: Liberal on the Right*, 86.
30 *Historical Sketches* (*Istoricheskie zapiski*) actually came out in print in late 1909, which explains the appearance of P. Struve's review in the December issue of *Russian Thought* (*Russkaia mysl'*).
31 P. Struve, review of *Istoricheskie zapiski* by M. Gershenzon, *Russkaia mysl'* 12 (1909) (republished in *Patriotica: sbornik statei za piat' let. 1905-1910*, 470).
32 M. Gershenzon, *Istoricheskie zapiski* (St. Petersburg: 1910), 94.
33 M. Gershenzon, "Otvet P. B. Struve, " *Russkaia mysl'* 2 (1910): 177.
34 Ibid.

vidual wills a single cosmic will circulates."[35] The second rule is that "our consciousness, rooted in unconscious will through all of its roots (*korniami koreniascheesia*) is in essence cosmic." By this, Gershenzon means that all the premises and categories of our consciousness emerge from our condition as representatives of cosmic holism. Finally, Gershenzon claimed that the sole correct way to live is to conform one's spirit and consciousness to the imperatives of the cosmic religion. This meant, above all, that one must modulate self-consciousness so that it reflects the idea of the "religious self-definition of the individual"—the understanding that the person is "one with all."[36] These axioms, Gershenzon continues, are fixed and represent a "scientific law of the human spirit, similar to those laws of material life, which Newton, Kepler, and Galileo have formulated."[37]

While not disagreeing that mystical feeling exists, Struve drew vastly different conclusions about its meaning. Attacking Gershenzon's religious philosophy as a form of "pantheism, " he noted its "abstract" quality; it neither treats religion as a social institution or set of socially conditioned rituals and beliefs, nor considers God or history as determining categories. Moreover, according to Struve, Gershenzon is a hidden rationalist. "Cosmic metaphysics, " he argued, actually destroys religious feeling, since by working as an iron-clad law, revealing how and why each person is connected to the force in the universe, it ultimately rationalizes religious feeling and takes something essentially transcendental and personal, i.e., religious experience, making it terrestrial and impersonal.[38]

In addition, Struve wondered about the social consequences of a cosmic religion. He doubted Gershenzon's unspoken premise that the positive release from reason necessarily leads to ethical behavior. "... Can the cosmic order or higher [spiritual] reason be expressed directly in moral law? Or, using a pretentious philosophical term, can the moral law be considered in line with the cosmic order?"[39] Assured that it could not and convinced that the rational aspects of cosmic religion made it unlike the irrational mysticism of Russian Orthodoxy, Struve asserted

---

35 Ibid.
36 Ibid.
37 Ibid.
38 Struve, rev. of *Istoricheskie zapiski*, 471.
39 Ibid., 474.

that Gershenzon was far from the Slavophiles, who "considered the Russian people righteous for being the carrier of Russian Orthodoxy," and from Tolstoy, who saw in the people "the carrier of God's truth and social justice." Rather, Gershenzon "found in it the carrier of cosmic feeling."[40] Repeating his criticism of "Creative Self-Consciousness," Struve held that, as a result of his religious philosophy, Gershenzon arrived at a mistaken view of the Russian people. "This characterization of the people is the most general, the most abstract, the most lifeless, the most murky of all the folk-adoring (*narodopoklonnicheskie*) characterizations."[41]

The reason Struve attacked Gershenzon has its explanation in Struve's political thinking around 1910. Rejecting any modernized version of Slavophilism, which he thought especially dangerous due to its romantic attractions, Struve thought Russia had entered a new era in which neither purely Slavophile nor Westernizer doctrines could be effective antidotes to the country's persistent political problems. The solution was not to borrow concepts from the West or to revive Russian national models, but rather to end dictates from above completely. Viewing the individual himself as the object of self-improvement, he called for the development of individual creativity, religious sensitivity and moral responsibility. The path toward achieving these goals, he claimed in *Landmarks*, is through "education" (*vospitanie*), which he described this way:

> We understand education completely in contrast to the idea of "organizing" the social environment and its pedagogical effect on the individual. This is the "socialist" idea of education, which has nothing in common with the idea of education in the religious sense. Education in this sense is completely foreign to socialist optimism. It believes not in organization, but only in creativity, in the positive work of the individual on his own self [perfection], in the struggle within himself in the name of creative tasks.[42]

---

40   Ibid., 480.
41   Ibid.
42   Struve, "Intelligent i revoliutsiia," 164.

Although Struve did not advocate any particular political party or political system in *Landmarks*, one recalls from his speeches in the second Duma and his other writings from the period that he envisioned a liberal monarchy in which political life would be governed democratically with representatives from the State Duma holding more legislative power than the tsar. In addition, he considered the Constitutional Democratic Party the best vehicle for the achievement of a free civil society.[43] In comparison, although we do not know Gershenzon's concrete political preference at this time, his radical, pro-Communist views in 1917 appear as a consistent result of the utopian strivings expressed in his cosmic religion.[44]

The intellectual polemics emerging in *Historical Sketches* point to differences that also appeared in *Landmarks*. Gershenzon's apolitical religiosity has definite ideological similarities with Bulgakov's position in his article, "Heroism and the Heroic" ("*Geroizm i podvizhnichestvo*") and, to a lesser degree, Berdiaev's "Philosophical Truth and Intelligentsia Truth" ("*Filosofskaia Pravda i intelligentnaia pravda*"). In those articles, as in Gershenzon's, the utopian drives of the intelligentsia did not come under assault, only the intelligentsia's mistaken aim. Instead of revolution, the authors wanted to direct the intelligentsia's intense passion toward the goal of religious perfection and social rebuilding. In contrast, Struve's focus on ethical responsibility and his critique of Russia's concrete political situation link his essay to those of the other contributors, S. Frank, B. Kistiakovsky and A. Izgoev. These individuals framed their questions in terms more in tune with contemporary Russian life, treating the political, legal, economic, and sexual consequences of the intelligentsia's uncompromising attitude toward revolution.

If the articles in *Landmarks*, as many have noted, contradict each other in a variety of ways, we might wonder why Struve was surprised at finding internal conflict. Again an examination of the relations of Struve and Gershenzon proves illuminating. By 1908 Gershenzon was

---

43 See Struve's writings on political issues and economic problems during 1908 and 1909; for example, "Razmyshleniia na politicheskie temy" (1908), "Kleveta na predkov i na konstitusiiu" (1908) and "Obshchee politicheskoe polozhenie: A. I. Guchkov i P. A. Stolypin" (1909). Struve's bibliography can be found in R. Pipes, *Struve: Liberal on the Right*, 470-508.

44 Gershenzon quickly grew cold to Bolshevism after 1917. For a discussion of Gershenzon's political views in 1917, see chapter 7 in this volume and also "The End of a Friendship: the Philosophical Rift Between N. A. Berdiaev and M. O. Gershenzon, " *Empire Jews: Jewish Nationalism and Acculturation in 19th- and Early 20th-Century Russia* (Bloomington: Slavica, 2009), 197-216.

a well-known historian who had published one book, *The History of Young Russia*, and many articles on Russian intellectual history. Furthermore, Gershenzon was a regular reviewer for the liberal journal *Vestnik Evropy*. More importantly, Struve knew Gershenzon well from earlier days. They had already collided in 1903, when Gershenzon had written a contentious letter to the editor against the ideological direction of Struve's illegal journal, *Osvobozhdenie* (*Liberation*), published in Geneva, and Struve had published the letter and his response to it in the first issue of that year.

In his 1903 "Letter from the Shores of Lake Geneva," Gershenzon, echoing Jean Jacques Rousseau, stood up for the laws of morality against the laws of politics. In much the same way as he later argued in *Landmarks*, Gershenzon complained that, in their quest to realize political goals, revolutionaries often sinned against moral norms that they would in any other case consider as absolute and inviolable. Furthermore, he claimed that there was a whole domain of morality outside the political sphere; the morality of people in their relations with others and within themselves. The government cannot take this internal freedom away from individuals. Finally, he declared that the *intelligenty* were hypocrites who lived a lie, since, while struggling for the liberation of the peasants, they did not renounce using servants and domestic help from the lower classes.[45]

Struve struck at Gershenzon mercilessly. Calling him a Tolstoyan and an ethical maximalist, Struve exclaimed that in Gershenzon's moral arguments "a great lie was hidden, which lazy minds and sleepy souls would always accept and which therefore sophists and apologists of force use with great ease."[46] Russian society, Struve maintained, needs true freedom, not illusions, and it will not have real freedom until it rids itself of the yoke of autocracy. Moreover, Struve claimed that the yearning for political freedom is not autonomous or separate from internal freedom, but comes out of an entire moral and religious worldview. He writes, "Outside of and without political freedom we cannot 'live by conscience' otherwise than in a ceaseless and irrecon-

---

[45] M. Gershenzon, "Pis'mo s beregov Zhenevskogo ozera," *Osvobozhdenie* (Stuttgart), 1-2 (1903-1904): 227.

[46] P. Struve, "Pis'mo s beregov Zhenevskogo ozera i otvet na nego redaktora 'Osvobozhdeniia,'" *Osvobozhdenie* (Stuttgart), 1-2 (1903-1904): 234.

cilable struggle with the state-ruler."[47]

Considering Struve's position in 1903, his unconditional adherence to political change as the basis for personal and social improvement in Russia, I think it is fair to say that by 1909 Struve had come closer to Gershenzon. Having come to regret the policy of "no enemies on the left," Struve was no longer convinced that political solutions automatically resolve the problems of social life or that the autonomous realms of truth and beauty should be sacrificed to political considerations. Nevertheless, knowing Gershenzon and having already been at swords' points with him, Struve was probably foolish to expect that the two would reach agreement in 1909. In fact, Gershenzon had changed little, his articles showed no repudiation of his adherence to Tolstoyanism and religious populism. Why then did Struve get involved with Gershenzon in an endeavor as important as *Landmarks*?

It seems to me that Struve, having wrested the choice of contributors from Gershenzon's control, was probably convinced that the final product would reflect his conception. What occurred, however, was something very different. Partially influenced by Struve and partially by Gershenzon, *Landmarks* was supposed to be a unified project, while in fact the essays were only marginally linked together. Sundered by internal contradictions and yet intending to offer a coherent message, *Landmarks* was neither a forum for intellectual sharing and mutual tolerance, nor a harmonious choir of unanimity. With two fathers it came out as best it could: it ended up as a biting negative critique, a response, a "symptom," as Georges Florovsky famously put it.

Landmarks was a symptom, but it was not just a sign of conflict in the Russian intelligentsia, one part still locked in a dead-end revolutionary mentality, the other moving forward toward a more balanced acceptance of the state. By arguing against the politicization of Russian thought, the authors of *Landmarks* were edging closer to the view that philosophy deserves its own disciplinary space independent of current affairs. Although the writers themselves could not achieve this goal, their complaints were indicative of a general trend in Russian thought before the 1917 Revolution.[48]

---

47   Ibid., 238.
48   One can consult Randal Poole's excellent articles for the confirmation of this idea. See also Andrzej Walicki's *Legal Philosophies of Russian Liberalism*.

Since *Landmarks* veered away from Struve's conception of unity, scholars have been quick to call it a failure. But is that really a fair evaluation? If we change our focus and measure success in terms of the reaction to it, the turmoil it created, and its publicity value, we might claim that *Landmarks* performed extremely well. We recall that it incited over 250 periodical articles in the first year alone, as well as numerous conferences and countless reviews and newspaper accounts.[49] Pavel Miliukov went on a lecture tour to repudiate it.[50] Even Lev Tolstoy bought a copy and wrote a review.[51] Furthermore, the volume went through five editions within the year and in the end sold over 15, 000 copies. To what can we attribute this marketing success?

I believe the lack of unity, rather than just a hindrance, was a vital factor in the volume's success. Without a central plan, the impression of genuine, heart-felt criticism was transmitted, as each contributor spoke not for any group, but about his own individual experience. Furthermore, the lack of unity revealed the extent of the fissure within the intelligentsia itself. This was not merely a unified group of dissidents or a single enemy. No, with a measure of ideological diversity, the contributors hit from different sides and the attack was therefore all the more surprising, damaging and sustained. Had the volume appeared without all its supposed flaws, could it have done more than it did? I think we can now agree that the volume found strength in its flaws and enjoyed such popularity not in spite of, but because of its internal contradictions.

---

49   For a list of reviews written during the first year after publication, see the appendix in the fifth edition of *Landmarks* (Moscow, 1910).
50   For more on Miliukov and *Landmarks*, see Nicholas Zernov, *The Russian Religious Renaissance of the Twentieth Century* (London: 1963), 126-31.
51   For more on Lev Tolstoy's attitude toward *Landmarks*, see "Lev Tolstoy and 'Vekhi,'" *Slavonic and East European Review* 42, no. 99 (June 1964): 332-52.

12. M. O. Gershenzon and Georges Florovsky: Metaphysical Philosophers of Russian History[1]

There are significant parallels in the historical approaches of M. O. Gershenzon and Georges Florovsky. They share a sensitivity to the metaphysical content of history and a marked respect for the religious truths contained in Russian culture. But the philosophical differences between them are numerous. They disagree about the purpose of history, the goal of the historian, and the meaning of the Russian intellectual tradition. Besides, they belong to two different generations: Gershenzon was a Silver-Age idealist thinker and a Jew by birth, whereas Florovsky was an Orthodox theologian who reached intellectual maturity in emigration. Gershenzon sought in Russian culture a universal idea, not associated with any institution, which he thought suitable for all time and all places. Florovsky, however, approached his studies from an Orthodox-Christian perspective. Therefore, while sharing a common attitude toward the past as a source for edification about the present, they are completely different with opposing worldviews, and their historical work reflects these differences.

Intellectual history in the modern sense used by Wilhelm Dilthey came late to Russia. Silver-Age historians and religious philosophers just before World War One were its first major practitioners. Earlier in the nineteenth century, Russian historians considered their subject devoid of disciplinary boundaries. The study of the past straddled the lines between social thought, political science, literary investigation, and ethnography. Furthermore, political motivations often underlay the study of intellectuals and the treatment of their ideas. However, *fin de siecle* with its modernism in literature and anti-positivism in various branches of science changed the focus of historical studies. To a large extent the practice of intellectual history became entwined in the search for spiritual values characteristic of Russia's Silver Age culture (1890-1920). This is explained in large part by the religious orientations of the practicing writers.

---

1   Georges Florovsky (1893-1979).

The development of intellectual history in Russia had as its basis a new attitude toward the individual set forth by Vladimir Solov'ev, and in his wake Symbolist writers, who questioned the positivist confidence in reason and rationality. They asserted that the individual belonged both to this world and the world beyond, and thus was capable of understanding far more than the knowledge gained from his reason or senses. Moreover, Solov'ev set forth a new anthropology, giving the individual a primary role in the fate of the universe. If a person in positivist systems was the sole arbitor of the world, then Solov'ev deified him, giving him a religious, world-historical dimension. Solov'ev's God-Man brought new tasks to the individual; each person became a hero of the spirit, whose life and will was inextricably connected with the most profound religious and historical issues facing humanity—salvation and eschatology.

The Symbolists produced a similar transformation in consciousness. Insisting that an unexplored world of the spirit existed, the Symbolists maintained that the poet served as a conduit by which this supra-rational world could be perceived. Just as his texts were filled with correspondences serving as a door into the other world, so too the poet's life was an artistic text of sacral meaning. Through the raising of the poet from a mere person to a messenger of the other world, the artist (intellectual) became a focal point for investigations of religious temperament.

These new attitudes were quickly applied to the historical sciences. With the help of Wilhelm Dilthey's concept of *Geistesgeschichte*, Mikhail Gershenzon and other Silver Age historians involved themselves with an examination of intellectuals in their concrete and unrepeatable historical contexts. This approach was similar to historicism as it was practiced in the West—the search to discover the "spirit" of an age so as to understand the hero from within the codes of his own time—except that the Silver Age philosophers were less rigorous, often relying on their own metaphysical-religious presumptions and applying them to their subject of inquiry. It is significant, for instance, that those engaged in these historical studies were foremostly religious philosophers.[2] Under

---

2   I am referring to D. Merezhkovsky, Iu. Aikhenval'd, A. Volynsky, N. Berdiaev, N. and S. Trubetskoi. There were of course, political historians and historians of literature who disparaged the religious approach, but I am concerning myself with historians and philosophers sympathetic to religion, such as members of the Petersburg Psychological Society and the Moscow Philosophical Society. See Randal Allan Poole, *Problems of Idealism: Essays in Russian Social Philosophy* (New Haven: Yale University Press, 2003).

the influence of the ideas of Henri Bergson and William James, many thinkers sought to show the universality, but also the subjectivity of religion and faith, making no distinction, however, between a hero's faith in nature, the cosmos, or a Christian God.

***

My decision to examine Gershenzon and Florovsky together arose because Florovsky wrote two articles about Gershenzon: a 1922 review of the *Correspondence from Two Corners* (1921) which Gershenzon co-authored with Viacheslav Ivanov, and a long essay devoted to Gershenzon's oeuvre in 1926, just after the latter's death.[3] In addition, Gershenzon is mentioned many times in *The Ways of Russian Theology* (*Puti russkogo bogosloviia*) albeit primarily as an opponent.[4]

According to Marc Raeff, the basic premises underlying Florovsky's historical methodology can be attributed to Gershenzon, who influenced Florovsky in three aspects. Raeff writes:

> In the first place, a thinker's intellectual make-up and development have a single spiritual source which provides a basic unity, as well as explanation, for his life work. ...Secondly, this task is best accomplished through empathy, *Einfuhlung*, for even rational thoughts and concepts do not come naked, but in an existential matrix that the historian must try to perceive and understand. ...Third and last, an individual's intellectual and spiritual life is to be understood only within the wider context of his cultural milieu, that is mainly from his spiritual and aesthetic ambiance.[5]

From these premises, Gershenzon, and later Florovsky, developed a historical method which permitted them to penetrate the individual's

---

3   Georges Florovsky, "V mire iskanii i bluzhdanii, " *Russkaia mysl'* 4 (1922): 129-42. Georges Florovsky, "Michael Gerschensohn, " *Slavonic Review* 5, no. 14 (1926): 315-31.
4   Gershenzon appears on pages 235, 245, 253, 266, 458, 491, 537, 546-49, 551, 563, 567 of the Russian fourth edition of the *Puti* (Paris: YMCA Press, 1988).
5   Marc Raeff, "Enticements and Rifts: Georges Florovsky as Historian of the Life of the Mind and the Life of the Church in Russia, " *Modern Greek Studies Yearbook* 6 (1990): 211.

psyche and gain an understanding of the many-sided self in its complex unity; it enabled them to detect the emotional core of the individual's religious strivings and to perceive the cultural context in which his spiritual accomplishments take place. To achieve these aims, Gershenzon and Florovsky had to be as much philosophers as historians.

Their idea of history is not indifferent to subjective evaluation. In fact, both historians purposely shape their historical explorations to show the inherent superiority of some ideas over others. Moreover, a philosophical dialogue between the present and the past is a strong component of both their work. Despite their common methods, each applied his own quite different metaphysical views to his historical research.

Gershenzon did not investigate the past merely in order to understand, rather he was attracted to the religious questions that Russian intellectuals of the nineteenth century asked and the solutions they offered; in their experience Gershenzon found a universal religious truth which he called the "cosmic unity."[6] Cosmic unity is a pantheism of sorts based on the premise that the whole universe, including humans, comes from a single source and is therefore eternally bound in total unity. This belief in unity, Gershenzon claims, is religious at its base, since it satisfies the religious needs of the individual; it resolves the mystery of the individual's relationship with the cosmos.[7] Stranger even than Gershenzon's cosmic theory is the fact that Gershenzon thought he had derived his ideas from the Slavophiles and, in particular, Ivan Kireevsky. Gershenzon claims that Kireevsky taught that reason, if permitted, will overrun man's other psychic forces and dominate his being. In this case, the individual becomes unhealthy psychologically and physically. The individual's best psychic state—inner holism—is achieved when reason is subordinated to the total of the individual's psyche, when reason is aligned and in balance with his intuition, faith, experience, and feelings. From Kireevsky's original ideas, however, Gershenzon retained the psychological aspects—the ways these ideas motivate individuals—using them to support his idiosyncratic theory of the cosmos.[8]

Gershenzon's search for a universal spirituality can be explained in part by his affiliation with the Silver-Age culture and in part by his back-

---

[6] For more about Gershenzon's idea of "cosmic unity," see his article, "Otvet P. V. Struve," 177.
[7] Vera Proskurina calls these ideas a "gnostic myth." See V. Proskurina, *Techenie Gol'strema*, 59-106.
[8] See chapter 3 of this book, "M. O. Gershenzon — Metaphysical Historian of Russia's Silver Age: Part 2."

ground. The Nietzschean drive to overturn all values was a conspicuous feature of the cultural life of the time. Writers and even historians took the opportunity to re-evaluate the Russian philosophical tradition for their own contemporary needs. As a Jew who never converted, Gershenzon needed to find a common culture in which he could believe without denying Judaism. Gershenzon "de-Christianized" his Russian heroes so that they could serve as the embodiment of universal values capable of appreciation by non-Russians, such as Gershenzon himself.

Florovsky-the-historian was also motivated by a metaphysical urge: the creative recovery of the past for use in the solution to the problems of the present.[9] Florovsky viewed history as a part of the present's intellectual inheritance by virtue of the Christian experience. He thought that all people are participants in the reality of terrestrial time to which the ultimate Christian purpose is attached. Here in life free individuals struggle to realize religious goals. The attempt to grasp religious accomplishment in the past made Florovsky sensitive to the role of the historian as a creative participant in the present. Florovsky outlines the historian's connection with the past in his 1926 article, "The Metaphysical Premises of Utopianism," writing: "Knowledge as a historical task is created by the combined and joined efforts of changing and successive generations, it is an accomplishment. This is a tragic struggle for experience, for the correct experience, the 'experience of truth.' Worldviews do not become dragged into one and a single evolutionary path. They have a polyphiletic nature."[10]

With this view of a free and imaginative continuity between the historian and the past, Florovsky fashioned a palpable closeness between his perspective and the experience of the early Greek fathers, the Russian theologians, and secular religious philosophers, especially those of nineteenth-century Russia. Of particular relevance are Florovsky's views of Russian thinkers of the nineteenth century, since these views best illustrate his differences with Gershenzon.

Florovsky found in select secular Russian thinkers predecessors who serve as partners of a sort in the spiritual heroism he endorses. Such individuals voice Florovsky's own metaphysical preoccupations, they

---

9   A fine study is by Andrew Blane, *Georges Florovsky: Russian Intellectual and Orthodox Churchman* (Crestwood, NY: St. Vladimir's Seminary Press), 1993.
10   G. Florovsky, "Metafizicheskie predposylki utopisma, " *Put'* 4 (June-July 1926): 30.

aid him in the creation of his judgments and call attention to the correct solutions to the problems of contemporary life. All the examples that follow come from articles written in the 1920s, during Florovsky's Eurasian period, when he concerned himself with the problems of the nineteenth-century Russian intelligentsia.

In his theoretical article, "The Purpose of History and the Purpose of Life" (1921), Florovsky allows Alexander Herzen to express views the historian himself embraces. Florovsky rejected utopian thinking, i.e. thinking which posits either a predetermined course or conscribed evolution to history, claiming that such thinking eliminates the value of human freedom and risk. Alexander Herzen expresses Florovsky's negative view of intellectual determinism:

> Herzen perceives in Hegelianism, in this new "scholasticism of the Protestant world, " a "Buddhist stagnation"; he sharply grasped that in such systems of individualism the authentic concept of personality was lost and replaced by surrogates; the personality is considered not a thing apart, not as an inimitable monad, but as a "carrier of the idea, " as an embodiment of "common" concepts....[11]

We might have thought that the ideas put forth were Florovsky's own, if we had not been told they were Herzen's. Herzen here serves as a sympathetic predecessor, a like thinker, who is compared to a "seed which matures not only for judgment, but for all eternity, " as Florovsky describes his predecessors.[12] The individual does not have to be Orthodox to contribute to humanity's synthesis. In the past there are concrete examples of eternal moral and metaphysical accomplishments that can aid us in our own religious struggles.

In a similar fashion Florovsky built upon Fedor Dostoevsky's psychological insights in his 1930 article, "The Deadend of the Romantic" ("Die Sackgassen der Romantik"), Tracing the development of Russian thought from Herzen to Dostoevsky, Florovsky shows how romantic aesthetics needed to be overcome. In Florovsky's view, Dostoevsky man-

---

11 G. Florovsky, "Smysl istory i smysl zhizni, " *Russkaia mysl'* (Sofia) (Aug.-Sept. 1921): 179-80.
12 G. Florovsky, "Christianity and Culture, " in *The Collected Works of Georges Florovsky* (Belmont, MA: Nordland, 1974), 2:64.

aged to "break through" the logical insularity of romanticism by basing his conception of human psychology on Christian principles. Florovsky explains Dostoevsky's view of the nature of personality and its relation to morality, writing "...The moral demise means for him [Dostoevsky] always the metaphysical deconstruction of the personality.... Only in good does a person come to himself, but a person stops being himself outside the good, the personality desolves in the whirl of masks and larva."[13] Florovsky claims that Dostoevsky shows "the dialectic of the personality, " the idea that personality remains whole only when it is close to the good, to God, otherwise it disintegrates.

In his analysis of romantic thought Florovsky employs this idea. The flaw in Vasily Leont'ev's worldview, for example, is that it falls victim to the basic contradiction in romanticism, the division between a belief in "organic theory" and the "violent formation of reality." In other words, one cannot simultaneously admire the inherent order of the world and the unique violent power of life. This contradiction led Leont'ev to acknowledge the eternal order found in Christianity, while he trembled before the stronger temporal power of nature. Christianity for Leont'ev was a philosophy of the final end and not of life. Such sacrilegious views, however, resulted in the destruction of his personality. Florovsky writes:

> He did not rescue himself either from contradictions or from death. The pathos of birth satisfies the thirst for immortality. But then it [the pathos] gives birth to the faceless, impersonal elemental energy, the personality melts in the ocean of life—and this birth is a birth toward death. Man can only get out of this deadend when he surrenders his romantic premises, only in the belief that man's personality is above nature.[14]

Here Florovsky relies on Dostoevsky's concept of the personality in his evaluation of romantic thought. In Dostoevsky, Florovsky discovered an intellectual source, a model who passed on to the historian the view that philosophies not grounded in Christianity have detrimental effects

---

13   G. Florovskij, "Die Sackgassen der Romantik, " in *Orient and Occident: Blatter fur Theologie und Soziologie* (Leipzig: Viertes Heft 1930), 36.
14   Ibid., 30.

on the personality. Of course, Florovsky creatively modified the concept by placing it in the context of an analysis of neo-Romantic thought.

In formulating a solution to the social problems of his own society in 1921, Florovsky finds a potent precedent in Slavophile thought. In his essay, "The Eternal and Transitory in the Teaching of the Russian Slavophiles" ("Vechnoe i prekhodiashchee v uchenii russkikh slavianofilov", 1921), Florovsky acknowledges his connection to the past, while reacting to the civil war period. He writes:

> Among the horrors of the Red and White terror, among the disappointments of the lost struggle for liberation, under the rattling of sabres and the profane cries of the conquerors, under the groans of the vanquished, at the twilight of a new century the problem of life's arrangement again forms before the consciousness of European humanity. Again the question is raised of the reconciliation of an all-powerful society with the postulate of a finished organization and the unique personality with the infinite demand for freedom. But the question should have been resolved in a new way, in the spirit of radical individualism. The individual of the beginning of the nineteenth century no longer wanted to be reconciled to the abstract concept of the "free and rational creature, " that had substituted for the concrete and changing living individual on which the philosophical idea of the Enlightenment was based. The idea of creating such a plan for a perfect society, which was equally relevant for Tasmania, England, and Russia, no longer satisfied him. To the rational equality of the eighteenth century the new century counterpoised the ideal of the creative autonomy of the individual and the idea of the inimitable originality of each historical age, of the "individuality of the people's spirit." The ideas of Heraclitus again became animated in man's consciousness.[15]

---

15 G. Florovsky, "Vechnoe i prekhodiashchee v uchenii russkikh slavianofilov, " *Nachala: Religiozno-filosofsky zhurnal* (Moscow) 3 (1991): 33-34. First published in 1921.

In this passage, as in the article as a whole, Bolshevism and the Enlightenment as bearers of determinism are contrasted with Orthodoxy and Slavophilism as bearers of freedom. In this way, Florovsky contrasts the Slavophile ideas of a historically-bound individuality with universal principles and sees the Slavophile worldview as aligned with the solution to the problems of war-torn Russia. Florovsky hails the Slavophiles because they gave voice to the principle of unique individuality and the prerogatives of freedom, ideas he himself holds sacred.

Although I have brought forth a few examples, I think it is safe to say that they are representative. Florovsky's metaphysical conception of history and his personalist idea of Orthodoxy led him to approve of a great deal in nineteenth-century Russian thought. He found in the Russian intellectual tradition a Christian ideal of individual freedom and community with the religious past. Florovsky reclaimed for Christian Orthodoxy the personages and ideas of Ivan Kireevsky and Fyodor Dostoevsky who had been interpreted in a non-Christian context by Silver Age thinkers.[16]

Although Florovsky used secular sources for his synthesis, he gave first priority to the interests of the modern Orthodox Church and the needs of his own Orthodox Christian theology. Despite refraining from distorting his figures to the degree that Gershenzon did, Florovsky also fashioned his heroes for his own ends. He toned down the romantic folk elements of Slavophile thought, since they clashed with his emphasis on the doctrine of individual freedom. Similarly, he ignored Herzen's admiration for the peasant commune and blocked from view Dostoevsky's unpleasant Russian chauvinism. Consequently, one finds in Florovsky's work a manipulative modeling of his heroes, a careful selection of their qualities, and a willful suppression of those aspects not useful for his overall synthesis. It should also be noted that Florovsky did not accept all Russian philosophers. He was critical of those with whom he disagreed, namely, Nikolai Fedorov, Vladimir Solov'ev and Vasily Rozanov, and his heated criticism of them also reveals Florovsky's unique Christian preoccupations.

Florovsky's interpretation of Russian intellectual history reacts

---

16 Examples of works in which Dostoevsky comes in for non-Christian treatment are: D. Merezhkovsky's *Tolstoi i Dostoevsky* (2 vols. 1901-02), A. Volynsky's *Tsarstvo Karamzinykh* (1901) and A. Gornfel'd's *Muki slova* (1906). Gershenzon drew a non-Orthodox portrait of I. Kireevsky in *Istoricheskie zapiski* (1910).

against Gershenzon and the Silver-Age's ecumenical treatment. Florovsky sought in Russian intellectual history of the nineteenth century neither an escape from history nor the creation of a new religious paradigm, but a continuity with and inspiration from the past. Although Florovsky resembles his Silver-Age predecessors in that he discovered the spiritual orientations of his heroes, he belongs in age and mentality to the second and third decade of the twentieth century, the time of an intense Christian-Orthodox revival. Just preceding the October revolution and then in emigration the Orthodox Church attracted new talent among the urban intellectual elite. Major thinkers like Sergei Bulgakov, Lev Kartashev, Lev Karsavin, and Florovsky turned to the priesthood as a reputable and challenging career.

On Florovsky's relation to Gershenzon as a historian, we can say in summation that, despite Gershenzon's influence on Florovsky's historical approach, their relations to the nineteenth-century Russian intelligentsia and their aims in the study of history are more dissimilar than similar. One can also distinguish the two as having very different views on the meaning of religion. For Gershenzon, religion was the individual's own creation, while for Florovsky, it was contained in Orthodoxy and its Church. The divergence in their religious perspectives explains the clash in their historical treatment of Russian heroes and views on tradition. While Gershenzon was an early nourishing source for Florovsky, it was in the ultimate negation of that source that Florovsky established his Christian principles.

13. From the Annals of the Literary Life of Russia's Silver Age: The Tempestuous Relationship of S. A. Vengerov and M. O. Gershenzon[1]

Within Russia's Silver Age it is difficult to find two scholar intellectuals seemingly more alike than Mikhail Osipovich Gershenzon and Semyon Afanas'evich Vengerov. By background, education and intellectual interests they were extremely similar. Both were born to Jewish families and educated at Russian universities. Both became major scholars of the work of Alexander Pushkin and historians of Russian culture of the first half of the nineteenth century. Politically, both shared a desire to transform Russian society. Despite these parallels, however, Gershenzon and Vengerov belonged to different generations and held divergent views about the purpose of art, Russian history, the role of the Russian intelligentsia, and the meaning of the Russian revolution of October 1917. This article is an investigation of these differences, based on their correspondence from 1903-1920.[2]

Semyon Vengerov (1855-1920), critic, literary historian, bibliographer and Professor of Petersburg University, was born near Poltava in Lubny to educated parents; his father was a banker and his mother a writer.[3] First certified as a lawyer, Vengerov studied literature at Yuriev University (Tartu), later doing graduate work at Petersburg University, although he never received a degree. By the mid-1870s, Vengerov already started publishing articles and reviews that revealed his strong commitment to the populist ideology. His first serious work of literary study, *Russian Literature in its Contemporary Shapes: Critical-Biographical Studies* (*Russkaia literatura v ee sovremennykh predstavleniakh. Kritiko-bi-*

---

[1] The author acknowledges the editorial aid and useful suggestions of Professor Stanley Rabinowitz.

[2] S. Vengerov's letters to M. Gershenzon are located in Gershenzon's archive in the Russian National Library-fond: 746-30-7. Gershenzon's letters to Vengerov are located in Vengerov's archive in the Pushkin House-fond: 377. I have left out a description of Gershenzon's biography because one can be found in chapter 1 of this volume.

[3] Pauline Wengeroff wrote *Memoiren einer Grossmutter*, 2 vol. (1910), 2: 192-93. They have recently appeared in English: Pauline Wengeroff, *Memoirs of a Grandmother: Scenes from the Cultural History of the Jews of Russia in the Nineteenth Century*, ed. Shulamit Magnes (Stanford: Stanford University Press, 2010-2012).

ograficheskie etiudy), about I. S. Turgenev appeared in 1875. In concert with his populist perspective, Vengerov devoted his major books to the heroes of the Russian intelligentsia. Among them, the most important are: *History of Contemporary Russian Literature: From Belinsky's Death to Our Day* (*Istoriia noveishei russkoi literatury. Ot smerti Belinskogo do nashikh dnei,* 1885) and *The Heroic Character of Russian Literature* (*Geroicheskii kharakter russkoi literatury,* 1911).

In addition to his scholarly oeuvre, Vengerov received acclaim for his bibliographical work. Vengerov was Russia's first serious bibliographer and under his direction many volumes of reliable bibliographical information about Russian culture were published. He also created the first organization committed to the compilation and publication of bibliography, the Book Chamber. His bibliographical labors are embodied in four works: *The Biographical Dictionary of Russian Writers and Scholars* (*Kritiko-biograficheskii slovar' russkikh pisatelei i uchenykh*), 6 vols. (1886-1904); *Russian Books, with Biographical Information about Authors and Translators (1708-1893)* (*Russkie knigi. S biograficheskimi dannymi ob avtorakh i perevodchikakh [1708-1893]*, 3 vols., 1895-1899); *Sources for a Dictionary of Russian Writers* (*Istochniki slovaria russkikh pisatelei*, 4 vols., 1900-1917); *A Preliminary List of Russian Writers and Scholars and the First Information about Them* (*Predvaritel'nyi spisok russkikh pisatelei i uchenykh i pervye o nikh spravki,* 1915-1918). Only 2 volumes appeared, although there are 33 thousand unpublished entries in Vengerov's archive in Pushkin House. Vengerov also organized the first Pushkin seminars at Petersburg University (from 1906) which served as a center for the development of formalist literary scholarship.

Although individual literary critics in Russia from 1890-1920 were eclectic in method, nevertheless distinct critical schools were identifiable. The main criterion, which permits a rough classification of literary critics, is a critic's didacticism: does the critic interpret literature to further a political or religious program? Literary critics such as M. Nevedomsky, A. Volynsky and G. Plekhanov, who would be difficult to classify in terms of their method, can easily be identified according to their goal. Plekhanov was politically engagé, A. Volynsky was a proselytizer of spiritual values, while Nevedomsky was neutral to both. Nevedomsky preferred a criticism that treated the author's psychology or intention. Looking at the goal of a critic helps to clarify the differences among the main tendencies in Russian criticism of the time: political, religious or psychological. The tempestuous relationship of Vengerov and Gershenzon exemplifies the conflict between politically committed critics and those inspired by spiritual convictions. Vengerov, a resolute populist, confronted Gershenzon, a religious thinker, in the prosaic business of literary criticism and historical studies.

The period in which Vengerov and Gershenzon worked was characterized by a general reevaluation of values. The values of didacticism and civic utility, which had exclusively guided the role and significance of literature since the 1850s, had finally come to an end and in their wake new religious and spiritual values were vying for ideological dominance. All of literature was up for grabs; not only the present and future, but also the past. Vengerov zealously asserted the superiority of the populist school of criticism, which claimed that Russian literature was aesthetically beautiful because of its morally laudable political goals. Gershenzon attached himself to the Symbolist movement, promulgating the importance of literature primarily as a means of understanding the mystical and spiritual truths of the universe. These debates took place in the unlikely context of the investigation of the biographies of Russia's past literary and intellectual heroes: A. Pushkin, P. Chaadaev, I. Kireevsky, A. Herzen and V. Belinsky.

The dispute between those two figures was as much emotional as intellectual in nature. Besides their ideological orientations, each had an individual temperament which conditioned how they faced and reacted to various issues. Vengerov revealed a marked need to belong to a collective and was sympathetic to arguments of a moral bent. He attached himself to the populists early in his career and never deviated from their ideological boundaries. In civic criticism, Vengerov found the moral justification for his life and the collective support of the entire Russian intelligentsia. In exchange, however, Vengerov had to sacrifice those aspects of his personality which he could not share with the collective, i.e. his Jewish identity; Vengerov voluntarily converted to Russian Orthodoxy.

In contrast, Gershenzon was an individualist. He believed in a personal mystical religion that declared that every person was united through will with the destiny of the cosmos. To live correctly, Gershenzon claimed, is to follow personal feeling which originates in will. Thus to be at one with the universe means to be an individual, single, inimitable and unique. Gershenzon himself was such an individual, and his personal transformation from provincial Jew to Russian intellectual reflects a conscious choice of identity. In addition, in his relation to his Jewish roots Gershenzon too was idiosyncratic. Although he did not practice Judaism, neither did he convert to Russian Orthodoxy. Rather, he tried to fashion a personal religion of the cosmos which could substitute for his loss of Judaism and supplant any need to convert.

The relationship between Vengerov and Gershenzon started in earnest in 1905. Far from the spontaneous fury of the revolution, Vengerov was intensely organizing his six-volume *Collected Works of A. S. Pushkin* (*Sobranie sochinenii A. S. Pushkina*), which appeared from 1907-1914. Vengerov intended the project to be "a collection of Pushkin's works and an investigation of his life and art." To complete the scholarship promised by these goals, Vengerov amassed the leading experts on Pushkin of the time, in particular calling on Gershenzon to contribute articles about Pushkin and his contemporaries. In requesting an article on Pushkin's relationship to Chaadaev, Vengerov wrote Gershenzon, specifying his needs: "I expect from your respected pen a full essay on Chaadaev. It should be an original monograph on Chaadaev in which his relations to Pushkin should be especially emphasized."[4]

The reasons why Vengerov called upon Gershenzon are clear. Vengerov needed a scholar to treat Chaadaev and Pushkin's Decembrist friends and Gershenzon had just published essays about these figures; moreover, his historical approach was not unfamiliar to Vengerov.[5] Just as Vengerov, Gershenzon investigated writers of primary and secondary importance in order to capture the general worldview of an entire epoch. To focus on Pushkin did not entail a drastic shift in approach; Gershenzon could still adhere to his preferred biographical-sociological method. All that his work with Vengerov involved was a change of emphasis.

During the period of his cooperation with Vengerov (1905-1919), Gershenzon's attitude to Pushkin and especially scholarship on poetry radically evolved. Having written one article on Pushkin's relationship with Chaadaev and another on the poet's friendship with Pavel Nashchokin for Vengerov, Gershenzon requested a change of roles.[6] Instead

---

4 S. Vengerov to M. O. Gershenzon, 13 April 1906. This letter was written in German.
5 See Gershenzon's articles, "Molodost' P. Ia. Chaadaeva," *Nauchnoe slovo* 6 (1905): 83-121, and "Sem'ia Dekabristov," *Byloe* 10 (1906): 288-317.
6 Gershenzon's article "Chaadaev i Pushkin," appeared in volume 6, and "Pushkin i Nashchokin"

of investigating Pushkin's biography, he craved a chance to analyze texts directly. In a letter from May 5, 1906 Gershenzon writes, "... It would be especially agreeable to me to write a long introductory article on *Evgeny Onegin* of a historical-aesthetic type and give a broad analysis of the poem's history, conception, content and form."[7]

Although *Evgeny Onegin* had already been portioned out to another scholar, Gershenzon got his chance with "The Queen of Spades." In this article, he demonstrated his new "metaphysical" approach to the study of literature. Arguing that Pushkin presented a elemental, vitalistic philosophy of existence, Gershenzon interprets Hermann this way: "Pushkin wants sort of to say that we all are ready at any minute for a scandal; our soul full of passion greedily looks in the world for food for its passion—so greedily that even the shadow of something is capable of seducing it and then our soul flairs for an instant and burns in painful happiness, one soul does it slowly, another quickly like Hermann."[8]

Pushkin, Gershenzon claimed, was the real-life prototype for Hermann. As a poet, he appeared calm and rational, but he too was vulnerable to losing his reason through an explosion of passion or artistic inspiration. In addition, Gershenzon drew wide-sweeping metaphysical conclusions: Pushkin and Hermann represented man's fate, man was either hot—blessed with inspiration and thus vulnerable to insanity—or cold and stolid, as were most people. In Gershenzon's view, Pushkin, like all poets, professed a philosophy of unlimited anarchistic freedom for humanity.

Although Vengerov accepted the article for his collection, he objected to Gershenzon's exclusive focus on Hermann to the exclusion of the other characters. In a letter from December 21, 1909, Vengerov tried to correct Gershenzon's exclusive preoccupation with Hermann, writing, "Of course I will send you the preface to 'The Queen of Spades.' It is very interesting, but you did not say anything about the old woman as a psychological type. I consider 'The Queen of Spades' the most brilliant depiction of an old person's egoism in world literature."[9]

Vengerov and Gershenzon's opposing images of Pushkin can be

---

appeared in volume 5 of *Sobranie sochinenii A. S. Pushkina* (St. Petersburg: Brokgauz i Efron, 1907-1914).
7 M. O. Gershenzon to S. Vengerov, 5 May 1906.
8 M. O. Gershenzon, *Mudrost' Pushkina* (Moscow, 1919), 99.
9 Vengerov to Gershenzon, 21 Dec. 1909.

clearly seen in their two interpretations of Pushkin's poem, "Exegi Monumentum ('Ia pamiatnik sebe vozdvig nerukotvornyi...')." Agreeing that the poem represents Pushkin's "last will and testament," both scholars share the view that Pushkin expresses his ideological credo in this piece. According to Vengerov, in this, his last statement on the value of literature, Pushkin reveals his mature opinion that poetry should serve the people.[10] Therefore, Pushkin repudiates his earlier views of art for art's sake and at the end of his life willy-nilly attaches himself to the great course of Russian literature.

In contrast, Gershenzon considers the poem as Pushkin's "sign" of resignation before those who interpret his poetry as having a didactic function. According to Gershenzon, the poet uses irony, which undercuts the poem's apparent meaning, and therefore, Pushkin's real credo—art for art's sake—is directly opposed to the literal message of the work. If Pushkin had been serious about serving the people, Gershenzon claims, then, "... The poet took the viewpoint of the 'crowd': he takes pride in the utility of his art, but not the art itself; he sees in it a means, but not an end. Such a metamorphosis as the culmination of his artistic work, if it was conscious, would be equivalent to suicide."[11] Following this line of reasoning, Gershenzon proposes that the poem contains two views of glory, one of glory deserved, and the other a vulgar glory. Pushkin accepts the glory he deserves for writing wonderful poetry, but rejects any glory for having served the people.

The differences between the two interpretations paralleled those between Vengerov and Gershenzon, for each found in Pushkin an image corresponding to his own personal viewpoint. For his part, Vengerov discovered in Pushkin a civic poet who saw his primary role in being useful to society and furthering the goals of justice, equality and freedom. Gershenzon, on the contrary, fashioned an aesthete. His Pushkin strongly defended the idea of art for art's sake.[12]

Gershenzon arrived at his conclusions by applying his method of analyzing literature, entitled *Slow Reading* (*medlennoe chtenie*). Gershenzon had first employed *Slow Reading* as a method for retrieving new

---

10   S. Vengerov, "Poslednyi zavet Pushkina," in *Sobranie sochinenii A. S. Pushkina*, 4: 48.
11   M. Gershenzon, *Mudrost' Pushkina*, 66.
12   Although Gershenzon and Vengerov disagreed, their debate entered into the long history of views concerning the poem. For a summary of these debates, see M. Alekseev, *Stikhotvorenie Pushkina "Ia pamiatnik sebe vozdvig..."* (Leningrad, 1967).

biographical facts about Pushkin through a close reading of his lyrics in essays such as "Pushkin's Northern Love" ("Severnaia liubov' Pushkina") (1907) and "Pushkin and Princess E. K. Vorontsova" ("Pushkin i Kniaginia E. K. Vorontsova") (1909). By 1910, though, he began to use it as a method to derive the poet's ideal vision lying beneath the text's exterior form. In his 1919 programmatic essay, *The Poet's Vision* (*Videnie poeta*), Gershenzon explains the role of the critic in reading literature: "Literary criticism is nothing other than the art of slow reading, i.e. the art of seeing the artist's vision through the fascination of form. The crowd slips on the ice, the critic goes slowly and sees life in the deep water. The tasks of the critic are not to judge a work, but, having seen, to teach others to see the poet's vision; actually to teach everyone to read slowly so that everyone can see because each will perceive it in his own way."[13]

Gershenzon's approach focused on the critic's subjective reading of the poet. Central to his technique was the ahistorical extraction of ideas and leitmotifs which supposedly revealed Pushkin's psychology. By reading extra-carefully, the reader was supposed to grasp those ideas Pushkin would not, or could not express directly for "fear of being branded as insane." Thus, Gershenzon, using a subjective and intuitive method, thought the practitioner of Slow Reading had exclusive access to Pushkin's transcendent worldview.

Vengerov's method of studying literature was quite different. Educated in an age dominated by populism and positivism, Vengerov clung to the idea that literature had a didactic function, to improve the moral climate of society. In contrast to his teachers, however, Vengerov did not subordinate aesthetics to ethics, but considered aesthetics and the pleasure received from art as proof of a work's genius. The best works, he claimed, were those in which aesthetics and ethics were perfectly joined. In his 1911 lecture, "What is the Charm of Russian Literature of the 19th Century" ("V chem ocharovanie russkoi literatury XIX veka?"), he clearly articulates his theory: And it seems to me that the basic task of any history of contemporary Russian literature leads to the presentation of its moral beauty, the demonstration of how aesthetics and ethics, artistic perfection with moral force are joined in a higher harmony."[14]

---

13   M. Gershenzon, *Videnie poeta* (Moscow, 1919), 18.
14   S. Vengerov, *V chem ocharovanie russkoi literatury XIX veka?* (Petersburg: 1912), 8.

Vengerov thought he found the synthesis of artistic merit and moral virtue in writers to whom he devoted full monographs: Ivan Turgenev, Vissarion Belinsky, Nikolai Gogol and Konstantin Aksakov. These writers were able to put forth their views in such a way that they were able to galvanize and influence society as a whole. The aesthetic beauty of their creations was equal to their moral message.

Since he believed in the potentially transformative power of the idea, Vengerov held that he was an "idealist." But, he added, an idealist of a particular type—an "idealist-realist." Antithetical both to the Marxist view that class membership defines the historian's perspective and the view that ideas exist for their own sake, independent of historical circumstances, Vengerov claimed that that an idea's significance depended on its useful effect on society. For Vengerov, individuals are important not for the originality of their thought, but for their ability to embody ideas important to a whole generation. In his evaluation of Belinsky, Vengerov writes: "Admiration for Belinsky should not remove the fact that the ideas that he expressed with such great talent and force, were ideas of an entire circle of people who inspired him. And one should not dispose of this fact not only 'because' it is true, but also because it does not contain anything at all that would diminish Belinsky's importance. After all, truly great people are those who are not alone and isolated, but who reflect great epochs."[15] Vengerov's view of literature as reflecting great epochs and only secondarily as products of individuals was the legacy of the positivist school of Alexander Pypin. The positivist approach, which was associated with ethnography, tended to see literature as merely source material for studying the history of social ideas in Russian culture.

With this view of art and history, Vengerov came into conflict with Gershenzon, who believed that the individual personality is always greater than the ideas expressed. Gershenzon claimed that an individual is always psychically "holistic, " which means that his whole being—the intellectual, emotional, conscious and unconscious aspects of his personality—was reflected in everything he said and did. Ideas, therefore, are only one aspect of a person and thus, if studied in isolation, give a distorted picture of an individual. In order really to know an individual, Gershenzon asserted, the historian has to study all the

---

15   S. Vengerov, *Ocherki po istorii russkoi literatury* (St. Petersburg: 1907), 248.

spheres of his being, especially his personal life. Using personal documents, such as letters, diaries and miscellaneous jottings, Gershenzon perceived the internal struggles and religious propensities of Russia's most important nineteenth-century writers and thinkers.

Gershenzon's perspective was conditioned in part by the age in which he was writing. Closely aligned with the Symbolists, Gershenzon held that all men were religious by nature. In their every action or thought they unconsciously expressed the "spiritual holism" believed inherent to every individual. This holism, Gershenzon claimed, was based on a pantheistic unity of the cosmos, a unity which insured that everything was linked together. Thus, all thinkers, whatever their outlook might seem, were in fact *a priori* struggling for religious unity. Faithful to this premise, Gershenzon placed Gogol' before Belinsky and Kireevsky before Herzen as more important thinkers, since the former supposedly internalized in their life and thought the truth that each person is endowed with a need for religion and they founded a moral program that conformed to this truth.

Not surprisingly Vengerov responded negatively to Gershenzon's biographies of Chaadaev and the Slavophiles, objecting not only to his images of Russia's heroes, but also to his scholarly methodology. In his review of Russian literature for the year 1909, Vengerov lashed out at Gershenzon, writing in the January 1 issue of *Russkie vedomosti*:

> In 1909, M. O. Gershenzon joined them [the writers of *Landmarks*] and pursued a belated lawsuit about Gogol''s 'Correspondence' with Belinsky and Pypin. In general lately this gifted writer has taken the dangerous road of 'new illuminations' of phenomena only interesting in a historical perspective. He depicts for us Chaadaev, but not the one who, in Herzen's solely correct definition, was a 'shot in the dark night,' but a mystic completely alien to politics whom no one has ever known. The Kireevsky he gives us is not the one who founded real Slavophilism, but an image that has been created anew by excerpts from letters unknown until now.[16]

---

16   S. Vengerov, "Literaturnoe nastroenie," *Russkie vedomosti* 1 (1910): 14.

Vengerov found Gershenzon's de-politicized, religious interpretations of Russia's heroes odious because they completely contradicted the traditional conception of Russian intellectuals. Vengerov's Belinsky, following Chernyshevsky's work, is depicted as the father of Russian liberalism; his idea of Chaadaev, following Herzen, is a political opponent to tsarist absolutism, and even his conception of Gogol' follows the traditional interpretation set down by Belinsky. In his book on Gogol', *Writer-Citizen (N. V. Gogol') (Pisatel'-Grazhdanin [N. V. Gogol']*), Vengerov, interpreting the *Selected Passages from a Correspondence with Friends (Vybrannye mesta iz perepiski s druz'iami)*, resolutely sides with Belinsky and his famous "Letter to Gogol'." In one place Vengerov even quotes it: "... One can only fully identify with Belinsky's feeling, when he, choking from terrible indignation, historically cried out to Gogol' in his letter: 'Preacher of the whip, apostle of ignorance, promoter of obscurantism, panegyrist of Tatar morals—what are you doing!'"[17]

Vengerov, however, wanting to soften the personal impact of his negative review (he and Gershenzon were still friends), wrote an apology to Gershenzon in a letter from January 7, 1910: "I hope that you did not feel insulted by me for my article in *Russkie vedomosti*. Having called you a 'talented' writer (I use such epithets very rarely) and called attention to your departure from *Vestnik Evropy*, I, it seems to me, have done everything to show that the difference in our political views does not stop me from esteeming and loving you."[18]

Their conflict over the study of Russian history reflected divergent views of the role of the Russian intelligentsia. The 1909 publication of *Landmarks (Vekhi)* brought these differences into the open.[19] In sending a copy to Vengerov, Gershenzon did not anticipate the strong reaction that the volume would elicit. In a letter from March 25, 1909 Gershenzon enthusiastically informs Vengerov about the volume's popularity: "*Landmarks* are making a splash and selling—like Leonid Andreyev. I can imagine what people in *Russkoe bogatstvo* are saying. In general we

---

17 Vengerov, *Ocherki*, 226.
18 Vengerov to Gershenzon, 7 Jan. 1910. In mentioning Gershenzon's dismissal from *Vestnik Evropy*, Vengerov was underscoring that Gershenzon had been unfairly fired and that the real cause may even have been anti-Semitism. For more about this incident, see Arthur Levin's dissertation, [what shortened title was used before?] "The Life and Work of Mikhail Osipovich Gershenzon (1869-1925): A Study in the History of the Russian Silver Age, " 114-16.
19 The writers of *Vekhi* were: N. Berdiaev, S. Bulgakov, S. Frank, M. Gershenzon, A. Izgoev, B. Kistiakovsky and P. Struve.

are going to get a lot of criticism. Today Ignatov in *Russkie vedomosti* in two pages confesses his stupidity about *Landmarks*."[20]

In his reply Vengerov describes his initial feelings:

> I still haven't read *Landmarks* seriously, but only glanced over it. I am happy for you personally if it makes a splash and therefore allows for a second edition.[21] But as an incorrigible "public activist" (*obshchestvennik*) I cannot be happy: I have only one feeling about the Russian intelligentsia—I worship it immeasurably and do not know why one has to curse it so bitterly. I also do not like church incense and it seems that there is enough of it in *Landmarks*. I say all this, however, not having acquainted myself with the volume in detail. I have only cut the pages and read yesterday's article by Levin.[22] Before my Moscow trip, I will read the book seriously and will fight with you personally.[23]

In his next letter to Gershenzon, following a close reading of *Vekhi*, Vengerov had harsher words:

> If I feel like it, I will fight with you till [we shed] blood over *Landmarks*. Now you are on the most dangerous of all literary paths—the path of Akim Volynsky. Luckily you are free of what makes Volynsky repulsive. You do not write under the influence of personal and shallow impulses. Nonetheless, it is fruitless and fatal to curse what gives Russian literature its brilliance. The whole beauty of Russian literature lies in the call to heroism, and you spit on heroism and the call to it. Ok, that's enough until our fight in person.[24]

---

20 Gershenzon to Vengerov, 25 March 1909. *Russkoe bogatstvo* was the central organ of the populists.
21 Following the appearance of *Vekhi*, a second volume was conceived in which the contributors would express their positive ideals. The idea never came to fruition.
22 Vengerov here is referring to D. Levin's article in *Rech'*, March 25, 1909.
23 Vengerov to Gershenzon, 26 March 1909.
24 Vengerov to Gershenzon, 15 June 1909.

In his reply Gershenzon revealed amazement at Vengerov's hostility, expressing that he felt he had been misunderstood. "I feel pity that you have formed a final judgment about me, but I can only explain in person; and now my wife will not let me go to Petersburg because of the cholera. Someday this thing will find its rightful place, as all things do. I read the condemnations in the papers with total indifference, but personally such mistaken accusations worry me, i.e. from people close who, I believe, would doubtless sympathize if they understood. It appears that to make oneself understandable isn't so easy."[25]

In his reply, Vengerov jokingly continues the dialogue, challenging Gershenzon to come to see him despite the cholera.

> You are afraid of cholera in vain: the only ones who die of it are those peasants from whom *Landmarks* saves the intelligentsia and therefore they don't obey the intelligentsia. But those intellectuals who do not drink untreated water, cholera does not affect them. But it would be good if you could come to Petersburg for a day. We could fight it out to the end. To calm your wife's fears we could even organize the fight in Sestroretsk where I spend time at my dacha and where there is no cholera.[26]

Although the exchange of letters is entertaining and gives us an insider's view of the spirited interaction of these two men, there are some points that need clarification. Why exactly did Gershenzon think he was misunderstood, and why did Vengerov find nothing redeemable in Gershenzon's *Landmarks* article, "Creative Self-Consciousness" ("Tvorcheskoe samosoznanie")? On Gershenzon's side, it seems that he naively believed his article was not, as so many thought, predominantly a criticism of the intelligentsia, but actually consisted of well-intended advice for its revival. The message he was propagating was that, by embracing the impersonal ideals of "equality and justice and sacrifice for the people, " the intellectual had forsaken his egoism, which is the motivating force of all things. Unfortunately this selflessness had fragmented the intellectual's personality, severing the unity between will

---

25 Gershenzon to Vengerov, 19 June 1909.
26 Vengerov to Gershenzon, 1 July 1909.

and consciousness and creating psychological cripples. In *Landmarks* Gershenzon explains the dangers of an impersonal ideology:

> What did the idea of our intelligentsia achieve in half a century? I am speaking of course of the mass of intellectuals. A large group of revolutionaries went from house to house and knocked at every door: "Out on the street! It's shameful to stay at home!" And all of life's creations spilled into the square, those with a limp, the blind and crippled: not a single one remained at home. For half a century they debate in the square, raise their voices and argue. At home there is dirt, poverty, and disorder, but the head of the household doesn't have time for that. He's with the others saving the people—after all it is easier and more interesting than the hard work at home.[27]

Not all intellectuals were crippled, however, and Gershenzon distinguished between healthy individuals and diseased ones, between those who followed their personal feeling and those who aped the ideas of others. The well-being of society, Gershenzon warned, depended on the individual strength of each of its members. Only the moral improvement of every single individual would correct the flaws in society as a whole. Gershenzon's political thinking reveals the influence of Lev Tolstoy. Gershenzon not only accepted Tolstoy's idea of personal morality, but he also absorbed his rational approach to religion and even his idealization of the peasants.[28]

As his review and personal letters show, Vengerov was personally stung by the venom of *Landmark*'s criticism, which he felt was "black ingratitude" toward the intelligentsia. In his review he exclaimed, "… The attack on the Russian intelligentsia and its representative literature, was executed with an unprecedented bitterness, and, one can even say, an intensive fury."[29] Vengerov's reaction was predicated on his image of the intelligentsia as the sole element responsible for all the

---

27 M. Gershenzon, "Tvorcheskoe samosoznanie," in *Vekhi*, 2nd ed. (Moscow: 1909), 80.
28 Gershenzon, "Tvorcheskoe samosoznanie," 87.
29 S. Vengerov, *Sobranie sochinenii* (St. Petersburg: 1911), 1:198.

social and spiritual improvement of Russian life and thus undeserving of such scathing criticism. Lauding the intelligentsia for its unassailable "striving for an ideal, " Vengerov claimed that the intelligentsia was motivated by self-sacrifice and the denial of personal happiness in the name of higher moral values. In *The Heroic Character of Russian Literature* (1911), Vengerov rejects *Landmarks*' notion of individualism, praising the intelligentsia's traditional imperative of serving the collective: "The essential element of melancholy is the deep consciousness that in each person lies an obligation one way or another to destroy evil in the world. The direct conclusion from this is that everyone has to be a fighter for truth whether through personal happiness, illegal means, or even pettiness."[30]

Vengerov's conflict with Gershenzon was clearly a microcosm of the heated debates elicited by *Landmarks* between the religious-inclined thinkers and the politically left-leaning members of the intelligentsia. Gershenzon, nodding to his colleagues, the Silver-Age religious philosophers, claimed that social improvement had to begin with individual growth and moral regeneration, while Vengerov offered the traditional populist idea that the intelligentsia's opposition to the government and self-sacrifice for the people would bring about political reform.

Interestingly, Vengerov's rejection of *Landmarks* reveals that his goals remained unchanged, since ideologically his position closely resembled his debate with the decadents a decade earlier. Criticizing decadent poetry in 1897 for its "apotheosis of egoism" and its solipsistic admiration for the "spiritless principle of beauty, " Vengerov denounced its detachment from the social needs of Russian life. In the same way, in 1910 Vengerov faulted *Landmarks* for its emphasis on individual self-actualization and neglect for the social struggle.

Once his initial anger over *Landmarks* had calmed, however, Vengerov found a way to defuse these two threatening movements. Thanks to Gershenzon's intercession, Vengerov realized that former decadents had become religious seekers, aiming to transform Russia's political and social landscape, and that the writers of *Landmarks*, although appearing apolitical, were actually trying to revive the intelligentsia's spiritual legacy. Vengerov writes:

---

30 S. Vengerov, *Geroichesky kharakter russkoi literatury* (St. Petersburg: 1911), 110-11.

> And an amazing thing happens: analyzing the historical-literary meaning of *Landmarks*, as soon as you take the proper scientific-genetic point of view, a kind of miracle occurs: *Landmarks* not only does not seem like a dissonance that pains one's ears, but on the contrary, like an organic link in a chain it belongs to the general appeal of the Russian intelligentsia and Russian literature for heroism—"deepen your self-consciousness, work on your own individuality"—permit me sirs, but this is terribly familiar to Lavrov's critical-thinking individual, which in its turn only repeats in scientific form what Belinsky called for. Both Lavrov and *Landmarks* in exactly the same way lead to the self-consciousness of the individual, in the same way place the whole weight of the world-historical process on the individual![31]

Vengerov's acceptance of *Landmarks* seemingly reverses his initial hostility. Thus, Gershenzon had been right all along in saying that had Vengerov understood, he would have lauded *Landmarks*. If, however, Gershenzon meant that he was merely repeating Lavrov and calling attention to the intelligentsia's small flaws and was not repudiating the revolutionary struggle, then why did he so vehemently rail against the intelligentsia and its goal of uniting with the people to overthrow the tsar? Why, for example, did Gershenzon write that inflammatory anti-revolutionary phrase: "As we are, we not only cannot dream of unity with the simple people, but should fear them more than all the punishments of the government and bless the government that alone with its bayonets and prisons protects us from the people's anger."[32] The points of agreement and disagreement over *Landmarks* were in fact simplified by both Vengerov and Gershenzon and could never have been so easily resolved if treated in all their true complexity.

The revolutionary year of 1917 upset the established roles of their friendship. In *Landmarks*, Gershenzon had argued for society's slow improvement through the spiritual regeneration of individuals. Now Gershenzon supported the October Revolution. This change astounded

---

31 Vengerov, *Sobranie sochinenii*, 1: 200-1.
32 Gershenzon, "Tvorcheskoe samosoznanie," 89.

Vengerov who, in a letter from January 22, 1918, confronted Gershenzon concerning the latest rumors, writing, "In conclusion I want to ask you: what is *Wahrheit* and what is *Dictung* in the rumor, inconceivable in my view, that you and Shestov have become Bolsheviks! Out of disgust is it for the actual bankrupt intelligentsia?"[33]

Although Gershenzon never answered Vengerov directly, he was hurt by accusations that he supported the Bolsheviks. His point of view, he insisted, was more complex than the "for or against" attitude that many intellectuals of the time offered. Gershenzon was not a Bolshevik, but he was uncertain. Sympathizing with the individual "man suffering today," he also knew the importance of the abstract values of Russian statehood and might.[34] Gershenzon ultimately supported the Revolution because he believed humanity needed a thorough transformation after the terrible war.

Gershenzon's support for the Revolution, however, signifies to a great extent a repudiation of his position in *Landmarks*. Gershenzon had taken up Vengerov's position, proposing that political action be used to transform society. Vengerov, for his part, did not support the Bolsheviks for fear that a destruction of the old world would mean unimaginable suffering and desecration of culture. Unfortunately, their correspondence is silent about these political reversals.

During the Civil War, Vengerov and Gershenzon found themselves reunited emotionally. In the face of political, social, economic, and cultural changes in the new Soviet state, these two individuals now had more in common than differences. They were both already intellectuals of the "old world," suffering from ill health, famine, and cultural obsolescence. Their emotional distance from the state gave them the chance to sum up their relationship and put their differences in a new perspective. In addition, appreciation for revolution had engendered in Gershenzon a new attitude toward literature. No longer was the study of literature itself important; of far more importance was his relationship with his friends and his feelings for the individual person. In a letter from July 23, 1919, Gershenzon shares his sympathy for Vengerov:

---

33   Vengerov to Gershenzon, 22 Jan. 1918.
34   For more information about Gershenzon's attitude toward the October Revolution, see chapter 4 in this volume.

I thank you sincerely for your book.³⁵ You know that I cannot agree with it, but I cut it and again read those familiar pages: what does it matter that we have different ideas! The main thing is that your heart is in the right place, suffers and loves as it should in this serious life—that is the main thing. Ideas go in different ways, struggle, die—their fate is the fate of things: the authentic essence in a person is his holistic spirit and especially his heart. You are a good, kind person and that kindness of yours enters your ideas, your truth and righteousness. That is why I love not only you, but your books too, your ideas that often seem false to my mind. That is why I have always read you, but never felt it so clearly as this time. Maybe I am wiser thanks to the experience of these years. True observations, correct ideas are like products: what man can make for his profit and use. But I do not look at the products of his hands—leave them in peace! How many products have already been collected and every day they multiply; how much true and subtle observations, witty juxtapositions, and brilliant thoughts are published! I look at the person himself, at his face, I hear his voice: how is he inside himself? This alone is important. That is why I also love you. I think about myself this way, about my books and myself. Are my ideas smart, my books interesting—isn't genuine humanism found in those things, seriousness, honesty, and kindness; isn't this the whole thing.³⁶

Gershenzon's view of the relation between literature and life had indeed changed. Due to the tragic experiences of the Bolshevik revolution and the Civil War, Gershenzon had become a skeptic. Ideas, he now understood, were merciless and impersonal. Only living, holistic individuals were capable of pursuing a politics of love which could transform human consciousness. In short, Gershenzon realized that

---

35   Gershenzon probably received the second volume of Vengerov's *Russkaia literatura XX veka*, 1914-1917.
36   Gershenzon to Vengerov, 23 July 1919.

to arrive at a better world, one had to take a different route than that offered by culture.

Vengerov also revealed his personal feelings in his final letter to Gershenzon, sharing all his woes with his friend.

> I received without delay the letter about your receiving my books. It touched me deeply with its sincerity as perhaps you would not have expected because I am immensely alone now. True, the infinitely dear beings, my children remain, and if I always loved them, then it's double now. But children always stay children and nothing can replace a wife, especially such one as Roza Aleksandrovna, one of the most sublime natures that I ever met in my life. In addition, my children, to my great dismay, are such fragile souls, so unaccustomed to endure life's pains that I never allow myself to share with them my sad feelings. On the contrary, I am always lively and don't show it. And my pain keeps growing. I am planning to come to Moscow, maybe I will share my feelings with you. Your letter gives me a reason to think that you will listen about them with sympathy. Until then, thank you once again.[37]

Although right before his death Vengerov had become emotionally close to Gershenzon, this reconciliation concealed new disagreements in their worldviews. Facing the common difficulties of life in post-revolutionary Russia, they approached the prospect of Bolshevik rule with differing attitudes. Vengerov, an epigone of populism, ended his life disappointed with the Revolution, holding that the Bolsheviks had distorted his vision of social justice and moral beauty. Gershenzon was also disappointed not only because a social utopia had not been realized, but, more importantly, because he had come to the view that the individual's true needs were themselves antithetical to culture, whether tsarist or Bolshevik.

The same differences that had characterized their relationship throughout their careers were felt here as well. In contrast to Vengerov,

---

37   Vengerov to Gershenzon, 26 Sept. 1919.

who placed his hopes in reason and culture, in the *Correspondence Across a Room* (1921) Gershenzon expressed his longstanding intuition that culture would never fulfill its promises; it would never bring the individual happiness or society a moral order. Only a world that superseded reason and culture, that overcame them, leading to a postcultural, spiritual world would result in human perfection. Thus by the end of his life Gershenzon ceased writing, thereby repudiating culture, while Vengerov, emboldened by unshakable optimism about reason and culture's virtues, continued the enormous self-assigned task of collecting a bibliographical reference for every book and every writer who ever wrote in Russian.

14. M. O. Gershenzon, the Intellectual Circle, and the Perception of Leader in Russia's Silver-Age Culture

At least since the beginning of the nineteenth century, Russian cultural life revolved around the intellectual "circle" or club in which members met to discuss shared philosophies, ideals, and moral visions. The many examples of intellectual circles in Russian culture include, "Beseda," "Arzamas," the "Lovers of Wisdom," the Petrashevtsy," "The People's Will," even up the "Moscow Conceptualists." From this historical experience emerged structures of group organization with clear patterns of self-perception. The circle's structure often led to the idealization of one individual, who became perceived as the embodiment of the highest values cherished by the group. This individual was given the sacred position of leader and he served as a model for adoration and emulation. In an article on Andrei I. Turgenev, the historian Marc Raeff described the qualities which the leader had to possess: "The hero of the circle had to be someone whose promise had remained unfulfilled—be it because of early death or political persecution. It also had to be someone capable of inspiring enthusiasm and worship by his character and example. Finally, the hero had to be a 'whole' (*tsel'nyi*) personality, that is, someone whose identity was perceived to be the source of unquestionable moral authority."[1]

In the early twentieth century, Mikhail Osipovich Gershenzon asserted himself as the leader of his own literary circle. In his emotional attachment to his subject matter, his conversations and personal relationships, his studies of Alexander Pushkin and Russian intellectual history, Gershenzon tried to embody the recognized values of a leader. Moreover, not only did he possess the above prerequisites for the role, but he consciously cultivated the image of a leader by linking his identity with other "leaders" in the Russian past. Through his biographical monographs he became perceived as indelibly associated with Ivan

---

1   Marc Raeff, "Russian Youth on the Eve of Romanticism: Andrei I. Turgenev and his Circle," in *Revolution and Politics in Russia: Essays in Memory of B. I. Nikolaevsky*, eds. Alexander and Janet Rabinowitch (Bloomington: Indiana University Press, 1972), 52.

Kireevsky, Alexander Herzen, Nikolai Stankevich, Nikolai Ogarev, Pushkin, Pyotr Chaadaev, and Vladimir Pecherin. This association lent him the role he desired, that of intellectual "culture-bearer" and moral conscience of his epoch.

Gershenzon's circle was different from its prototype in the nineteenth century because his home was more a place for intimate visits than an acknowledged meeting-place of an official group. In addition, those who came were friends and guests. This informal relationship between Gershenzon and his friends reflects not only Gershenzon's open, sharing personality, but also corresponds to the state of the intellectual circle in Russia's Silver Age. While in the nineteenth century the circle was held together by the ideological unanimity and personal fidelity of its members, in the twentieth century such demands were relaxed. People belonged to several groups simultaneously and could be ideologically independent or even rivals. In her memoirs, Evgeniia Gertsyk explains the difference between the circle in the nineteenth and twentieth centuries:

> But what united such dissimilar thinkers as Viach[eslav] Ivanov and Gershenzon, Shestov and Berdiaev? It was not a group of allies, as it was in the past, for example the Slavophile and Westernizer circles. Nonetheless it wasn't the caprice of individual taste, but something deeper that united them. Was it not that in each of them was hidden an explosive force aimed against intellectual superstitions and the values of the old world, illusions and liberalism, but also against the trappings of decadence that seemed to many at the time the latest word. Certainly it was an anarchistic revolt; each had his vision of the future, a polished, austere vision that defined his entire creative path.[2]

Nonetheless, the circle was still perceived as linked with its original prototype through the self-conscious attitude towards the institution. Already by the end of the century the intelligentsia recorded a note of self-consciousness about their intellectual "circles" and the whole con-

---

2   Evgeniia Gertsyk, *Vospominaniia* (Paris: YMCA, 1973), 162.

stellation of ideas, models and behavioral norms originating in the first third of the nineteenth century. While self-consciousness may have lent a tint of irony or conventionality to statements about cultural life during the Silver Age, by viewing their epoch in terms of the past, intellectuals saw themselves as part of a historical continuum. Overt and hidden references to historical precedents anchored the modern circle more firmly in the Russian tradition, creating a dialogue with the past. In his autobiography, published in 1949, Nikolai Berdiaev describes the self-consciousness of Russian intellectual life.

> In Russia at the time of our old debates we were concerned with last, ultimate, and crucial problems, with primary, not secondary things, and not just the reflection [of reality]. That is how it was not only in the religious-philosophical societies, but also in arguments in private homes that resembled the debates of the Westernizers and Slavophiles of the 40s. Belinsky said after a fight that had gone on all night: we cannot go home, we still haven't resolved the question of God. That is how it was for us when S. Bulgakov, M. Gershenzon, L. Shestov, V. Ivanov, A. Bely, G. Rachinsky and others gathered together.[3]

Perhaps due to the greater diversity of the members of the intelligentsia and the multifaceted intellectual opportunities of modern cultural life, the monolithic circle was gradually replaced by something which resembled it formally, but differed from it internally. Typical for the Silver Age was something akin to an "open house"; intellectuals opened their homes or offices for visits from literary acquaintances and friends. Although the demands of the circle had changed, the historically grounded attitudes of intellectuals to their vocation and personal relationships remained intact. Thus, despite the fact that no one ever

---

3   Nikolai Berdiaev, *Samopoznanie*, 3rd ed. (Paris: YMCA, 1989), 182. See also Fedor Stepun's memoirs regarding evenings in the offices of "Musaget": "Besides the almost daily meetings of the basic core of the contributors, in 'Musaget' open evenings were organized to which fifty and sometimes more came." Stepun, *Byvshee i nesbyvsheesia* (New York: Chekhov, 1956), 1: 272. In addition, Evgeniia Gertsyk describes her "open house, " where the "intense life" of Moscow's intelligentsia took place. Gertsyk, *Vospominamia*, 145-65.

acknowledged a "Gershenzon circle," Gershenzon's visitors could perceive the historian in images suitable to a "leader."

In her memoirs of the period, Gershenzon's daughter adumbrates the contours of the intellectual circle which met in the historian's home between 1910-1917. Nataliia Mikhailovna Chegodaeva-Gershenzon describes its activities and lists its members:

> At the time the circle of writers and philosophers in Moscow lived a particularly intense intellectual life and interaction between them was extremely lively. They often gathered, heatedly argued, read and discussed their new works. From 1913-17 to our home frequently came L. I. Shestov, V. Ivanov, A. Bely, the philosophers G. Shpet, Ern, N. Berdiaev, D. N. Zhukovsky, the lawyer B.A. Kistiakovsky, the historian D. M. Petrushevsky, the Pushkinist M. A. Tsiavlovsky, the poets Iu. N. Verkhovsky and V. F. Khodasevich, the publisher M. B. Sabashnikov, A. Remizov, and many others, who came less often. From among the literary ladies, A. N. Chebotarevskaia was an especially close friend.[4]

The members of this circle were Gershenzon's Symbolist friends, the contributors to *Vekhi* (*Landmarks*), fellow Pushkinists, and younger poets. In their memoirs of that period, so many individuals describe their stimulating visits to Gershenzon. Andrei Bely in his memoirs openly announces what others merely hint at, writing, "The apartment on Nikol'sky pereulok many years represents for me a true symbol of the brilliant cultural work of Moscow, perhaps, of all Russia."[5]

Although Nataliia Chegodaeva-Gershenzon does not claim that Gershenzon was the group's leader, from my study it is clear that he

---

4   See Brian Horowitz, "Les premiers pas dans la vie: les années de mon immortalité," *La revue des etudes slaves* 63 (1991): 623.

5   Andrei Bely, "M. O. Gershenzon," *Rossiia* 5, no.14 (1925): 248. In her memoirs, Evgeniia Gertsyk comments about Gershenzon's home, writing, "I'm not sure if it seemed to me or it was true that nowhere else was the fireplace the hottest, nowhere else was as informal as in Gershenzon's kitchen where we sat in the evening with our tea" (*Vospominaniia*, 160). Gershenzon figures in the memoirs of V. Khodasevich, A. Bely, E. Gertsyk, N. Valentinov, N. Berberova, V. Lidin, B. Zaitsev, M. Sabashnikov, N. Krandievskaia-Tolstaia, A. Batrakh, N. Gershenzon-Chegodaeva, and F. Stepun.

wanted and made conscious efforts to play that role. According to Pavel Sakulin, Gershenzon wanted to be a representative of the Russian intelligentsia. Writing in an unpublished eulogy, "Apology of the Spirit: M. O. Gershenzon and the Russian Intelligentsia" ("Apologiia dukha: M. O. Gershenzon i russkaia intelligentsiia"), Sakulin claims:

> M. O. Gershenzon considered his task to be the same as for the whole Russian intelligentsia. He united his spiritual interests entirely with the interests of the Russian intelligentsia. He constantly expressed himself, "We Russian intellectuals." He knew that in the course of many decades the finest representatives of the Russian intelligentsia stubbornly thought about the same things that he did. Therefore he so lovingly studied the history of the Russian intelligentsia, the history of its errors and searches.[6]

Marc Raeff has pointed out that the leader must be perceived as worthy of veneration. In a 1925 meeting of the Leningrad Society of Bibliophiles, N. I. Pozharsky declared, "It is strange that M. O. Gershenzon, a person of the second half of the nineteenth and first quarter of the twentieth century was a typical representative of Slavophilism. He was uncommonly practical, although he could not adapt to life, was uncorruptable—almost a saint. He works are not eternal, no genius; but as a person, a figure, he takes on enormous significance."[7] Pozharsky emphasizes the contradictions of Gershenzon's persona. He was perhaps not a genius, his works were not classics (sic), but still Russian culture pays tribute to his memory because of his symbolic figure.

In his synthetic and creative works on Pushkin, Gershenzon established an indelible association between himself and the poet. From these works participants in the Silver-Age culture aligned Gershenzon with Pushkin. These identifications are broad. At once we find sympathetic juxtapositions and angry accusations that Gershenzon projected

---

[6] Pavel Sakulin, "Apologiia dukha: M. O. Gershenzon i russkaia intelligentsiia," unpublished essay. Pavel Sakulin papers located in TsGALI: 444-1-14.

[7] N. Pozharsky, unpublished notes from meeting on March 20, 1925. A. G. Bisnek Papers 247, (Leningradskoe obshchestvo bibliofilov, Protokoly [1-51] obshchikh sobranii [1923-1927]), located at the Russian National Library, St. Petersburg, fond 76 no. 65.

his own person onto the poet's legacy.

To explain the significance of Pushkin in the cultural life of Gershenzon's time, I quote from Boris Gasparov's introduction to a collection of essays concerning the influence of Russia's Golden Age on the Silver Age. About the significance of the symbol of Pushkin Gasparov writes, "Life seemed to be saturated with Pushkin's image; his various attributes glimmered, signs of his eternal, absolute presence were found in all aspects of art and life. He was everywhere: in the artistic monuments of the Modernist age, in philosophical and aesthetic debates, in historical events and in real-life situations, in the topographical signposts of the cultural scenery, in the symbolism of dates and names and, finally, in individuals' physical appearance and personality."[8]

In his spiritual characteristics and physical appearance, the twentieth-century Pushkinist was perceived in terms of the nineteenth century poet. Fedor Stepun observed, for example (1956), " M. O. Gershenzon, a small, stout, modestly dressed man with a seething temperament, but balanced, bright, a spirit fortified by Pushkin . . ." [9] Andrei Bely also confirmed the image, referring to the idea of Gershenzon as a "black man" with an explosive, destructive temperament (this depiction corresponds to the popular image of Pushkin during the Silver Age, expressed originally by Vladimir Solov'ev in his 1897 essay, "Pushkin's Fate" ["Sud'ba Pushkina"]). In his memoirs Bely writes:

> ... And I thought, this respected figure has a temperament truly negroid, and a young boy's quickness.
> ...That's him, Gershenzon!
> In other words, not typical, not a whitebeard; not Natanson, but a "coffee perculator": boiling over, pouring out its hot coffee....[10]

---

8   Boris Gasparov, "Introduction: The 'Golden Age' and its Role in the Cultural Mythology of Russian Modernism, " in *Cultural Mythologies of Russian Modernism: From the Golden Age to the Silver Age*, eds. B. Gasparov, Robert P. Hughes, and Irina Paperno, *California Slavic Studies*, ser. 15, 1 (Berkeley: University of California Press, 1992): 3-18.
9   Fedor Stepun, *Byvshee i nesbyvsheesia* (New York: Chekhov, 1956), 1: 265-66.
10 Andrei Bely, "M. O. Gershenzon, " *Rossiia* 5, no.14 (1925): 248. In her article, "Pushkin v zhizni cheloveka serebrianogo veka, " Irina Paperno sees a link between Andrei Bely's description of Gershenzon and the description of "Dudkin" in the novel *Petersburg,* writing, "In his memoirs, *Mezhdu dvukh revoliutsii* (Between Two Revolutions), Andrei Bely describes Gershenzon as a Negro Pushkinist: 'African', with a dark-brown nose', 'on his brown dark face lips that were puffed like plums.' (Gershenzon's unexpected visit is described in vocabulary that is very close to the

Mark Andreevich Natanson (1850-1919) (peudonym Bobrov), the Populist and revolutionary and later left-Socialist Revolutionary here symbolizes the boring and ineffectual populists who ruled Russian culture a decade earlier. Natanson was also a Jew and with the adjective "whitebeard" Bely hints at Gershenzon's Jewish identity. Moreover, by calling him a negroid, Bely alludes to Gershenzon's semitic appearance, his dark skin, and his impulsiveness.

Gershenzon himself established an identification with Pushkin by participating in the culture's "mythologization" of the poet, one aspect of which was the desire to resurrect and reanimate Pushkin. Among others, Dmitry Merezhkovsky, Zinaida Gippius, Valery Briusov, Marina Tsvetaeva and Andrei Bely participated in this endeavor. In "Article for a Certain Daily Paper" ("Stat'ia dlia odnoi dnevnoi gazety") Gershenzon describes his own attempts to get "closer" to the person of Pushkin, emphasizing his relation to the living monuments connected with the poet (1924):

> My generation is probably the last that still saw in their own lives even weak traces of the living Pushkin. We still knew people who had seen Pushkin; for late-comers there only remains what is preserved in museums, his things and manuscripts. In my youth my grandfather who lived all his life in Kishinev, told me how he saw Pushkin in the city gardens during his walk, Pushkin running in plaid pants with a cane. Later in Moscow as a student I met a few times in Red Square A. A. Pushkin, the poet's eldest son, a tall, lanky old man in a general's grey overcoat, and I passed by his front door with the copper sign: "A. A. Pushkin..." ...I felt happy to hear these Pushkin names, not from books, but names of living places where this man lives and walks.[11]

It is not chance that Gershenzon used the present tense ("lives and walks"). Gershenzon linked his life with Pushkin's in various ways. His

---

depiction of Dudkin's vision of the Bronze Horseman in the novel, *Peterburg*.) 'Neighing like a train releasing steam, ' 'expelled steam from his wide nostrils.'" Irina Paperno, "Pushkin v zhizni cheloveka Serebrianogo veka, " 35.

11 M.O. Gershenzon, "Stat'ia dlia odnoi dnevnoi gazety, " in *Stat'i o Pushkine* (Leningrad: 1926), 111.

hometown, Kishinev, was Pushkin's home for a time and his grandfather saw the poet and "genetically" passed the experience to his grandson. In the passage, Kishinev and Moscow become two sister cities linking Pushkin's and Gershenzon's fates.

Gershenzon was not alone in linking the Russian Silver and Golden Ages. Mikhail Tsiavlovsky explained that, "Gershenzon conceived of the publication of the collection, 'Pushkin Annual for 1925,' in which, besides various articles and materials about Pushkin, there was going to be a 'memorial' part devoted to Pushkin's life and works in 1825 and a bibliography of work on Pushkin in 1924. Such an annual Mikhail Osipovich proposed bringing out every year."[12]

The significance of Gershenzon's death, 'the death of the Pushkinist' was also creatively interpreted as linked to Pushkin's. In each case, death symbolized the end of a creative epoch and the commencement of a cruel and materialistic age. According to Irina Paperno, we find this image in Khodasevich's article, "Bloody Victuals" ("Krovavaia pishcha") in which Khodasevich describes Gershenzon's death "as an example of the death of the poet, a repeating symbolic event which has Pushkin's death as its original prototype."[13] In Ol'ga Forsh's novel, *Sumasshedshy korabl'* (*The Ship of Fools*, 1931) we also find a similar interpretation of Gershenzon's death. Forsh describes a scene which has a real-life prototype. It seems that at Gershenzon's funeral, despite the fact that no speeches were to be made, a Communist began to talk, saying that although Gershenzon was not "ours," the proletariat still pays tribute to this "survivor" of bourgeois culture. "He was useful, like a cog-wheel in a carriage, and hopefully he will soon be replaced by another." At this moment Aleksandra Chebotarevskaia, the sister of Sologub's wife and a poet in her own right, couldn't control herself and expressed everything which had gathered in her soul, saying it was quite unlikely that such a one as Gershenzon could ever be replaced. When everyone had left the cemetery, she couldn't calm herself the whole day, and in the evening, she went to the Bolshoi Kamenny Most and threw herself from the bridge into the icy waters.[14]

---

12 Mikhail Tsiavlovsky, *Moskovsky Pushkinist* (Moscow: 1927), 3.
13 Paperno, "Pushkin v zhizni cheloveka Serebrianogo veka," 35.
14 For the description of this scene in Ol'ga Forsh's novel, see *Sumasshedshii korabl'* (Washington D.C.: Inter-Language Literary Associates, 1964), 202. I am indebted to Irina Paperno for directing me to Forsh's novel. In her article, "Pushkin v zhizni cheloveka Serebrianogo veka," Paperno

Gershenzon's funeral, decorated with the contrasting imagery of the two epochs, the pre-revolutionary and the Soviet, manifested in the conflict between the individual versus the collective, the human being versus the machine, plus the accompanying suicide of Chebatorevskaia, was perceived symbolically as a critical event. Gershenzon's death was seen in terms of Pushkin's death as carrying a tragic message; it signaled the end of a creative epoch and the rise of a new and terrible era.

In his works on Russian history Gershenzon displayed personal devotion and love for his subject. This love was a byproduct of his intuitive historical method founded on personal empathy; Gershenzon believed that through personal identification with his heroes, he could mystically grasp their psychology and extract the religious essence of the ideas. At the same time, the scholar's empathy and love came to be seen as a virtue in itself, both by Gershenzon and by his contemporaries. For at least one section of the intelligentsia, spiritual identification with and personal commitment to Russian culture served as a category of aesthetic judgment which redeems the faults in a writer's personality or the mistakes in his work. In his review of N. O. Lerner's *Pushkin's Works and Days* (*Trudy i dni Pushkina*), for example, Gershenzon writes (1910):

> It is understandable how great is the exhaustive knowledge of the subject and how inexhaustible one's patience must be in order to carry out this work; only love generates such knowledge and such patience and this touching selfless love for Pushkin lends Mr. Lerner's book, in my view, the character of a morally beautiful act. Pushkin's personality and poetry are one of the phenomena of eternal beauty... Only a person whose soul, perhaps in secret and unaware, reaches inexorably for the sun, only such a person can so tenderly and with such devotion love the poet, as Mr. Lerner loves Pushkin.[15]

---

writes, "...One of the central scenes of the novel is the funeral of the Pushkinist—prototype Gershenzon—and the central ideas are expressed in a quoted passage from the notes of the main character devoted to Pushkin and the end of the Petersburg culture. 'Amazing,' the hero writes, 'how everything originates with Pushkin and everything returns to Pushkin.'" ("Pushkin v zhizni cheloveka Serebrianogo veka," 36)

[15] M.O. Gershenzon, review of *Trudy i Dni Pushkina*, by N. Lerner, *Russkaia Mysl'* 10 (1910): 328.

Gershenzon's evaluation points to love for Russian culture as a value higher than objective truth. Sympathetic critics praised Gershenzon's work precisely for this "love." About his book *Krivtsov the Decembrist and His Brothers* (*Dekabrist Krivtsov i ego brat'ia*) A. Izgoev writes, "What explains the power of M. O. Gershenzon's beautiful and idiosyncratic talent? [The power] lies in his unusual deep but balanced love for Russian society of the last century [nineteenth century]. ...He reanimates his life with his love."[16] Leonid Grossman expressed a similar idea: "A profound artist in the difficult art of painting souls, an amazing actor of the word, a subtle portrait painter of past people and generations, he was not only able to draw his heroes with rare clarity, but to inspire the reader with the whole of reserve of charm contained in them and infect us with his inexhaustible love for the forgotten images of the past."[17]

Despite their different ideological affiliations, critics admired Gershenzon's love for Russian culture and assigned it aesthetic value. Relying exclusively on a subjective method, however, Gershenzon made grave mistakes. Besides eliciting criticism, these mistakes also paradoxically lent him the aura of an ideal person. Khodasevich writes: "In some sense Gershenzon's mistakes are more valuable and deeper than many truths. He divined in Pushkin a great deal that our wisemen never even dreamed of."[18] V. Veresaev expresses the same idea:

> His method is useless, but he himself is so smart and interesting, knows Pushkin so well and so touchingly loves him, has thought about him so much, that you read any of his works: immediately you do not agree with a single word, you mark up the whole article with question and exclamation marks, but you finish reading and in your head so many questions come up that you begin to feel Pushkin anew; you begin clearly to realize the need for a more sustained, deeper, and sharper reading of Pushkin that you get more from this article than from one with which you agreed with entirely.[19]

---

16 A.S. Izgoev, review of *Dekabrist Krivtsov*, by M. Gershenzon, *Rech'* 100, 14 April 1914: 3.
17 Leonid Grossman, "M.O. Gershenzon, " *Iskusstvo trudiashchimsia* 14 (1925): 12.
18 Khodasevich, *Nekropol'*, 155.
19 Ibid., 154.

Personal conversations are culturally significant among Gershenzon's friends, crossing the borders of personal life and spilling into the public realm of collective creation. In this context Gershenzon's conversations are seen as genuine artifacts of culture, solidifying his role as an ideal intellectual. For example two of the epoch's most important works, *Landmarks* (*Vekhi*) (1909), the collection of essays criticizing the Russian intelligentsia, of which Gershenzon was the volume's editor, and *Correspondence Across a Room* (*Perepiska iz dvukh uglov*, 1920) emerged from such conversations. Gershenzon's leadership position emerges in the light of *Landmarks*, since he suggested to friends in 1908 that the time had come for idealist thinkers to make their views known regarding the revolutionary intelligentsia and its failure in 1905.

The *Correspondence Across a Room* also emerged from personal conversations with a friend, this time the poet Viacheslav Ivanov. Evgeniia Gertsyk explains the work's origins: "There is a small book, *Correspondence Across a Room*, which brings to the reader the full freshness of the spirit and sound of conversations from the time. It consists of actual letters by Gershenzon and Viach[eslav] Ivanov when they, starving in 1919, found refuge in a sanatorium outside Moscow. They found a place in a single room together with other people and irrepressible talkers, in order not to bother the others, they wrote, each sitting on his cot."[20]

As the *Correspondence Across a Room* shows, personal relationships did not remain confined in a separate category, but became themselves the focus of artistic expression, and just as in Russia's Golden Age when correspondences were often creative works in their own right.[21] Parts of Andrei Bely's correspondence with Alexander Blok, for example, were published at the time they were written. In Symbolist circles the poet or artist was supposed to live "aesthetically, " realizing the theurgic principle of the artist as creator. Khodasevich alludes to this attitude when he writes in *Nekropolis* (*Nekropol'*) (1936), "At first glance it is strange that at this time and among these people the 'gift of writing' and 'gift of living' was valued almost equally."[22] Life, then, is as valuable as art, or even more valuable, since art can never express or realize the personality fully. Bely alluded to this aspect, writing about Gershenzon: "I loved

---

20 Gertsyk, *Vospominaniia*, 161.
21 William Todd, *The Familiar Letter as a Literary Genre in the Age of Pushkin* (Princeton: Princeton University Press, 1976).
22 Khodasevich, *Nekropol'*, .9.

him as a writer, but his main [idea] he did not express in books."[23] In his life, even more than in art, Gershenzon expressed his genuine self.

Gershenzon's physical home off the Arbat on Nikol'sky pereulok became a symbolic location representative of Russian culture. The symbolic image of the house is conjured up in the description of its as a magical and mysterious place. Bely writes, "…One had to climb up the stairs. From the entrance hall one had to climb a second time to find oneself in two little, clean, illuminated rooms, where Gershenzon carried out his magic, spraying living water over the dead museum artifacts that he had collected; in these actions he seemed to me like a kind of Merlin."[24] In Ol'ga Forsh's novel, *Ship of Fools*, the hero describes as cultural events in their own right her talks with a character drawn from Gershenzon. She views them as mystical, unusual, and a creative revival of the Silver Age during the days of Bolshevism. "To the Chaldean many people came before because he was full of talent, erudition, culture, and interaction with him enriched one. But now they came even when he didn't invite, they didn't extort erudition from him, each spoke his own; they had forgotten how to talk this way and even didn't know that one could speak in such a way. And now he was able especially to listen. He gave himself over not to intellect or thirst for knowledge, but so it seemed, to contemplation."[25]

In addition, the furniture and decorations in Gershenzon's home had a symbolic function, a metonymic resonance in connection with Russian culture. The writer Vladimir Lidin, in his 1925 eulogy, wrote, "A bookshelf, three portraits—Pushkin, Herzen, Chaadaev—in black frames on white walls, and nothing else."[26] The chair on which Gershenzon sat also linked him to the Russian intellectual tradition; it was a chair that had belonged to Chaadaev. Khodasevich certifies, "It was a historical armchair, from Chaadaev's study."[27] Such symbolic images reflect the reverential attitude towards Gershenzon and allude to his commanding role within the group of Moscow intellectuals.

In his private life Gershenzon had the reputation of ethical uprightness. In memoirs about him his asceticism and altruism are empha-

---

23 Bely, *Rossiia*, 212.
24 A. Bely, *Mezhdu dvukh revoliutsii* (Leningrad: Izd-vo Pisatelei v Leningrade, 1934), 284.
25 Forsh, *Sumasshedshii korabl'*, 200-1.
26 Vladimir Lidin, *Rossiia* 5, no. 14 (1925): 249.
27 Khodasevich, *Nekropol'*, 144.

sized and this image of moral incorruptibility allowed him to be judged favorably against the strict criteria for the behavior of a Russian intellectual. It is true that Gershenzon lived simply, modestly, without luxuries. Partially this was the result of free choice, partially of economic necessity, since his family, consisting of his wife and two children, lived solely on the earnings from his writings. In his oftentimes miserable poverty, however, many contemporaries saw in Gershenzon rare spiritual qualities. "He lived simply, even sparsely, like a true Russian writer."[28] Gershenzon's work in organizing the first writer's union in Moscow after the Bolshevik Revolution and his requests on behalf of writers became legend. Khodasevich, usually a cruel judge of people, tenderly writes: "Those who lived in Moscow during the most difficult years, eighteen, nineteen and twenty, will never forget how great a comrade Gershenzon was. It was precisely he who conceived of the Writers' Union which eased our life so much and without which, I believe, many writers simply would have disappeared. He was the most active of the union's organizers and its first premier. But, having put the union on a solid footing, he withdrew from the leader position and remained an ordinary union member."[29]

Gershenzon's self-sacrificing and generous actions correspond to a cultural model of the ideal individual. Poverty, suffering, but also selflessness are qualities considered obligatory for a Russian intellectual. Bely describes Gershenzon as someone who aided those in need and put the interest of others before his own. For Bely he is also a personalization of the biblical maxim, "Bear fruit and multiply." Thus, Gershenzon was seen not only as charitable, but also as fertile. "Gershenzon did not have a sense of ownership: he gave others selflessly not ideas really, but kernels of thought. It was as though he said to his thought, 'Be fruitful and multiply.' Others wanted to cut them back, he grew more."[30] In his attitudes and behavior his friends perceived disciplined self-negation and generosity, and one might add, genuine asceticism. Khodasevich writes, "Anecdotes aside, I believe that in his self-denial there was true aceticism."[31]

One of the features that allowed Gershenzon to be perceived as em-

---

28 Lidin, *Rossiia*, 259.
29 Khodasevich, *Nekropol'*, 150-51.
30 Bely, *Mezhdu dvukh revoliutsii*, 292-93.
31 Khodasevich, *Nekropol'*, 150.

bodying his culture is his ability to mutate and appear in association with contemporary trends, movements, and ideas. He is described as a synthesizer of contradictions and opposites; he is at once young, old, helpful, and helpless, a genius and an imposter, Russian and non-Russian, a man of light and erudition and an underground man, an obscurantist. These paradoxes, instead of dispelling the idea of Gershenzon as a "Kulturträger," reinforce and underscore that identification.

Although some described him as an ugly old Jew, it was this appearance that served as evidence of his ideal role. Khodasevich sketches a Semitic monster. "...A small man, thick eyebrows with a moustache, a puffy mouth, a fat nose, a pince-nez, typical Jew."[32] But only pages later Khodasevich praises this Jew, "He was one of the deepest and subtlest critics of poetry that I ever met."[33] Georgy Chulkov sees Gershenzon's Judaism as an emblematic symbol of high spiritual qualities. In an unpublished poem, "You Prefer to Live in Darkness" ("Ty volish zhit' vo t'me"), dedicated to Gershenzon, written while both writers were relaxing in Gaspra in 1925, Chulkov ties the historian's Semitic appearance to his interior image as an Old-Testament seeker of spiritual truths.

> Потомок странников пустыни,
> Искатель истины! Во мрак
> Ты устремил свой взор – и ныне
> Во тьме ты ищешь вещий знак.
> Найдешь ли? Знает Бог, – но совесть
> Тебе – как верная жена,
> И жизнь твоя как сердца повесть:
> То отчей правды письмена.
> Ты в них увидел правду Божью,
> Как свет зарниц во мраке туч...
> И вот бредешь по придорожью,
> Лелея сердце веры ключ.[34]

Descendent of wanderers in the desert

---

32 Ibid.
33 Ibid., 154.
34 G. Chulkov, "Ty volish' zhit' vo t'me," an unpublished poem dedicated to M.O. Gershenzon, Gershenzon's papers, TsGALI (130-1-115).

> Seeker of truth! In darkness
> You directed your sight-and now
> In darkness you search for a prophetic sign.
> Will you find it? God knows, —but conscience is to you
> Like a faithful wife,
> And your life is like a story of the heart:
> The words of ancient truth
> In them you see God's truth,
> Like summer's light in the darkness of storm clouds…
> And you walk along the side of the road,
> cherishing the heart of a key of faith.[35]

Leonid Grossman attributes Gershenzon's success as an artist to his Jewish background, remarking that, by virtue of his race, he has become one of the great figures of Russian culture. In his article, "Gershenzon-Writer" ("Gershenzon-pisatel'") (1926), Grossman writes, "He gave to Russian literature his Jewish heart in love with the Slavic soul and with true righteousness in the fulfillment of his mission with simplicity and unintentionally he completed his life's work and found himself unexpectedly even to himself at the apex of Russian literature together with its great and unforgettable names."[36]

His contemporaries applauded the contradictions in his personality. This attitude can be explained by the fact that the Silver-Age culture was itself characterized by contradictions. Georges Florovsky describes the period: "It was a time of searching and seductions. Paths strangely crossed and diverged. And more than anything else were contradictions…"[37] Paradoxes pursue the portait of Gershenzon too. Bely attributes his contradictory personality to his unique capacity to conjoin the head and the heart, reason and emotions where usually people are forced to choose between them: "Antimonies of life are explained by the most rare, concrete transferrals of consciousness, his heart was embodied in his thought: he thought acutely; and he thought sincerely; in his heartbeats, momentary outbursts there was hidden an instinct of the most penetrating wisdom; he behaved as a wiseman; perceived as

---

35 My translation.
36 Leonid Grossman, "Gershenzon - pisatel', " published in M. O. Gershenzon's *Stat'i o Pushkine* (Moscow: 1926), 12.
37 G. Florovsky, *Puti russkogo bogosloviia*, 3rd. ed. (Paris: YMCA, 1982), 452-53.

a lover; in this he differed from everyone around him whom you meet who have the ordinary division of reason and feeling."[38]

In this bizarre omnipresence Gershenzon represents all of Russian culture... Bely again writes, "He made a home in various branches of culture: a materialist in one, an idealist in another, a realist in a third, and a Symbolist in the fourth. He was not just an 'ist,' he knew the ideal, but without 'ism'; he lived in the 'real' without 'ism,' interpreting in the material the symbols of the living life."[39]

The idealized perception of Gershenzon was motivated by concrete reasons and supported by the historical experience of the intelligentsia. The Russian intelligentsia has always seen itself in heroic categories, venerating its members, as priests or saints in a quasi-religious organization. Moreover, self-consciousness, or the study of the consciousness of the intelligentsia itself has traditionally been the main subject matter of the Russian inteligentsia. In his article, "Russian Intellectual History and its Historiography," Marc Raeff has written, "The notion of intellectual history, as Isaiah Berlin has pointed out, is a particularly Russian one in the sense that it is not strictly speaking a history of ideas—i.e. an investigation of the inner relationships and filiations of ideas in specific fields such as philosophy, politics and the like. It is rather an account of the tradition by which succeeding generations of the intelligentsia defined themselves and which they used as their guide to action."[40]

In view of this emphasis on self-definition, Gershenzon deserved the role lent him by fellow intellectuals, since he dedicated himself to the idealization of Russian intellectuals. In a sense, Gershenzon as Russian intellectual was enormously self-referential: he fostered a laudatory view of the ideal intellectual (a spiritual seeker, exactingly moral, honest, etc...), and then he set about living out these codes in his own life. It is not at all surprising that through a kind of metonymic attachment, Gershenzon came himself to represent the figures about whom he wrote.

It should be remembered that this sympathetic identification was not shared by all Russian intellectuals, but only by a small group of

---

38   Bely, *Mezhdu dvukh revoliutsii*, 282.
39   Bely, *Rossiia*, 249.
40   Marc Raeff, "Russian Intellectual History and its Historiography," *Forschungen zur Osteuropäischen Geschichte* 25 (1978): 279.

writers, who for the most part lived in Moscow and befriended Gershenzon. The limited number of adherents does not, however, invalidate the fact nor reduce the importance of Gershenzon's image. In Gershenzon these intellectuals found the embodiment of their ideal individual and by studying their perception, we learn not only more about this unique man, but also about the value system of the age itself. There is much, if one were to study the question, that links the Silver Age to the other spiritual movements in Russian culture, and the idealization of "leader" is a repeating ritual in Russian cultural life.

Bibliography

Aronson, Grigory. "Evrei v russkoi literature, kritike, zhurnalistike i obshchestvennoi zhizni." In *Kniga o russkom evreistve ot 1860-kh godov do revoliutsii 1917 g.: sbornik statei*. New York: Soiuz russkikh evreev, 1960.

Aronson, Michael. *Troubled Waters: The Origins of the 1881 Anti-Jewish Pogroms in Russia*. Pittsburgh: University of Pittsburgh Press, 1990.

Avineri, Shlomo. *The Making of Modern Zionism: The Intellectual Origins of the Jewish State*. New York: Basic Books, 1981.

Bartal, Israel. "Dubnov's Image of Medieval Autonomy." In *A Missionary for History: Essays in Honor of Simon Dubnov, Yearbook Supplement*, 11-18. Minneapolis: University of Minnesota, 1998.

———. *Jews of Eastern Europe, 1771-1881*. Philadelphia: University of Pennsylvania Press, 2005.

Bartal, Israel, Antony Polonsky, and Scott Ury, eds. *Polin: Studies in Polish Jewry, Volume: 24 Jews and their Neighbours in Eastern Europe since 1750*. Oxford: The Littman Library of Jewish Civilization, 2012.

Beckerman, Gal. *When They Come for Us We'll Be Gone: the Epic Struggle to Save Soviet Jewry*. New York: Houghton Mifflin Harcourt, 2010.

Beizer, Mikhail. *Evrei Leningrada. Natsional'naia zhizn' i sovetizatsiia: 1917-1939*. Jerusalem: Gesharim, 1999.

Berger, David, ed. *The Legacy of Jewish Migration: 1881 and its Impact*. New York: Brooklyn College Press, 1983.

Berkowitz, Michael. *Zionist Culture and West European Jewry Before the First World War*. Cambridge: Cambridge University Press, 1993.

Biale, David. *Not in the Heavens: the Tradition of Jewish Secular Thought*. Princeton: Princeton University Press, 2010.

Brann, Ross, and Adam Sutcliffe. *Renewing the Past, Reconfiguring Jewish Culture: From al-Andadlus to the Haskalah*. Philadelphia: University of Pennsylvania, Center for Advanced Judaic Studies, 2004.

Brenner, Michael. *Prophets of the Past: Interpreters of Jewish History*. Princeton: Princeton University Press, 2010.

Brutskus, Iu. "Iz moskovskikh vospominanii." In *Sbornik A. D. Idel'sona*. Berlin, 1925.

Cherikover, Elias. *Istoriia Obshchestva dlia rasprostranenmiia prosveshcheniia mezhdu evreiami v Rossii: kul'turno-obshchestvennye techeniia v russkom evreistve, 1863-1913*. St. Petersburg: s. n., 1913.

Chernov, Viktor. "Memoir about Leon Bramson." Unpublished in YIVO Archives in the Center for Jewish History (Tcherikower archive 1095, file 81109-81115).

Dahlmann, Dittmar, and Pascal Trees, eds. *Von Duma zu Duma: Hundert Jahre Russischer Parlamentarismus*. Bonn: Bonn University Press, 2008.

Di ershte sprach konferents: barikht, dokumenten und opklangen fun der Tshernovitser konferents, 1908. Vilna: Der Institut, 1931.

Dubnov, Semyon. *Epokha pervoi emancipatsii, 1789-1815: Noveishaia istoriia evreiskogo naroda*. Vols. 1-3. Jerusalem: Gesharim, 2002.

———. *Fun zhargon tsu idish*. Vilna: Kletzkin, 1929.

———. *Kniga zhizni, materialy dlia istorii moego vremeni: vospominaniia i razmyshleniia*. Moscow-Jerusalem: Gesharim, 2004.

———. "Letters on Old and New Judaism." In *Nationalism and History: Essays on Old and New Judaism*, ed. Koppel S. Pinson. Philadelphia: Jewish Publication Society, 1958.

———. "O sovremennom sostoianii evreiskoi istoriografii." *Evreiskaia starina* 1 (1910).

———. "Vospominaniia o S.M. Fruge." *Evreiskaia starina* 4 (1916).

———. *Ob izuchenii istorii russkikh evreev i ob uchrezhdenii russko-evreiskogo istoricheskogo obshchestva*. St. Petersburg: 1891.

———. *Pis'ma o starom i novom evreistve*. 2nd ed. St. Petersburg: Obshchestvennaia pol'za, 1907.

———. "Survival of the Jewish People: The Secret of Survival and the Law of Survival." In *Nationalism and History: Essays on Old and New Judaism*, ed. Koppel S. Pinson, 327. Philadelphia: Jewish Publication Society, 1958.

———. *Volkspartei: Evreiskaia Narodnaia Partiia*. St. Petersburg: Ts. Kraiz, 1907.

Dubnov-Erlich, Sophia. *Khleb i matsa: vospominaniia, stikhi raznykh let*. St. Petersburg: Maksima, 1994.

_____. *The Life and Work of S. M. Dubnov: Diaspora Nationalism and Jewish History*. Bloomington: Indiana University Press, 1990.

Elon, Amos. *The Pity of It All: A Portrait of the German Jewish Epoch, 1743-1933*. New York: Picador, 2002.

Encyclopedia Judaica. 16 Vols. Jerusalem: Keter Publishing, 1973.

Endelman, Todd, ed. *Jewish Apostasy in the Modern World*. New York: Holmes & Meier, 1987.

Evreiskaia entsiklopediia: svod znanii o evreistve i ego kul'ture v proshlom i nastoiashchem. 16 vols. St. Petersburg: Brokgauz-Efron, 1907-1913.

Feiner, Shmuel. *Haskalah and History: the Emergence of a Modern Jewish Historical Consciousness*. Translated by C. Naor and S. Silverston. Portland: Littman Library of Jewish Civilization, 2002.

Feldman, Eliyahu. *Yehudi Rusyah bi'yeme ha-mahpekhah ha-rishonah veha'pogromim*. Jerusalem: Magnes Press, 1999.

Fishman, David. *The Rise of Modern Yiddish Culture*. Pittsburgh: University of Pittsburg Press, 2000.

Frankel, Jonathan. "Crisis of 1881-82 as a Turning Point in Modern Jewish History." In *The Legacy of Jewish Migration: 1881 and its Impact*, ed. David Berger. New York: Columbia University Press, 1983.

_____. *Crisis, Revolution, and Russian Jews*. Cambridge: Cambridge University Press, 2008.

_____. *Prophecy and Politics: Socialism, Nationalism, and the Russian Jews, 1862-1917*. Cambridge: Cambridge University Press, 1981.

Frankel, J., and S. Zipperstein, eds. *Assimilation and Community: the Jews in Nineteenth-Century Europe*. Cambridge: Cambridge University Press, 1992.

Freeze, G. "The Soslovie (Estate) Paradigm and Russian Social History." *American Historical Review* 91, 1 (1986): 11-36.

Frede, Victoria. *Doubt, Atheism and the Nineteenth-Century Russian Intelligentsia*. Madison: Wisconsin University Press, 2011.

Gassenschmidt, Christoph. *Jewish Liberal Politics in Tsarist Russia, 1900-1914: The Modernization of Russian Jewry*. New York: New York University Press, 1995.

Gessen, Iulii. *Istoriia evreiskogo naroda v Rossii*. 2 vols. V. Kel'ner and V. Gessen, eds. Moscow: Evreiskii Universitet v Moskve, 1993.

Gimpel'son, Ya. I. *Zakony o evreiakh, sistematicheskii obzor deistvuiush-chikh zakonopolozhenii o evreiakh s raz'iasneniiami pravitel'stvennykh ustanovlenii*. Petersburg: Iurisprudentsiia, 1914.

Gintsburg, Shaul. *Amolike Peterburg: forshungen un zikhroynes vegn Yidishn lebn*. New York: Tsiko Bikher-Verlag, 1944.

———. "Iz zapisok pervogo evreia-studenta v Rossii," *Perezhitoe: sbornik posviashchennyi obshchestvennoi i kul'turnoi istorii evreev v Rossii*, in 4 vols., 1 (St. Petersburg: 1908-1913), 1-50.

———. *Minuvshee: istoricheskie ocherki, stat'i i kharakteristiki*. Petrograd: Izdanie avtora, 1923.

———. "O russko-everiskoi intelligentsii." *Evreiskii mir* 1 (Paris: 1939).

Gitelman, Zvi. *Century of Ambivalence: the Jews of Russia and the Soviet Union, 1881 to the Present*. 2nd ed. Bloomington: University of Indiana Press, 2001.

———. *Jewish Nationality and Soviet Politics: the Jewish Sections of the CPSU, 1917-1930*. Princeton, NJ: Princeton University Press, 1972.

Goldshtein, Yosef. *Ben tsionut medinit le-tsionut ma'asit: ha-tnuah ha-tsionit be-rusiyah be-ra'ashita*. Jerusalem: Magnes Press, 1991.

Goldstein, Alexander, et al., ed. *Sefer Idelsohn: Divre ha'arkakhah ve zikhronot, toldot hayav u-ketavav*. Tel Aviv: Va'ad Lehotsaat, 1946.

———. *Usishkin-biyografiyah: ha-tekufah ha-rusit, 1863-1919*. Jerusalem: Magnes, 1999.

Graetz, Heinrich. *Geschichte der Juden von den ältesten Zeiten bis aud die Gegenwart: Aus den Quellen neubearb*. Vol. 1-11. Leipzig: 1874-1902.

Groberg, Kristi, and Abraham Greenbaum, eds. *A Missionary for History: Essays in Honor of Simon Dubnov*. Minneapolis: University of Minnesota Press, 1998.

Grüner, Frank. "'Russia's Battle Against the Foreign': the Anti-Cosmopolitanism Paradigm in Russian and Soviet Ideology." *European Review of History* 7 (2010).

Gruzenberg, O. O. *Yesterday: Memoirs of a Russian-Jewish Lawyer*. Translated by D.C. Rawson and T. Tipson. Berkeley: University of California Press, 1981.

Haberer, Erich. *Jews and Revolution in Nineteenth Century Russia*. New York: Cambridge University Press, 1995.

Harshav, Benjamin. *The Meaning of Yiddish*. Berkeley: University of California Press, 1990.

He-Avar: Le divre yemei ha-yihudim ve-ha-yahadut be-russiyah. Tel Aviv: 1953-1958.

Herman, Luc. *Concepts of Realism.* New York: Camden House, 1996.

Horowitz, Brian. *Empire Jews: Jewish Nationalism and Acculturation in Nineteenth- and Early Twentieth-Century Russia.* Bloomington: Slavica, 2009.

____. *Jewish Philanthropy and Enlightenment in Late-Tsarist Russia.* Seattle: University of Washington Press, 2009.

____. *Myth of A.S. Pushkin in Russia's Silver Age, M.O. Gershenzon-Pushkinist.* Evanston, IL: Northwestern University Press, 1997.

Hosking, Geoffrey. *The Russian Constitutional Experiment: Government and Duma, 1907-1914.* Cambridge: Cambridge University Press, 1973.

Idel'son, Avram. *Bazel'skaia programma.* Petrograd: Vostok, 1917.

____. *Evreiskoe natsional'noe sobranie.* St. Petersburg: Vostok, 1906.

____. *Sionism: Lektsiia pervaia (teoreticheskoe obosnovanie).* Saratov: I.M. Rotshtein & S.I. Ginzburg, 1903.

____. *Sobranie sochinenii.* Petrograd: Kadima, 1919.

____. *Voina, evreistvo i Palestina: stat'i.* Petrograd: Vostok, 1916.

Jabotinsky, Vladimir. *Fel'etony.* St Petersburg: 1913.

Kantor, L. "Chem my sdelalis' v poslednie dvadtsat' piat' let?" *Russkii evrei* 4 (1880).

Kawalec, Krzyszt. *Roman Dmowski: 1864-1939.* Wroclaw: Zaklad Narodowy, 2002.

Kassow, Samuel. "Historiography." In *YIVO Encyclopedia of Jews in Eastern Europe.* Ed. Gershon Hundert. 2 vols. New Haven: Yale University Press, 2008.

Katsir: kovets le-korot ha-tenu'ah ha-tisyonit be-Rusyah. Tel Aviv: Masadah be-shituf ha-va'ad ha-tsiburi le-toldot ha-tenu'ah ha-tsionit be-Russyah, 1964.

Katz, Jacob. *Out of the Ghetto: the Social Background of Jewish Emancipation, 1770-1870.* Cambridge, MA: Harvard University Press, 1973.

Kaufman, A. *Druz'ia i vragi evreev i D. I. Pikhno.* St Petersburg: Pravda, 1907.

Kel'ner, Viktor. "Dva intsidenta: iz russko-evreiskikh otnoshenii v

nachale XX v." *Vestnik Evreiskogo Universiteta v Moskve* 3, 10 (1995).
____. *Missioner istorii: zhizn' i trudy Semena Markovicha Dubnova*. St. Petersburg: Mir, 2008.
Klausner, Yosef. *Opozitsyah le-Hertsl*. Jerusalem: Hotsa'at Ahi'ever, 1960.
Klier, John. *Imperial Russia's Jewish Question*. Cambridge: Cambridge University Press, 1995.
____. *Russians, Jews, and the Pogroms of 1881-1882*. Cambridge: Cambridge University Press, 2011.
____. "Concept of 'Jewish Emancipation' in a Russian Context." In *Civil Rights in Imperial Russia*, edited by O. Chrisp and L. Edmondson. Oxford: Clarendon Press, 1989.
Klier, John D., and Shlomo Lambroza, eds. *Pogroms: Anti-Jewish Violence in Modern Russian History*. Cambridge: Cambridge University Press, 1992.
Kucherov, S. L. *Kniga o russkom evreistve ot 1860-kh godov do revoliutsii 1917 g.* New York: Soiuz russkikh evreev, 1960.
Kurzman, Charles. *Democracy Denied, 1905-1915: Intellectuals and the Fate of Democracy*. Cambridge, MA: Harvard University Press, 2008.
Kuznits, Cecile. "The Origins of Yiddish Scholarship and the YIVO Institute for Jewish Research." PhD thesis, Stanford University, 2000.

Labroza, Shlomo. "Jewish Responses to Pogroms in Late Imperial Russia." In *Living with Antisemitism: Modern Jewish Responses*, edited by Jehuda Reinharz. Hanover: Brandeis University Press, 1987.
____. "Plehve, Kishinev and the Jewish Question: A Reappraisal." *Nationalities Papers* 12, 1 (1984): 117-27.
Lederhandler, Eli. *The Road to Modern Jewish Politics: Political Tradition and Political Reconstruction in the Jewish Community of Tsarist Russia*. New York: Oxford University Press, 1989.
Lestschinsky, Jacob. "Jewish Migrations, 1840-1946." In *The Jews*, edited by L. Finkelstein, vol. 4. Philadelphia: Jewish Publication Society, 1949.
Levanda, L. *Goriachee vremia*. St. Petersburg, 1872.
____. "Neskol'ko slov o evreiakh zapadnogo kraia Rossii. Pis'mo v redaktsiiu (Iz goroda Igumena, Minsk[oi] guber[nii])." *Rassvet* May 27 (1860): 7-9.
Levin, Alfred. *The Third Duma: Election and Profile*. Hamden, Connecticut: Archon Books, 1973.

Levin, Vladimir. "Russian Jewry and the Duma Elections, 1906-1907." *Jews and Slavs* 7. Jerusalem: Kyiv, 2000.

Lilienblum, M. L. *Hatt'ot neurim, o, Vidui ha-gadol shel ehad ha-sofrim ha-'ivrim*. Vienna: Buchdruckerei von Georg Brög, 1876.

List of Russian, Other Slavonic, and Baltic Periodicals in the New York Public Library. New York: the Library, 1916.

Litvak, Olga. *Conscription and the Search for Modern Russian Jewry*. Bloomington: Indiana University Press, 2006.

Loewe, Heinz-Dietrich. "From Charity to Social Policy: The Emergence of Jewish 'Self-Help' Organizations in Imperial Russia, 1800-1914." *East European Jewish Affairs* 27, no. 2 (1997): 53-75.

____. *Tsars and the Jews: Reform, Reaction and Anti-Semitism in Imperial Russia, 1772-1917*. Chur, Switzerland: Harwood Academic Publishers, 1993.

Maklakov, Vasily. *M. M. Vinaver i russkaia obshchestvennost' nachala XX veka*. Paris, 1905.

____. *Rechi: sudebnye, dumskie i publichnye lektsii, 1904-1926*. Paris: Izdanie Iubileinogo komiteta 1869 - 1949 gg, 1949.

____. *Vlast' i obshchestvennost' na zakate staroi Rossii (vospominaniia)*. Paris, 1936.

Maor, Yitzhak. *Sionistskoe dvizhenie v Rossii*. Translated by O. Mints. Jerusalem: Biblioteka Alia, 1977.

Maslennikov, Boris. *Morskaia karta rasskazyvaet*. Moscow: Voenizdat, 1986.

Meir, Natan M. *Kiev, Jewish Metropolis: A History, 1859-1914*. Bloomington: Indiana University Press, 2010.

Menashe, Louis. *Alexander Guchkov and the Origins of the Octobrist Party: The Russian Bourgeoisie in Politics, 1905*. New York: New York University Press, 1966.

Mendelsohn, Ezra. *Class Struggle in the Pale: The Formative Years of the Jewish Workers' Movement in Tsarist Russia*. Cambridge: Cambridge University Press, 1970.

____. *On Modern Jewish Politics*. New York: Oxford University Press, 1993.

Mendelsohn, Ezra, and Stefani Hoffman, eds. *The Revolution of 1905 and Russia's Jews*. Philadelphia: University of Pennsylvania Press, 2008.

Morgulis, Mikhail. "Evreiskii vopros v ego osnovaniiakh i chastnostiakh." *Voskhod* 1 (1881).

_____. "Natsional'nye i prakticheskie vzgliady na znachenie drevne-evreiskogo iazyka." *Den'* 3 & 6 (1869).

_____. *Voprosy evreiskoi zhizni: sbornik statei*. 2nd ed. St. Petersburg: Tip. A. N. Mikhailova, 1903.

Murav, Harriet. *Music from a Speeding Train: Jewish Literature in Post-Revolution Russia*. Stanford: Stanford University Press, 2011.

Nakhimovsky, Alice Stone. *Russian-Jewish Literature and Identity: Jabotinsky, Babel, Grossman, Galich, Roziner, Markish*. Baltimore: John Hopkins University Press, 1992.

Nathans, Benjamin. *Beyond the Pale: The Jewish Encounter with Late-Tsarist Russia*. Los Angeles: University of California Press, 2002.

_____. "Russian-Jewish Historiography." In *Historiography of Imperial Russia: The Profession and Writing of History in a Multinational State*. London: M. C. Sharpe, 1999.

_____. "Jews, Law, and the Legal Profession in Late Imperial Russia." *Evrei v Rossii, istoriia i kul'tura*. St. Petersburg: Petersburg Jewish University, 1998.

Niger, Shmuel. "Simon Dubnow as Literary Critic, " *YIVO Annual of Jewish Social Science* 1 (1946): 335-58.

Orbach, Alexander. *New Voices of Russian Jewry: A Study of Russian-Jewish Press of Odessa in the Era of the Great Reforms 1860-1871*. Leiden: E.J. Brill, 1980.

Orlinsky, Harry M. "Jewish Biblical Scholarship in America." *Jewish Quarterly Review. New Series* 47, no. 4. April (1947): 343-353.

Orshansky, Il'ia. *Evrei v Rossii: ocherki ekonomicheskogo i obshchestvennogo byta russkikh evreev*. St. Petersburg: Sh. I. Bakst, 1877.

Osorgin, M. "Vladimir Zhabotinskii." *Evreiskii mir: sbornik 1944 goda*. New York: Union of Russian Jews, 1944.

Paperno, Irina. *Cherynshevsky and the Age of Realism*. Stanford: Stanford University Press, 1988.

Petrovsky-Shtern, Yohanan. *Jews in the Russian Army, 1827-1914*. Cambridge: Cambridge University Press, 2009.

Pinson, Koppel S. "Simon Dubnow: Historian and Political Philosopher." In *Nationalism and History: Essays on Old and New Judaism*, 1-65.

Philadelphia: Jewish Publication Society, 1958.

Pisarev, Dmitry. "Bazarov." In *Sochineniia v chetirekh tomakh*, Vol. 2, 7-50. Moscow: Gosudarstvennoe Izdatel'stvo Khudozhestvennoi Literatury, 1955.

Polishchuk, Mikhail. *Evrei Odessy i Novorossii: sotsial'no-politicheskaia istoriia evreev Odessy i drugikh gorodov Novorossii, 1881-1904*. Jerusalem: Gesharim, 2002.

Polonsky, A. *The Jews in Poland and Russia: 1350-1881*. Portland, OR: Littman Library, 2010.

Posner, S. "Rol' A. I. Braudo v dele razoblacheniia Azefa." In *Aleksandr Isaevich Braudo, 1864-1924, ocherki i vospominaniia*, edited by Leon Bramson. Paris: Izdanie Kruzhka russko-evreiskoi intelligentsii v Parizhe, 1937.

Pozner, S. B. "Bor'ba za ravnopravie." *M. M. Vinaver i russkaia obshchestvennost' nachala XX veka*. Paris: Imp. Cooperative Etoile, 1937.

Rabinovich, Osip. "Odessa." *Rassvet* 5, June 17 (1860).

____. "Odessa." *Rassvet* 15, December 2 (1860).

Rabinovitch, Simon. "The Dawn of a New Diaspora: Simon Dubnov's Autonomism, from St. Petersburg to Berlin." *The Leo Baeck Institute Yearbook*. Vol. 50. Oxford: Oxford University Press, 2005.

Raeff, Mark. *Origins of the Russian Intelligentsia: The Eighteenth-Century Nobility*. New York: Harcourt, Brace & World, 1996.

____. *Russia Abroad: A Cultural History of the Russian Emigration, 1919-1939*. New York: Oxford University Press, 1990.

____. *Understanding Imperial Russia: State and Society in the Old Regime*. New York: Columbia University Press, 1984.

Raisin, Jacob. *The Haskalah Movement in Russia*. Philadelphia: Jewish Publication Society of America, 1913.

Rawson, D. C. *Russian Rightists and the Revolution of 1905*. Cambridge: Cambridge University Press, 1995.

Rechtman, A. "The Jewish Ethnographical Expedition." *Tracing An-sky, Jewish Collections from the State Ethnographical Museum in St. Petersburg*. New York: Jewish Museum, 1992.

Reinhartz, Jehuda. *Chaim Weizmann: the Making of a Statesman*. New York: Oxford University Press, 1993.

Rogachevsky, Vasilii L'vovich. *A History of Russian Jewish Literature*. Edited by Alfred Levin. Ann Arbor: Ardis, 1979.

Rogger, Hans. "Government, Jews, Peasants and Land in Post-Emancipation Russia." *Cahier du Monde Russe et Soviétique* 17, no. 1-3 (1976): 5-21, 171-211.

―――. *Jewish Policies and Right-Wing Politics in Imperial Russia*. Berkeley and Los Angeles: University of California Press, 1986.

―――. "Jewish Policy of Late Tsarism: A Reappraisal." *Weidner Library Bulletin* 25, 1-2 (1971): 42-51.

―――. *Russia in the Age of Modernization and Revolution, 1881-1917*. London and New York: Longman, 1983.

Rosenberg, William G. *Liberals in the Russian Revolution: The Constitutional Democratic Party, 1917-1921*. Princeton: Princeton University Press, 1974.

Rosenthal, Leon. *Toledot hevrat marbe haskalah be-Yisrael be-erets rusiyah*. 2 vols. St. Petersburg, 1886-90.

Roskies, David. *Against the Apocalypse: The Responses to Catastrophe in Modern Jewish Culture*. Syracuse: Syracuse University Press, 1999.

Rozental, Yehudah. "Ha-historiografiya ha-yehudit be-rusiya ha-sovyetit ve Shim'on Dubnov." In *Sefer Shim'on Dubnov*, edited by Simon Rawidowicz. London: Arat Publishing Company, 1954.

Safran, Gabriella. *Wandering Soul: The Dybbuk's Creator, S. An-sky*. Cambridge, MA: Harvard University Press, 2010.

Sbornik statei po evreiskoi istorii i literature, izdavaemyi obshchestvom dlia rasprostraneniia prosveshcheniia mezhdu evreiami v Rossii. St. Petersburg, 1866-67.

Schwarcz, Vera. *Bridge Across Broken Time: Chinese and Jewish Cultural Memory*. New Haven: Yale University Press, 1998.

Shneer, David. *Yiddish and the Creation of Soviet Jewish Culture*. Cambridge: Cambridge University Press, 2004.

Schneer, Jonathan. *The Balfour Declaration: the Origins of the Arab-Israeli Conflict*. New York: Random House, 2010.

Seltzer, Robert. "Coming Home: The Personal Basis of Simon Dubnow's Ideology." *Association for Jewish Studies Review* 1 (1976).

―――. "Simon Dubnow: A Critical Biography of his Early Years." PhD diss., Columbia University, 1970.

Serman, Ilya. "Spory 1908 goda o russko-evreskoi literature i posleoktiabr'skoe desiatiletie." *Cahiers du Monde Russe et Soviétique* 36, no. 2 (Avril-Juin 1985): 167-74.

Shimoni, Gideon. *The Zionist Ideology.* Hanover: University Press of New England, 1995.
Shrayer, Maxim, ed. *An Anthology of Russian-Jewish Literature: Two Centuries of Dual Identity in Prose and Poetry.* 2 vols. Armonk, NY: M. E. Sharpe, 2007.
Slezkine, Yuri. *The Jewish Century.* Princeton: Princeton University Press, 2004.
Sliozberg, G. *Dela minuvshikh dnei: zapiski russkogo evreia.* 3 vols. Paris, 1933.
____. *Evrei v dorevoliutsionnoi Rossii.* St. Petersburg, 1907.
____. "Lichnost' A. I. Braudo." In *Aleksandr Isaevich Braudo, 1864-1924, ocherki i vospominaniia,* edited by Leon Bramson. Paris: Izdanie Kruzhka Russko-evreiskoi Intelligentsii v Parizhe, 1937.
____. *Pravovoe i ekonomicheskoe polozhenie evreev v Rossii.* St. Petersburg, 1907.
Slutzky, Yehudah. *Ha-'itonut ha-yehudit-rusit ba'me'ah ha-esrim (1900-1918).* Tel Aviv: ha-Agudah le-Heker Toldot ha-Yehudim ha-Makhon le-Heker ha Tefutsot, 1978.
Solov'ev, Vladimir. "Evreistvo i khristianskii vopros." In *Taina Izrailia,* edited by V. Boikov. St. Petersburg: Sofiia, 1993.
____. "Natsional'nyi vopros v Rossii." *Sobranie socheinenii v 10 tomakh,* vol. 5. Bruxelles: Foyer Oriental Chrétien, 1966.
Sosis, Izrael. "Natsional'nyi vopros v literature 60-kh godov." *Evreiskaia Starina* 1 (1913).
____. "Period 'obruseniia': natsional'nyi vopros v literature kontsa 60-kh i nachala 70-x godov." *Evreiskaia starina* 1 (1915): 129-42.
Stampfer, Shaul. *Ha-Yeshivah be-Lita, ibe-hithavutah.* Jerusalem: Zalmon Shazar Center, 1995.
Stanislawski, Michael. *Zionism and the Fin de Siècle: Cosmopolitanism and Nationalism from Nordau to Jabotinsky.* Berkeley: University of California Press, 2001.
Struve, Pyotr. *Patriotica: Politika, kul'tura, religiia, sotsialism.* Moscow: Respublika, 1997.

Terras, Victor. *Belinskii and Russian Literary Criticism: The Heritage of Organic Aesthetics.* Madison, WI: University of Wisconsin Press, 1974.
____, ed. *The Handbook of Russian Literature.* New Haven: Yale University Press, 1985.

Trunk, Isaiah. "Istoriki russkogo evreistva." *Kniga o evreistve ot 1860-kh godov do revoliutsii 1917 g.: sbornik statei*. New York: Soiuz russkikh evreev, 1960.

Tsitron, Sh. *Shtadlanim: interesante yidishe tipn fun noyentn ever*. Warsaw, 1926.

Turgenev, I. S. "Neschastnaia." In *Polnoe sobranie sochienii i pisem v dvadtsati vos'mi tomakh*. Vol. 10. Moscow-Leningrad: Nauka, 1965.

Urussoy, Sergei. *Memoirs of a Russian Governor*. London: Harper & Brothers, 1908.

Veidlinger, Jeffrey. *Jewish Public Culture in the Late-Tsarist Empire*. Bloomington: Indiana University Press, 2009.

____. *Moscow State Yiddish Theater: Jewish Culture on the Soviet Stage*. Bloomington: Indiana University Press, 2000.

____. "Simon Dubnow Recontextualized: The Sociological Conception of Jewish History and the Russian Intellectual Legacy." In *Simon Dubnow Institute Year Book* 3. Leipzig: 2004.

Vengerov, Semyon, ed. *Kritiko-biograficheskii slovar' russkikh pistaelei i uchenykh*. 2nd ed. Petrograd: 1915.

Vinaver, M. *Istoriia vyborgskogo vozzvaniia (vospominaniia)*. Moscow: 1913.

____. *Kadety i evreiskii vopros*. Odessa: 1912.

____. *Konflikty v pervoi dume*. St. Petersburg: 1907.

____. *Nedavnee: vospominaniia i kharakteristiki*. 2nd ed. Paris: D'art Voltaire, 1926.

____. *Po vekham: sbornik statei ob intelligentsii i 'natsional'nom litse'*. Moscow: 1909.

____. *Rechi M. M. Vinavera (partiia narodnoi svobody)*. St. Petersburg: 1907.

Vital, David. *Zionism: The Crucial Phase*. Oxford and New York: Claredon Press, 1987.

Volkspartei, evreiskaia narodnaia partiia. St. Petersburg: Ts. Kraiz, 1907.

Vladimir Medem: tsum tsvantsiksten yartseit. New York, 1943.

Walicki, Andrzej. *A History of Russian Thought: From the Enlightenment to Marxism*. Stanford: Stanford University Press, 1979.

Wengeroff, Pauline. *Memoirs of a Grandmother: Scenes from the Cultural

History of the Jews of Russia of the Nineteenth Century. Vol. 1. Edited by Shulamit Magnus. Palo Alto: Stanford University Press, 2010.

Wolitz, Seth. "Inscribing An-sky's *Dybbuk* in Russian and Jewish Letters." In *The Worlds of S. An-sky, A Russian-Jewish Intellectual and the Turn of the Century*, edited by G. Safran and S. Zipperstein. Stanford: Stanford University Press, 2006.

Zaslavskii, D., and S. Ivanovich. *Kadety i evrei*. Petrograd: 1916.

Zeltser, Arkady. *Evrei sovetskoi provintsii: Vitebsk i mestechki, 1917-1941*. Moscow: Rosspen, 2006.

Zimmerman, Joshua. *Poles, Jews and the Politics of Nationality: The Bund and the Polish Socialist Party in Late Tsarist Russia, 1892-1914*. Madison, WI: University of Wisconsin Press, 2003.

Zinberg, Israel. *The Haskalah Movement in Russia*. Jerusalem: Ktav, 1978.

Zipperstein, Steven. *Elusive Prophet: Ahad-Ha'am and the Origins of Zionism*. Berkeley: University of California Press, 1993.

_____. *Imagining Russian Jewry: Memory, History, Identity*. Seattle: University of Washington Press, 1999.

Zohar, Zion, ed. *Sephardic and Mizrachi Jewry: From the Golden Age of Spain to Modern Times*. New York: New York University Press, 2005.

Appendix A:
Jewish Monuments in Russia at the Turn of the 20th Century
(From the William Brumfield Collection)

1. Synagogue at Preobrazhenskoe Jewish Cemetery. Photograph by William Brumfield.

2a. Preobrazhenskoe Jewish Cemetery, south area, Main Allee. Abram M. Varshavskii mausoleum. Photograph by William Brumfield.

2b. Mark Antokol'skii grave. Photograph by William Brumfield.

Appendix A

3. Voronezh synagogue, southeast view. Photograph by William Brumfield.

4. Voronezh synagogue, east facade. Photograph by William Brumfield.
5. Voronezh synagogue, west facade, main entrance. Photograph by William Brumfield.

6. Cheliabinsk synagogue, Pushkin Street, east facade. Photograph by William Brumfield.
7. Chita synagogue, northeast view. Photograph by William Brumfield.

Appendix B: Rare Photographs of Mikhail Osipovich Gershenzon and his Family

1. Maria Borisovna Gershenzon (née Gol'denveizer), Natal'ia Mikhailovna Gershenzon- Chegodaeva, Sergei Mikhailovich Gershenzon, Mikhail Osipovich Gershenzon, Ekaterina Nikolaevna Orlova. Photograph provided courtesy of Maria Andreevna Chegodaeva.

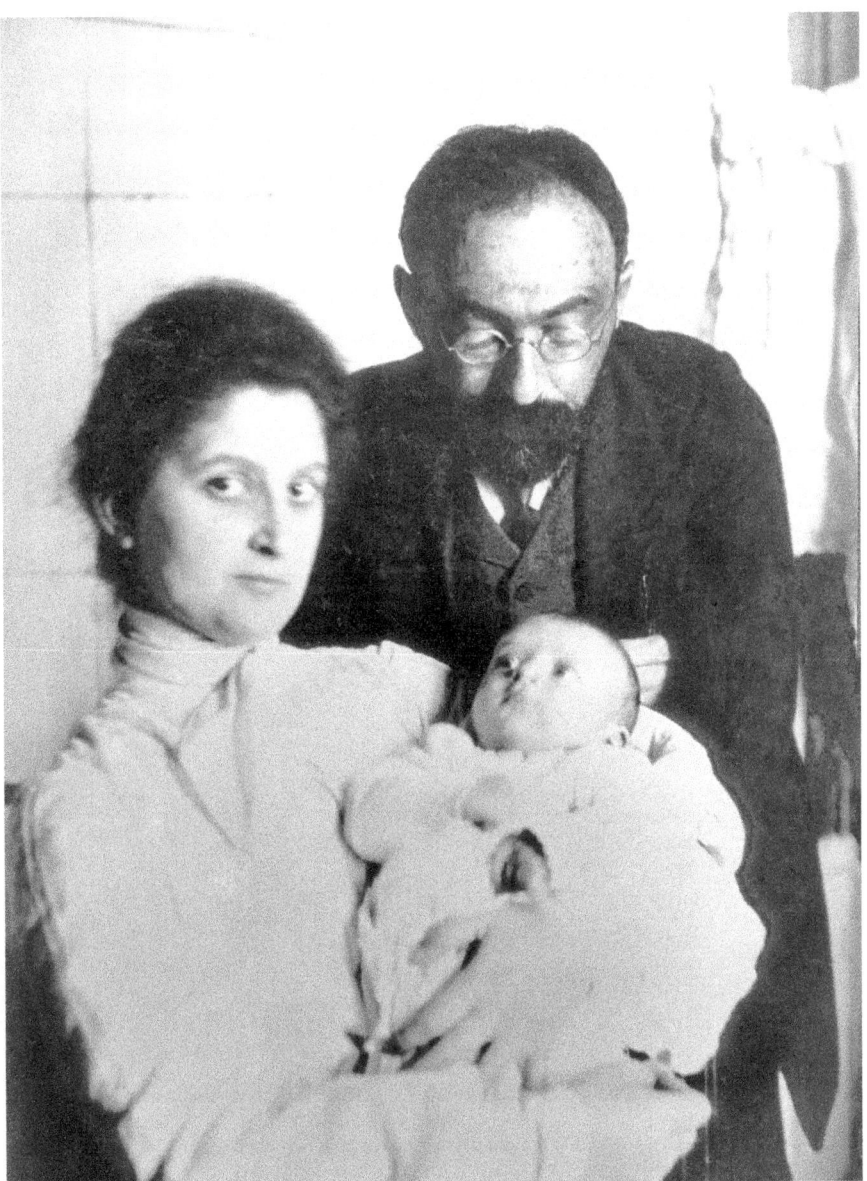

2. Maria Borisovna Gershenzon, Mikhail Osipovich Gershenzon, & Sergei Mikhailovich Gershenzon. Photograph provided courtesy of Maria Andreevna Chegodaeva.

3. Mikhail Osipovich Gershenzon and his golden retriever circa 1900. Photograph provided courtesy of Maria Andreevna Chegodaeva.

4. Maria Borisovna Gershenzon (née Gol'denveizer) & Mikhail Osipovich Gershenzon circa 1920. Photograph provided courtesy of Maria Andreevna Chegodaeva.

5. Mikhail Osipovich Gershenzon with his children Sergei Mikahilovich Gershenzon and Nataliia Borisovna Gershenzon-Chegodaeva. Photograph provided courtesy of Maria Andreevna Chegodaeva.

6. Group photo at Mikhail Osipovich Gershenzon's wake in 1925, apparently at GAKhN (The State Academy of the Arts), where Mikhail Osipovich Gershenzon taught in his final years. In the center is Pyotr Semyonovich Kagan, the president of the academy. Photograph provided courtesy of Maria Andreevna Chegodaeva.

7. Group photo at GAKhN (The State Academy of the Arts), where Mihkail Osipovich Gershenzon was a professor in the 1920s and until his death in 1925. Photograph provided courtesy of Maria Andreevna Chegodaeva.

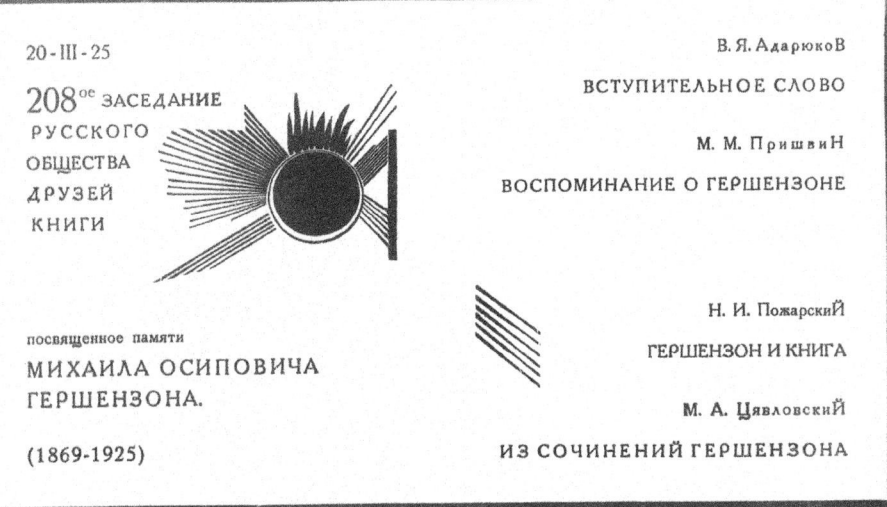

8. Invitation card to an evening of lectures dedicated to the memory of Mikhail Osipovich Gershenzon, March 20, 1925. Photograph provided courtesy of Maria Andreevna Chegodaeva.

9. Portrait of Maria Borisovna Gershenzon (née Gol'denveizer). Photograph provided courtesy of Maria Andreevna Chegodaeva.

INDEX

1881 Pogroms, 105, 112, 120, 121, 137
1905 Revolution, 27, 38, 47, 58-61, 103, 106, 114-121, 216-219, 221
Ahad-Ha'am (Asher Ginsburg), 54, 57, 62, 65, 72, 82
Aikhenval'd, Yuly, 215
Aksakov, Konstantin, 24, 182, 187, 246
Alexander II, 89, 105, 106, 109, 119, 120, 121
Alexander III, 13, 121, 137
All-Russian Jewish Congress, 59
An-sky, Shimon (Rappaport), 20n.8, 99-102, 128-132
Anti-semitism, 35, 57, 63, 64, 66, 110, 125, 126, 133, 134, 135, 136, 210
Asch, Shalom, 125
Assimilatio (integration), 24-26, 62-64, 72-75, 82-85, 106-109, 114, 120-122, 132, 136
Autonomists (anti-integrationists, or "nationalists"), 63-65, 82-85, 119
Azef, Yevno, 125

Balfour Declaration, 67-70
Bal Shem Tov (Yisroel ben Eliezer), 95-96
Basel Program, 67
Baten'kov, G.G., 156, 157
Beilis, Mendel, 33, 113, 133-134
Belinksy, Vissarion, 24, 179, 180, 241, 246-248, 253
Bely, Andrei, 19, 206, 218, 259-261, 263, 264, 268-273

Ben-Ami, Mark (Mordechai) Rabinovich, 82
Ben Gurion, 54
Berdiaev, Nikolai, 13, 141, 182, 203, 206, 213, 217, 225, 259-261
Bergson, Henri, 231
Berlin, 56, 69, 124, 151, 167
Bialik, Hayim Nachman, 57
Bialystok pogrom, 50, 51
Blok, Alexsandr, 19, 205n24, 212, 219, 268
Bogrov, Grigorii, 132
Bolsheviks, 68, 70, 135-137, 198, 205, 206, 236, 237, 254-256, 268
Bramson, Leon, 127
Braudo, Alexander, 127, 130
Briullov, Karl, 48
Briusov, Valery, 218, 264
Brodsky, Abraham, 73, 77
Brutskus, Yuly, 54, 55
Buber, Martin, 54
Bulgakov, Sergei, 213-215, 219, 225, 237, 260
Bund (General Jewish Labor Bund in Lithuania, Poland, and Russia), 87, 114, 117, 118

Carlyle, Thomas, 152
Chaadaev, Pyotr, 13, 154, 161-168, 194, 241, 242, 247, 248, 269
Chebotarevskaia, Anastasia, 261, 265, 266
Cherneshevsky, Nikolai, 23, 24, 130, 248
Chulkov, Georgy, 271, 272
Civil War (Russian), 125, 135-137, 212, 236, 254, 255

Communism, 19, 70, 225
Constituent Assembly, 51
Consciousness,
    cosmic, 208, 222-223
    historical, 30, 63, 89, 130, 144, 173-174, 183, 187-188, 192, 202, 208
    holistic, 150-155, 175-177, 191-192, 195, 204, 211, 247, 255
    self-, 130, 152, 171, 178-181, 188
    religious, 221
    romantic, 144, 145, 150,
    national consciousness,
    Jewish, 13, 91, 117-120, 130
    Russian, 149, 187, 209
Conversion to Christianity, 33, 81, 84, 92, 111, 153, 208, 233, 241
Cosmic unity or whole, 26, 211, 232, 241, 247
Czernowitz Language Conference of 1908, 87, 99

Decembrists, 131, 154, 155, 156, 157, 160, 161, 163, 186, 187, 196, 242
Defense Bureau, 37
Den', 92, 93
Diaspora Nationalists, 19-20, 33-35, 59-65, 98, 118-119, 125
Dilthey, Wilhelm, 229, 230
Dizengoff, Meir, 82
Dmowski, Roman, 27
Dolbroliubov, Nikolai, 24
Dostoevsky, Feodor, 30, 234, 235, 237
Dubnov, Semyon (Shimon),
    Introduction, 13, 14,
    early life, 17-21
    historiographical development, 22-26
    influence of Solov'ev, 26, 27
    development of views on nationalism, 27-30
    relationship with Semyon Vengerov, 31-34
    as Silver Age intellectual generally, 34-37
    and diaspora nationalism, 62, 63, 72, 82
    lack of training, 88
    as nationalist historiographer, 94-99
    as influence on S. An-Sky, 101, 102
    autonomy debate, 105n1
    founder of Folkspartai, 112-115
    First Duma, 115-120
    view on assimilation, 121, 122
    emigré memoirist, 124, 125
    Works:
    Epokha pervoi emansipatsii, 1789-1815, Noveishaia istoriia evreiskogo naroda, 26
    Kniga zhizni, 17-33, 98
    "O sovremennom sostoianii evreiskoi istoriografii," 34, 118
    "Ob izuchenii istorii russkikh evreev i uchrezhdenii Istoricheskogo obshchestva," 29, 30, 97
    Pis'ma o starom i novom evreistve, 25-35, 63
    Volkspartei: Evreiskaia Narodnaia Partiia, 27
    "Vosniknovenie Khasidizma," 95-97
    "Vospominaniia o S. M. Fruge," 22, 23
Dubnov-Erlich, Sophia, 34, 131
Duma, First, 37-52, 61, 106, 118

Emancipation, 109, 119
Emigration, 135, 136, 137, 184
England, 27, 115
Ern, Vladimir, 141, 261
Evreiskaia starina, 13, 23n.17, 24n.25
Evreiskaia zhizn', 59, 64, 66, 115, 207

Fedorov, Nikolai, 237
Fedotov, Georgy, 141
Filosofov, A., 194
Filosofov, Dmitry, 219
Fishman, David, 27
Florovsky, Georges,
  introduction, 13,
  critic of Gershenzon, 148, 177, 182-185, 211
  metaphysical historian, 227-233
  writings on Russian intelligentsia, 235-238
  remarks on his milieu, 272-273
Folkspartai, 27, 29, 114, 115
Forsh, Ol'ga, 265, 269
Frank, Semyon, 213, -218, 225
French Revolution, 24
Frug, Semyon, 22, 132

Gabrilovich, Leonid, 213-215
Gegenwartsarbeit, 13, 59, 114, 118
Gershenzon-Chegodaeva, Natalia, 261
Gershenzon, Mikhail,
  introduction, 13, 15,
  as metaphysical historian of "feeling," 141-147
  theory of break in Russian consciousness, 148-150
  early life, 150-154
  on Decembrists, 155-169
  on Slavophiles, 171-185
  focus on "everyday life, 186-194
  compiles *Russian Propylaea*, 194-196
  influence of WWI and 1917 Revolution on *Correspondence Across a Room*, 198-212
  early development of *Landmarks*, 213-219
  disagreements with Pyotr Struve, 219-228
  philosophical influences, 229-231
  compared with Florovsky, 232-238
  as Pushkin scholar, compared with Semyon Vengerov, 239-245
  "Slow Reading," 244-245
  debate with Semyon Vengerov over *Landmarks*, 246-257
  as leader of Silver Age circle, 258-262
  identification with Pushkin, 262-268
  home as salon, 269-274
  Works:
  Dekabrist Krivtsov i ego brat'ia, 142-144, 186-189, 267
  Griboedov's Moscow, 146-147, 186, 189-192, 198
  The History of Young Russia, 144, 145, 155, 157, 184, 185, 198, 226
  Istoricheskie zapiski, 171-184, 195, 222, 225, 259
  Landmarks (Vekhi), 171, 198, 213-228, 247, 248, 249, 250, 251, 252, 253, 254, 261, 268
  "Otvet P. B. Struve," 148, 149, 183, 222-223, 232
  P. Ia. Chaadaev: zhizn' i myshlenie, 155, 161-165, 198, 247
  Perepiska iz dvukh uglov, 198-212, 231, 257, 268
  Tvorcheskoe samosoznanie, 171, 180, 219, 224, 250, 251, 253
  Troistvennyi obraz sovershenstva, 203, 204, 208
  V. S. Pecherin, 155, 166, 167, 168, 169, 198, 259
Gertsyk, Evgeniia, 259, 260, 261, 268
Gessen, Yuly, 88, 117, 124, 133
Gintsburg, Baron Ezekiel, 107
Ginzburg, Shaul, 124, 125, 130, 132, 135
Gippius, Zinaida, 264
Gofman, Modest, 195
Gogol', Nikolai, 171, 179-182, 246-248
Gol'denveizer, Alexander, 128

Gol'denveizer, Mariia Borisovna, 208
Goldshtein, Abraham, 55
Gol'dshtein, I., 217, 218
Goncharov, Ivan, 21
Gordon, Yehuda (Judah)-Leib, 132
Gornfel'd, Arkady, 215
Gotlober, Abraham, 87
Graetz, Heinrich, 17, 30, 95
Grossman, Leonid, 267, 272
Gruzenberg, Oscar, 124, 133, 134
Gurevich, A, 58

Ha-Olam, 59, 68, 69, 70
Hasidism, 95, 107
Haskalah (maskilim), 20, 23, 26, 66, 74, 75, 81, 89-96, 107, 109, 129
Helsingfors, 54, 59, 114
Herzen, Alexander, 158, 159, 163, 194, 234, 241, 247, 259, 269
Herzl, Theodor, 57, 66, 67, 118
Hibbat Tsion, 54
Histadrut (Labor Zionists), 69, 117
Hovovei Zion, 57, 114
Humanism, 35, 94, 95, 138, 203, 255

Idealists, 160, 161, 246, 273
Idel'son, Avram,
   introduction, 13,
   biography, 54-59
   Synthetic Zionism, 60-67
   editor of Ha-Olam, 67-70
   Territorialism, 114-115
   Gegenswartarbeit, 118
Ivanov, Viacheslav (Razumnik), 13, 141, 198-212, 213, 215, 216, 218, 260, 261, 268
Izgoev, Aleksandr, 215, 225, 267

Jabotinsky, Vladimir, 49-50, 54-56, 60, 70, 125
Jaffe, Leib, 55, 131
James, William, 172, 178, 185, 231
Jewish Ethnographic and Historical Society, 13
Jewish Ethnographic Expedition, 100
Jewish folk culture, 93, 94, 99-103, 119
Jewish Literary Society, 98, 102
Jewish National Constitutional Assembly, 116
Jewish People's Group, 47
Jewish People's Party, 47
"Jewish Question, " 45-50, 67, 111, 193

Kant, 160, 221
Kadets (Constitutional Democrats), 13, 27, 28, 37-51, 61, 98, 114-117, 129, 225
Karsavin, Lev, 141, 239
Kartashev, Lev, 238
Katsenel'son, Lev (Leib) 125, 130
Khin, Rakhel, 132
Khodasevich, Vladislav, 261, 265-271
Kireevsky, Ivan, 171-176, 179, 182, 195, 232, 237, 241, 247, 259
Kishinev, 150, 181, 264-265
Khomiakov, Aleksei, 179, 182
Kliuchevsky, Vasily, 148
Kokoshkin, Fyodor, 52
Kol'tsov, Nikolai, 217
Korobka (Korobochnyi sbor; meat tax), 107-110
Korsakova, Varvara Aleksandrovna, 147
Kistiakovsky, Bogdan, 213-218, 225, 261
Kriticheskoe obozrenie, 216, 217, 218
Kulisher, Reuven, 74, 130

Landau, Alfred, 121
Lavrov, Petr, 24n.21, 253
Lemke, Semyon, 164,
Lemke, Mikhail, 218
Lermontov, Mikhail, 19, 20, 130
Lerner, Nikolai, 165, 166, 266
Lenin, Vladimir, 206, 213

Leningrad Society of Bibliophiles, 262
Leont'ev, Vasily, 235
Levanda, Lev, 13, 87, 90-91, 121, 132
Levitan, Isaac, 48, 193-194
Lidin, Vladimir, 269, 270
Lilienblum, Moses Leib, 20n.8, 23, 66, 121, 132
London, 68, 124, 166

Maeterlinck, Maurice, 175
Maklakov, Vasily, 40, 45-50
Mandel'shtam, Lev, 75
Marek, Pyotr (Pinhas), 114
Marxism, 150, 166, 168, 213, 218, 246
May Laws (Decree of the Third of May), 78, 87, 112, 121
Maze, Jacob, 70
Medele Moicher Sforim (Abramovitch), 22
Merezhkovsky, Dmitri, 219, 264
Merkaz (Zionist organization), 59
Meyers, Frederick W.H., 175
Miliukov, Pavel, 40, 44, 50, 141, 160, 228
Mill, John Stuart, 17, 95
Mochul'sky, Konstantin, 141
Morgulis, Mikhail, 13, 24, 25n27, 77-85, 91-94, 111, 121, 130
Moscow, 13, 57, 66, 124, 151, 205, 257, 268
Motzkin, Leo, 55
Mstislav, 23
Mysticism, 35, 163, 168, 223

Naidich, Isaac, 58
Narodnost', 26, 174
Nashchokin, Pavel, 242
Natanson, Mark (Bobrov), 264
Nekrasov, Nikolai, 131, 154
Nevedomsky, Mikhail, 240
Nicholas I, 137, 172
Nicholas II, 42, 46, 51, 120, 137

Nietzsche, Fredrich, 175, 210, 233

October Revolution, 14, 51, 52, 68, 70, 135, 137, 198, 205, 225, 227, 238, 239, 253-256, 270
Octobrist party, 40, 41, 61
Odessa, 13, 24, 72-87, 89, 91, 109, 119
Odessa Pogrom (1871), 76-78, 87, 91
Ogarev, Nikolai, 154, 194, 259
Orlov, Mikhail, 155
Orlova, Elizaveta, 217
Orshansky, Ilya, 88, 93, 112, 130
Osvobozhdenie (Liberation), 226

Pale of Settlement, 100, 112, 118, 150
Pasmanik, Daniil, 54, 70
Passover, Abraham, 124, 129
Pecherin, Vladimir, 167-169, 194, 259
Peretz, Itzhak Leib, 22
Peter the Great, 158-159, 220
Petrushevsky, Dmitry, 217-218, 261
Philanthropy, 72-87, 92, 107, 109
Pinsker, Leo, 54, 65, 74, 84
Pisarev, Dmitri, 24, 130
Pisemsky, Aleksei, 130
Plekhanov, Georgy, 168-169, 240
Poliakov family, 77
Polish nationalism, 27-29
Positivism, 102, 245
Pozharsky, Nikolai, 262
Provisional Government, 51, 119
Pushkin, Aleksandr, 20, 130, 195, 199, 202, 239-244, 258, 262-269
  "Elegy", 30
  "Evgeny Onegin", 243, 244

Rabinnical Commision of 1861, 87
Rabinovich, Osip, 108, 109, 110, 120, 132
Rassvet, 54, 58, 68, 90, 91, 107, 109, 130

Ravnitsky, Yehoshua, 82
Remizov, Aleksei, 261
Renan, Ernest, 17, 95
Rimsky-Korsakov Family, 191
Rozanov, Vasily, 13, 141, 193-194, 237
Russian Orthodox Christianity, 13, 33, 75, 81-84, 133, 172-183, 194, 208, 223, 229, 233-242
Russian Symbolists (literature), 101, 173, 230, 240, 241, 247, 261, 273
Russification, 74, 77, 81, 107, 119
Russkii evrei, 130
Rutenberg, Pinkhus, 55

Sabashnikov, Mikhail, 261
Sabbatai Zvi, 95
Saker, Jacob, 82
Sakulin, Pavel, 262
Samarin, Yury, 171, 177-182
Schelling, Friedrich, 177
Second Aliya, 55
Shakhovskoi, Dmitry, 165
Shalom Aleichem (Sholem Rabinovitch), 22
Sheftel, Mikhail, 124
Shestov, Lev, 125, 199, 200, 206, 254, 259-261
Shletser, Boris, 199
Shneerson, Zalman, 96
Shpet, Gustav, 218, 261
Shtadlanut, 73, 85, 106, 107, 109, 119
Shternberg, Lev, 129
Shwabacher, Shimon, 73
Slavophiles, 13, 19, 24, 102, 141-144, 149-150, 158-159, 171-173, 176, 177, 181-183, 196, 211, 219, 222, 224, 232, 236, 237, 247, 259, 260
Sliozberg, Henrik, 38, 117, 124-127, 130, 133
Socialism, 24, 158-159, 196
Society for the Promotion of Crafts and Practical Knowledge in Odessa (Trud), 76-78
Society for the Promotion of the Enlightenment Among the Jews of Russia, 24, 38, 58, 72-87, 89, 110, 114
Sologub, Fyodor, 101
Soloveichik, M., 58
Soloveichik, Emmanuel, 74, 76, 77
Solov'ev, Vladimir, 26, 230, 237, 263
Soviets, 119, 266
Speransky, Mikhail, 218
Spinoza, Baruch (Benedict), 95
Stankevich, Nikolai, 142, 157, 259
Steinberg, Aron, 125
Stolypin, Pyotr, 41
St. Petersburg, 13, 33, 37, 38, 66, 72, 76-78, 107, 127-130, 151, 250
as Petrograd, 68
Struve, Pyotr, 13, 28, 45, 47, 48, 50, 129, 183, 213-228

Tarbut school, 66
Tarnopol', I. (Joachim), 87
Tarnovsky, I., 74
Teitel', Jacob, 124, 125
Trudoviki, 42, 43
Tchelnov, Viktor, 70, 125
Tolstoy, Lev, 130, 168, 189-190, 210, 226-228, 251
Tsvetaeva, Marina, 264
Tsiavlovsky, Mikhail, 261, 265
Turgenev, Ivan, 19-23, 130, 145, 240, 246, 258

Union of Unions, 38
Union of Equal Rights, 47
Union for the Attainment of Full Equality for the Jewish People in Russia, 38
United States, 13, 14, 137
Usishkin, Menachem, 54, 70

Veinshtein, G.E., 79
Vengerov, Pauline, 33
Vengerov, Semyon, 31, 32, 33, 141, 164, 239-257
   Critical-Biographical Dictionary of Russian Writers, 31, 32, 33, 240, 257
   "Poslednii zavet Pushkina, "247
   Sobranie sochinenii A. S. Pushkina, 242-243, 251-253
   "V chem ocharovanie russkoi literatury XIX veka?, "245, 255
Veresaev, V., 267
Verkhovsky, Iu. N., 261
Veselovsky, A., 218
Vestnik Evropy, 226
Vilna Congress, 38
Vinaver, Maxim,
   Introduction, 13,
   early years, 37-38
   his account of the First Duma, 39-43
   in Vyborg, 44-45
   his critics, 46-49
   and the 1917 revolution, 49-52
   as memoirist, 124, 125, 128-129
   Works:
   Istoriia vyborgskogo vozzvaniia, 37, 44-47
   Ka-dety i evreiskii vopros, 48-49
   Konflikty v pervoi Dume, 37-43
   Nashe pravitel'stvo: Krymskie vospominaniia, 1918-1919, 52
   Nedavnee, 128, 129
   "Otkrytoe pis'mo P. B. Struve", 48, 129
Vinogradov, Nikolai, 217, 218
Vinogradov, Pavel, 153
Volynsky, Akim, 30, 240
Voskhod, 22, 24, 58, 98, 99
Vyborg Appeal, 38, 43, 44, 45

Warsaw, 37, 124
Weizmann, Hayim, 54, 55

Westernizers, 19, 141, 149-150, 158-162, 221, 224, 259-260
World War I, 37, 59, 67, 68, 100, 102, 198, 200, 207, 208, 229
World Zionist Organization, 59

Yishuv, 59, 60, 65, 68

Zaideman, A., 58
Zangwill, Israel, 64
Zhukovsky, D. N., 261
Zionism, 13,
   First Duma period, 48-51
   Russian Zionism generally, 54-70
   Synthetic Zionism, 59-61, 64, 69
   in Odessa, 72, 84-85,
   Territorialism, 114, 115
Zion (periodical), 130

www.ingramcontent.com/pod-product-compliance
Ingram Content Group UK Ltd.
Pitfield, Milton Keynes, MK11 3LW, UK
UKHW021847140426
5217IPUK00022B/1639